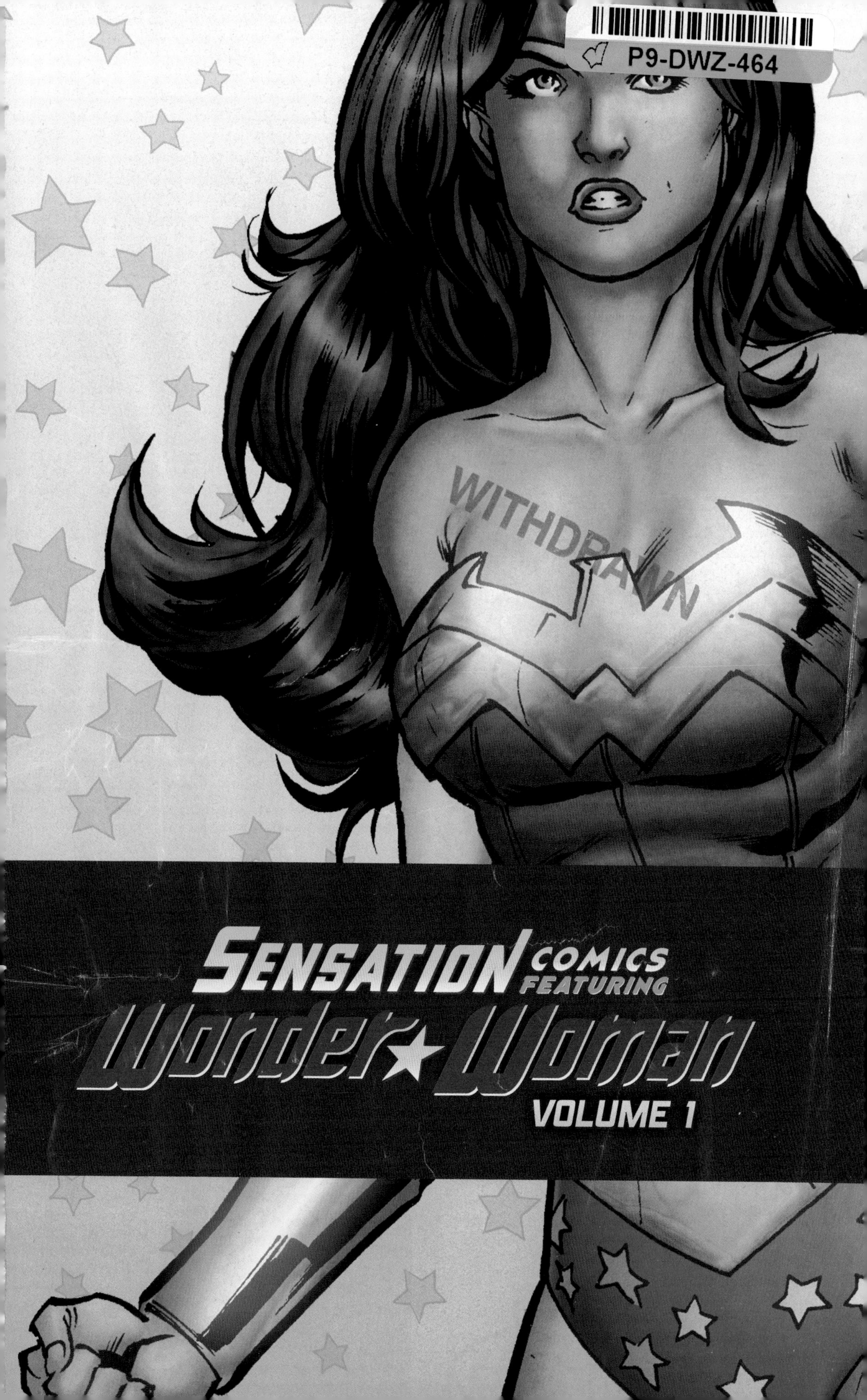

SENSATION COMICS FEATURING WONDER WOMAN

VOLUME 1

KRISTY QUINN Editor – Original Series
JESSICA CHEN Assistant Editor – Original Series
RACHEL PINNELAS Editor
ROBBIN BROSTERMAN Design Director – Books
SARABETH KETT Publication Design

HANK KANALZ Senior VP – Vertigo and Integrated Publishing

DIANE NELSON President
DAN DIDIO and JIM LEE Co-Publishers
GEOFF JOHNS Chief Creative Officer
AMIT DESAI Senior VP – Marketing and Franchise Management
AMY GENKINS Senior VP – Business and Legal Affairs
NAIRI GARDINER Senior VP – Finance
JEFF BOISON VP – Publishing Planning
MARK CHIARELLO VP – Art Direction and Design
JOHN CUNNINGHAM VP – Marketing
TERRI CUNNINGHAM VP – Editorial Administration
LARRY GANEM VP – Talent Relations and Services
ALISON GILL Senior VP – Manufacturing and Operations
JAY KOGAN VP – Business and Legal Affairs, Publishing
JACK MAHAN VP – Business Affairs, Talent
NICK NAPOLITANO VP – Manufacturing Administration
SUE POHJA VP – Book Sales
FRED RUIZ VP – Manufacturing Operations
COURTNEY SIMMONS Senior VP – Publicity
BOB WAYNE Senior VP – Sales

SENSATION COMICS FEATURING WONDER WOMAN VOLUME 1

DC Comics, 1700 Broadway, New York, NY 10019
A Warner Bros. Entertainment Company.
Printed by RR Donnelley, Salem, VA, USA. 3/6/15.
First Printing.
ISBN: 978-1-4012-5344-8

Library of Congress Cataloging-in-Publication Data

Simone, Gail.
  Sensation Comics featuring Wonder Woman / Gail Simone ;
illustrated by Ethan Van Sciver.
     pages cm
  ISBN 978-1-4012-5344-8 (paperback)
  1. Graphic novels. I. Van Sciver, Ethan. II. Title.
PN6728.W6S47 2015
741.5'973—dc23
                                              2014049013

SENSATION COMICS FEATURING WONDER WOMAN

VOLUME 1

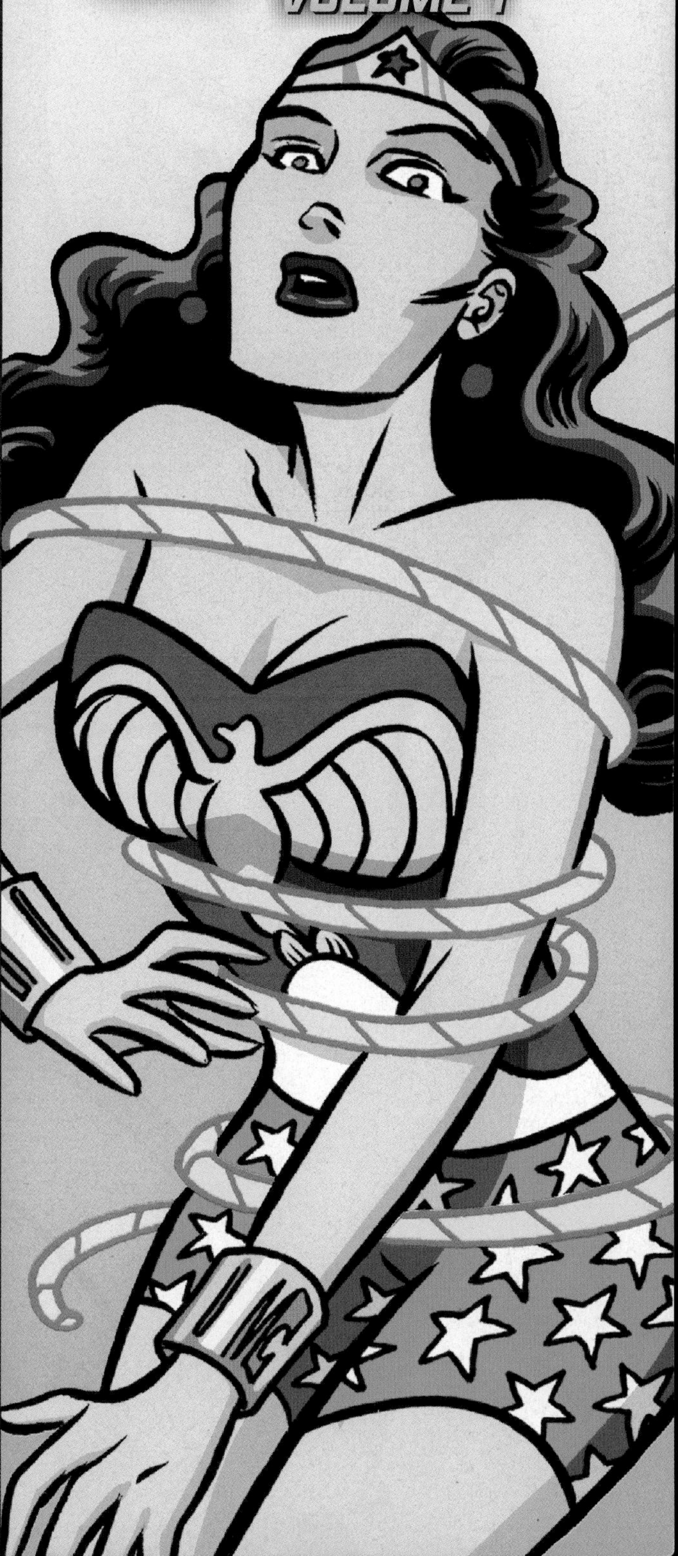
WMC

Gail Simone
Amanda Deibert
Ivan Cohen
Jason Bischoff
Sean E. Williams
Ollie Masters
Gilbert Hernandez
Neil Kleid
Rob Williams
Corinna Bechko
Gabriel Hardman
WRITERS

Ethan Van Sciver
Marcelo Di Chiara
Cat Staggs
Marcus To
David A. Williams
Marguerite Sauvage
Amy Mebberson
Gilbert Hernandez
Dean Haspiel
Tom Lyle
Gabriel Hardman
ARTISTS

Brian Miller of
Hi-Fi Colour Design
John Rauch
Andrew Dalhouse
Wendy Broome
Marguerite Sauvage
Amy Mebberson
Allen Passalaqua
Jordan Boyd
COLORISTS

Saida Temofonte
Deron Bennett
LETTERERS

Gene Ha
COLLECTION COVER ARTIST

WONDER WOMAN created by
William Moulton Marston

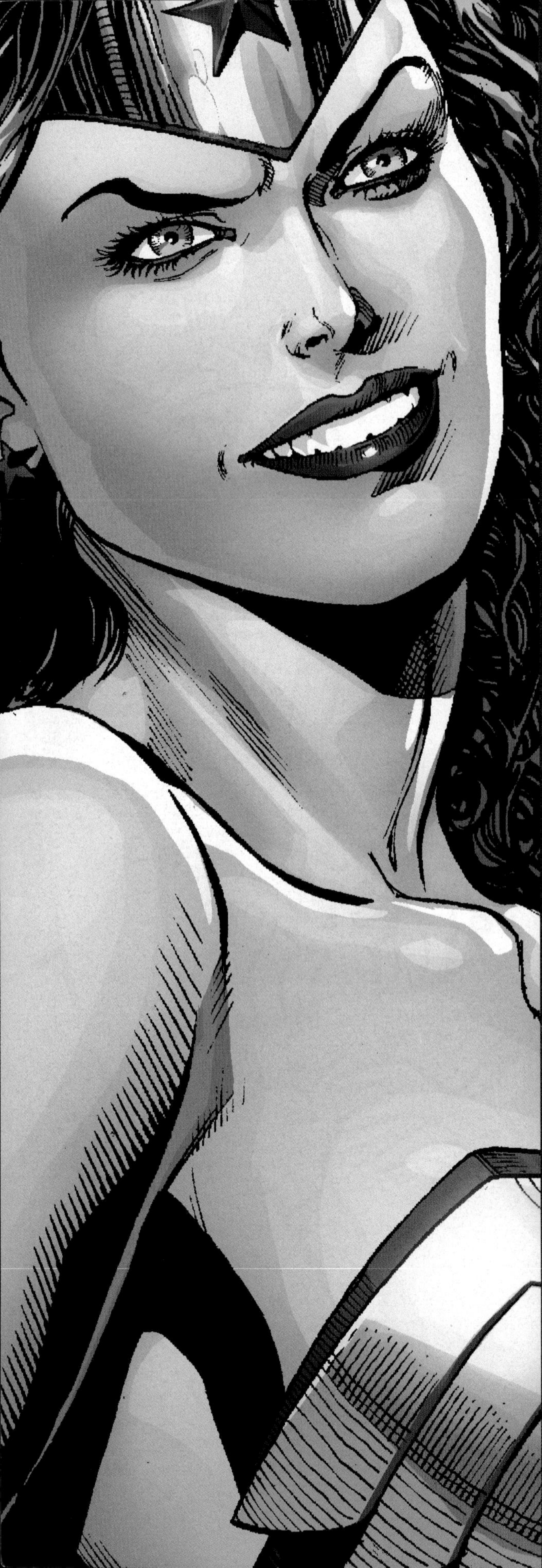

GOTHAMAZON

GAIL SIMONE
WRITER

ETHAN VAN SCIVER & MARCELO DI CHIARA
ARTISTS

BRIAN MILLER OF HI-FI COLOUR DESIGN
COLORISTS

SAIDA TEMOFONTE
LETTERER

THERE IS A SECRET MATH IN GOTHAM, A NUMERICAL CERTAINTY THAT HAS PREVENTED THE ENTIRE SYSTEM FROM BURNING TO THE GROUND.

IT IS SIMPLY THIS: WITH THIS GROUP, ONE AND ONE NEVER EQUAL TWO.

AND THANKFULLY, ONE AND ONE AND ONE AND ONE AND ONE AND ONE AND ONE HAVE NEVER, EVER EQUALED ANY COMBINED AGGREGATE.

THEY DON'T WORK TOGETHER. THEY HATE EACH OTHER ALMOST AS MUCH AS THEY HATE US.

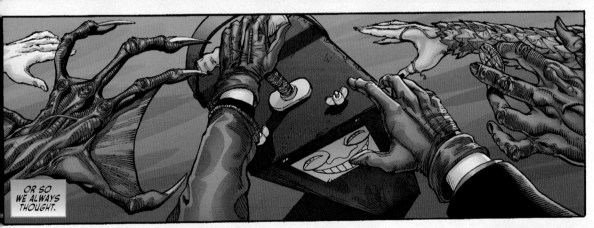

OR SO WE ALWAYS THOUGHT.

UNTIL ONE NIGHT, THIS PARTICULAR LOT DECIDED NOT TO BE COWARDLY AND SUPERSTITIOUS.

AND THE MATH OF GOTHAM CITY CHANGED IN BRUTAL FASHION.

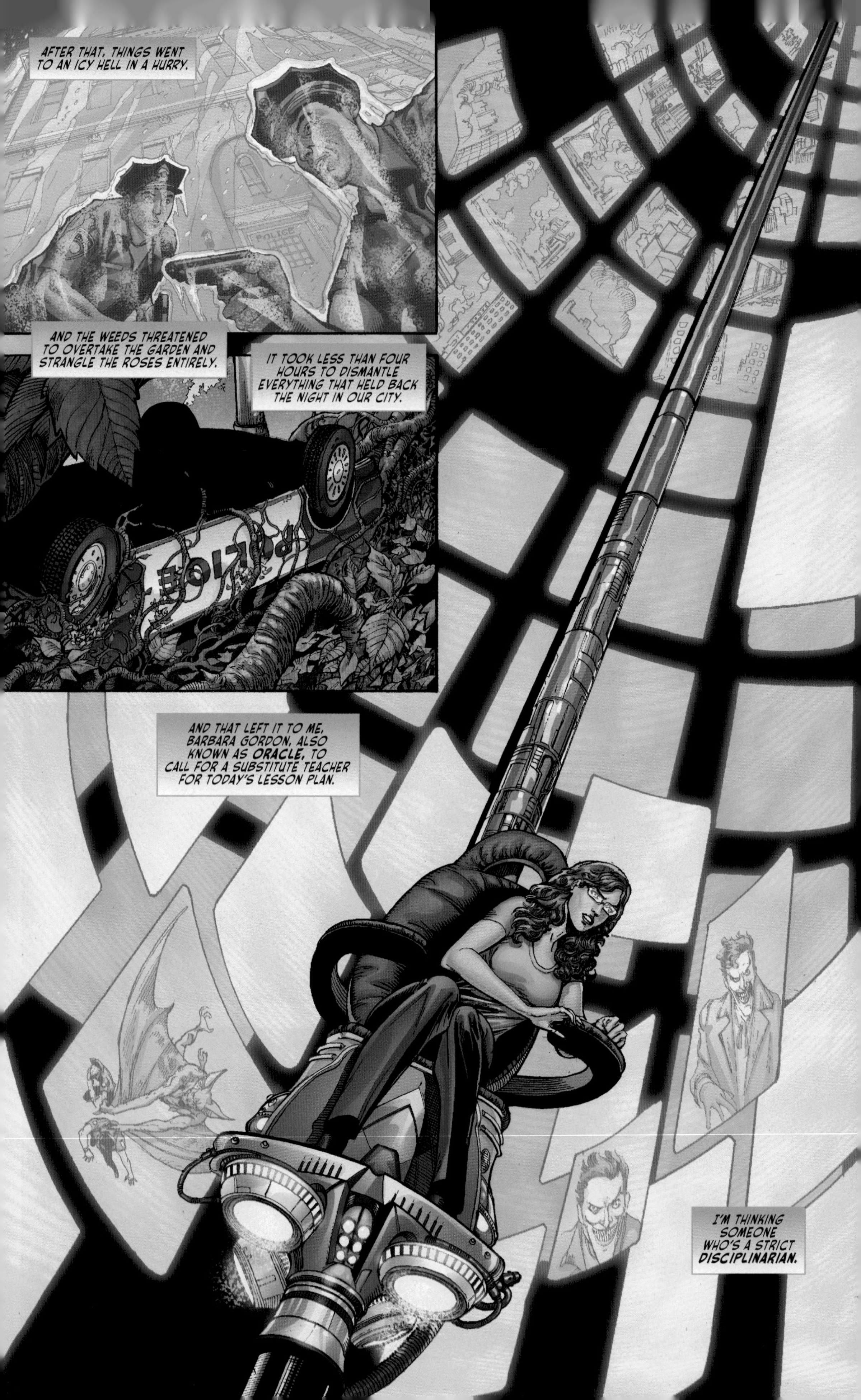
AFTER THAT, THINGS WENT TO AN ICY HELL IN A HURRY.
POLICE
AND THE WEEDS THREATENED TO OVERTAKE THE GARDEN AND STRANGLE THE ROSES ENTIRELY.
IT TOOK LESS THAN FOUR HOURS TO DISMANTLE EVERYTHING THAT HELD BACK THE NIGHT IN OUR CITY.
AND THAT LEFT IT TO ME, BARBARA GORDON, ALSO KNOWN AS ORACLE, TO CALL FOR A SUBSTITUTE TEACHER FOR TODAY'S LESSON PLAN.
I'M THINKING SOMEONE WHO'S A STRICT DISCIPLINARIAN.

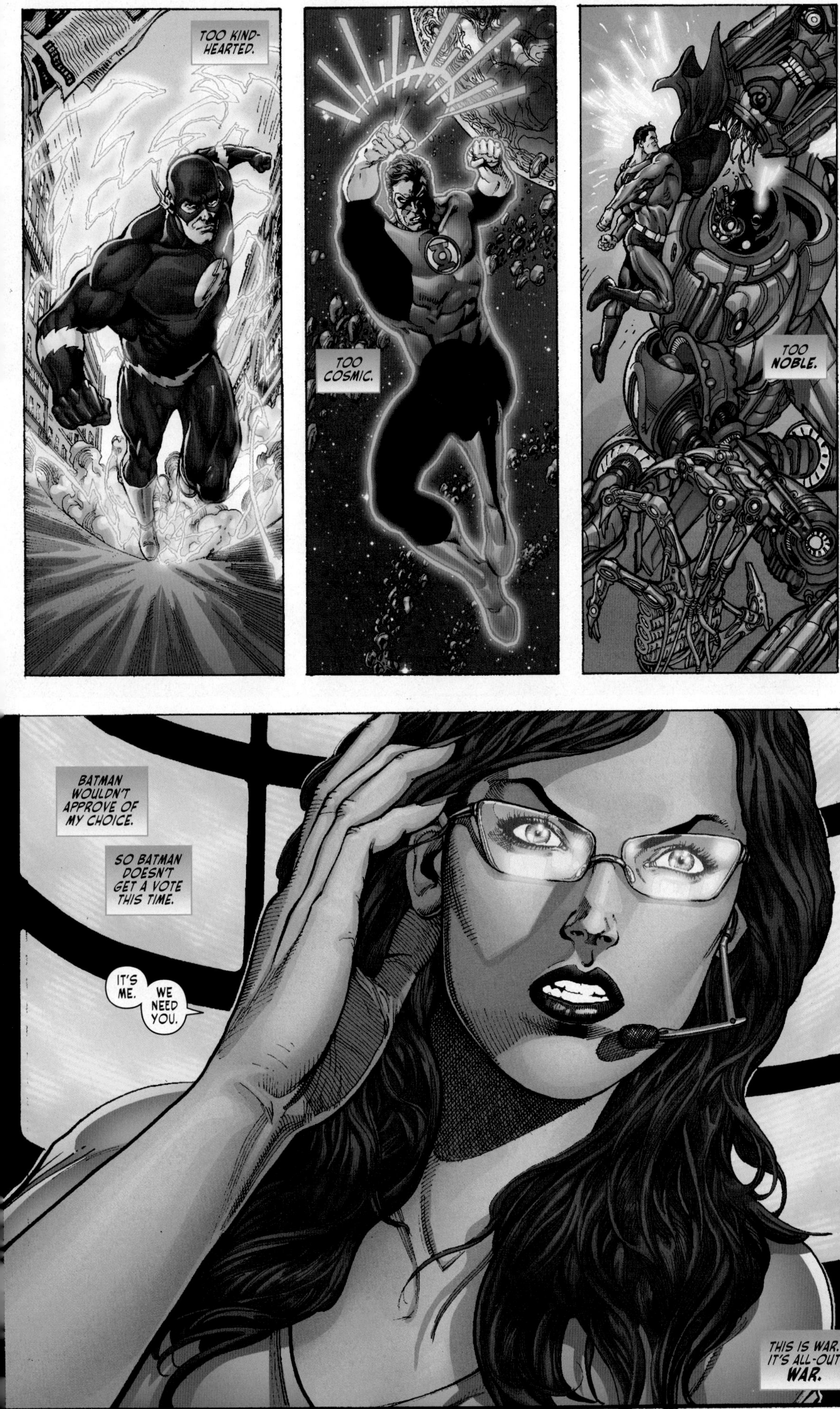
TOO KIND-HEARTED.
TOO COSMIC.
TOO NOBLE.
BATMAN WOULDN'T APPROVE OF MY CHOICE.
SO BATMAN DOESN'T GET A VOTE THIS TIME.
IT'S ME.
WE NEED YOU.
THIS IS WAR. IT'S ALL-OUT WAR.

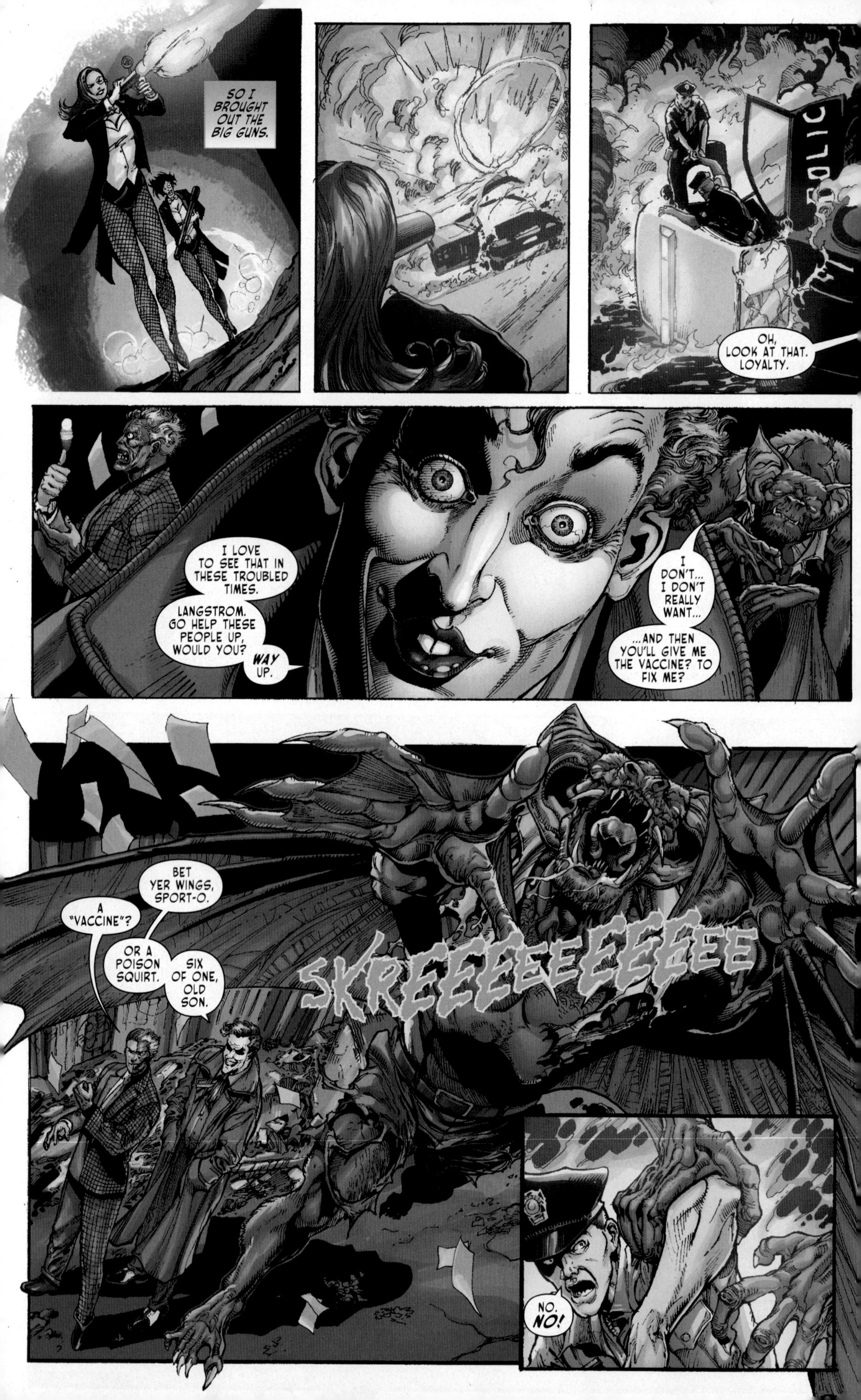
SO I BROUGHT OUT THE BIG GUNS.
OH, LOOK AT THAT. LOYALTY.
I LOVE TO SEE THAT IN THESE TROUBLED TIMES.
LANGSTROM. GO HELP THESE PEOPLE UP, WOULD YOU? WAY UP.
I DON'T... I DON'T REALLY WANT...
...AND THEN YOU'LL GIVE ME THE VACCINE? TO FIX ME?
A "VACCINE"?
OR A POISON SQUIRT.
BET YER WINGS, SPORT-O.
SIX OF ONE, OLD SON.
SKREEEEEEEEEEEE
NO. NO!

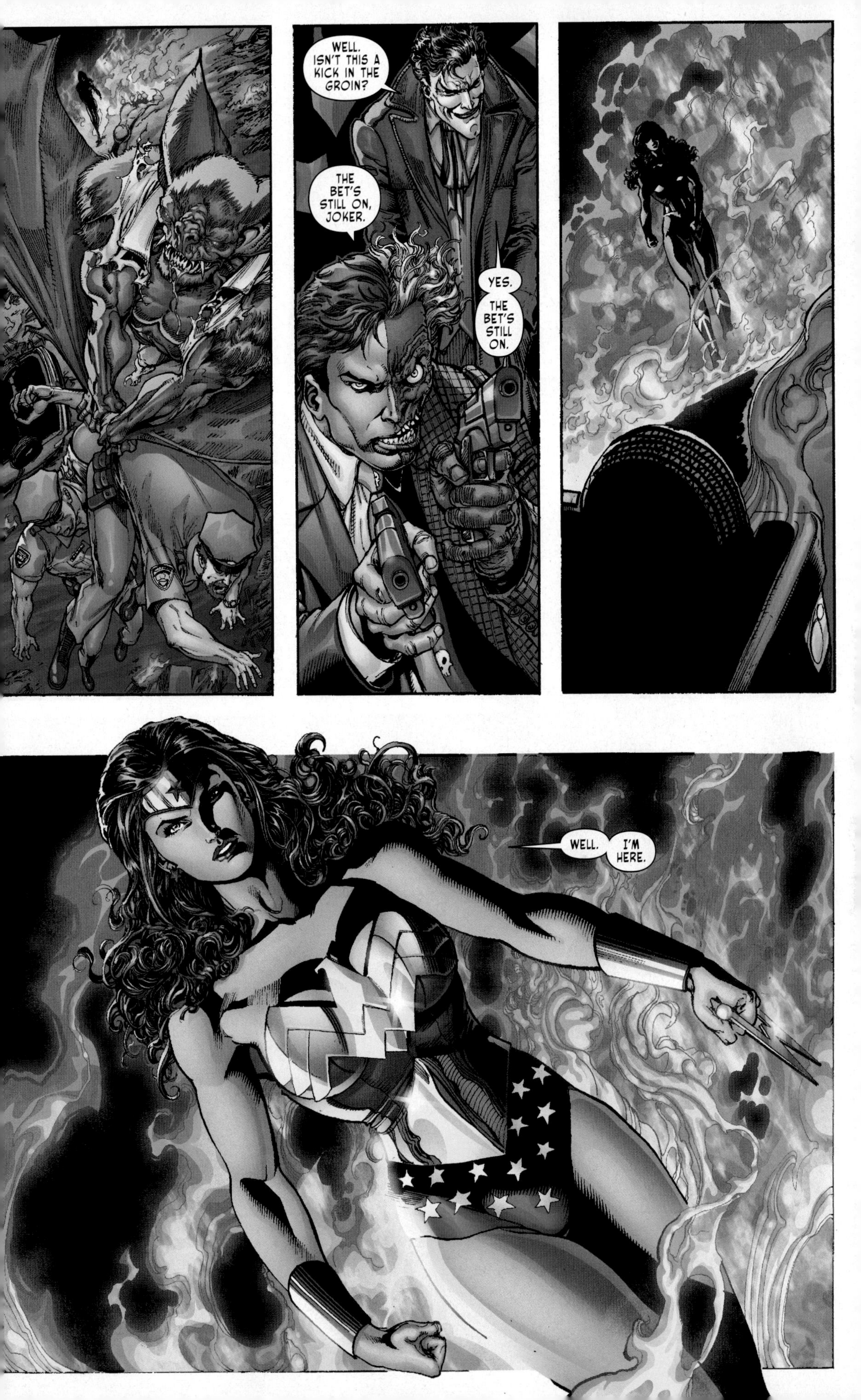

WELL. ISN'T THIS A KICK IN THE GROIN?
THE BET'S STILL ON, JOKER.
YES. THE BET'S STILL ON.
WELL. I'M HERE.

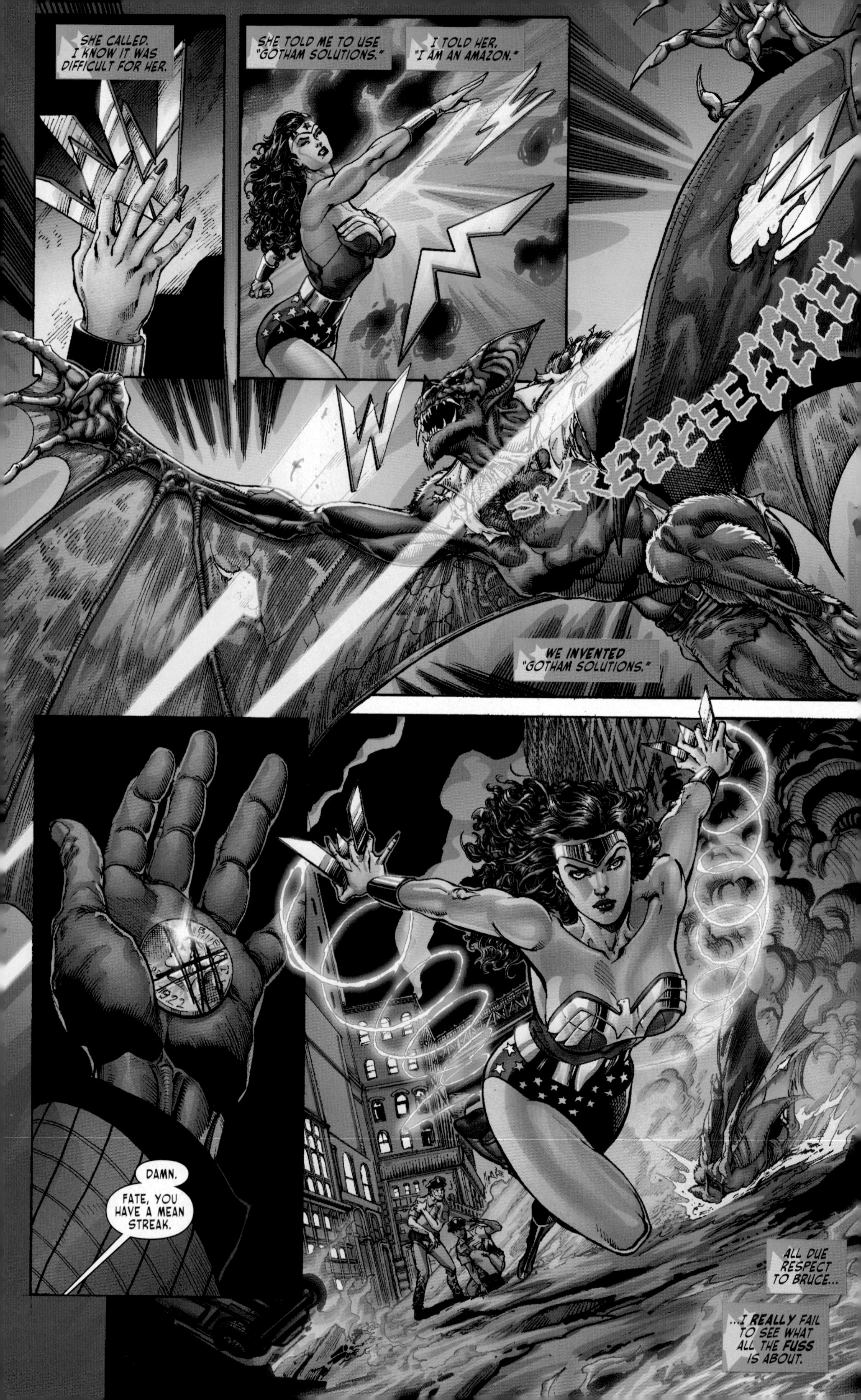
SHE CALLED. I KNOW IT WAS DIFFICULT FOR HER.
SHE TOLD ME TO USE "GOTHAM SOLUTIONS."
I TOLD HER, "I AM AN AMAZON."
SKREEEEEEEEEEET
WE INVENTED "GOTHAM SOLUTIONS."
DAMN.
FATE, YOU HAVE A MEAN STREAK.
ALL DUE RESPECT TO BRUCE...
...I REALLY FAIL TO SEE WHAT ALL THE FUSS IS ABOUT.

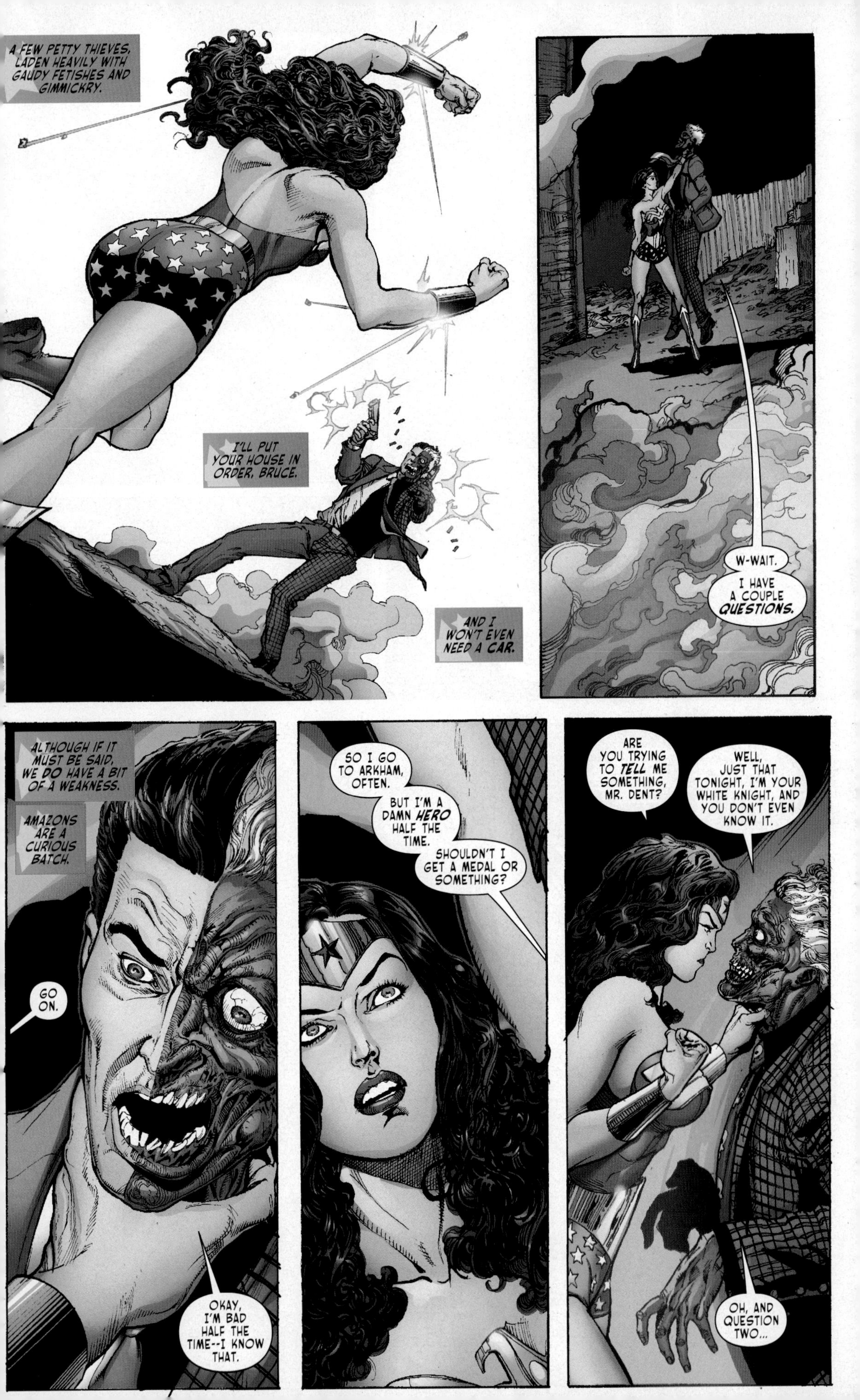
A FEW PETTY THIEVES, LADEN HEAVILY WITH GAUDY FETISHES AND GIMMICKRY.
I'LL PUT YOUR HOUSE IN ORDER, BRUCE.
AND I WON'T EVEN NEED A CAR.
W-WAIT. I HAVE A COUPLE QUESTIONS.
ALTHOUGH IF IT MUST BE SAID, WE DO HAVE A BIT OF A WEAKNESS.
AMAZONS ARE A CURIOUS BATCH.
GO ON.
OKAY, I'M BAD HALF THE TIME--I KNOW THAT.
SO I GO TO ARKHAM, OFTEN.
BUT I'M A DAMN HERO HALF THE TIME.
SHOULDN'T I GET A MEDAL OR SOMETHING?
ARE YOU TRYING TO TELL ME SOMETHING, MR. DENT?
WELL, JUST THAT TONIGHT, I'M YOUR WHITE KNIGHT, AND YOU DON'T EVEN KNOW IT.
OH, AND QUESTION TWO...

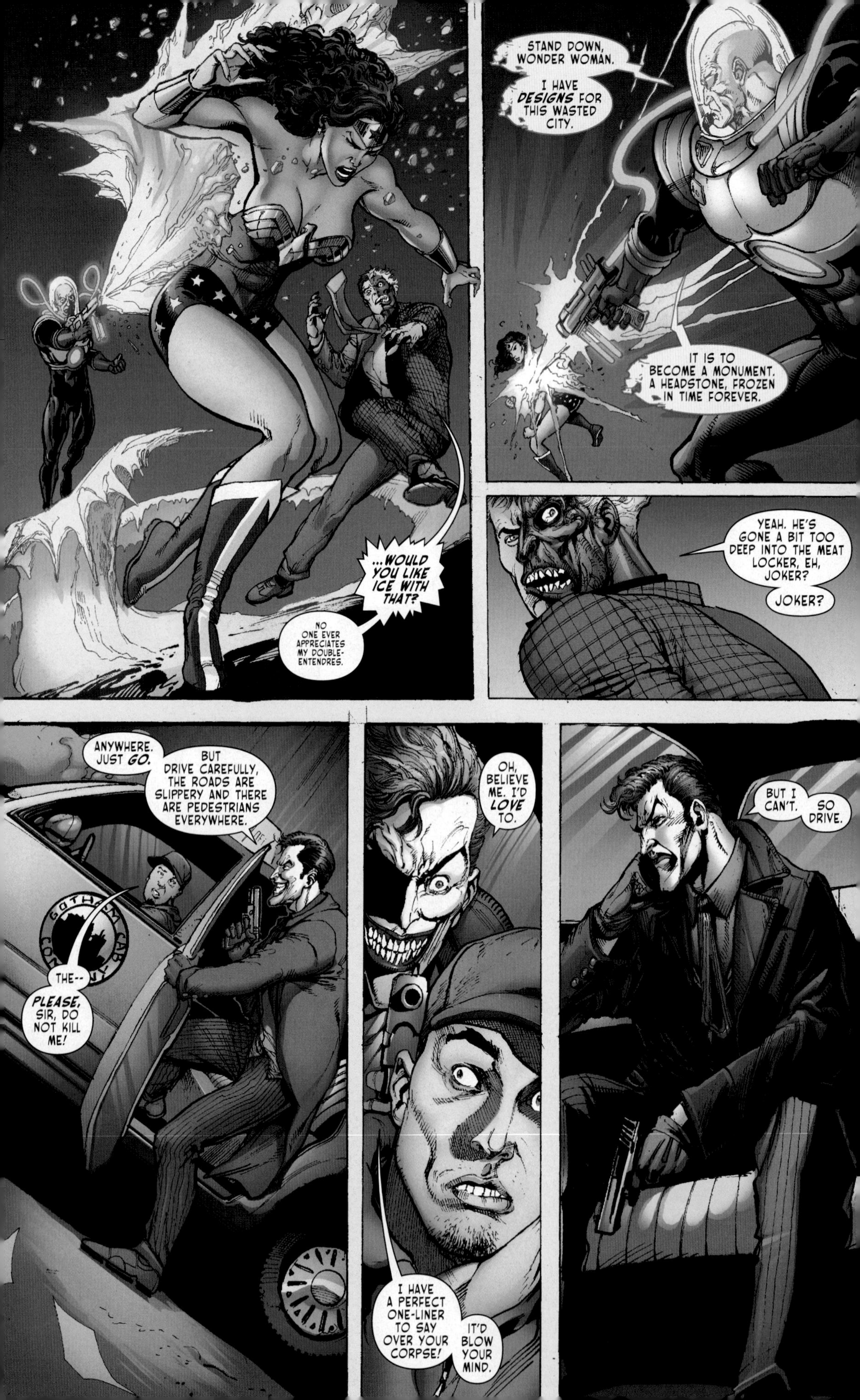
...WOULD YOU LIKE ICE WITH THAT?
NO ONE EVER APPRECIATES MY DOUBLE-ENTENDRES.
STAND DOWN, WONDER WOMAN.
I HAVE DESIGNS FOR THIS WASTED CITY.
IT IS TO BECOME A MONUMENT. A HEADSTONE, FROZEN IN TIME FOREVER.
YEAH. HE'S GONE A BIT TOO DEEP INTO THE MEAT LOCKER, EH, JOKER?
JOKER?
ANYWHERE. JUST GO.
BUT DRIVE CAREFULLY, THE ROADS ARE SLIPPERY AND THERE ARE PEDESTRIANS EVERYWHERE.
THE--
PLEASE, SIR, DO NOT KILL ME!
OH, BELIEVE ME. I'D LOVE TO.
I HAVE A PERFECT ONE-LINER TO SAY OVER YOUR CORPSE!
IT'D BLOW YOUR MIND.
BUT I CAN'T.
SO DRIVE.

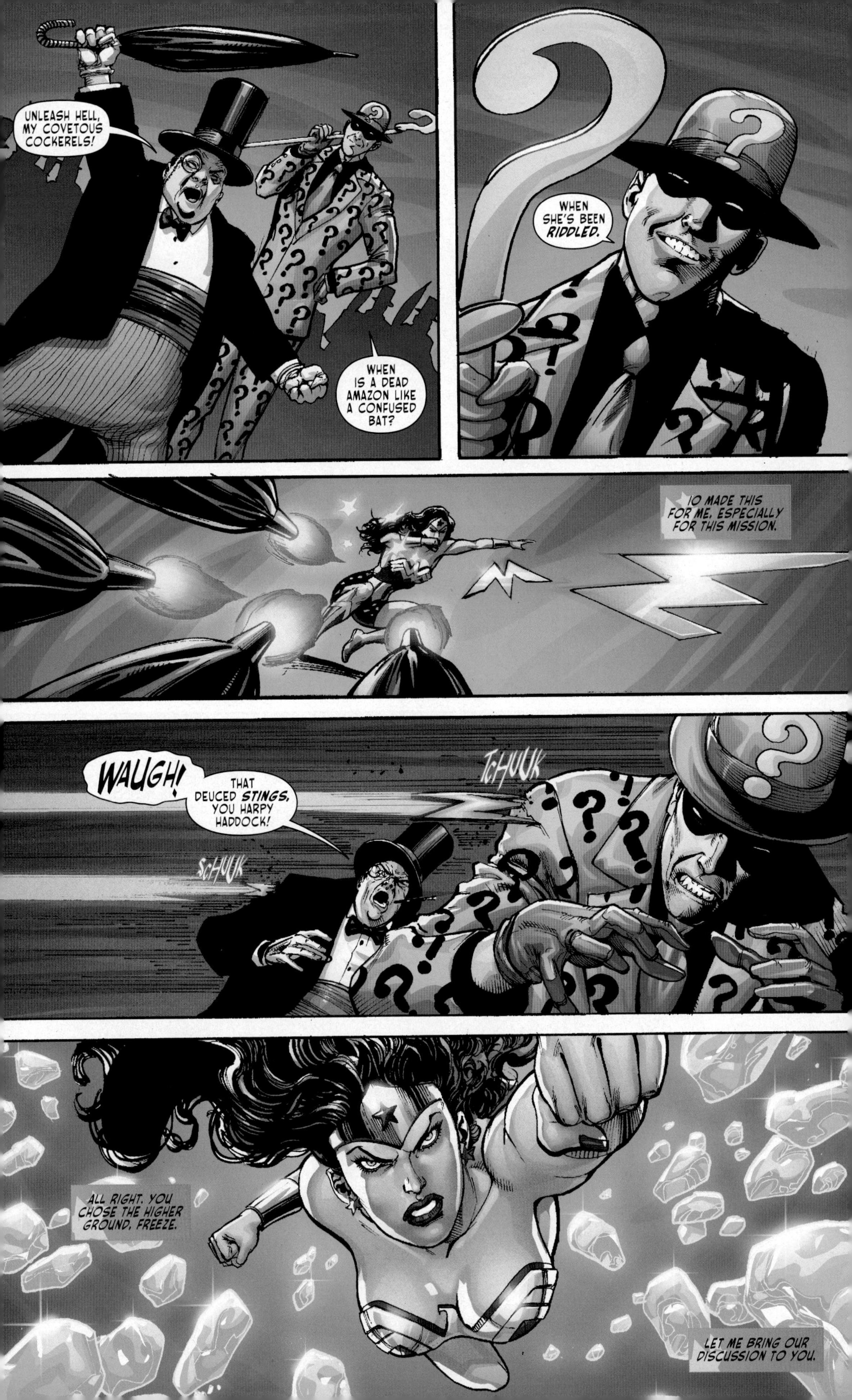
UNLEASH HELL, MY COVETOUS COCKERELS!
WHEN IS A DEAD AMAZON LIKE A CONFUSED BAT?
WHEN SHE'S BEEN RIDDLED.
IO MADE THIS FOR ME, ESPECIALLY FOR THIS MISSION.
WAUGH!
THAT DEUCED STINGS, YOU HARPY HADDOCK!
TCHUUK
SCHUUK
ALL RIGHT. YOU CHOSE THE HIGHER GROUND, FREEZE.
LET ME BRING OUR DISCUSSION TO YOU.

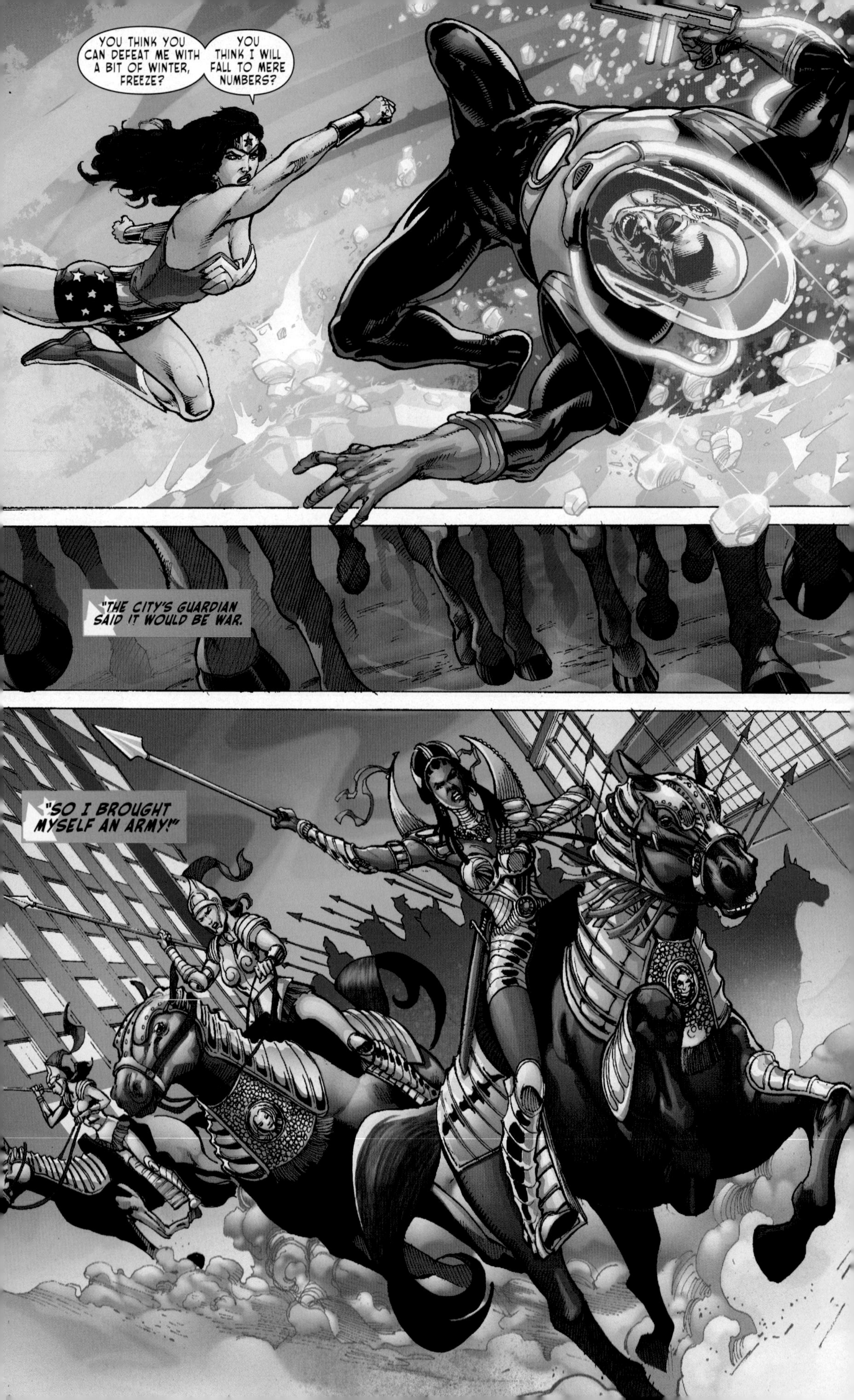
YOU THINK YOU CAN DEFEAT ME WITH A BIT OF WINTER, FREEZE?
YOU THINK I WILL FALL TO MERE NUMBERS?
"THE CITY'S GUARDIAN SAID IT WOULD BE WAR.
"SO I BROUGHT MYSELF AN ARMY!"

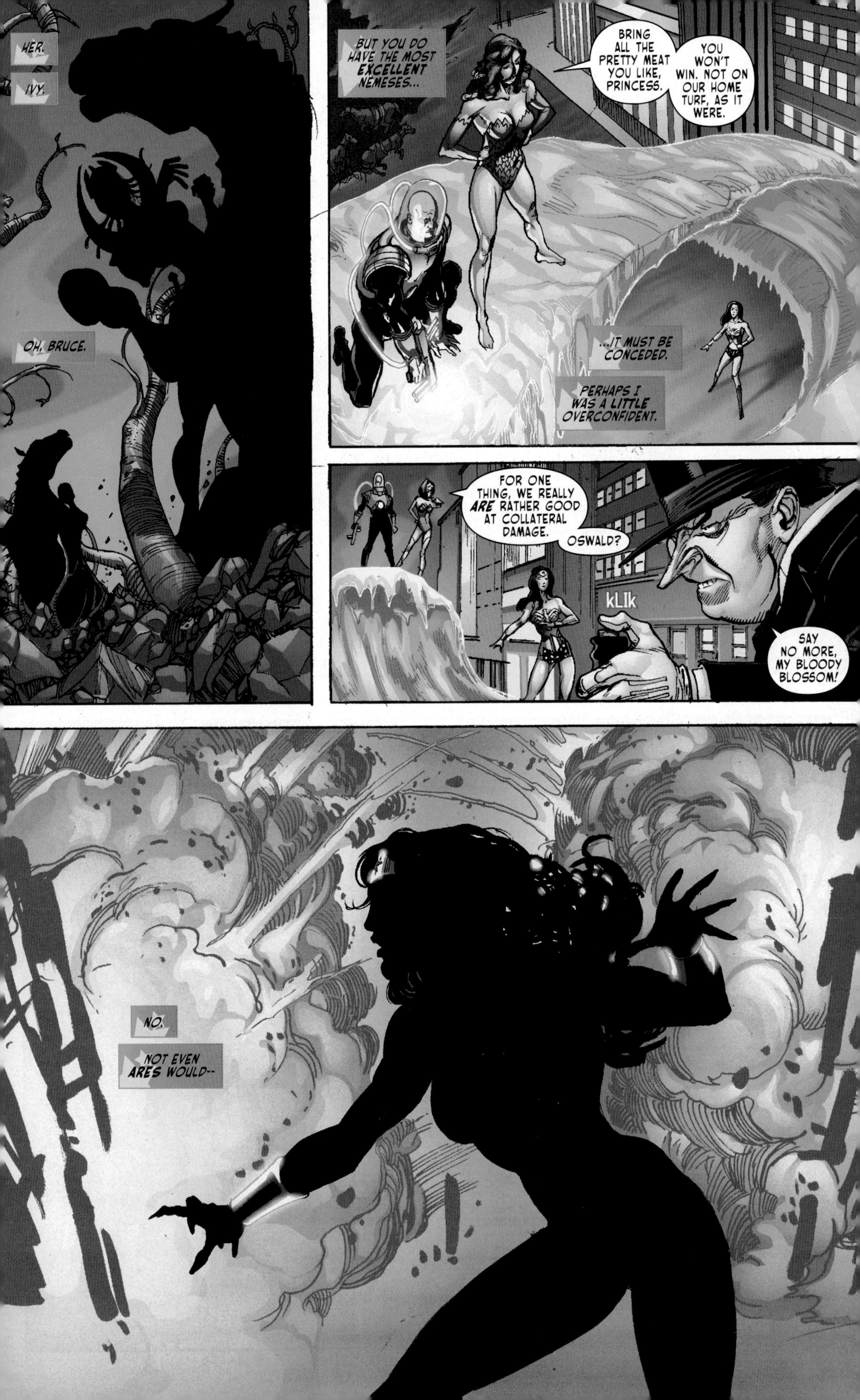
HER.
IVY.
OH, BRUCE.
BUT YOU DO HAVE THE MOST EXCELLENT NEMESES...
BRING ALL THE PRETTY MEAT YOU LIKE, PRINCESS.
YOU WON'T WIN. NOT ON OUR HOME TURF, AS IT WERE.
...IT MUST BE CONCEDED.
PERHAPS I WAS A LITTLE OVERCONFIDENT.
FOR ONE THING, WE REALLY ARE RATHER GOOD AT COLLATERAL DAMAGE.
OSWALD?
kLIk
SAY NO MORE, MY BLOODY BLOSSOM!
NO.
NOT EVEN ARES WOULD--

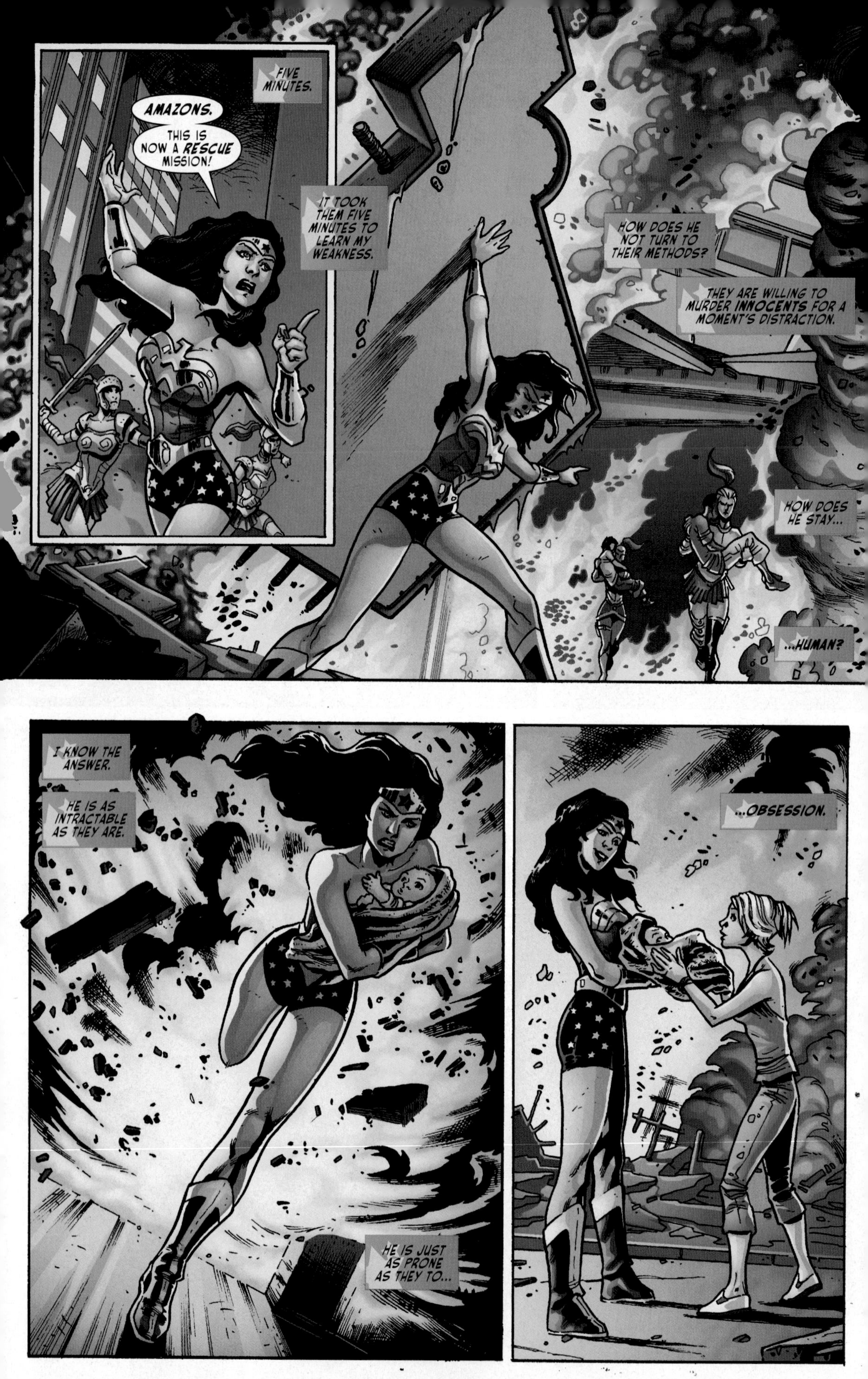

FIVE MINUTES.
AMAZONS.
THIS IS NOW A RESCUE MISSION!
IT TOOK THEM FIVE MINUTES TO LEARN MY WEAKNESS.
HOW DOES HE NOT TURN TO THEIR METHODS?
THEY ARE WILLING TO MURDER INNOCENTS FOR A MOMENT'S DISTRACTION.
HOW DOES HE STAY...
...HUMAN?
I KNOW THE ANSWER.
HE IS AS INTRACTABLE AS THEY ARE.
HE IS JUST AS PRONE AS THEY TO...
...OBSESSION.

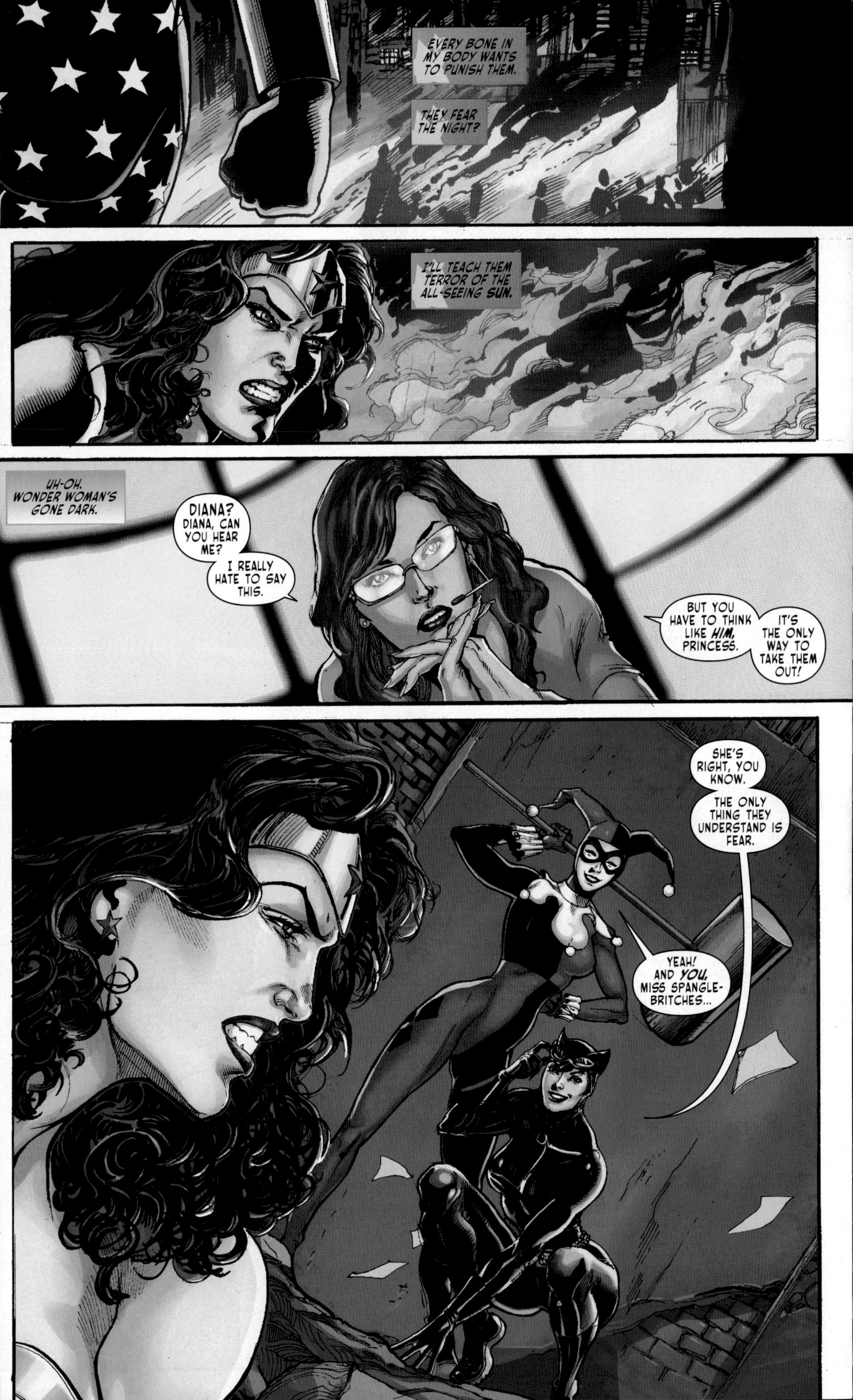
EVERY BONE IN MY BODY WANTS TO PUNISH THEM.
THEY FEAR THE NIGHT?
I'LL TEACH THEM TERROR OF THE ALL-SEEING SUN.
UH-OH. WONDER WOMAN'S GONE DARK.
DIANA? DIANA, CAN YOU HEAR ME?
I REALLY HATE TO SAY THIS.
BUT YOU HAVE TO THINK LIKE HIM, PRINCESS.
IT'S THE ONLY WAY TO TAKE THEM OUT!
SHE'S RIGHT, YOU KNOW.
THE ONLY THING THEY UNDERSTAND IS FEAR.
YEAH! AND YOU, MISS SPANGLE-BRITCHES...

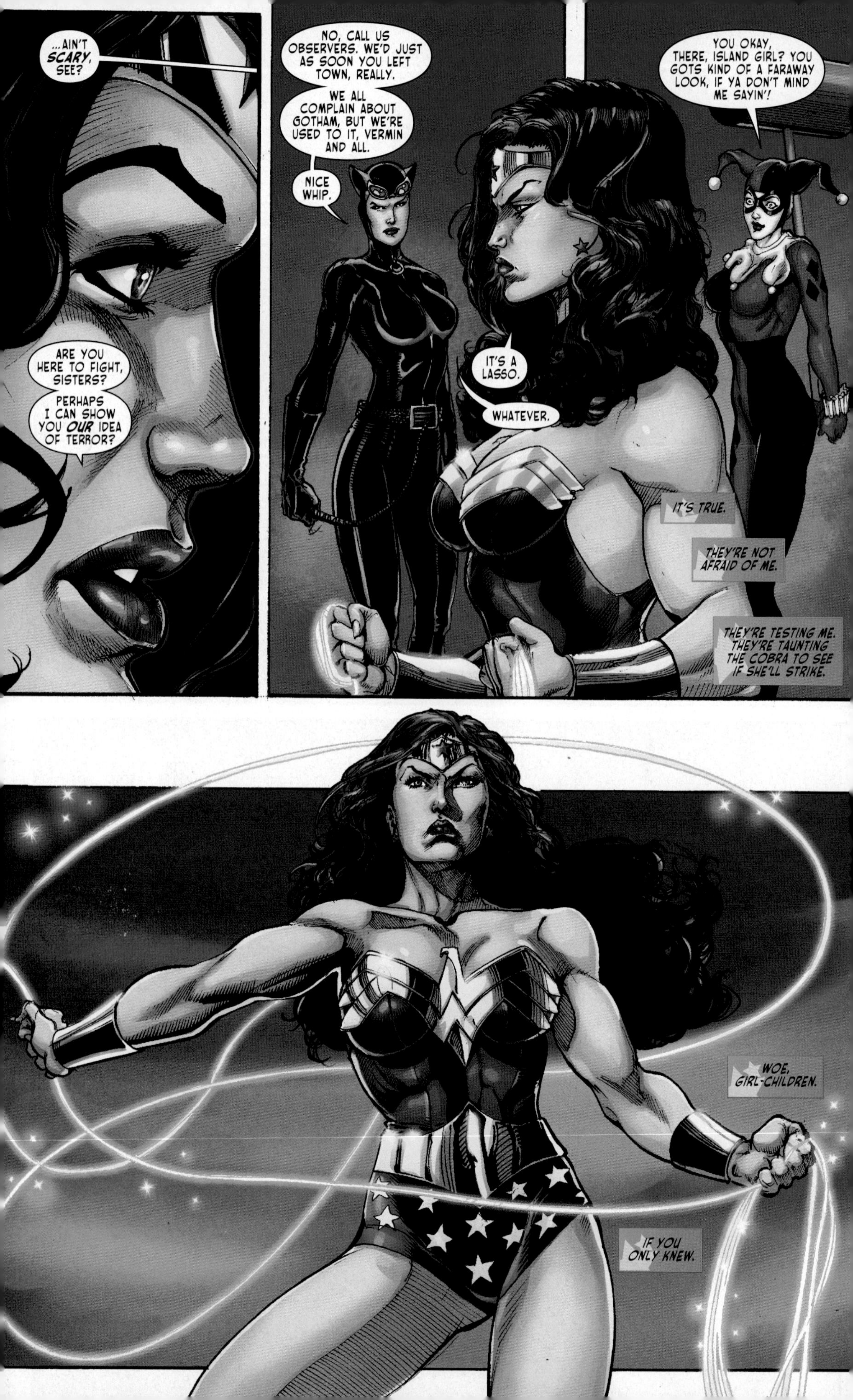
...AIN'T SCARY, SEE?
ARE YOU HERE TO FIGHT, SISTERS?
PERHAPS I CAN SHOW YOU OUR IDEA OF TERROR?
NO, CALL US OBSERVERS. WE'D JUST AS SOON YOU LEFT TOWN, REALLY.
WE ALL COMPLAIN ABOUT GOTHAM, BUT WE'RE USED TO IT, VERMIN AND ALL.
NICE WHIP.
YOU OKAY, THERE, ISLAND GIRL? YOU GOTS KIND OF A FARAWAY LOOK, IF YA DON'T MIND ME SAYIN'!
IT'S A LASSO.
WHATEVER.
IT'S TRUE.
THEY'RE NOT AFRAID OF ME.
THEY'RE TESTING ME. THEY'RE TAUNTING THE COBRA TO SEE IF SHE'LL STRIKE.
WOE, GIRL-CHILDREN.
IF YOU ONLY KNEW.

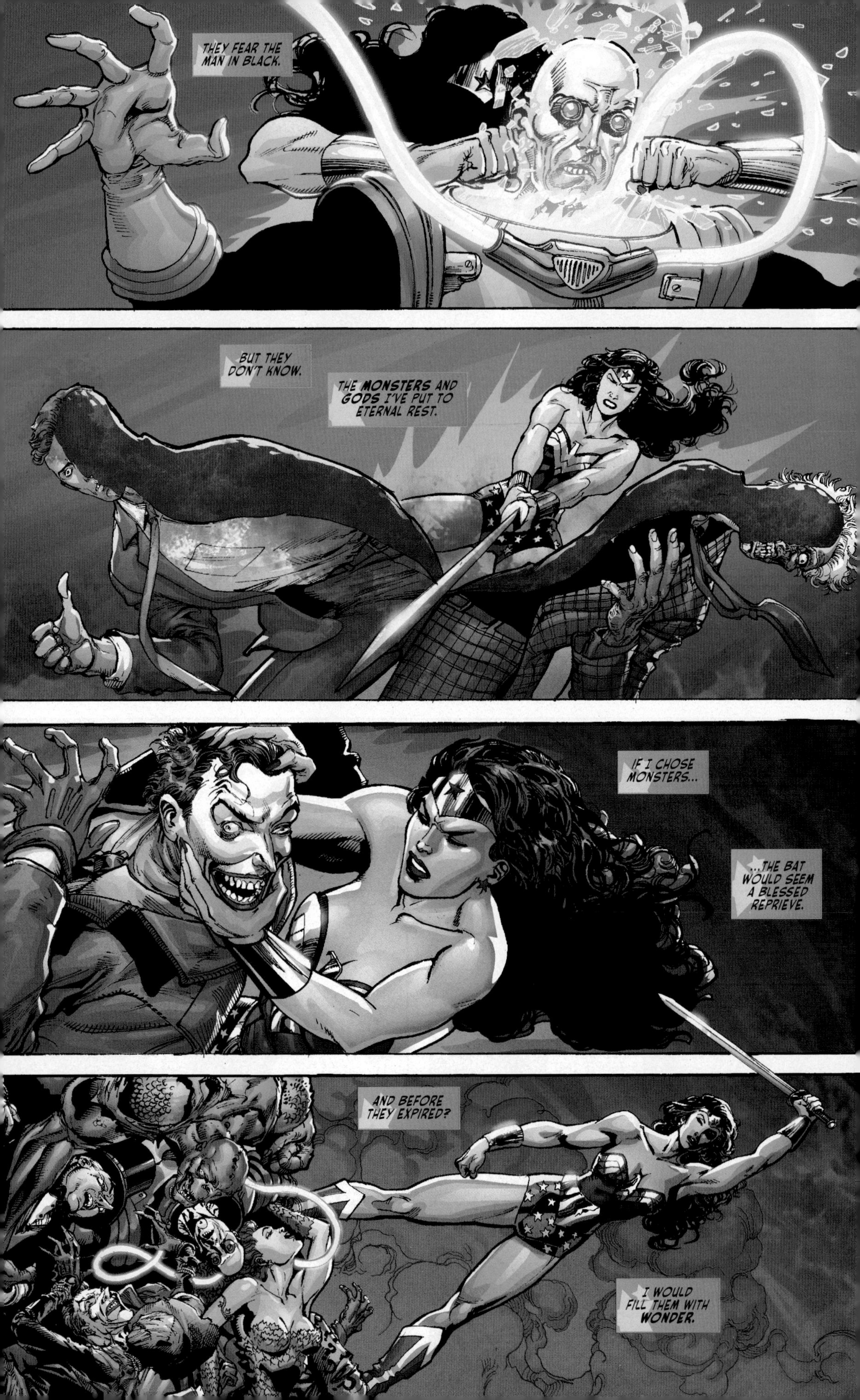

THEY FEAR THE MAN IN BLACK.
BUT THEY DON'T KNOW.
THE MONSTERS AND GODS I'VE PUT TO ETERNAL REST.
IF I CHOSE MONSTERS...
...THE BAT WOULD SEEM A BLESSED REPRIEVE.
AND BEFORE THEY EXPIRED?
I WOULD FILL THEM WITH WONDER.

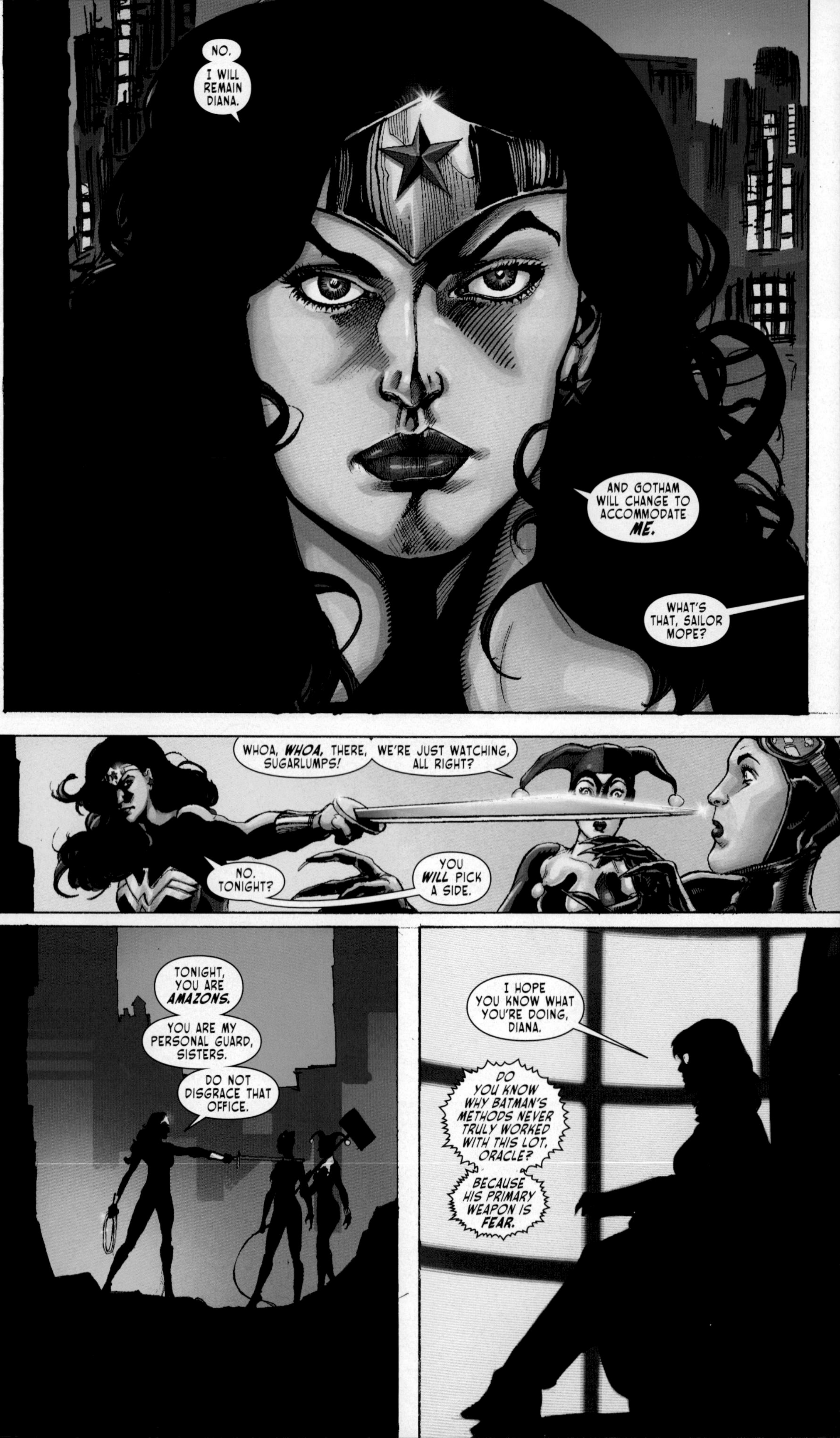
NO.
I WILL REMAIN DIANA.
AND GOTHAM WILL CHANGE TO ACCOMMODATE ME.
WHAT'S THAT, SAILOR MOPE?
WHOA, WHOA, THERE, SUGARLUMPS!
WE'RE JUST WATCHING, ALL RIGHT?
NO. TONIGHT?
YOU WILL PICK A SIDE.
TONIGHT, YOU ARE AMAZONS.
YOU ARE MY PERSONAL GUARD, SISTERS.
DO NOT DISGRACE THAT OFFICE.
I HOPE YOU KNOW WHAT YOU'RE DOING, DIANA.
DO YOU KNOW WHY BATMAN'S METHODS NEVER TRULY WORKED WITH THIS LOT, ORACLE?
BECAUSE HIS PRIMARY WEAPON IS FEAR.

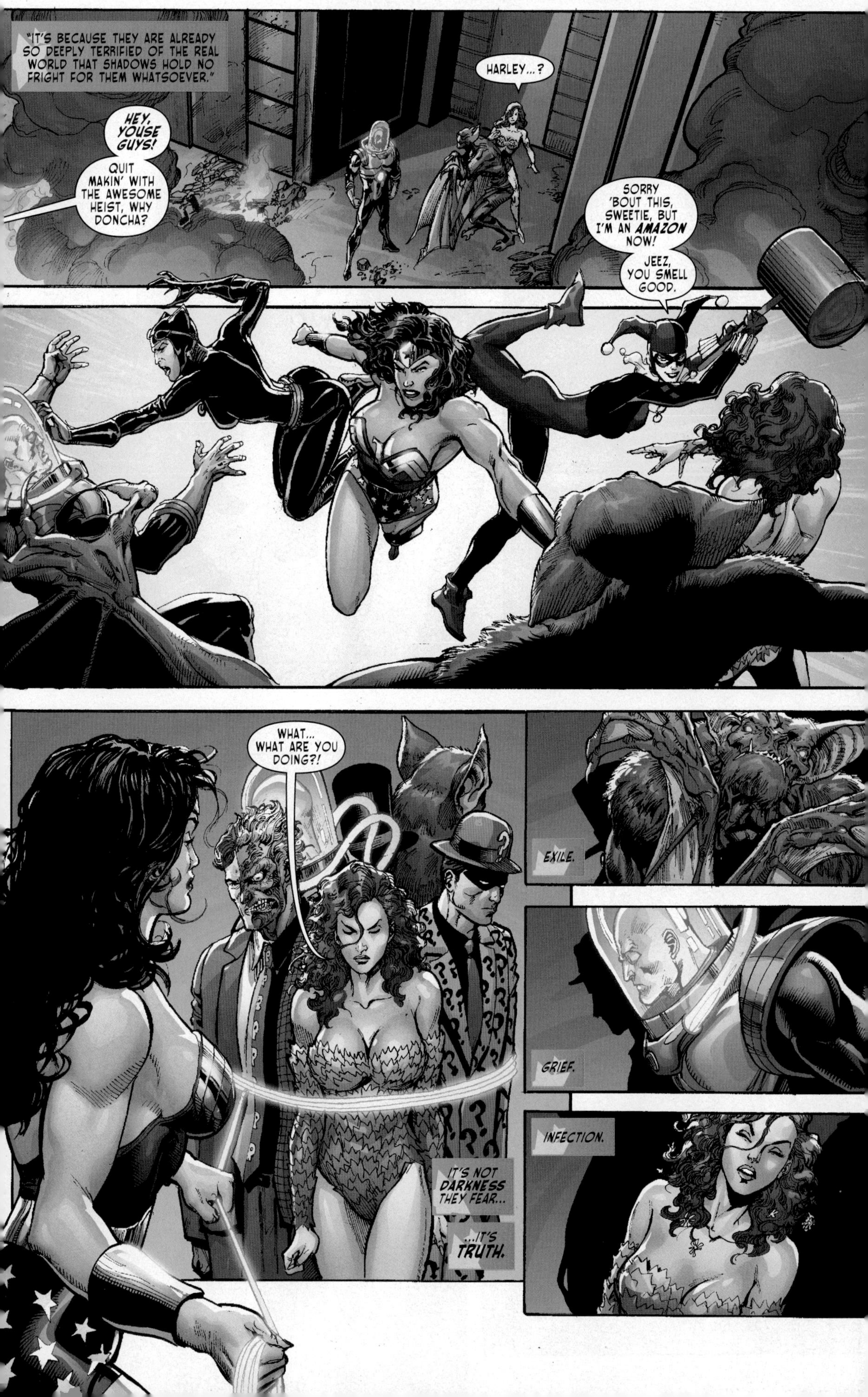
"IT'S BECAUSE THEY ARE ALREADY SO DEEPLY TERRIFIED OF THE REAL WORLD THAT SHADOWS HOLD NO FRIGHT FOR THEM WHATSOEVER."
HARLEY...?
HEY, YOUSE GUYS!
QUIT MAKIN' WITH THE AWESOME HEIST, WHY DONCHA?
SORRY 'BOUT THIS, SWEETIE, BUT I'M AN AMAZON NOW!
JEEZ, YOU SMELL GOOD.
WHAT... WHAT ARE YOU DOING?!
IT'S NOT DARKNESS THEY FEAR...
...IT'S TRUTH.
EXILE.
GRIEF.
INFECTION.

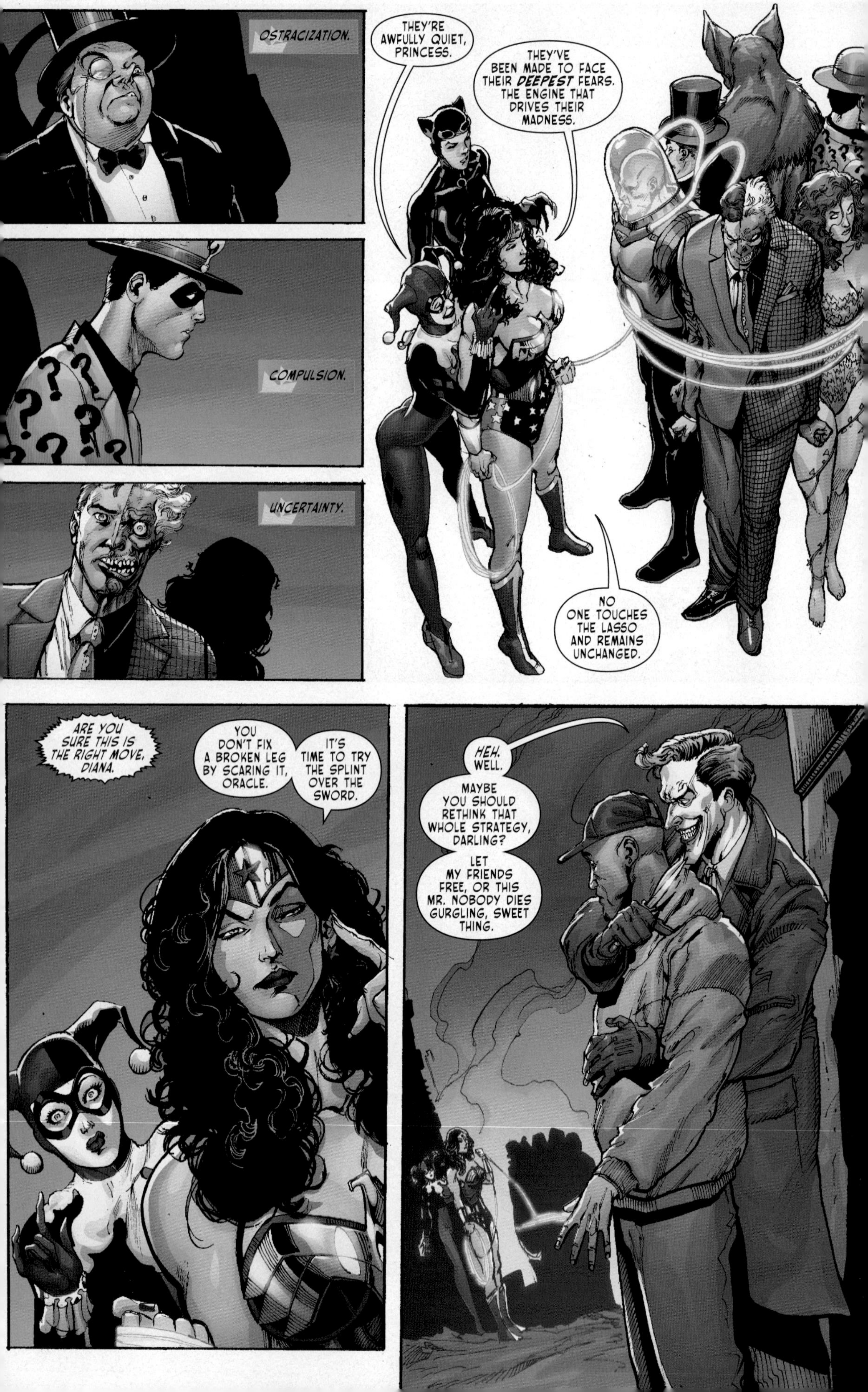
OSTRACIZATION.
COMPULSION.
UNCERTAINTY.
THEY'RE AWFULLY QUIET, PRINCESS.
THEY'VE BEEN MADE TO FACE THEIR DEEPEST FEARS. THE ENGINE THAT DRIVES THEIR MADNESS.
NO ONE TOUCHES THE LASSO AND REMAINS UNCHANGED.
ARE YOU SURE THIS IS THE RIGHT MOVE, DIANA.
YOU DON'T FIX A BROKEN LEG BY SCARING IT, ORACLE.
IT'S TIME TO TRY THE SPLINT OVER THE SWORD.
HEH. WELL.
MAYBE YOU SHOULD RETHINK THAT WHOLE STRATEGY, DARLING?
LET MY FRIENDS FREE, OR THIS MR. NOBODY DIES GURGLING, SWEET THING.

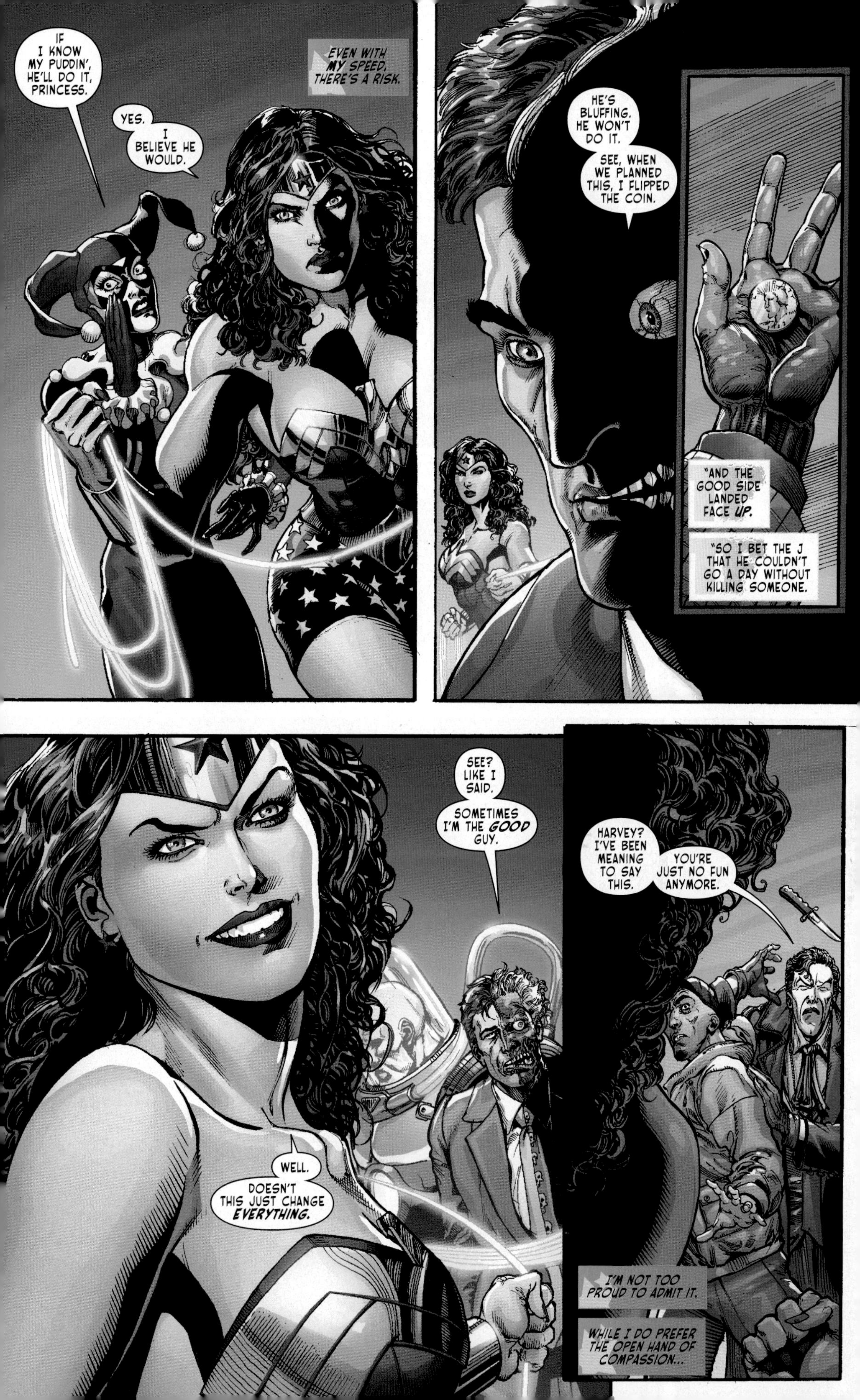
IF I KNOW MY PUDDIN', HE'LL DO IT, PRINCESS.
EVEN WITH MY SPEED, THERE'S A RISK.
YES. I BELIEVE HE WOULD.
HE'S BLUFFING. HE WON'T DO IT.
SEE, WHEN WE PLANNED THIS, I FLIPPED THE COIN.
"AND THE GOOD SIDE LANDED FACE UP.
"SO I BET THE J THAT HE COULDN'T GO A DAY WITHOUT KILLING SOMEONE.
SEE? LIKE I SAID.
SOMETIMES I'M THE GOOD GUY.
WELL.
DOESN'T THIS JUST CHANGE EVERYTHING.
HARVEY? I'VE BEEN MEANING TO SAY THIS.
YOU'RE JUST NO FUN ANYMORE.
I'M NOT TOO PROUD TO ADMIT IT.
WHILE I DO PREFER THE OPEN HAND OF COMPASSION...

I WIN, HARVEY. I WI--

...THE CLOSED FIST HAS ITS CHARMS, AS WELL.

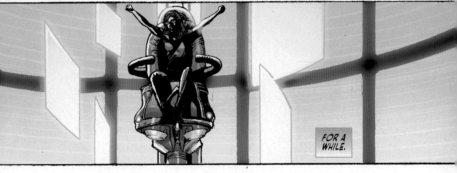

AND I ADMIT IT... I WAS A SKEPTIC.

BUT SHE REALLY DID CHANGE GOTHAM IN HER IMAGE.

FOR A WHILE.

SOME OF THE VILLAINS SHE TOUCHED WENT TO REHAB, AND A COUPLE EVEN WENT STRAIGHT ENTIRELY. WHO'DA THUNK?

EVEN BATMAN, WHEN HE CAME BACK, SEEMED IMPRESSED.

A LITTLE.

I WOULDN'T HAVE THOUGHT IT LIKELY, BUT GOTHAM WILL MISS HER.

SHE WAS STRONG, BUT KIND, AND COMPASSIONATE. HUMAN.

AND BRAVE.

DID I FORGET TO SAY BRAVE?

DEFENDER OF TRUTH

AMANDA DEIBERT
WRITER

CAT STAGGS
ARTIST

JOHN RAUCH
COLORIST

SAIDA TEMOFONTE
LETTERER

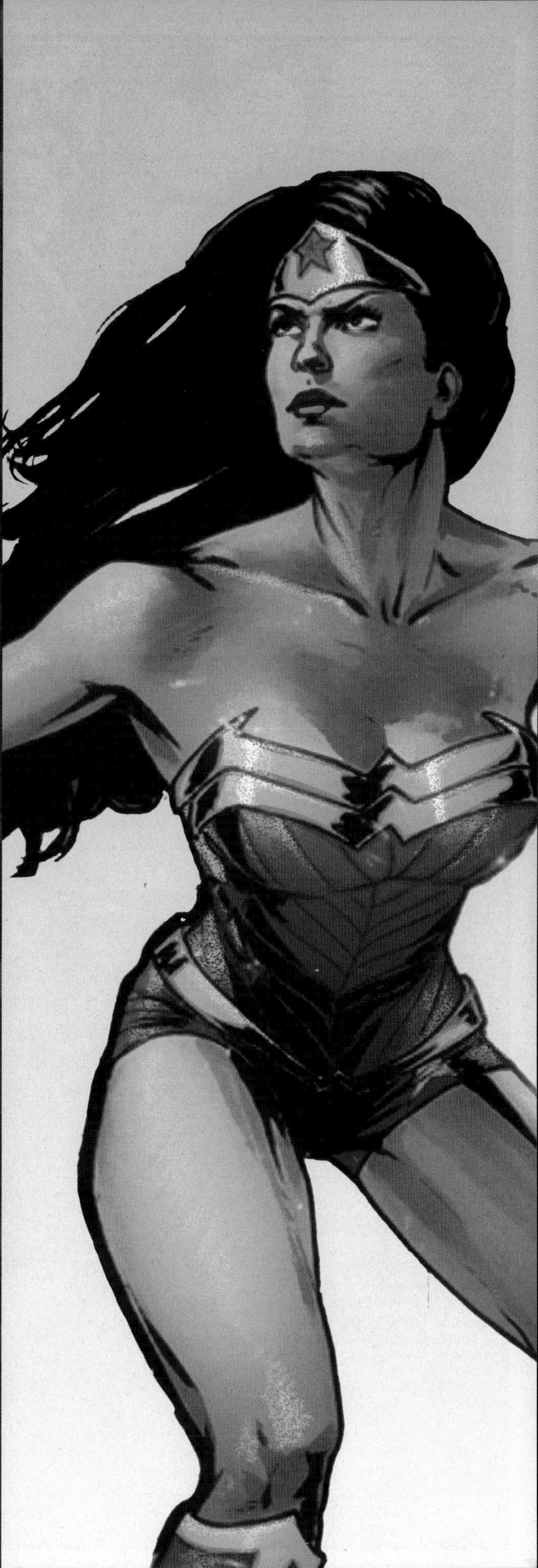

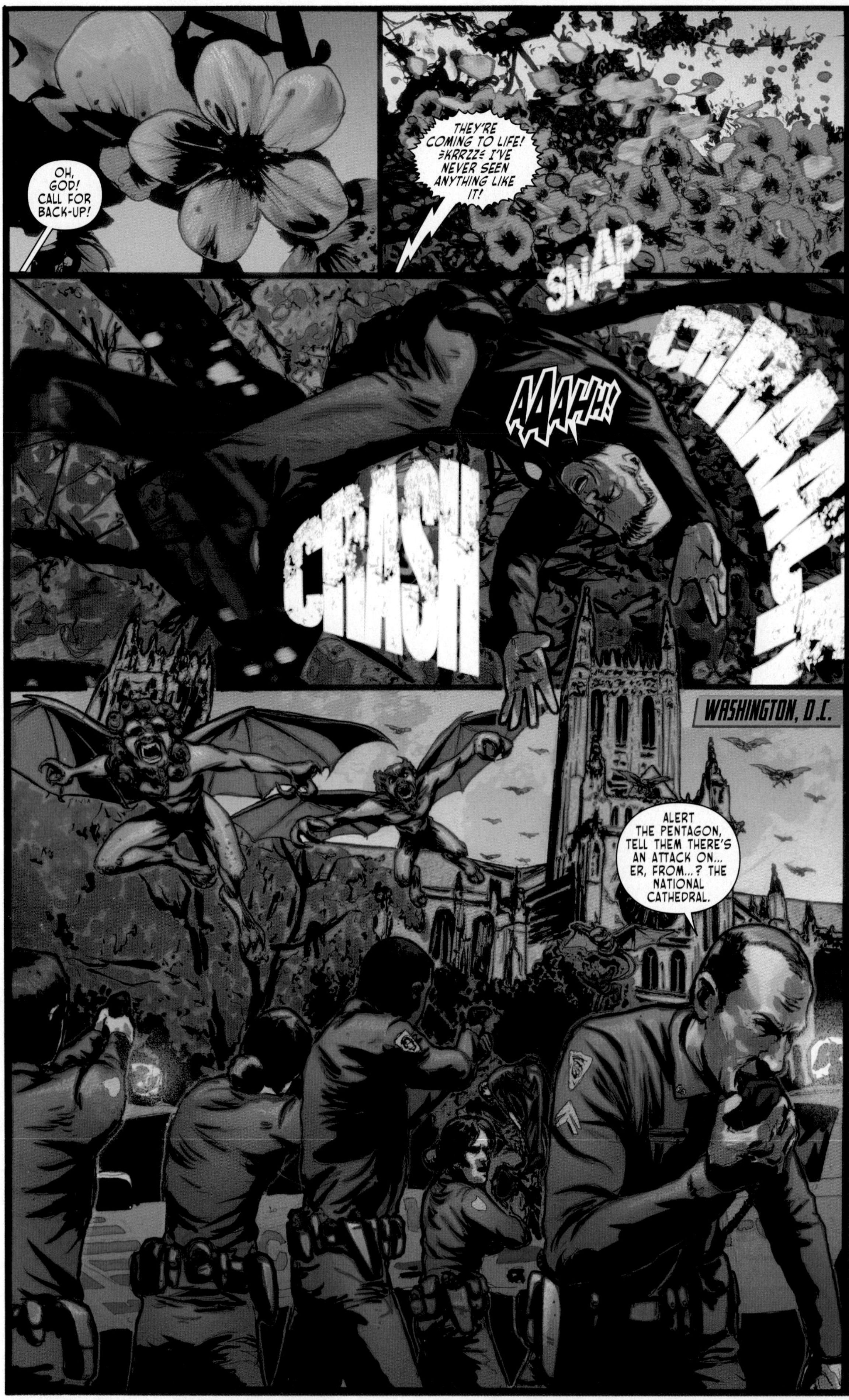
OH, GOD! CALL FOR BACK-UP!
THEY'RE COMING TO LIFE! ≠KRRZZ≠ I'VE NEVER SEEN ANYTHING LIKE IT!
SNAP
CRAAAACK
AAAHH!
CRASH
WASHINGTON, D.C.
ALERT THE PENTAGON, TELL THEM THERE'S AN ATTACK ON... ER, FROM...? THE NATIONAL CATHEDRAL.

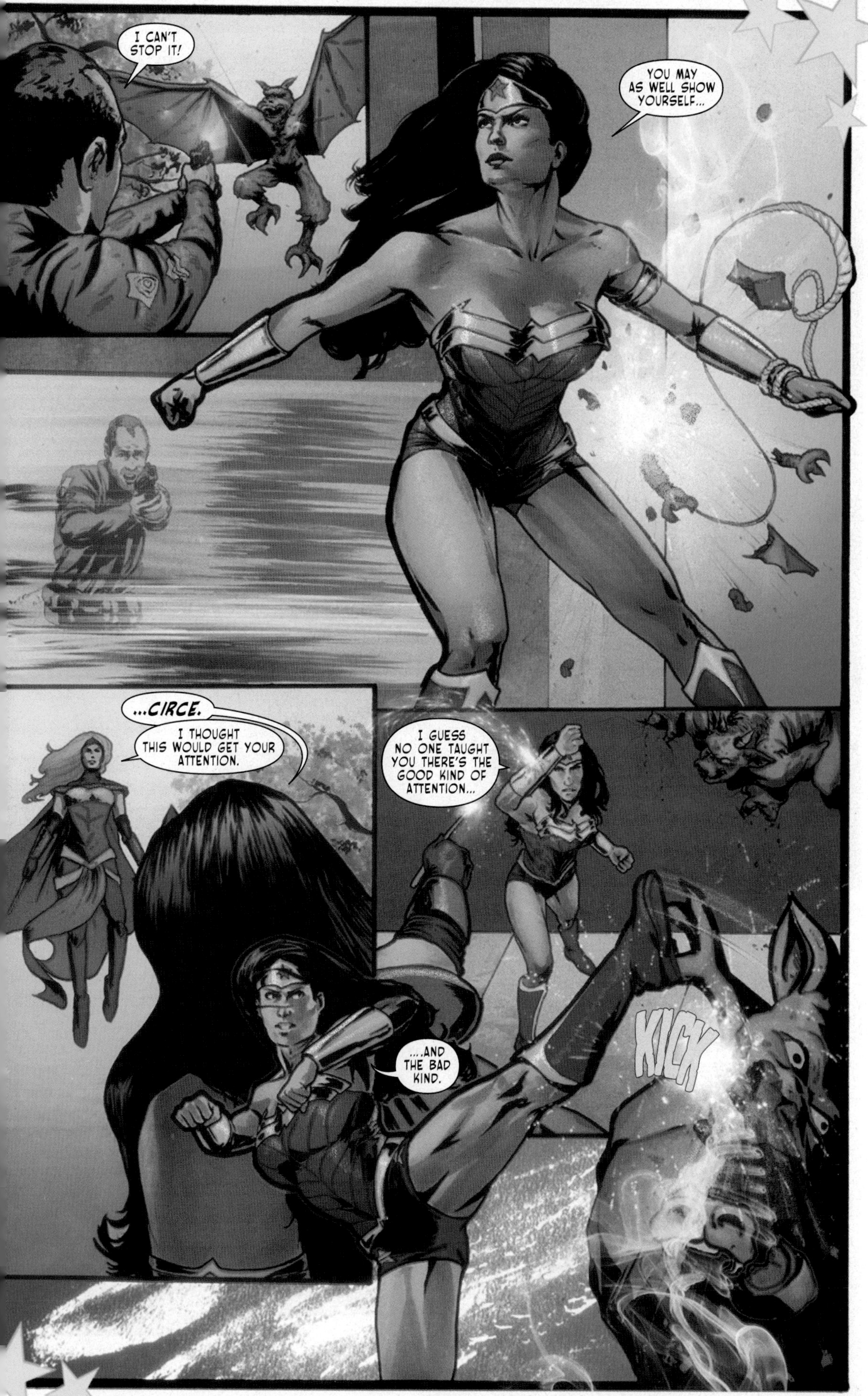

I CAN'T STOP IT!
YOU MAY AS WELL SHOW YOURSELF...
...CIRCE.
I THOUGHT THIS WOULD GET YOUR ATTENTION.
I GUESS NO ONE TAUGHT YOU THERE'S THE GOOD KIND OF ATTENTION...
....AND THE BAD KIND.
KICK

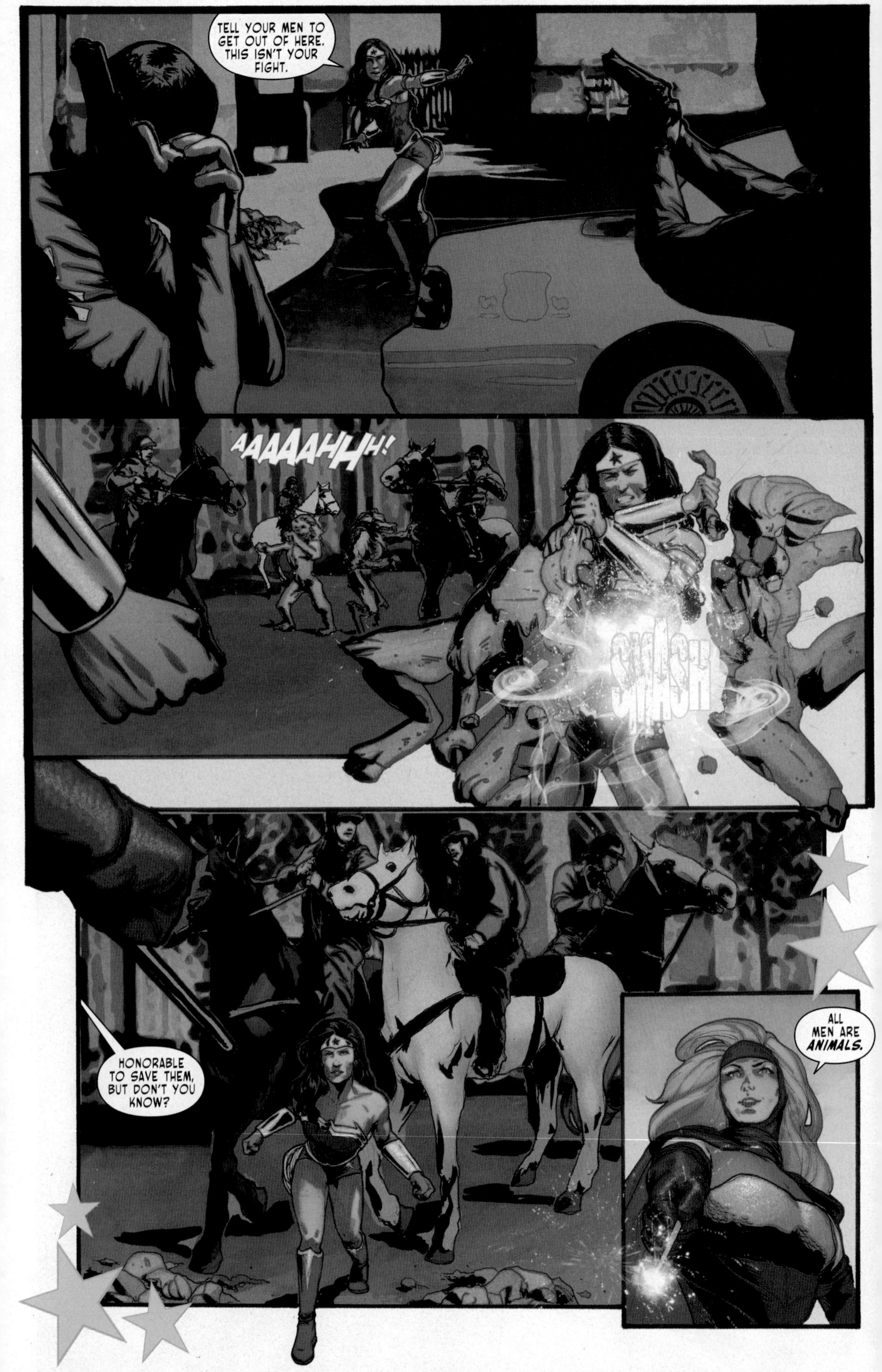
TELL YOUR MEN TO GET OUT OF HERE. THIS ISN'T YOUR FIGHT.
AAAAAHHH!
HONORABLE TO SAVE THEM, BUT DON'T YOU KNOW?
ALL MEN ARE *ANIMALS.*

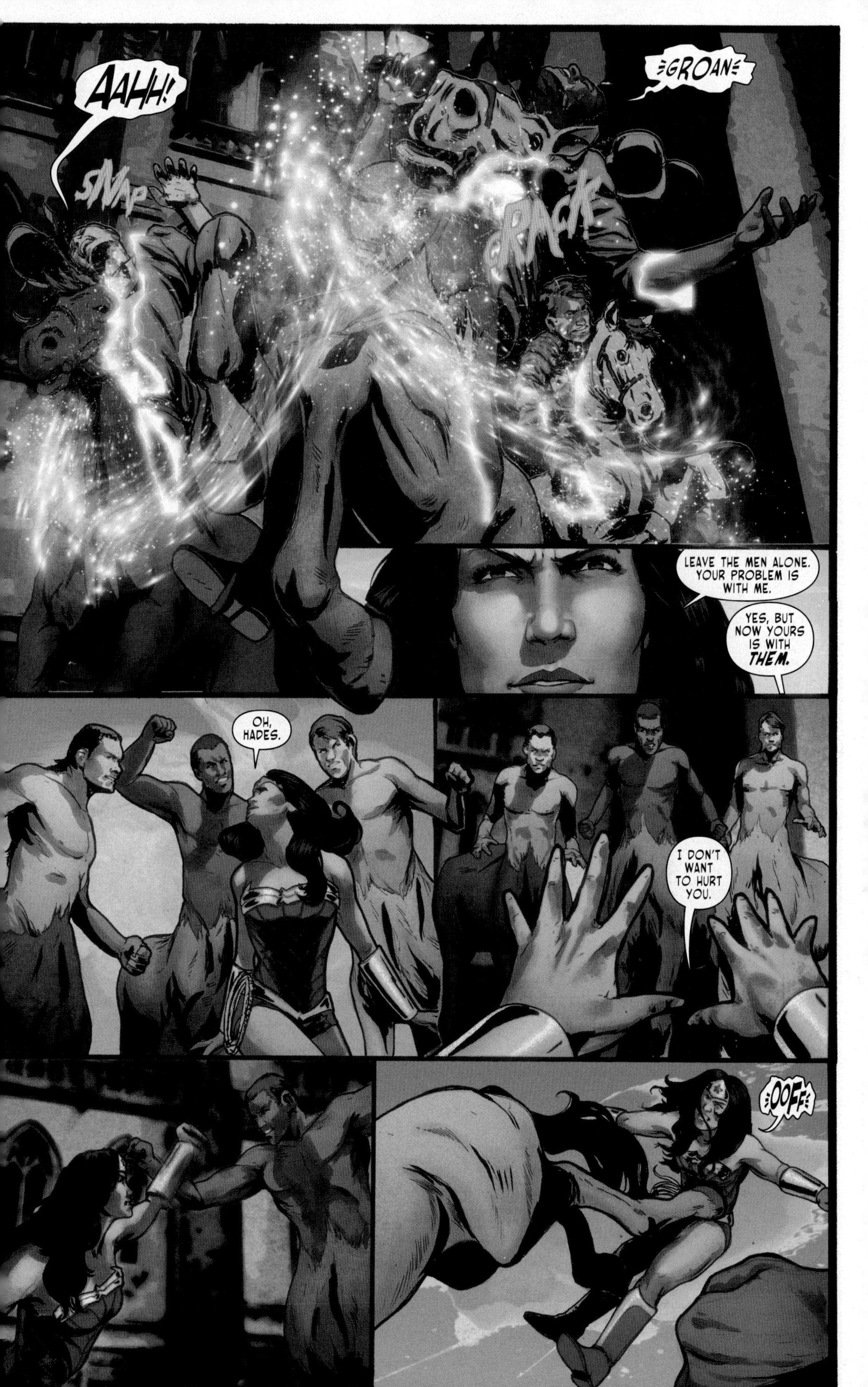
AAHH!
SNAP
GROAN
CRACK
LEAVE THE MEN ALONE. YOUR PROBLEM IS WITH ME.
YES, BUT NOW YOURS IS WITH THEM.
OH, HADES.
I DON'T WANT TO HURT YOU.
OOFF

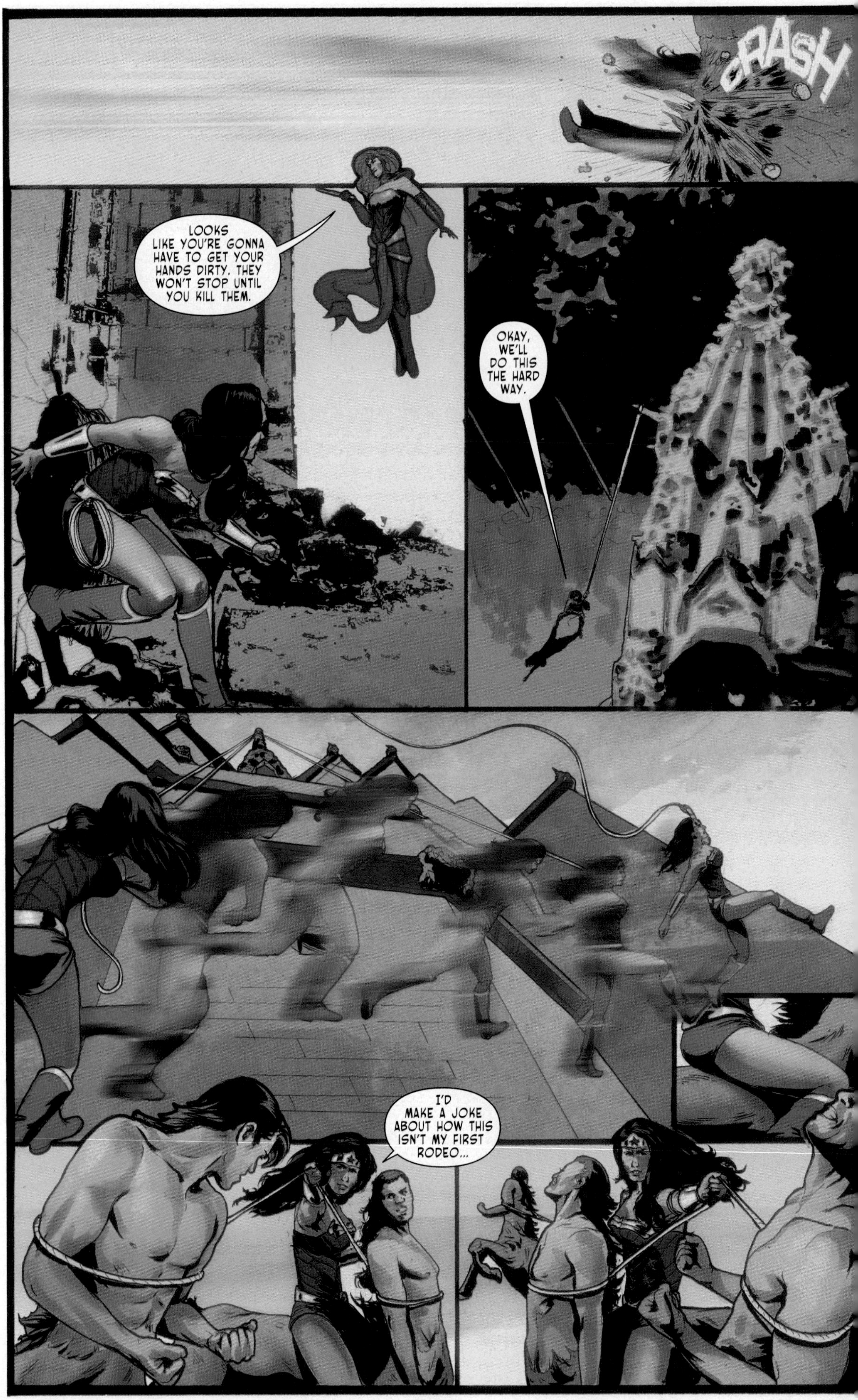
CRASH
LOOKS LIKE YOU'RE GONNA HAVE TO GET YOUR HANDS DIRTY. THEY WON'T STOP UNTIL YOU KILL THEM.
OKAY, WE'LL DO THIS THE HARD WAY.
I'D MAKE A JOKE ABOUT HOW THIS ISN'T MY FIRST RODEO...

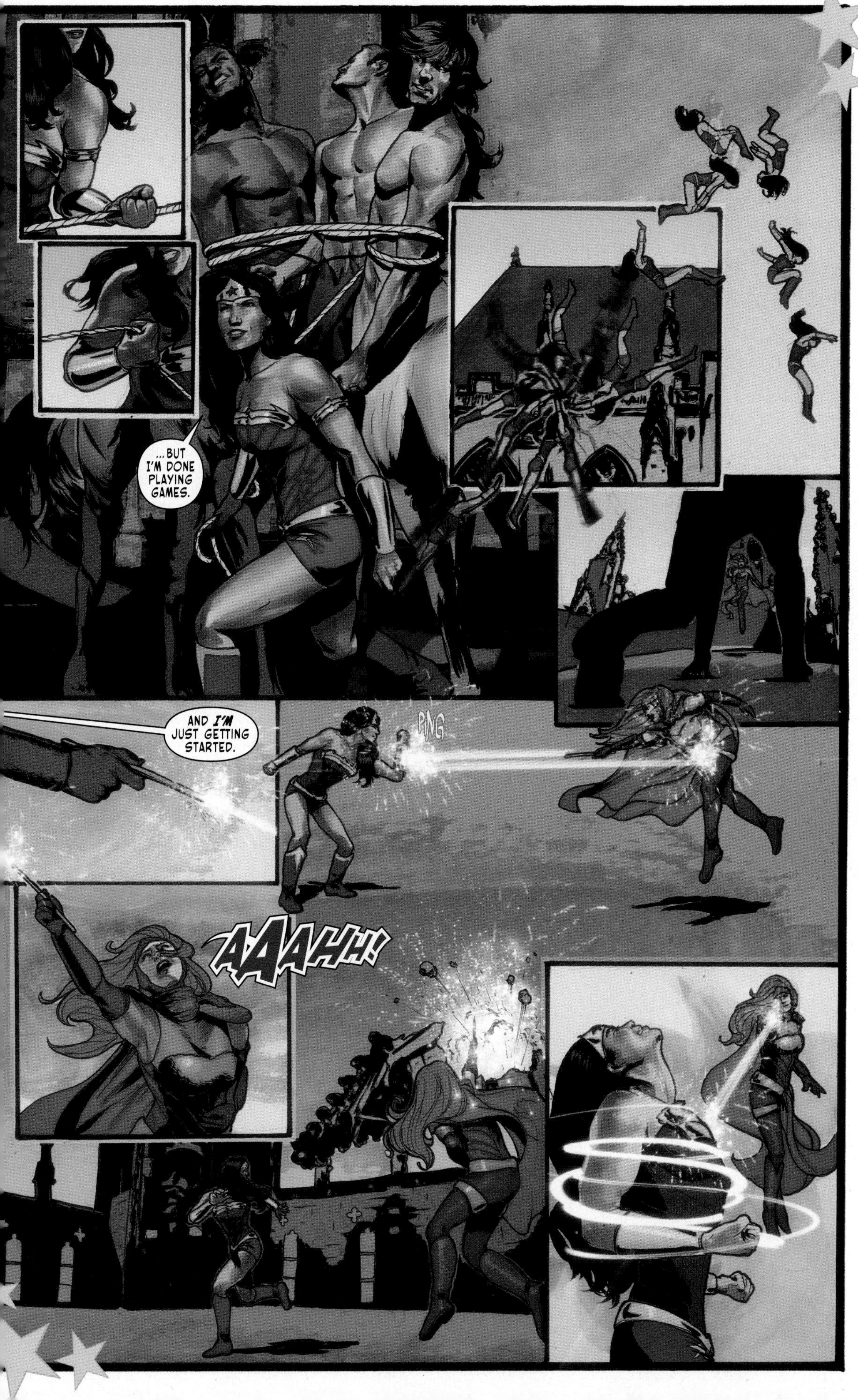
...BUT I'M DONE PLAYING GAMES.
AND I'M JUST GETTING STARTED.
PING
AAAHH!

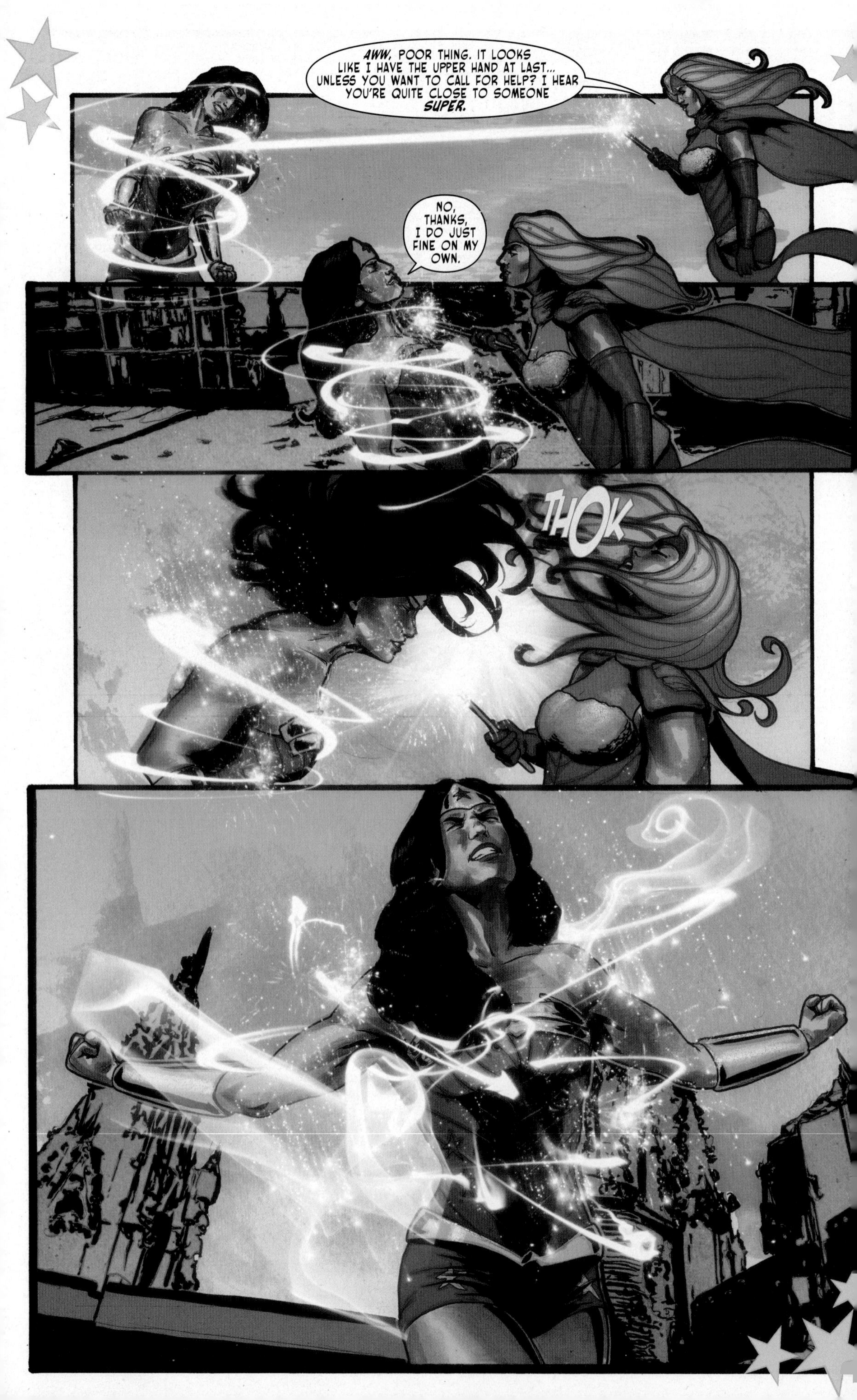
AWW, POOR THING. IT LOOKS LIKE I HAVE THE UPPER HAND AT LAST... UNLESS YOU WANT TO CALL FOR HELP? I HEAR YOU'RE QUITE CLOSE TO SOMEONE SUPER.
NO, THANKS, I DO JUST FINE ON MY OWN.
THOK

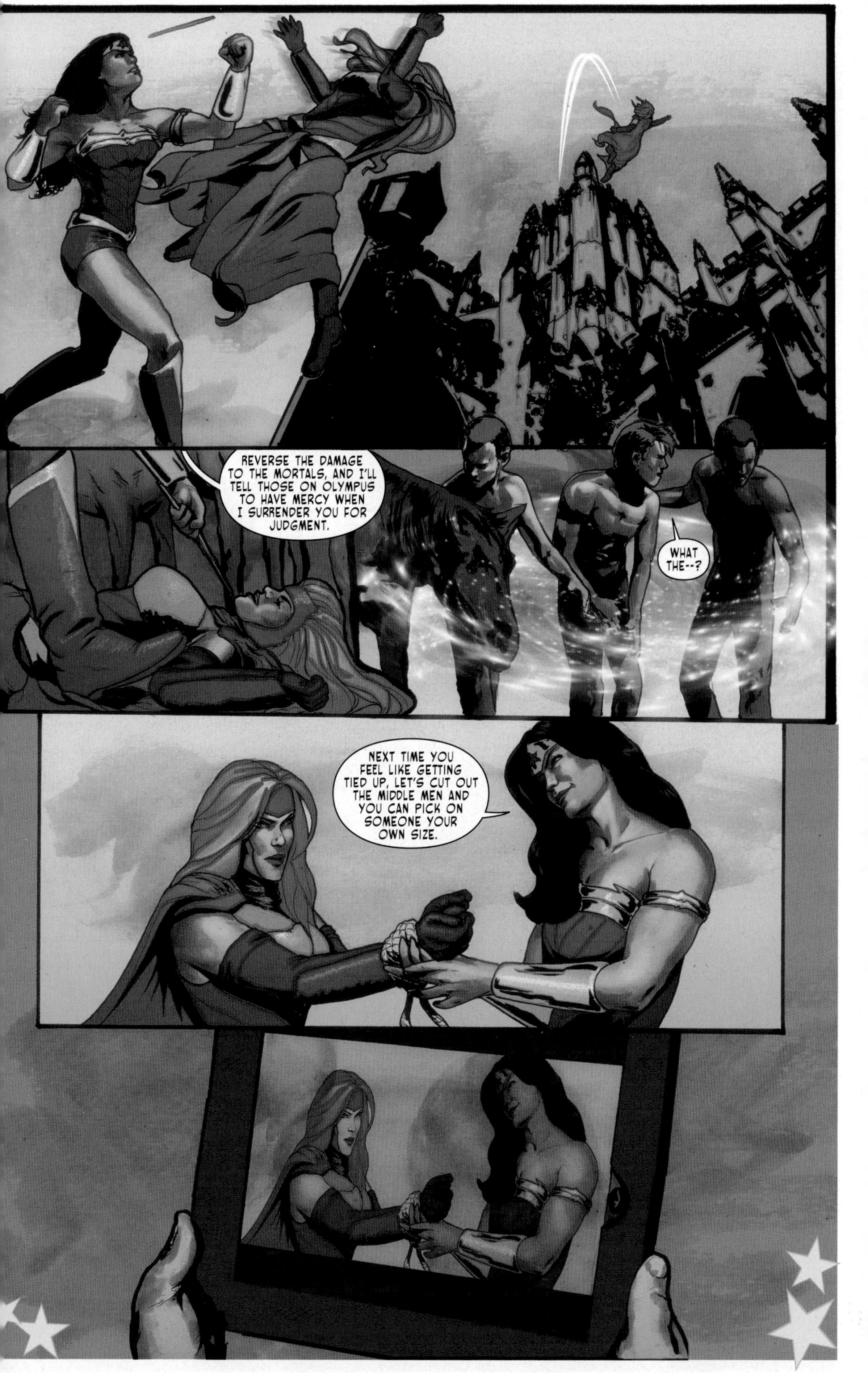
REVERSE THE DAMAGE TO THE MORTALS, AND I'LL TELL THOSE ON OLYMPUS TO HAVE MERCY WHEN I SURRENDER YOU FOR JUDGMENT.
WHAT THE--?
NEXT TIME YOU FEEL LIKE GETTING TIED UP, LET'S CUT OUT THE MIDDLE MEN AND YOU CAN PICK ON SOMEONE YOUR OWN SIZE.

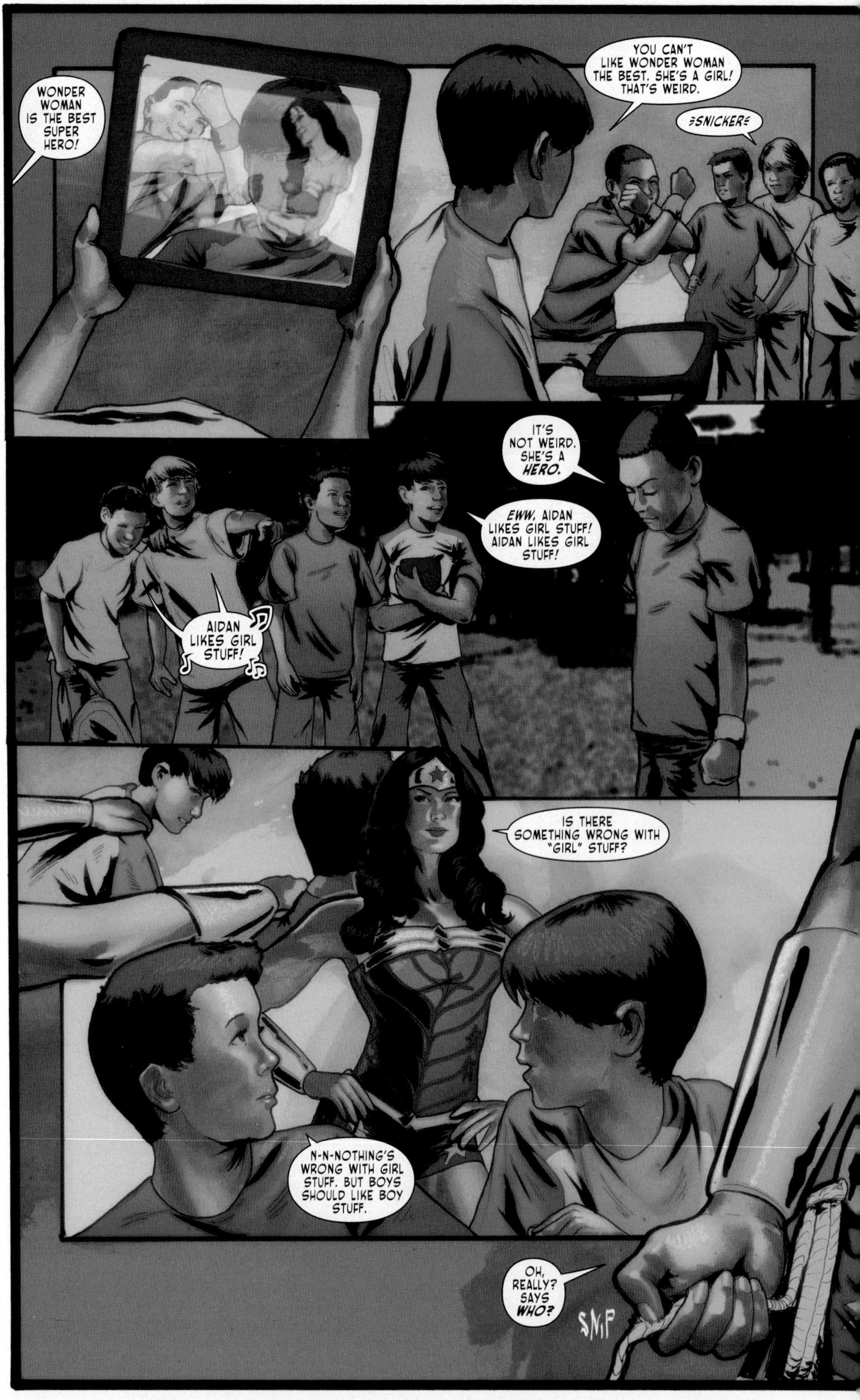
WONDER WOMAN IS THE BEST SUPER HERO!
YOU CAN'T LIKE WONDER WOMAN THE BEST. SHE'S A GIRL! THAT'S WEIRD.
SNICKER
IT'S NOT WEIRD. SHE'S A HERO.
EWW, AIDAN LIKES GIRL STUFF! AIDAN LIKES GIRL STUFF!
AIDAN LIKES GIRL STUFF!
IS THERE SOMETHING WRONG WITH "GIRL" STUFF?
N-N-NOTHING'S WRONG WITH GIRL STUFF. BUT BOYS SHOULD LIKE BOY STUFF.
OH, REALLY? SAYS WHO?
SNIP

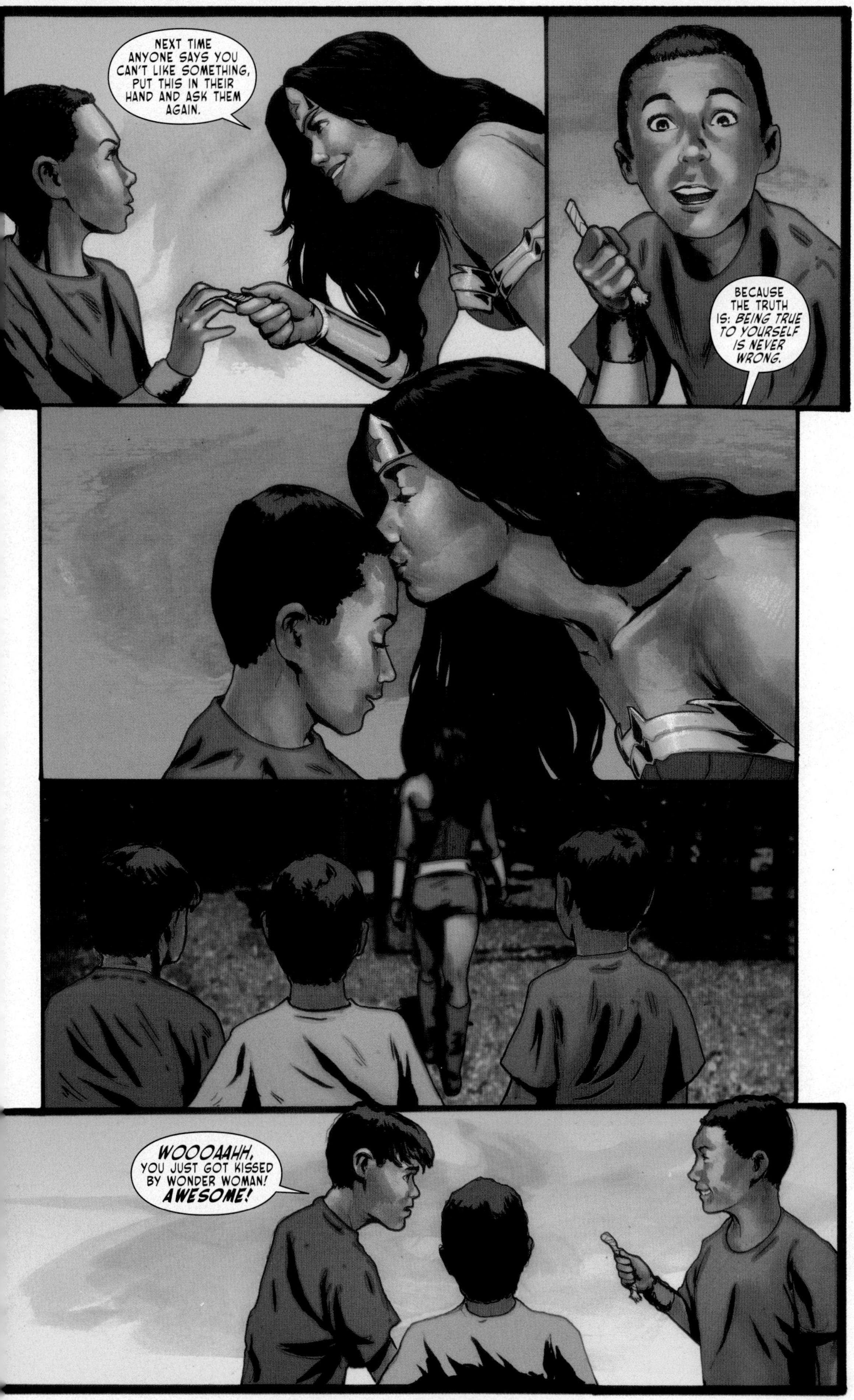
NEXT TIME ANYONE SAYS YOU CAN'T LIKE SOMETHING, PUT THIS IN THEIR HAND AND ASK THEM AGAIN.
BECAUSE THE TRUTH IS: *BEING TRUE TO YOURSELF IS NEVER WRONG.*
WOOOAAHH, YOU JUST GOT KISSED BY WONDER WOMAN! ***AWESOME!***

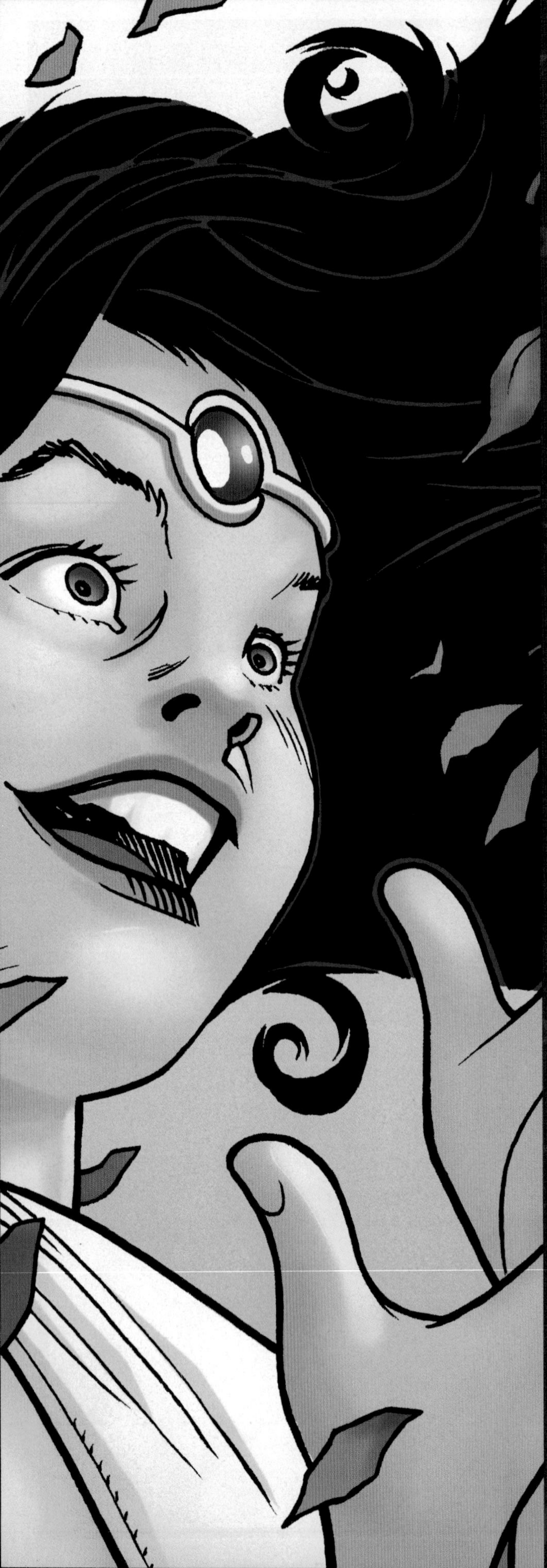

BRACE YOURSELF

JASON BISCHOFF
WRITER

DAVID A. WILLIAMS
ARTIST

WENDY BROOME
COLORIST

SAIDA TEMOFONTE
LETTERER

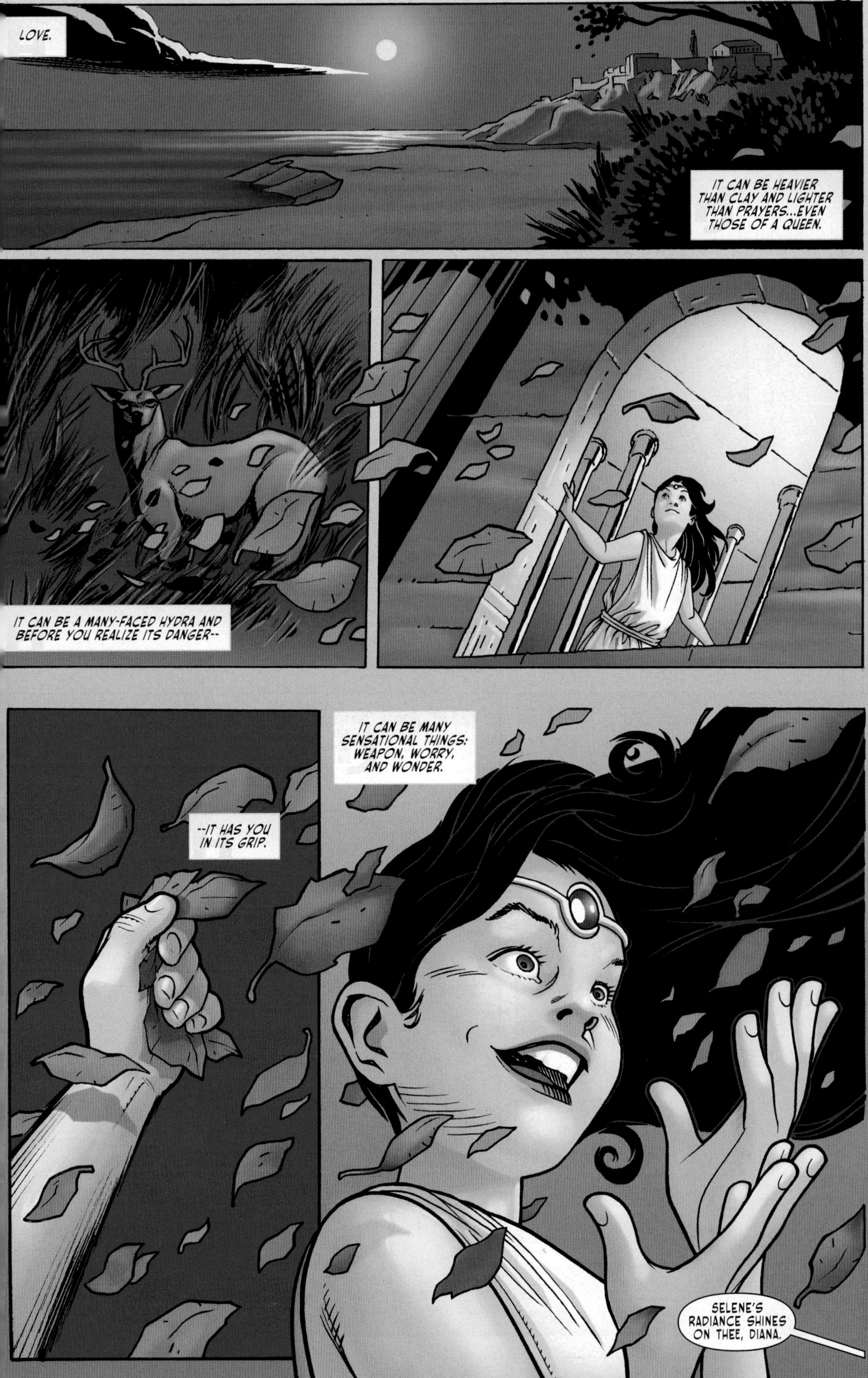
LOVE.
IT CAN BE HEAVIER THAN CLAY AND LIGHTER THAN PRAYERS...EVEN THOSE OF A QUEEN.
IT CAN BE A MANY-FACED HYDRA AND BEFORE YOU REALIZE ITS DANGER--
IT CAN BE MANY SENSATIONAL THINGS: WEAPON, WORRY, AND WONDER.
--IT HAS YOU IN ITS GRIP.
SELENE'S RADIANCE SHINES ON THEE, DIANA.

MOTHER, NOT IN FRONT OF THE IMPERIAL GUARD!

GODS, WHAT MUST DAMALI AND CALLIDORA THINK? IT'S BAD ENOUGH YOU DO IT AT ALL!

AM I NOT A LION? AM I NOT A WARRIOR?! AM I NOT A--

--FRAID?

WHAT IS IT?

THE CATACOMBS OF THE ISLAND, PRINCESS, THE WATCH OF OUR SLEEPING SISTERS.

A LION YOU MAY BE, DAUGHTER, BUT TONIGHT, BEYOND THIS DOOR, YOU ARE AN AMAZON MADE!

COME, THERE IS MUCH TO LEARN.

SOME ON OLYMPUS INSIST OUR TALE A TRAGEDY, OTHERS, STILL A COMEDY UNWRIT. I BELIEVE IT IS ONE OF HOPE.

FROM THE SHACKLES OF MORTAL DEATH, WE AMAZONS WERE RAISED IN THE WATERS OF JUSTICE.

OUR MISSION WAS PEACE.

JUSTICE!

PEACE!

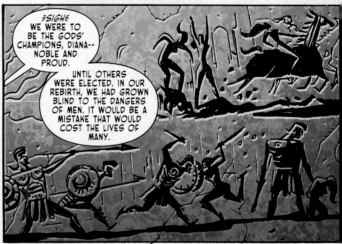

≡SIGH≡ WE WERE TO BE THE GODS' CHAMPIONS, DIANA-- NOBLE AND PROUD.

UNTIL OTHERS WERE ELECTED. IN OUR REBIRTH, WE HAD GROWN BLIND TO THE DANGERS OF MEN. IT WOULD BE A MISTAKE THAT WOULD COST THE LIVES OF MANY.

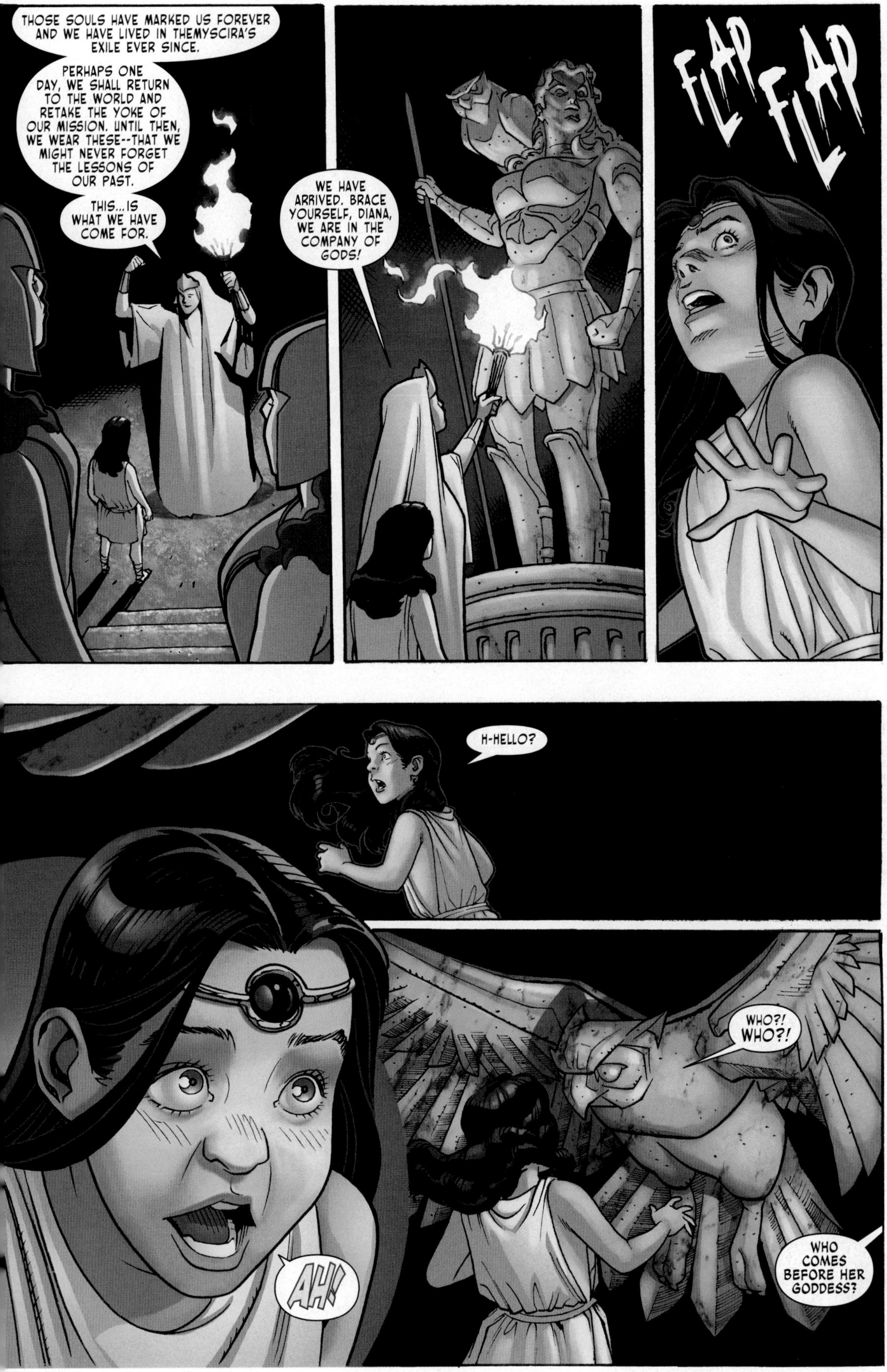
THOSE SOULS HAVE MARKED US FOREVER AND WE HAVE LIVED IN THEMYSCIRA'S EXILE EVER SINCE.
PERHAPS ONE DAY, WE SHALL RETURN TO THE WORLD AND RETAKE THE YOKE OF OUR MISSION. UNTIL THEN, WE WEAR THESE--THAT WE MIGHT NEVER FORGET THE LESSONS OF OUR PAST.
THIS...IS WHAT WE HAVE COME FOR.
WE HAVE ARRIVED. BRACE YOURSELF, DIANA, WE ARE IN THE COMPANY OF GODS!
FLAP FLAP
H-HELLO?
WHO?! WHO?!
WHO COMES BEFORE HER GODDESS?
AH!

ME, DIANA.

ARE-- ARE YOU ATHENA?

I AM ONE AND THE SAME.

YOUR OWL'S SCARY.

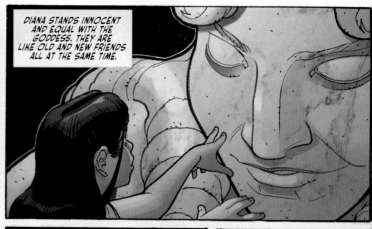

DIANA STANDS INNOCENT AND EQUAL WITH THE GODDESS. THEY ARE LIKE OLD AND NEW FRIENDS ALL AT THE SAME TIME.

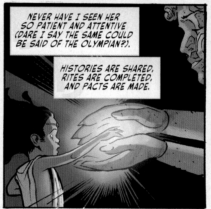

NEVER HAVE I SEEN HER SO PATIENT AND ATTENTIVE (DARE I SAY THE SAME COULD BE SAID OF THE OLYMPIAN?).

HISTORIES ARE SHARED, RITES ARE COMPLETED, AND PACTS ARE MADE.

REMEMBER YOUR OATHS ALWAYS, LITTLE AMAZON. MAY HOPE, TRUTH, PEACE, AND JUSTICE BE YOUR LEGACY.

WHAT I WOULD GIVE TO SEE THE WORLD MY DAUGHTER INHERITS, THE WORLD SHE SHAPES!

IT'S HEAVY.

NO LESS HEAVY THAN THE RESPONSIBILITY WE BEAR.

I WANT ANOTHER! YOU HAVE TWO, DAMALI.

THE SECOND WAS EARNED IN COMBAT, MY PRINCESS.

SUCH IS THE TRADITION. IF THIS IS YOUR DESIRE, DAUGHTER, BE WARNED: THERE IS ONLY ONE ON THIS ISLAND WORTHY OF A PRINCESS'S CHALLENGE--

--ME. THE PRIZE IS YOURS IF YOU CAN BEST ME AND ONLY ME, MY CHEEKY LAMB!

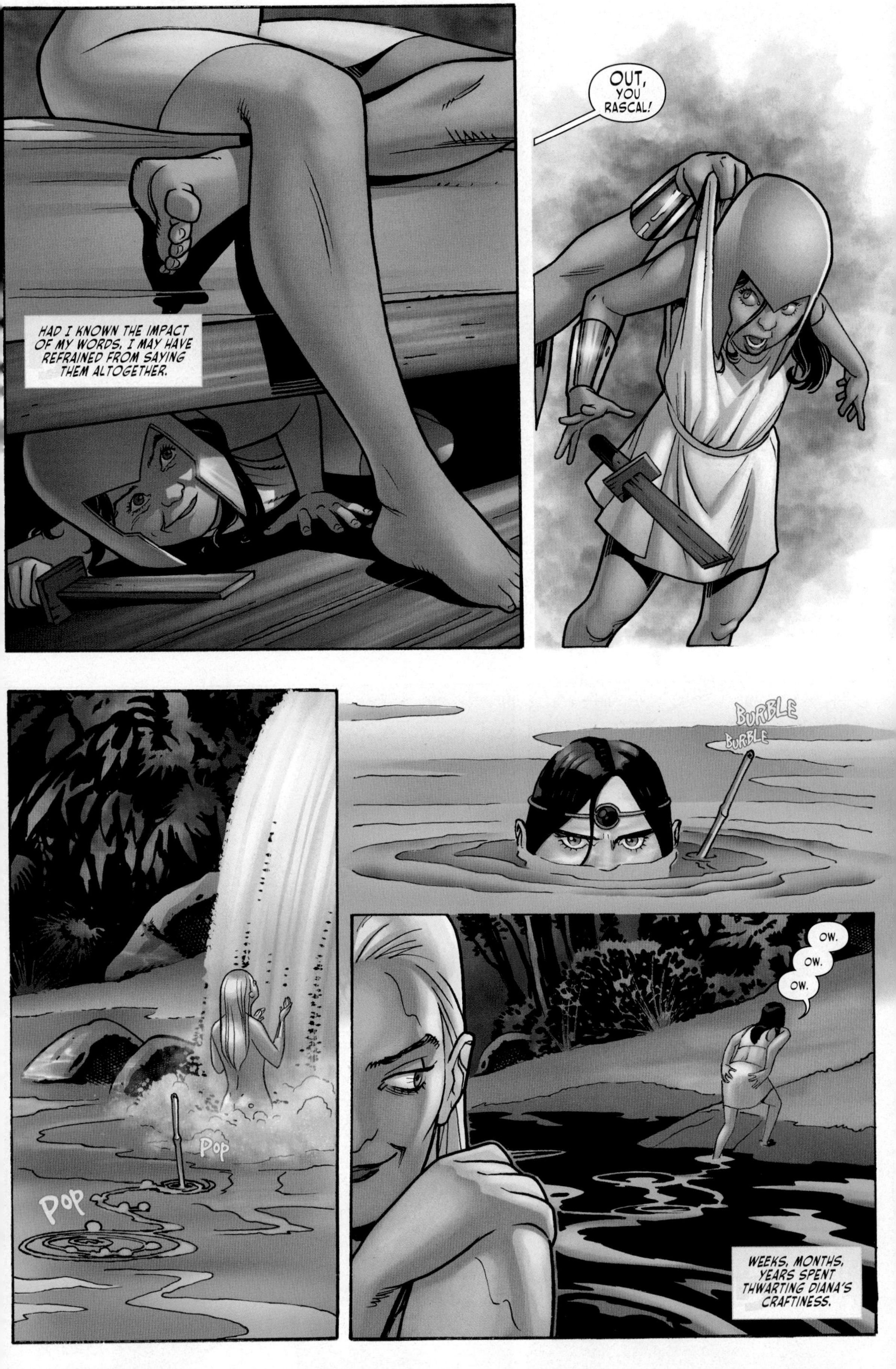
HAD I KNOWN THE IMPACT OF MY WORDS, I MAY HAVE REFRAINED FROM SAYING THEM ALTOGETHER.
OUT, YOU RASCAL!
BURBLE
BURBLE
POP
POP
OW.
OW.
OW.
WEEKS, MONTHS, YEARS SPENT THWARTING DIANA'S CRAFTINESS.

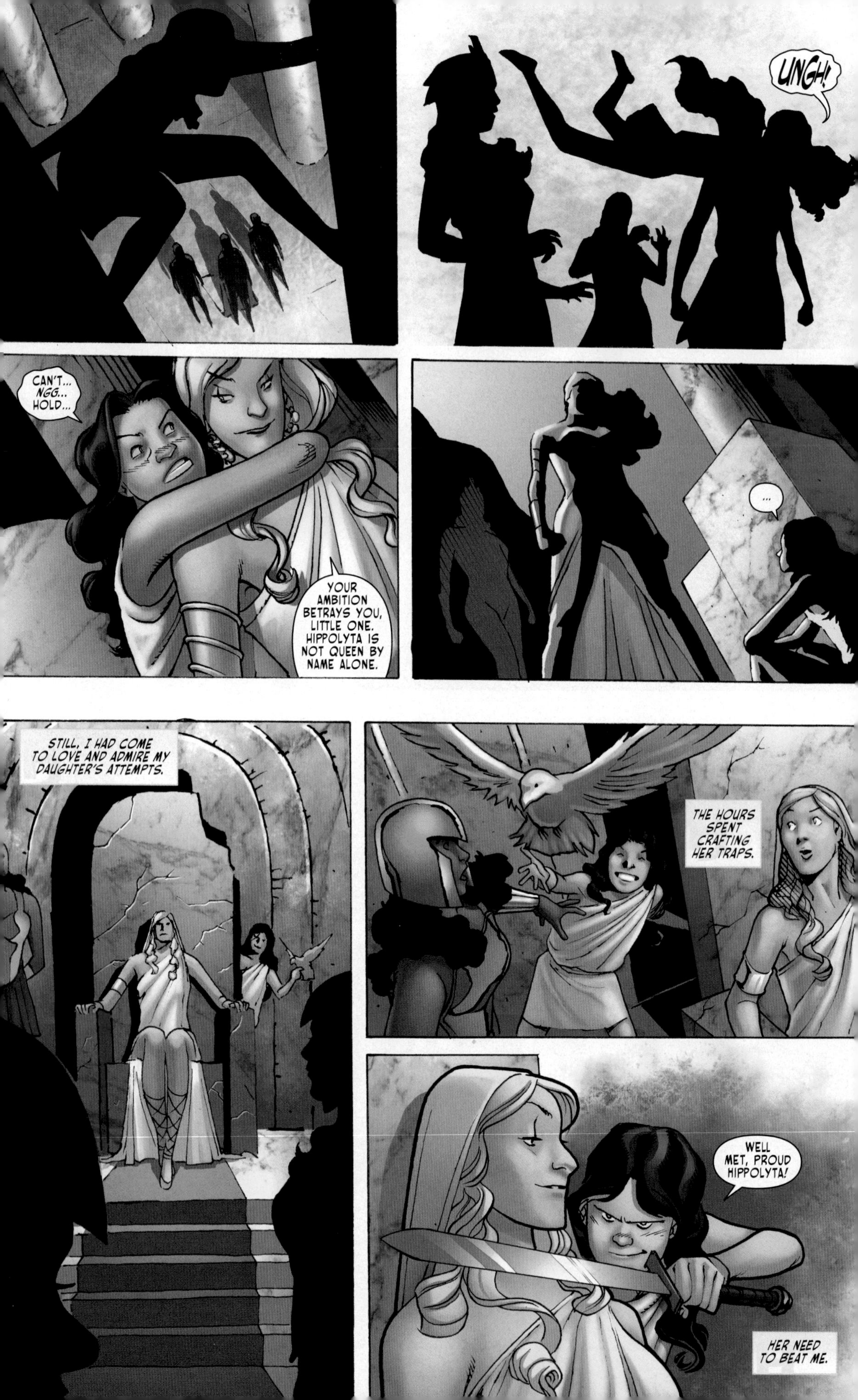
UNGH!
CAN'T... NGG... HOLD...
YOUR AMBITION BETRAYS YOU, LITTLE ONE. HIPPOLYTA IS NOT QUEEN BY NAME ALONE.
...
STILL, I HAD COME TO LOVE AND ADMIRE MY DAUGHTER'S ATTEMPTS.
THE HOURS SPENT CRAFTING HER TRAPS.
WELL MET, PROUD HIPPOLYTA!
HER NEED TO BEAT ME.

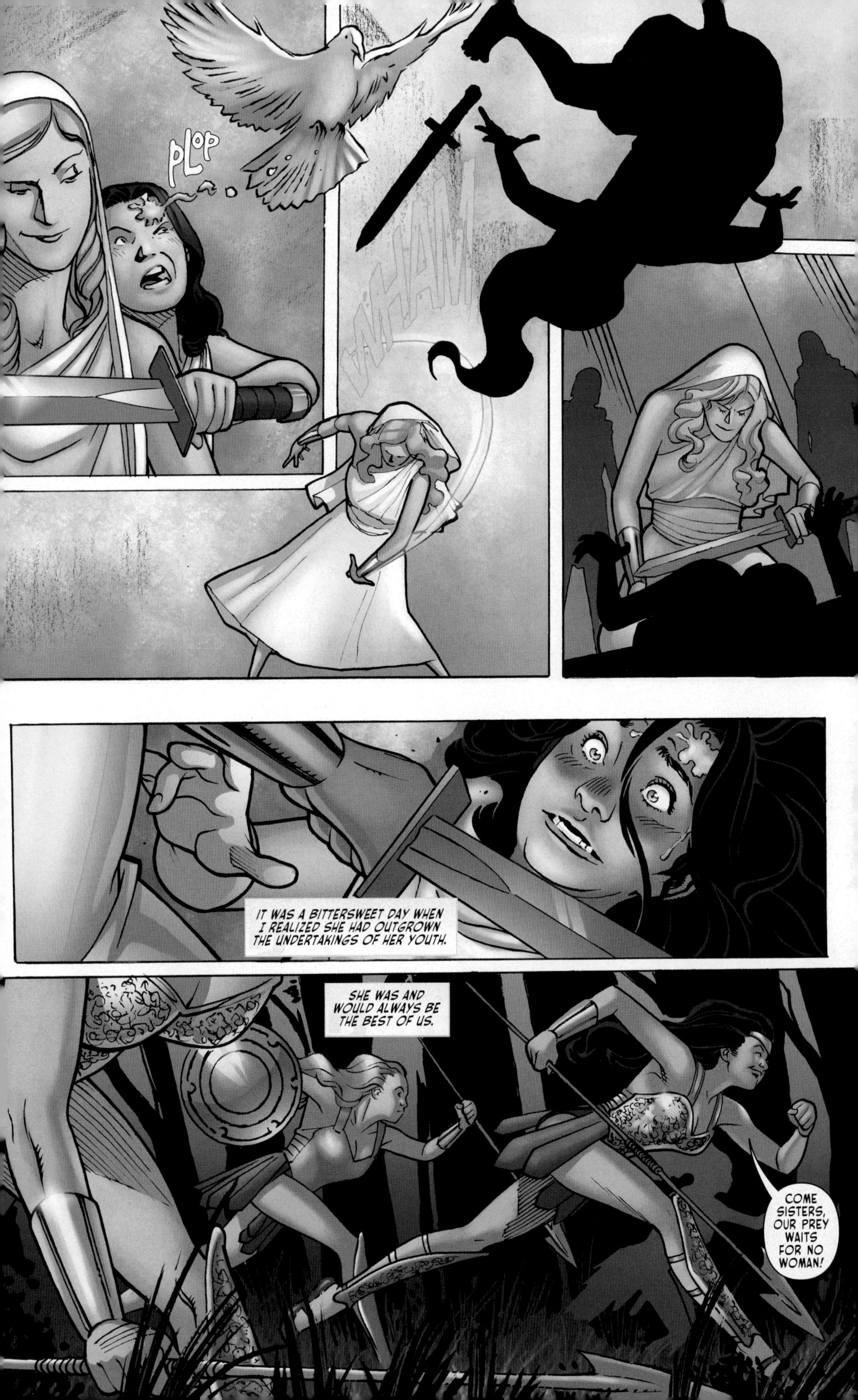
PLOP
WHAM
IT WAS A BITTERSWEET DAY WHEN I REALIZED SHE HAD OUTGROWN THE UNDERTAKINGS OF HER YOUTH.
SHE WAS AND WOULD ALWAYS BE THE BEST OF US.
COME SISTERS, OUR PREY WAITS FOR NO WOMAN!

DIANA IS THE EMBODIMENT OF OUR IDEALS, UNENCUMBERED WITH THE BURDENS OF OUR PAST.

HOW COULD I LET HER GO?

THIS CONTEST SHALL DETERMINE THE MOST CAPABLE AMONG YOU TO BE OUR EMISSARY TO THE OUTSIDE WORLD.

FIGHT WITH HONOR!

AS YOU SEE, MY QUEEN, HE IS NO THREAT TO OUR PEOPLE. HE NEEDS OUR HELP.

LET US MAKE OF HIM AN EXAMPLE. LET US SEE HIS SAFE RETURN!

TO MUCH PROTEST, I HAD FORBIDDEN MY DAUGHTER TO ENTER. LITTLE DID I KNOW, I HAD ONLY STOKED THE FIRE OF HER INDEPENDENCE.

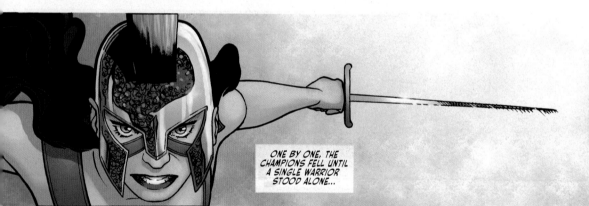

ONE BY ONE, THE CHAMPIONS FELL UNTIL A SINGLE WARRIOR STOOD ALONE...

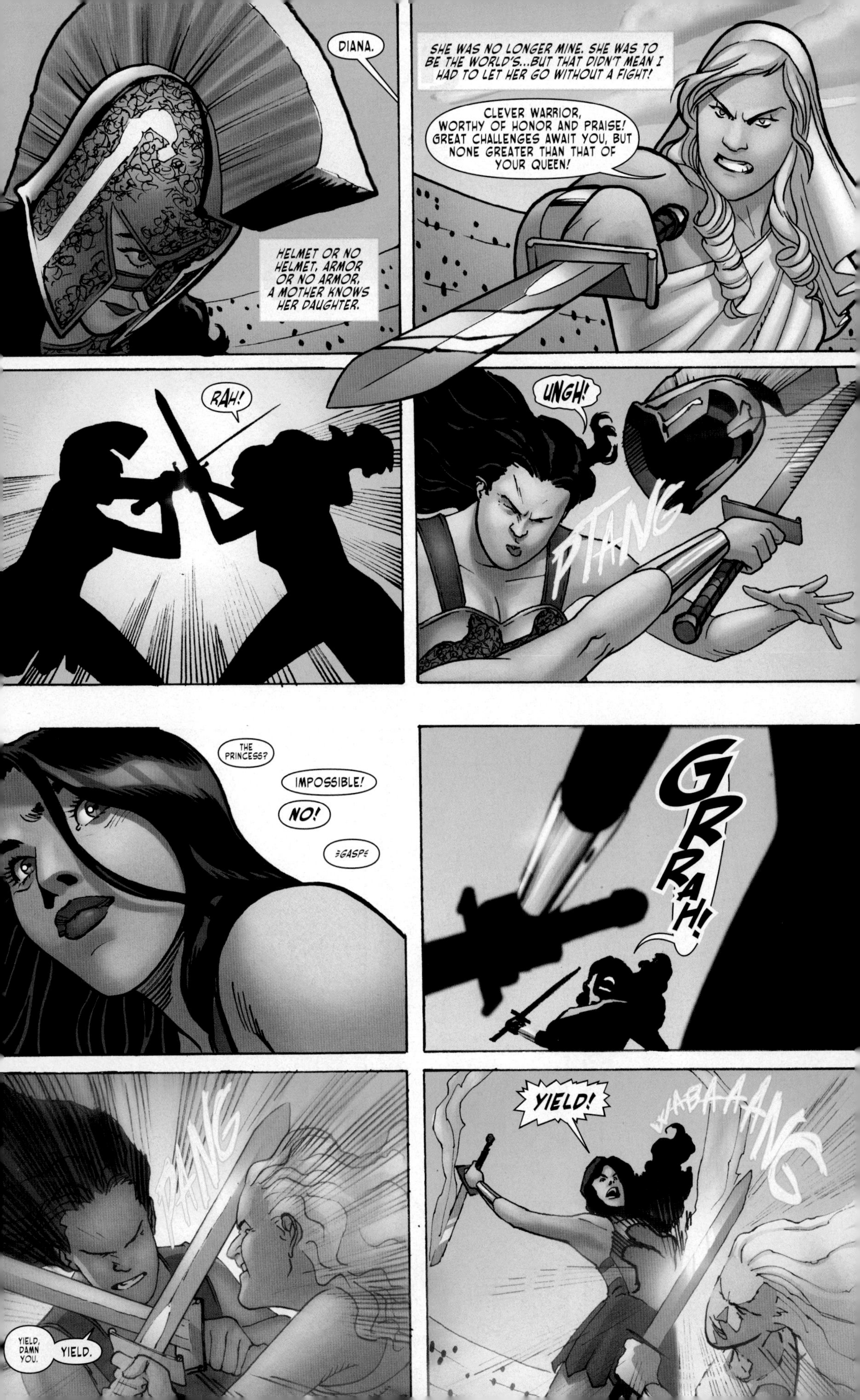
DIANA.
HELMET OR NO HELMET, ARMOR OR NO ARMOR, A MOTHER KNOWS HER DAUGHTER.
SHE WAS NO LONGER MINE. SHE WAS TO BE THE WORLD'S...BUT THAT DIDN'T MEAN I HAD TO LET HER GO WITHOUT A FIGHT!
CLEVER WARRIOR, WORTHY OF HONOR AND PRAISE! GREAT CHALLENGES AWAIT YOU, BUT NONE GREATER THAN THAT OF YOUR QUEEN!
RAH!
UNGH!
PTANG
THE PRINCESS?
IMPOSSIBLE!
NO!
GASP
GRRAAH!
PANG
YIELD, DAMN YOU.
YIELD.
YIELD!
WABAAANG

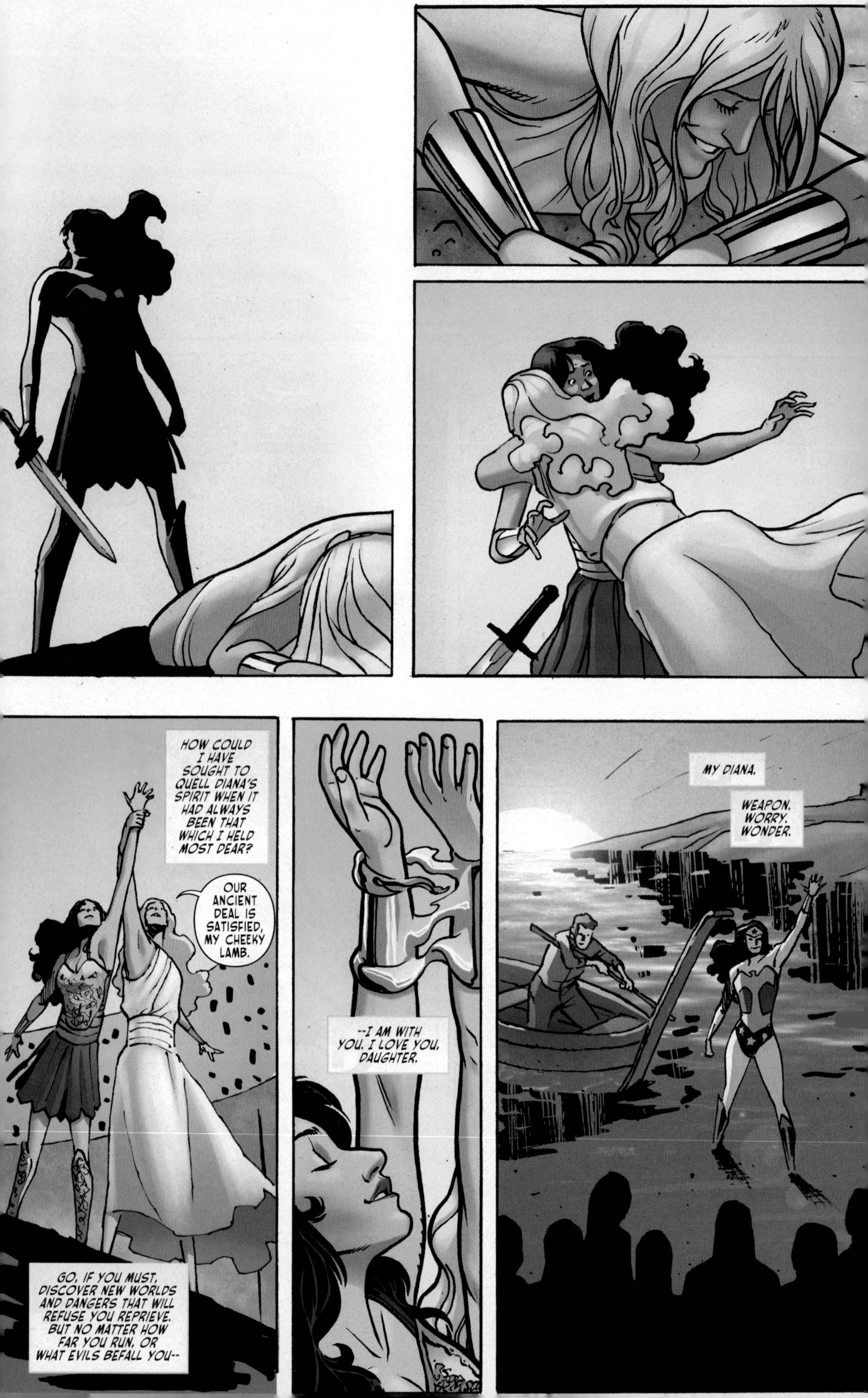
HOW COULD I HAVE SOUGHT TO QUELL DIANA'S SPIRIT WHEN IT HAD ALWAYS BEEN THAT WHICH I HELD MOST DEAR?
OUR ANCIENT DEAL IS SATISFIED, MY CHEEKY LAMB.
GO, IF YOU MUST, DISCOVER NEW WORLDS AND DANGERS THAT WILL REFUSE YOU REPRIEVE. BUT NO MATTER HOW FAR YOU RUN, OR WHAT EVILS BEFALL YOU--
--I AM WITH YOU. I LOVE YOU, DAUGHTER.
MY DIANA.
WEAPON. WORRY. WONDER.

TAKETH AWAY

IVAN COHEN
WRITER

MARCUS TO
ARTIST

ANDREW DALHOUSE
COLORIST

DERON BENNET
LETTERER

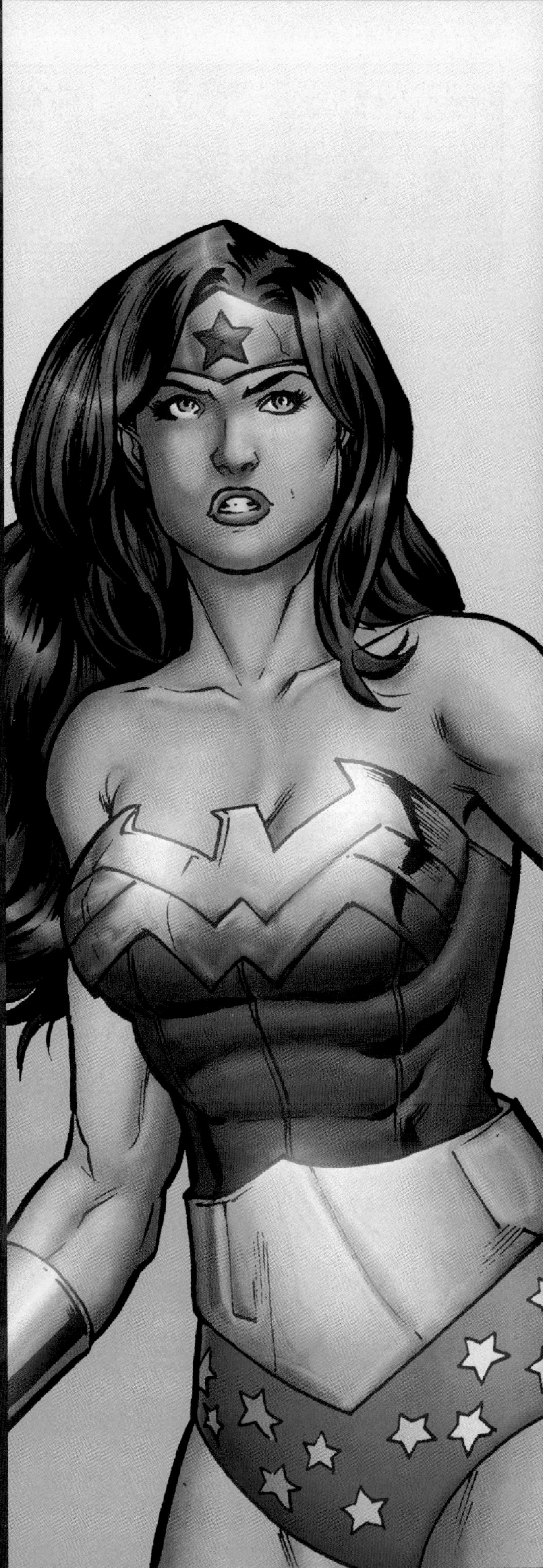

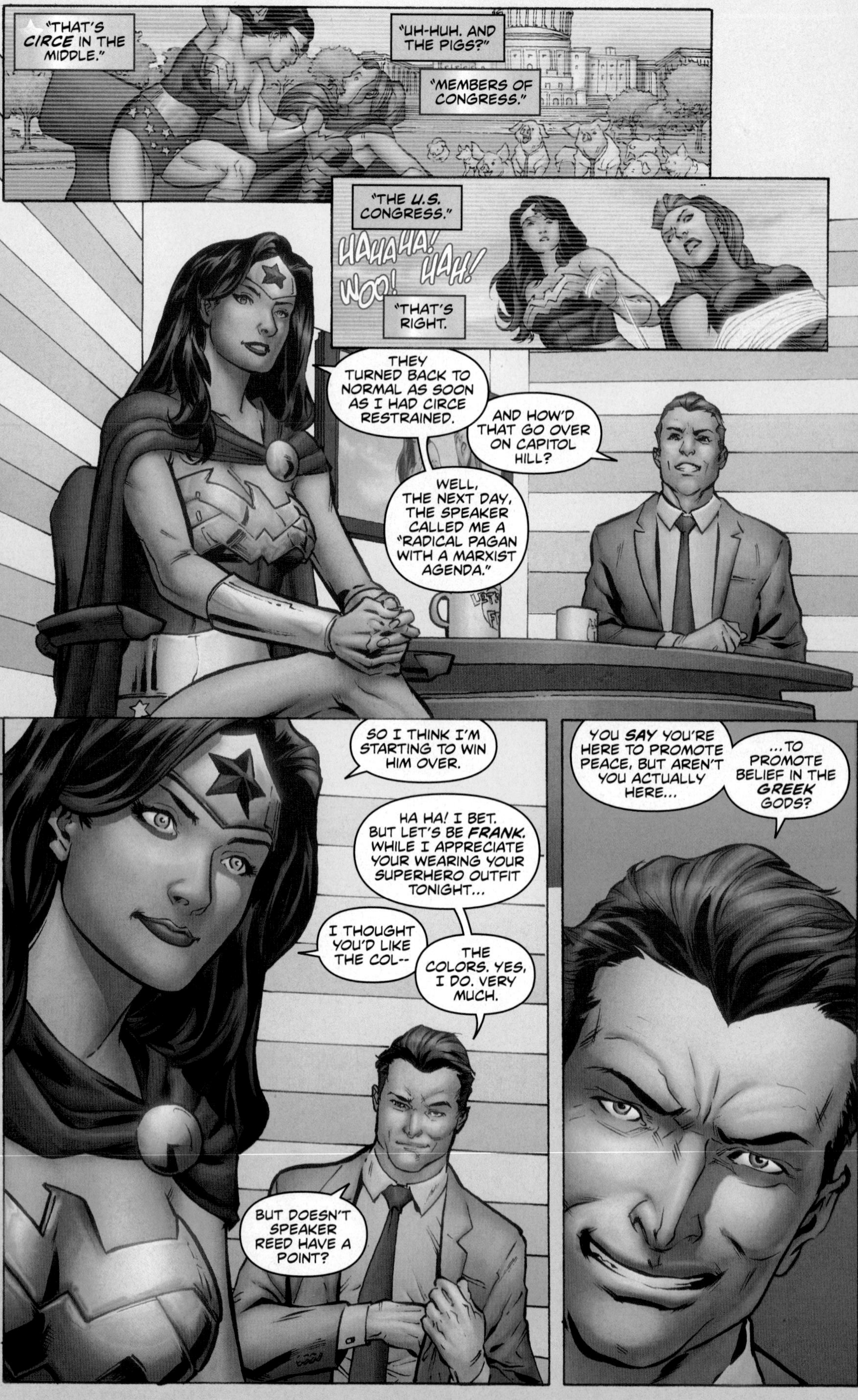
"THAT'S CIRCE IN THE MIDDLE."
"UH-HUH. AND THE PIGS?"
"MEMBERS OF CONGRESS."
"THE U.S. CONGRESS."
HAHAHA! HAH! WOO!
"THAT'S RIGHT.
THEY TURNED BACK TO NORMAL AS SOON AS I HAD CIRCE RESTRAINED.
AND HOW'D THAT GO OVER ON CAPITOL HILL?
WELL, THE NEXT DAY, THE SPEAKER CALLED ME A "RADICAL PAGAN WITH A MARXIST AGENDA."
SO I THINK I'M STARTING TO WIN HIM OVER.
HA HA! I BET. BUT LET'S BE FRANK. WHILE I APPRECIATE YOUR WEARING YOUR SUPERHERO OUTFIT TONIGHT...
I THOUGHT YOU'D LIKE THE COL--
THE COLORS. YES, I DO. VERY MUCH.
BUT DOESN'T SPEAKER REED HAVE A POINT?
YOU SAY YOU'RE HERE TO PROMOTE PEACE, BUT AREN'T YOU ACTUALLY HERE...
...TO PROMOTE BELIEF IN THE GREEK GODS?

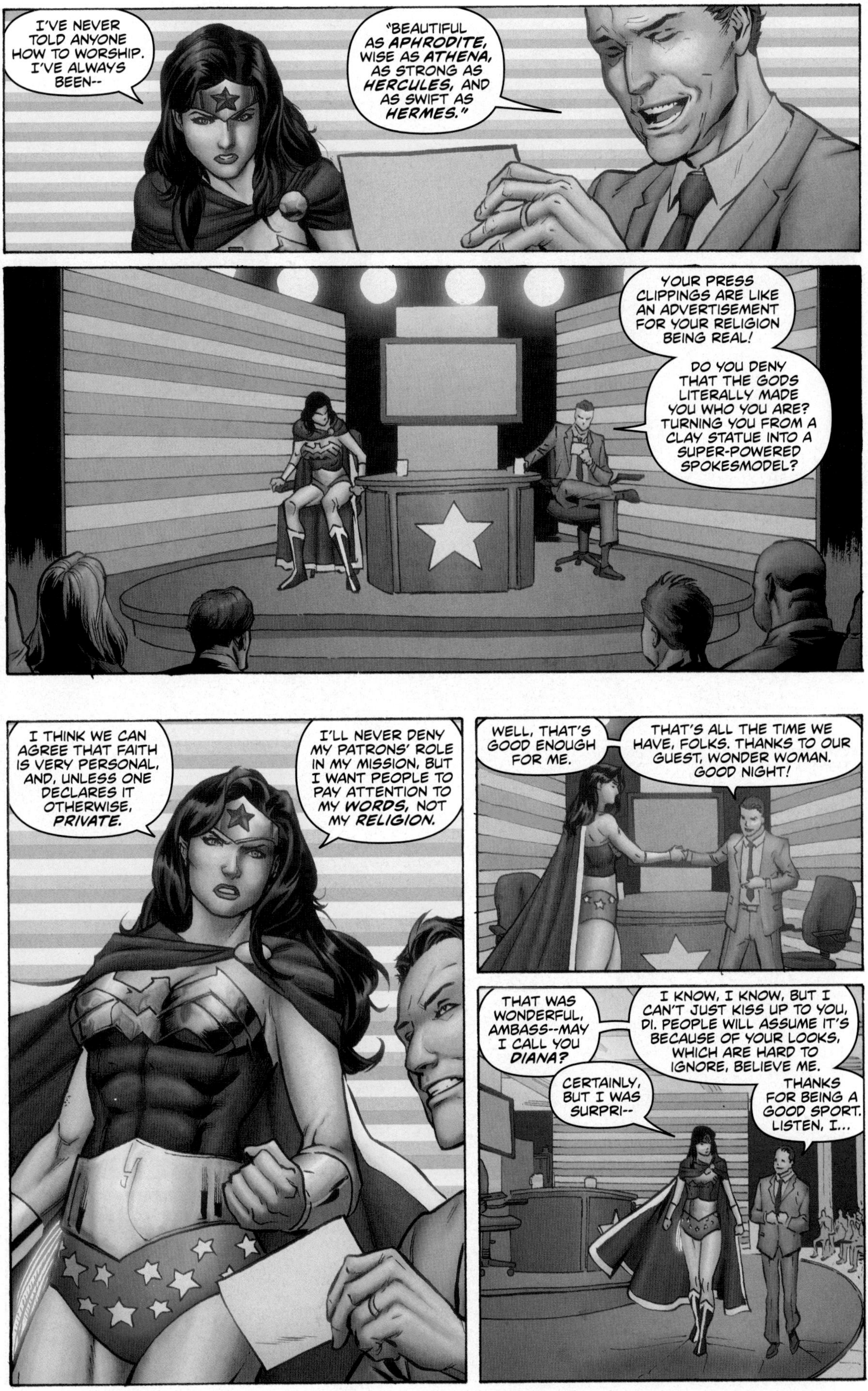
I'VE NEVER TOLD ANYONE HOW TO WORSHIP. I'VE ALWAYS BEEN--
"BEAUTIFUL AS APHRODITE, WISE AS ATHENA, AS STRONG AS HERCULES, AND AS SWIFT AS HERMES."
YOUR PRESS CLIPPINGS ARE LIKE AN ADVERTISEMENT FOR YOUR RELIGION BEING REAL!
DO YOU DENY THAT THE GODS LITERALLY MADE YOU WHO YOU ARE? TURNING YOU FROM A CLAY STATUE INTO A SUPER-POWERED SPOKESMODEL?
I THINK WE CAN AGREE THAT FAITH IS VERY PERSONAL, AND, UNLESS ONE DECLARES IT OTHERWISE, PRIVATE.
I'LL NEVER DENY MY PATRONS' ROLE IN MY MISSION, BUT I WANT PEOPLE TO PAY ATTENTION TO MY WORDS, NOT MY RELIGION.
WELL, THAT'S GOOD ENOUGH FOR ME.
THAT'S ALL THE TIME WE HAVE, FOLKS. THANKS TO OUR GUEST, WONDER WOMAN. GOOD NIGHT!
THAT WAS WONDERFUL, AMBASS--MAY I CALL YOU DIANA?
CERTAINLY, BUT I WAS SURPRI--
I KNOW, I KNOW, BUT I CAN'T JUST KISS UP TO YOU, DI. PEOPLE WILL ASSUME IT'S BECAUSE OF YOUR LOOKS, WHICH ARE HARD TO IGNORE, BELIEVE ME.
THANKS FOR BEING A GOOD SPORT. LISTEN, I...

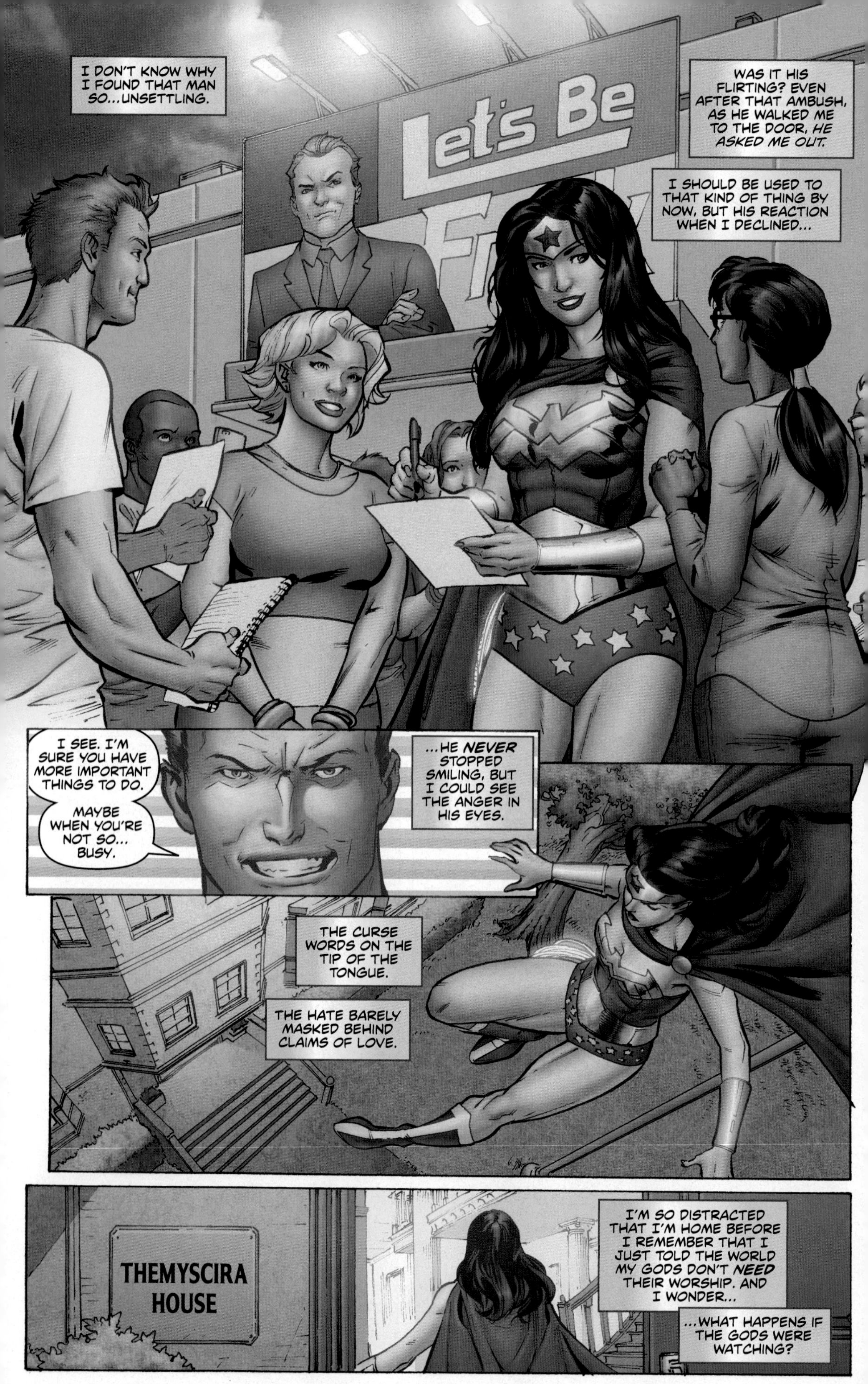

I DON'T KNOW WHY I FOUND THAT MAN SO...UNSETTLING.
Let's Be Fr
WAS IT HIS FLIRTING? EVEN AFTER THAT AMBUSH, AS HE WALKED ME TO THE DOOR, HE ASKED ME OUT.
I SHOULD BE USED TO THAT KIND OF THING BY NOW, BUT HIS REACTION WHEN I DECLINED...
I SEE. I'M SURE YOU HAVE MORE IMPORTANT THINGS TO DO.
MAYBE WHEN YOU'RE NOT SO... BUSY.
...HE NEVER STOPPED SMILING, BUT I COULD SEE THE ANGER IN HIS EYES.
THE CURSE WORDS ON THE TIP OF THE TONGUE.
THE HATE BARELY MASKED BEHIND CLAIMS OF LOVE.
THEMYSCIRA HOUSE
I'M SO DISTRACTED THAT I'M HOME BEFORE I REMEMBER THAT I JUST TOLD THE WORLD MY GODS DON'T NEED THEIR WORSHIP. AND I WONDER...
...WHAT HAPPENS IF THE GODS WERE WATCHING?

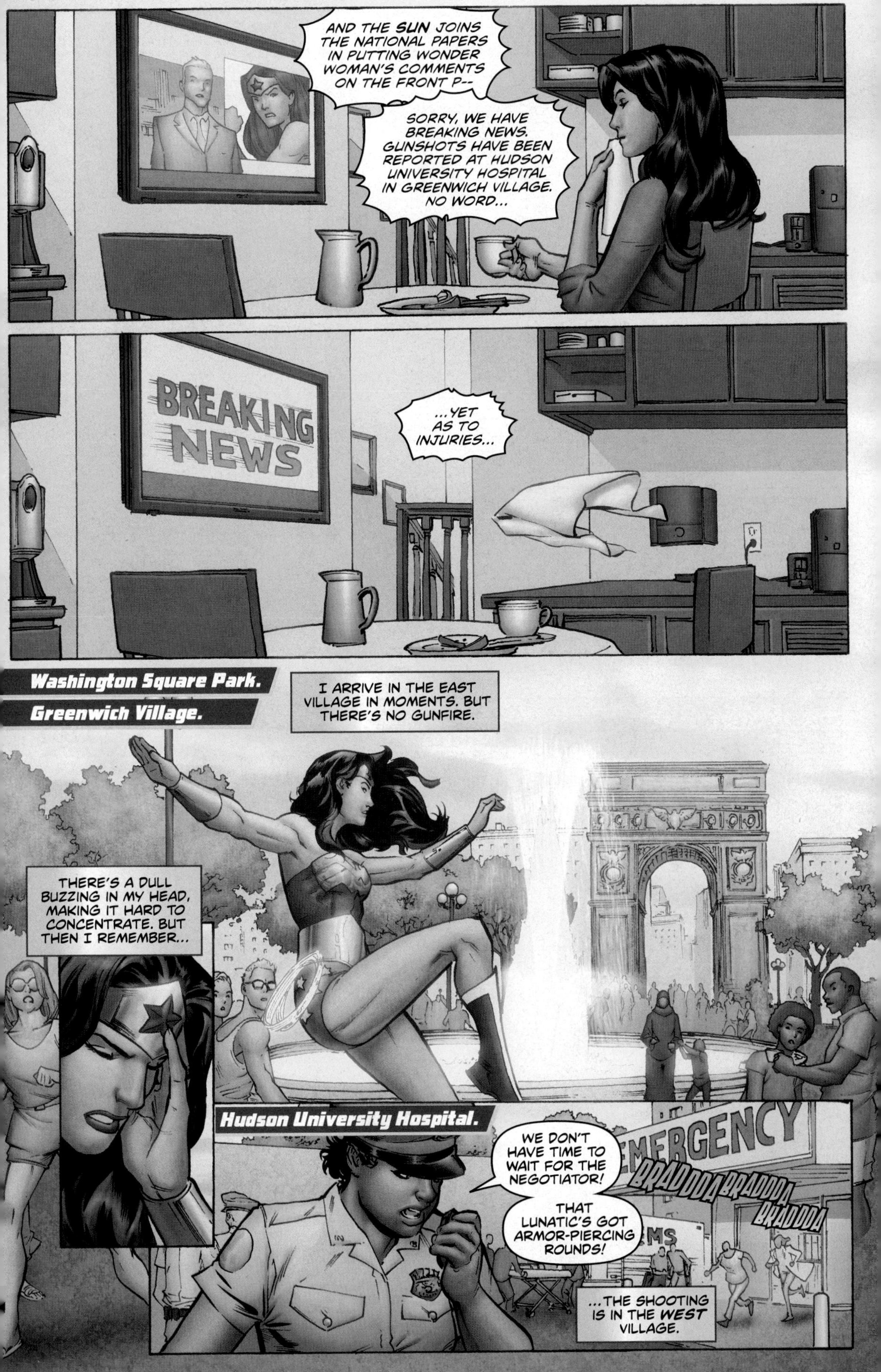
AND THE SUN JOINS THE NATIONAL PAPERS IN PUTTING WONDER WOMAN'S COMMENTS ON THE FRONT P--
SORRY, WE HAVE BREAKING NEWS. GUNSHOTS HAVE BEEN REPORTED AT HUDSON UNIVERSITY HOSPITAL IN GREENWICH VILLAGE. NO WORD...
BREAKING NEWS
...YET AS TO INJURIES...
Washington Square Park.
Greenwich Village.
I ARRIVE IN THE EAST VILLAGE IN MOMENTS. BUT THERE'S NO GUNFIRE.
THERE'S A DULL BUZZING IN MY HEAD, MAKING IT HARD TO CONCENTRATE. BUT THEN I REMEMBER...
Hudson University Hospital.
EMERGENCY
WE DON'T HAVE TIME TO WAIT FOR THE NEGOTIATOR!
THAT LUNATIC'S GOT ARMOR-PIERCING ROUNDS!
BRADDDA BRADDDA BRADDDA
...THE SHOOTING IS IN THE WEST VILLAGE.

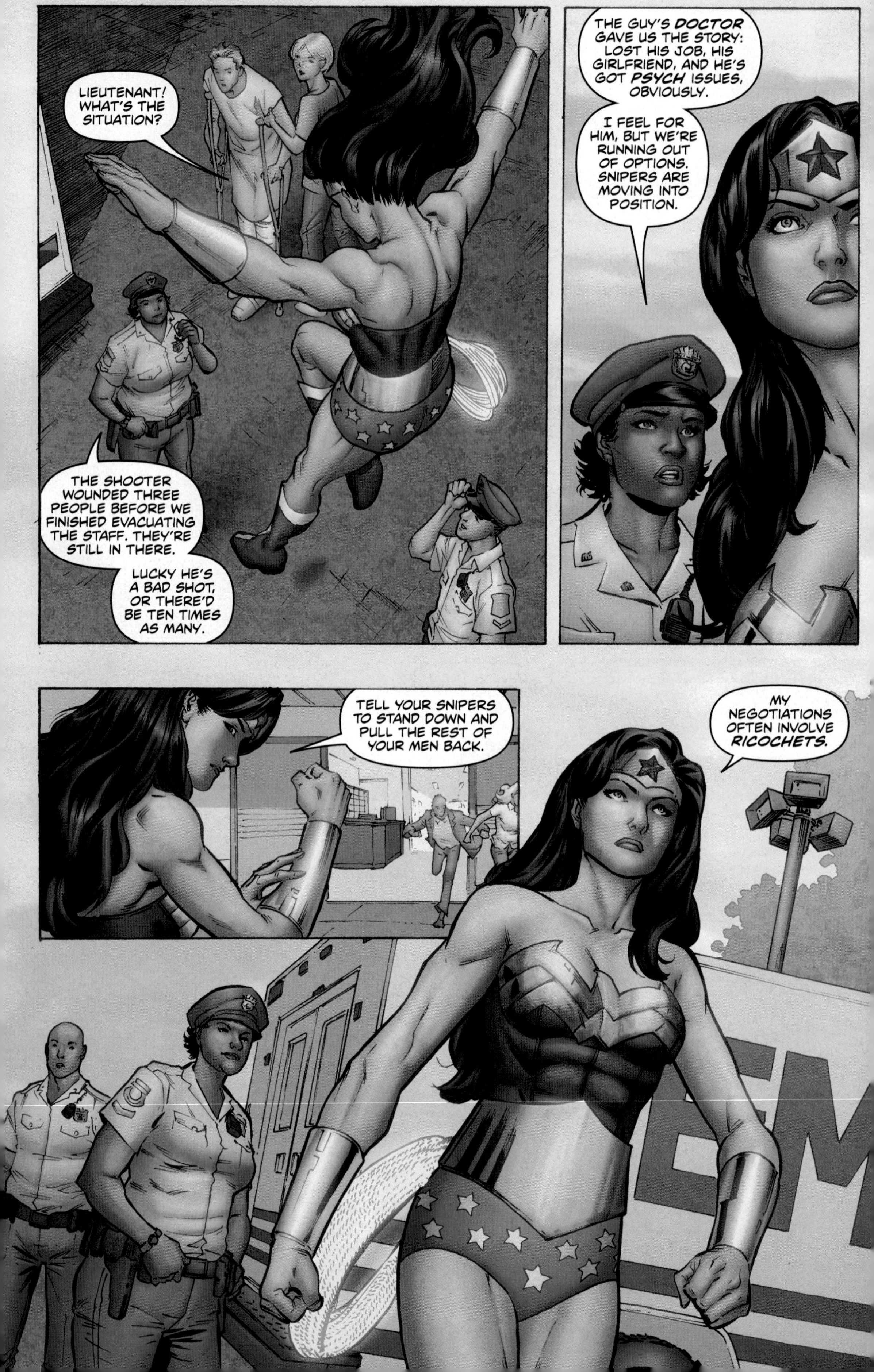
LIEUTENANT! WHAT'S THE SITUATION?
THE SHOOTER WOUNDED THREE PEOPLE BEFORE WE FINISHED EVACUATING THE STAFF. THEY'RE STILL IN THERE.
LUCKY HE'S A BAD SHOT, OR THERE'D BE TEN TIMES AS MANY.
THE GUY'S DOCTOR GAVE US THE STORY: LOST HIS JOB, HIS GIRLFRIEND, AND HE'S GOT PSYCH ISSUES, OBVIOUSLY.
I FEEL FOR HIM, BUT WE'RE RUNNING OUT OF OPTIONS. SNIPERS ARE MOVING INTO POSITION.
TELL YOUR SNIPERS TO STAND DOWN AND PULL THE REST OF YOUR MEN BACK.
MY NEGOTIATIONS OFTEN INVOLVE RICOCHETS.
EM

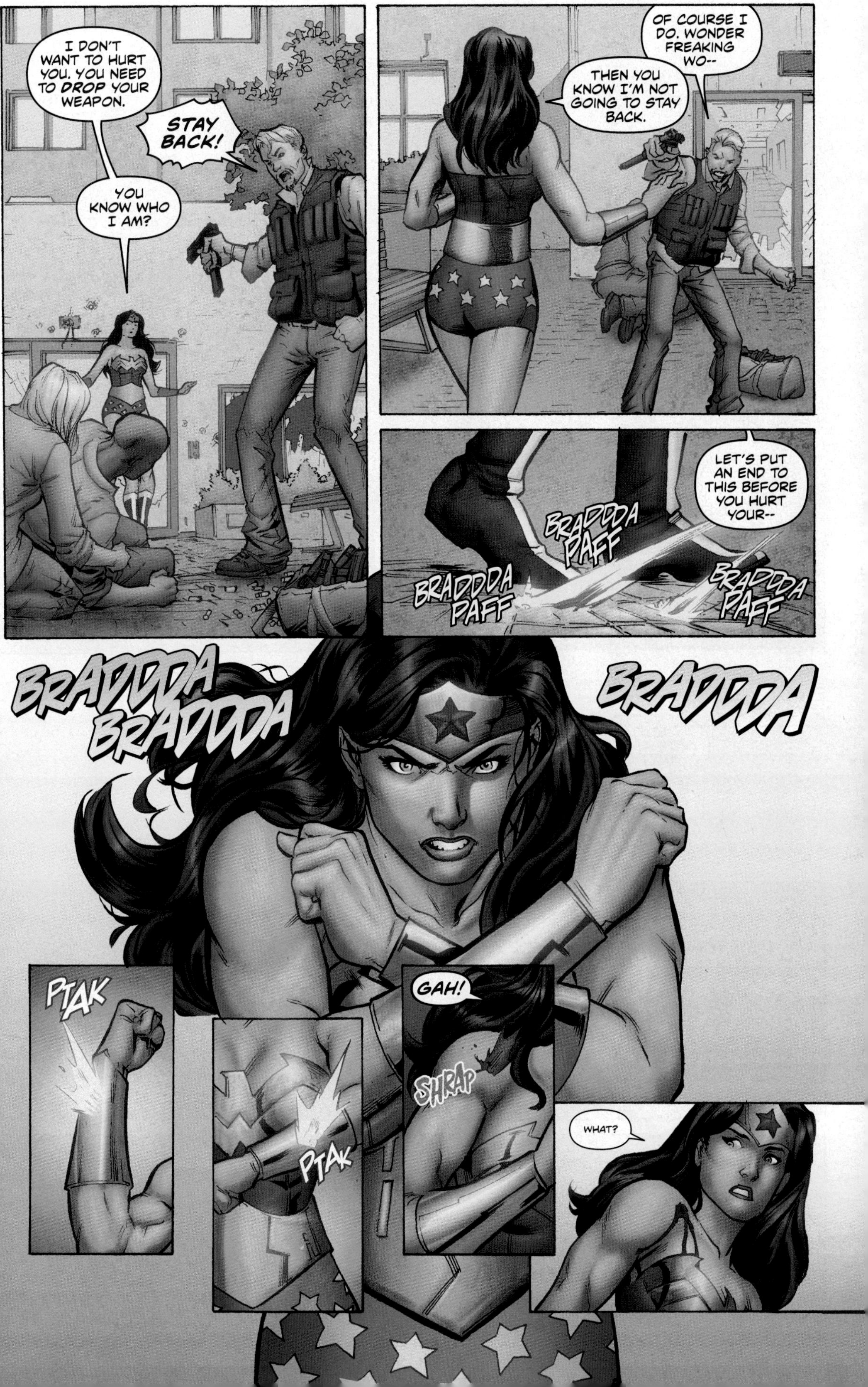
I DON'T WANT TO HURT YOU. YOU NEED TO DROP YOUR WEAPON.
STAY BACK!
YOU KNOW WHO I AM?
OF COURSE I DO. WONDER FREAKING WO--
THEN YOU KNOW I'M NOT GOING TO STAY BACK.
LET'S PUT AN END TO THIS BEFORE YOU HURT YOUR--
BRADDDA PAFF
BRADDDA PAFF
BRADDDA PAFF
BRADDDA
BRADDDA
BRADDDA
PTAK
PTAK
GAH!
SHRAP
WHAT?

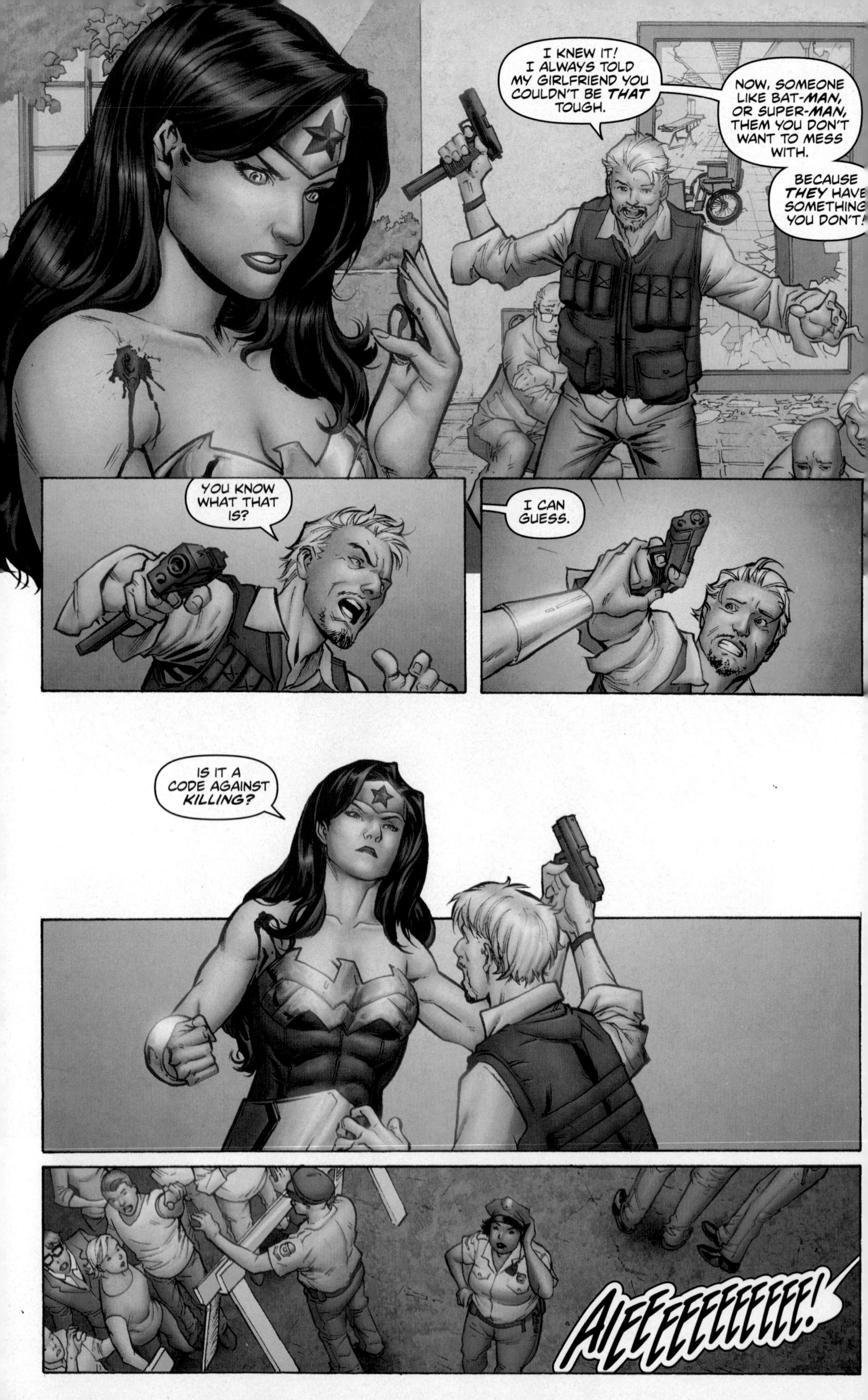
I KNEW IT! I ALWAYS TOLD MY GIRLFRIEND YOU COULDN'T BE *THAT* TOUGH.
NOW, SOMEONE LIKE BAT-*MAN*, OR SUPER-*MAN*, THEM YOU DON'T WANT TO MESS WITH.
BECAUSE *THEY* HAVE SOMETHING YOU DON'T!
YOU KNOW WHAT THAT IS?
I CAN GUESS.
IS IT A CODE AGAINST *KILLING*?
AIEEEEEEEEEEEE!

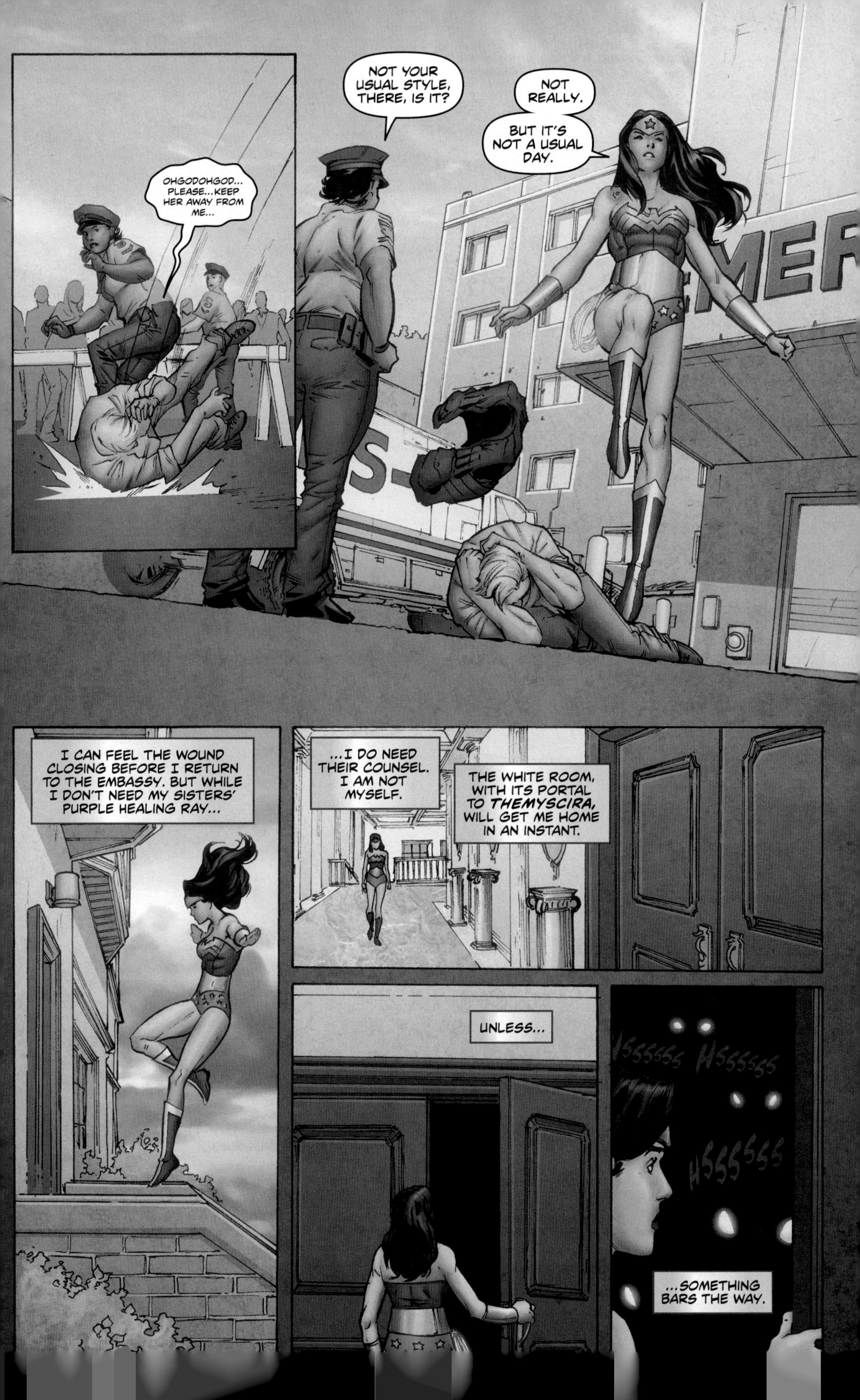
OHGODOHGOD... PLEASE...KEEP HER AWAY FROM ME...
NOT YOUR USUAL STYLE, THERE, IS IT?
NOT REALLY.
BUT IT'S NOT A USUAL DAY.
I CAN FEEL THE WOUND CLOSING BEFORE I RETURN TO THE EMBASSY. BUT WHILE I DON'T NEED MY SISTERS' PURPLE HEALING RAY...
...I DO NEED THEIR COUNSEL. I AM NOT MYSELF.
THE WHITE ROOM, WITH ITS PORTAL TO THEMYSCIRA, WILL GET ME HOME IN AN INSTANT.
UNLESS...
HSSSSSS HSSSSSS
HSSSSSS
...SOMETHING BARS THE WAY.

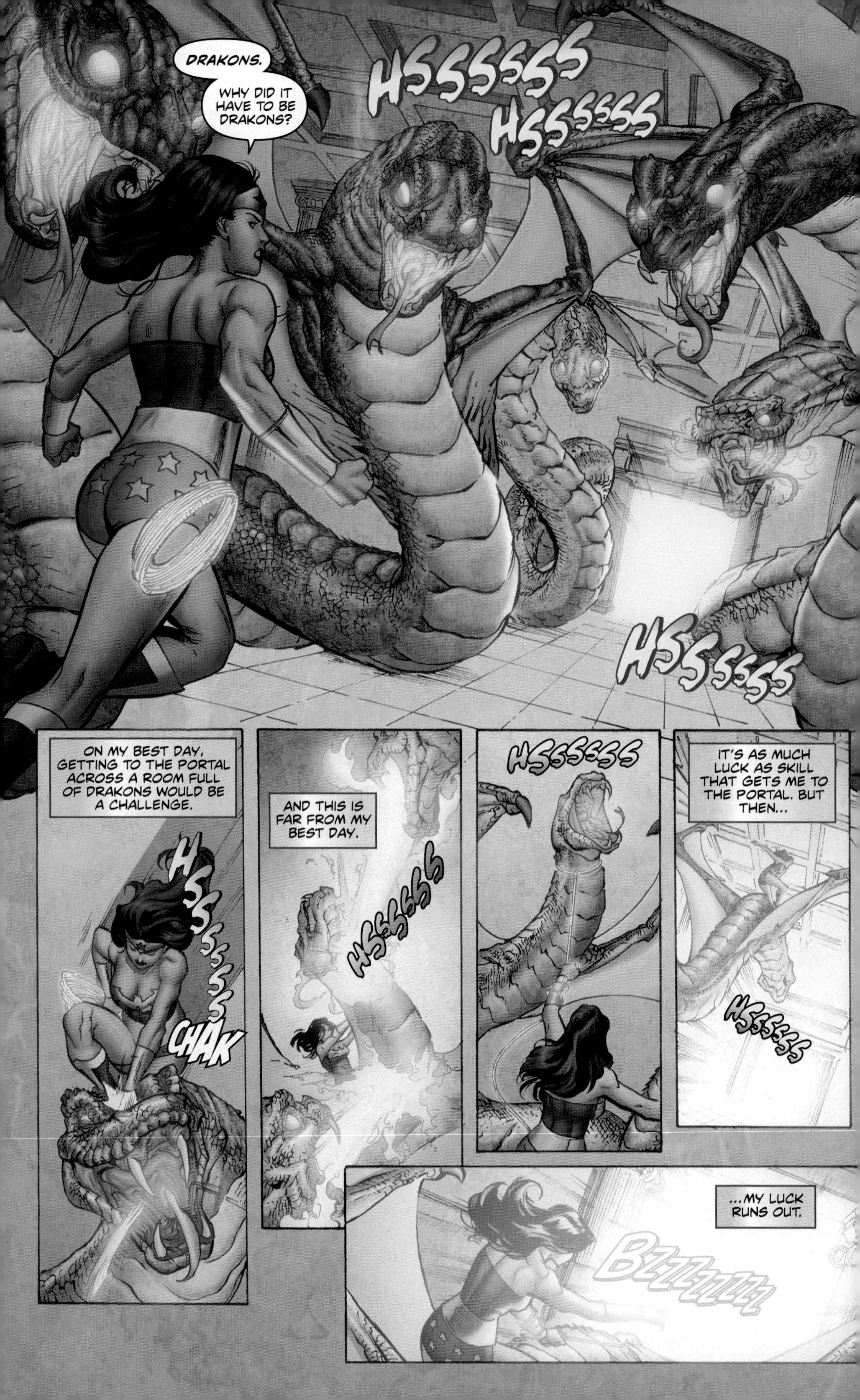
DRAKONS.
WHY DID IT HAVE TO BE DRAKONS?
HSSSSSS
HSSSSSS
HSSSSSS
ON MY BEST DAY, GETTING TO THE PORTAL ACROSS A ROOM FULL OF DRAKONS WOULD BE A CHALLENGE.
HSSSSSSS
CHAK
AND THIS IS FAR FROM MY BEST DAY.
HSSSSSSS
HSSSSSS
IT'S AS MUCH LUCK AS SKILL THAT GETS ME TO THE PORTAL. BUT THEN...
HSSSSSS
...MY LUCK RUNS OUT.
BZZZZZZZ

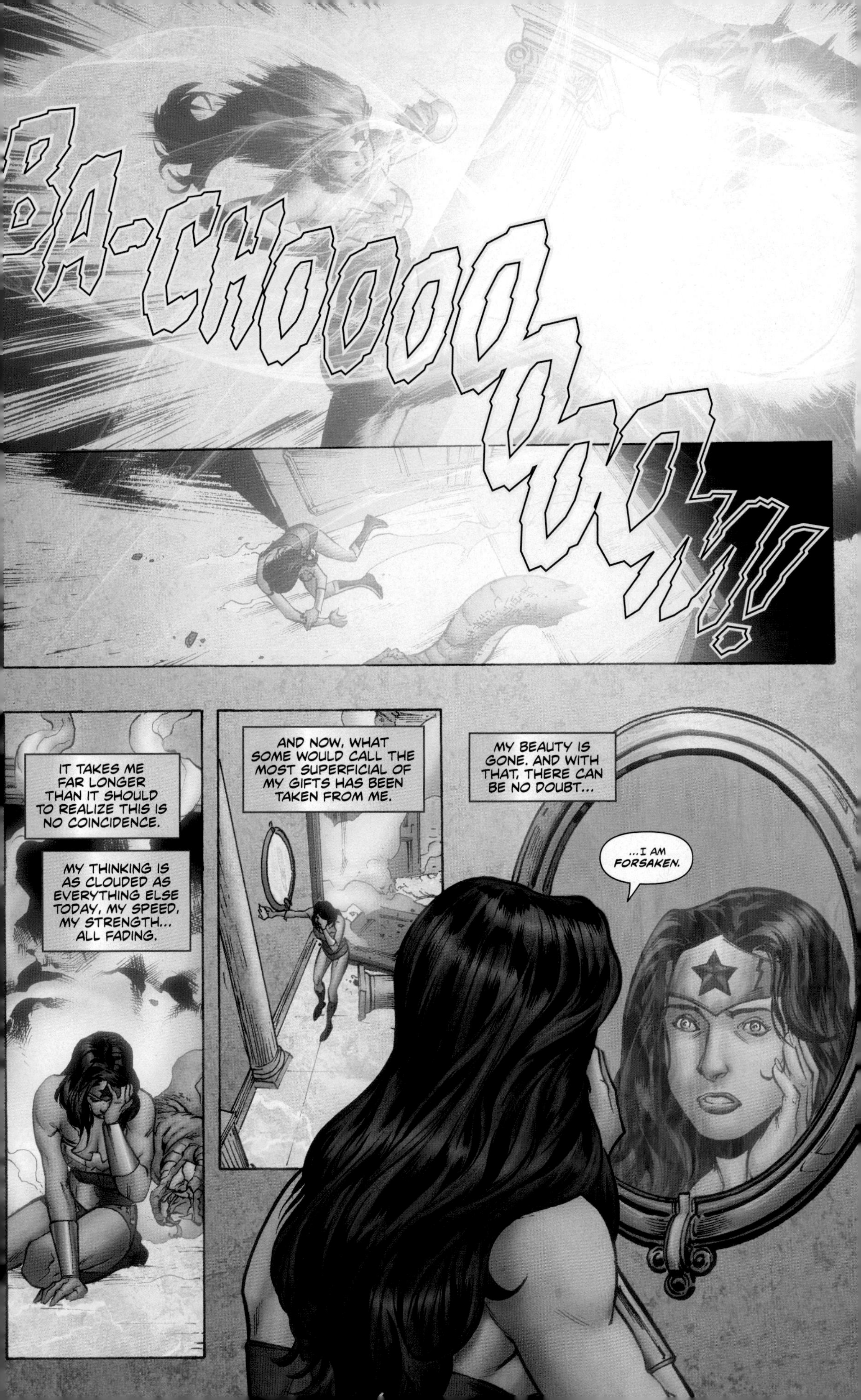
A-CHOOOOOOOOO!!
IT TAKES ME FAR LONGER THAN IT SHOULD TO REALIZE THIS IS NO COINCIDENCE.
MY THINKING IS AS CLOUDED AS EVERYTHING ELSE TODAY, MY SPEED, MY STRENGTH... ALL FADING.
AND NOW, WHAT SOME WOULD CALL THE MOST SUPERFICIAL OF MY GIFTS HAS BEEN TAKEN FROM ME.
MY BEAUTY IS GONE. AND WITH THAT, THERE CAN BE NO DOUBT...
...I AM FORSAKEN.

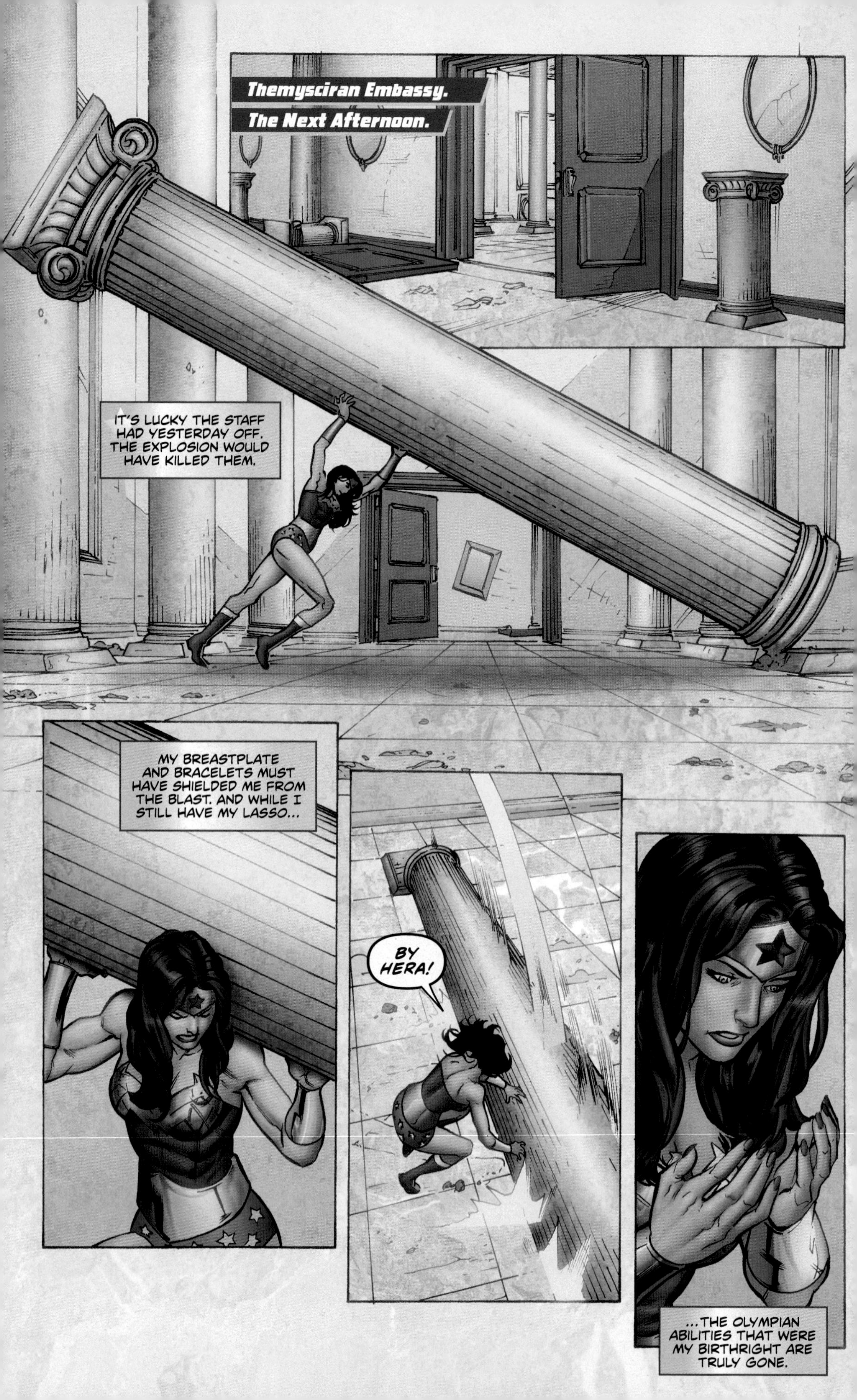
Themysciran Embassy.
The Next Afternoon.
IT'S LUCKY THE STAFF HAD YESTERDAY OFF. THE EXPLOSION WOULD HAVE KILLED THEM.
MY BREASTPLATE AND BRACELETS MUST HAVE SHIELDED ME FROM THE BLAST. AND WHILE I STILL HAVE MY LASSO...
BY HERA!
...THE OLYMPIAN ABILITIES THAT WERE MY BIRTHRIGHT ARE TRULY GONE.

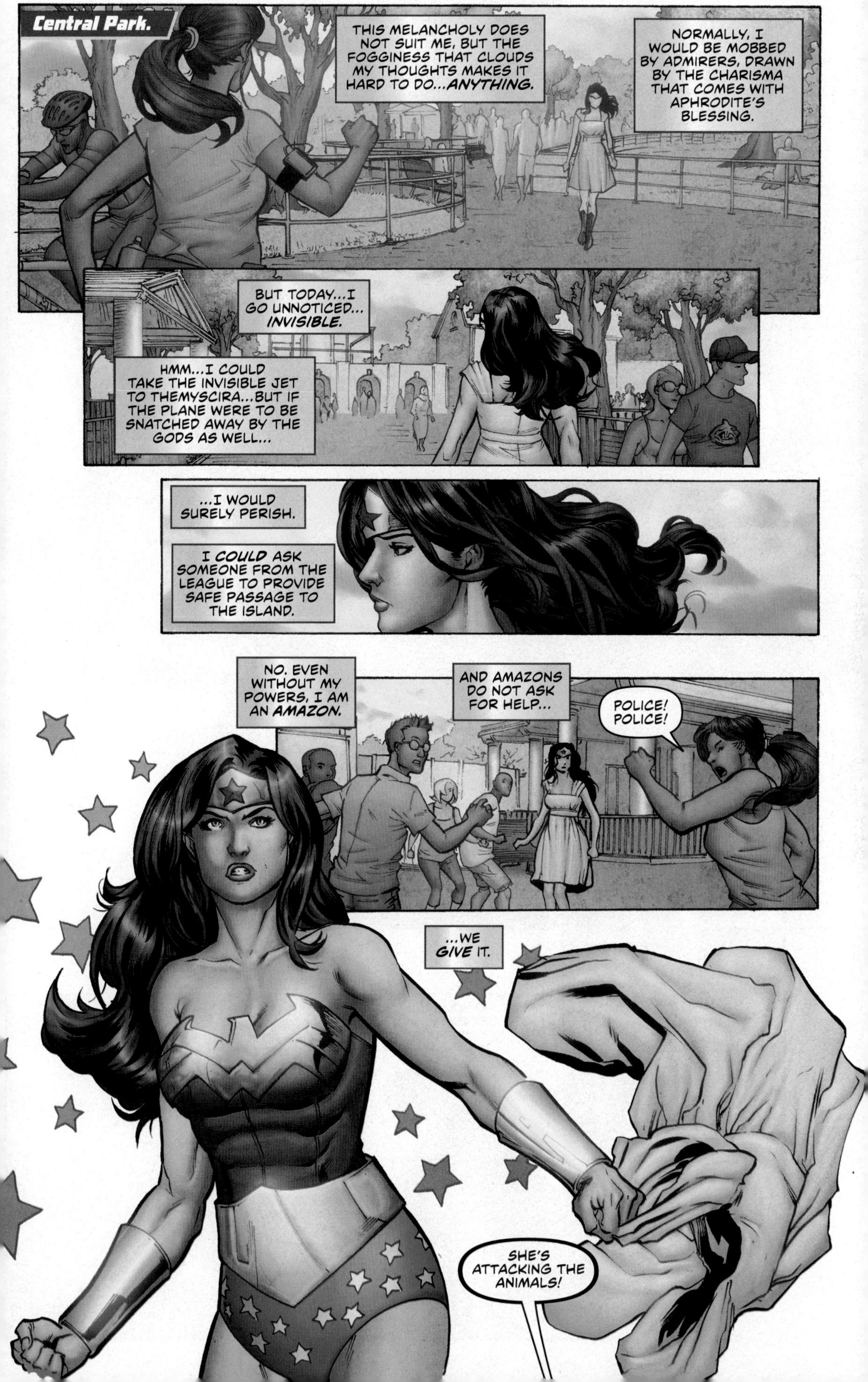
Central Park.
THIS MELANCHOLY DOES NOT SUIT ME, BUT THE FOGGINESS THAT CLOUDS MY THOUGHTS MAKES IT HARD TO DO...ANYTHING.
NORMALLY, I WOULD BE MOBBED BY ADMIRERS, DRAWN BY THE CHARISMA THAT COMES WITH APHRODITE'S BLESSING.
BUT TODAY...I GO UNNOTICED... INVISIBLE.
HMM...I COULD TAKE THE INVISIBLE JET TO THEMYSCIRA...BUT IF THE PLANE WERE TO BE SNATCHED AWAY BY THE GODS AS WELL...
...I WOULD SURELY PERISH.
I COULD ASK SOMEONE FROM THE LEAGUE TO PROVIDE SAFE PASSAGE TO THE ISLAND.
NO. EVEN WITHOUT MY POWERS, I AM AN AMAZON.
AND AMAZONS DO NOT ASK FOR HELP...
POLICE! POLICE!
...WE GIVE IT.
SHE'S ATTACKING THE ANIMALS!

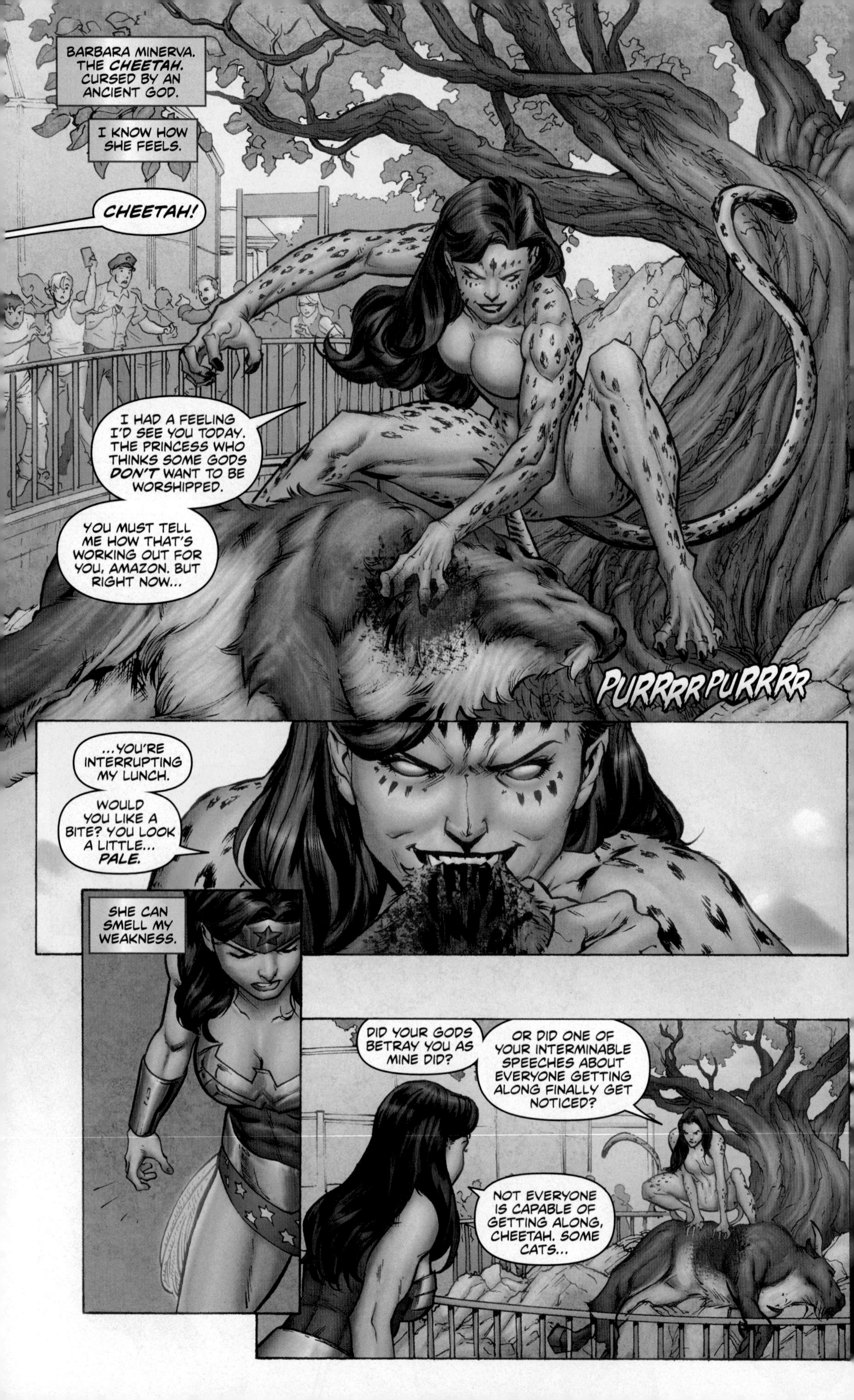
BARBARA MINERVA. THE *CHEETAH*. CURSED BY AN ANCIENT GOD.
I KNOW HOW SHE FEELS.
CHEETAH!
I HAD A FEELING I'D SEE YOU TODAY. THE PRINCESS WHO THINKS SOME GODS *DON'T* WANT TO BE WORSHIPPED.
YOU MUST TELL ME HOW THAT'S WORKING OUT FOR YOU, AMAZON. BUT RIGHT NOW...
PURRRR PURRRR
...YOU'RE INTERRUPTING MY LUNCH.
WOULD YOU LIKE A BITE? YOU LOOK A LITTLE... *PALE*.
SHE CAN SMELL MY WEAKNESS.
DID YOUR GODS BETRAY YOU AS MINE DID?
OR DID ONE OF YOUR INTERMINABLE SPEECHES ABOUT EVERYONE GETTING ALONG FINALLY GET NOTICED?
NOT EVERYONE IS CAPABLE OF GETTING ALONG, CHEETAH. SOME CATS...

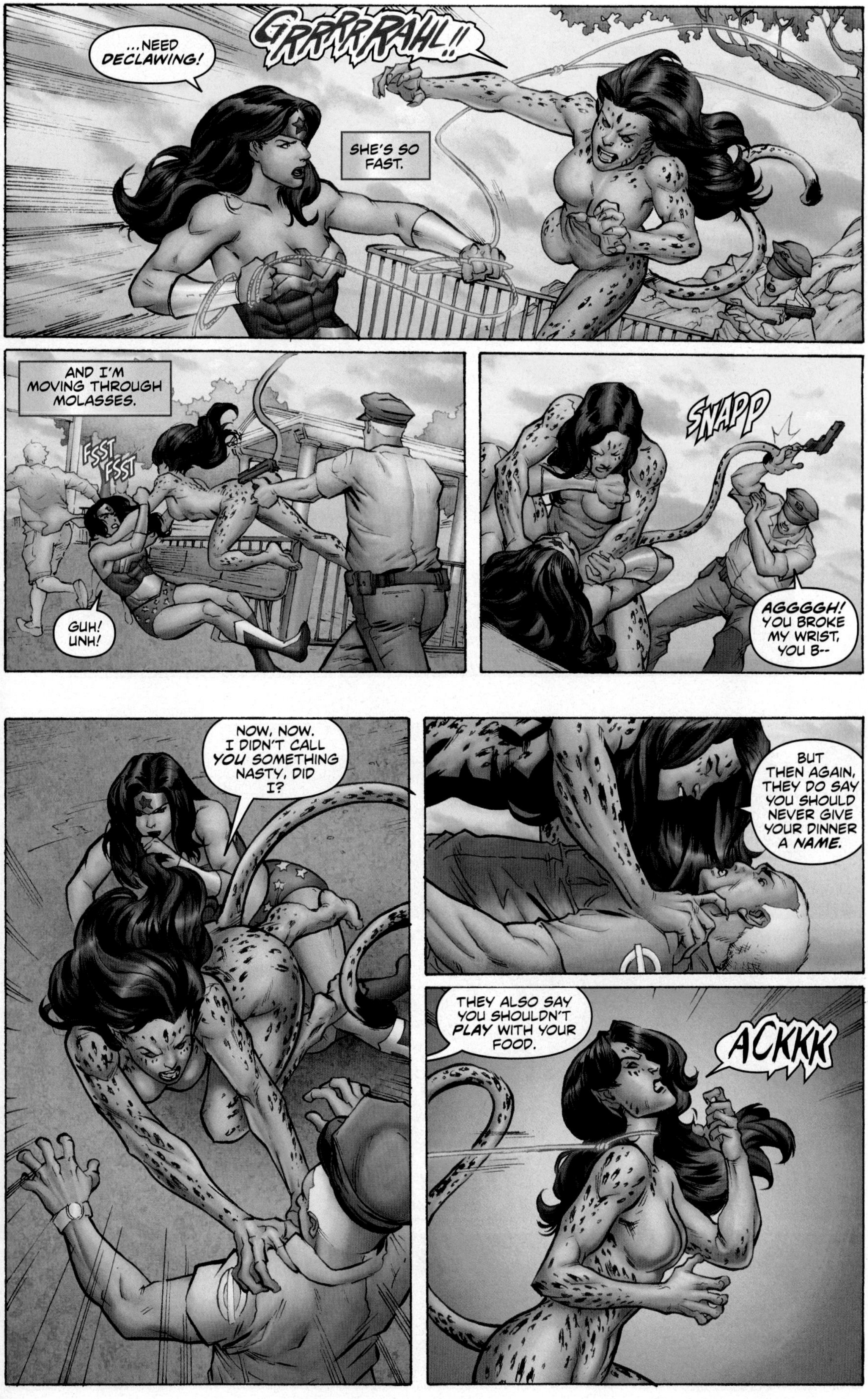
...NEED DECLAWING!
GRRRRRAHL!!
SHE'S SO FAST.
AND I'M MOVING THROUGH MOLASSES.
FSST FSST
GUH! UNH!
SNAPP
AGGGGH! YOU BROKE MY WRIST, YOU B--
NOW, NOW. I DIDN'T CALL YOU SOMETHING NASTY, DID I?
BUT THEN AGAIN, THEY DO SAY YOU SHOULD NEVER GIVE YOUR DINNER A NAME.
THEY ALSO SAY YOU SHOULDN'T PLAY WITH YOUR FOOD.
ACKKK

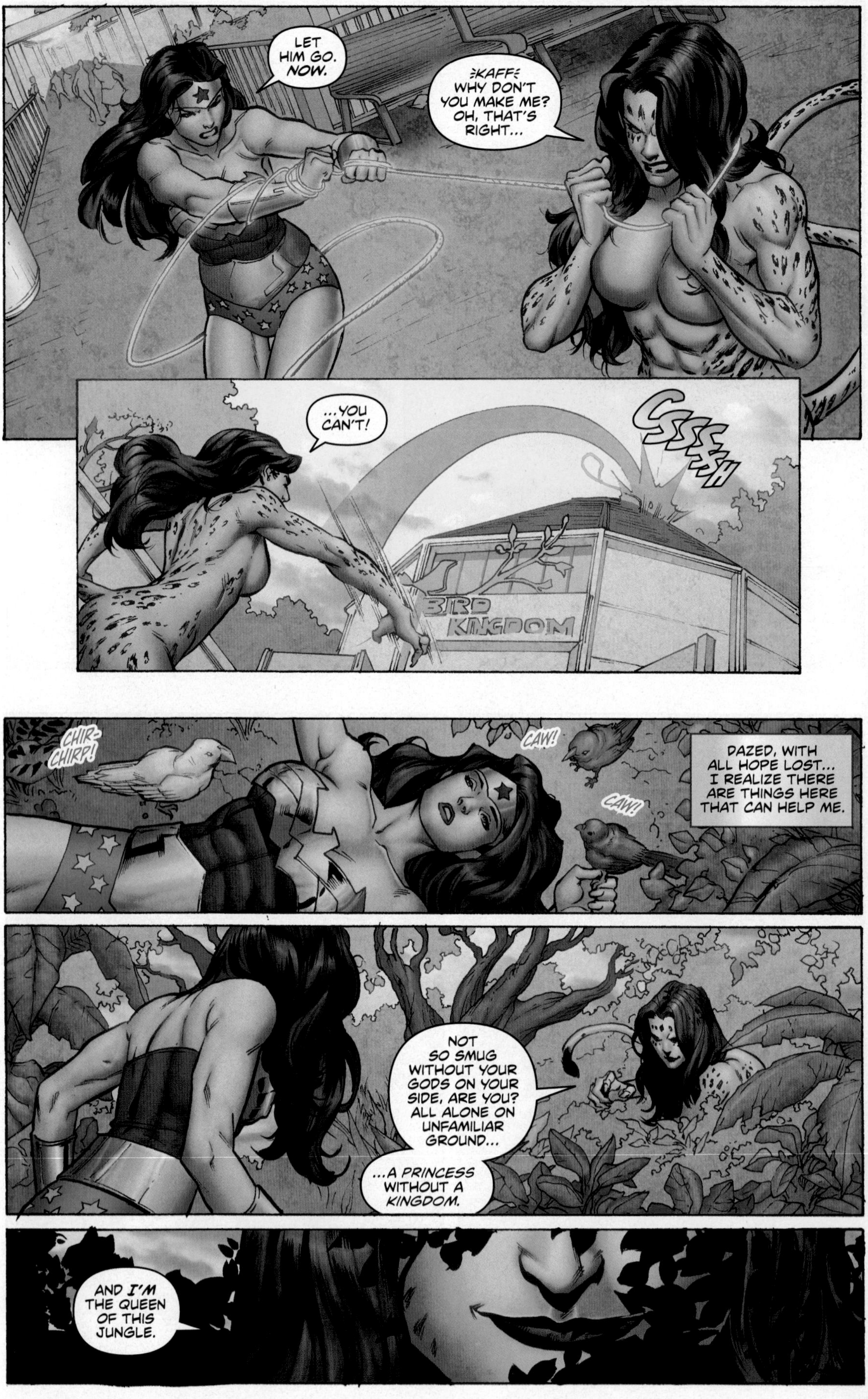
LET HIM GO. NOW.
=KAFF= WHY DON'T YOU MAKE ME? OH, THAT'S RIGHT...
...YOU CAN'T!
CSSSSH
BIRD KINGDOM
CHIR-CHIRP!
CAW!
CAW!
DAZED, WITH ALL HOPE LOST... I REALIZE THERE ARE THINGS HERE THAT CAN HELP ME.
NOT SO SMUG WITHOUT YOUR GODS ON YOUR SIDE, ARE YOU? ALL ALONE ON UNFAMILIAR GROUND...
...A PRINCESS WITHOUT A KINGDOM.
AND I'M THE QUEEN OF THIS JUNGLE.

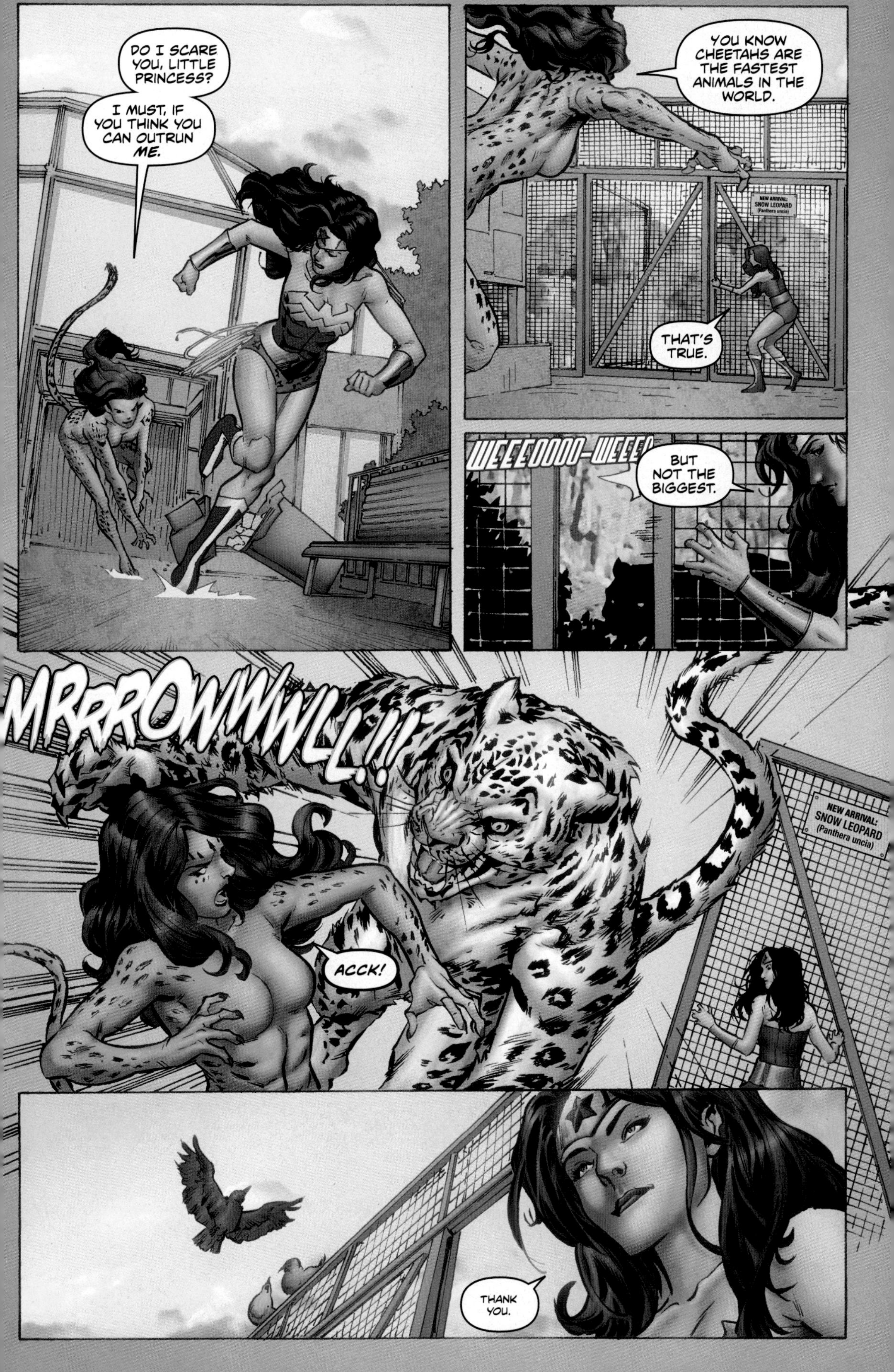
DO I SCARE YOU, LITTLE PRINCESS?
I MUST, IF YOU THINK YOU CAN OUTRUN ME.
YOU KNOW CHEETAHS ARE THE FASTEST ANIMALS IN THE WORLD.
NEW ARRIVAL: SNOW LEOPARD (Panthera uncia)
THAT'S TRUE.
WEEEOOOO-WEEE
BUT NOT THE BIGGEST.
MRRROWWWLL!!!
NEW ARRIVAL: SNOW LEOPARD (Panthera uncia)
ACCK!
THANK YOU.

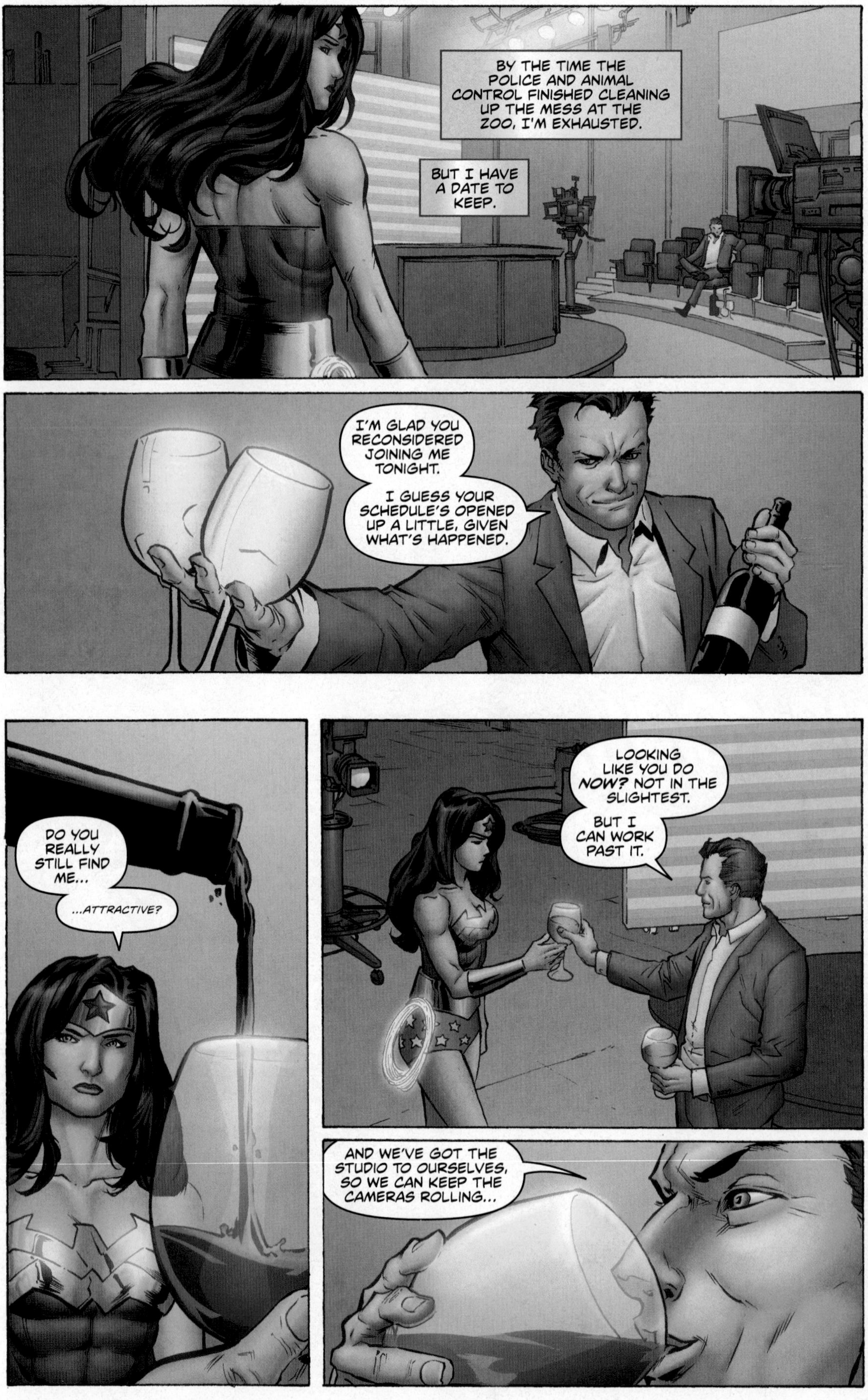
BY THE TIME THE POLICE AND ANIMAL CONTROL FINISHED CLEANING UP THE MESS AT THE ZOO, I'M EXHAUSTED.
BUT I HAVE A DATE TO KEEP.
I'M GLAD YOU RECONSIDERED JOINING ME TONIGHT.
I GUESS YOUR SCHEDULE'S OPENED UP A LITTLE, GIVEN WHAT'S HAPPENED.
DO YOU REALLY STILL FIND ME...
...ATTRACTIVE?
LOOKING LIKE YOU DO NOW? NOT IN THE SLIGHTEST.
BUT I CAN WORK PAST IT.
AND WE'VE GOT THE STUDIO TO OURSELVES, SO WE CAN KEEP THE CAMERAS ROLLING...

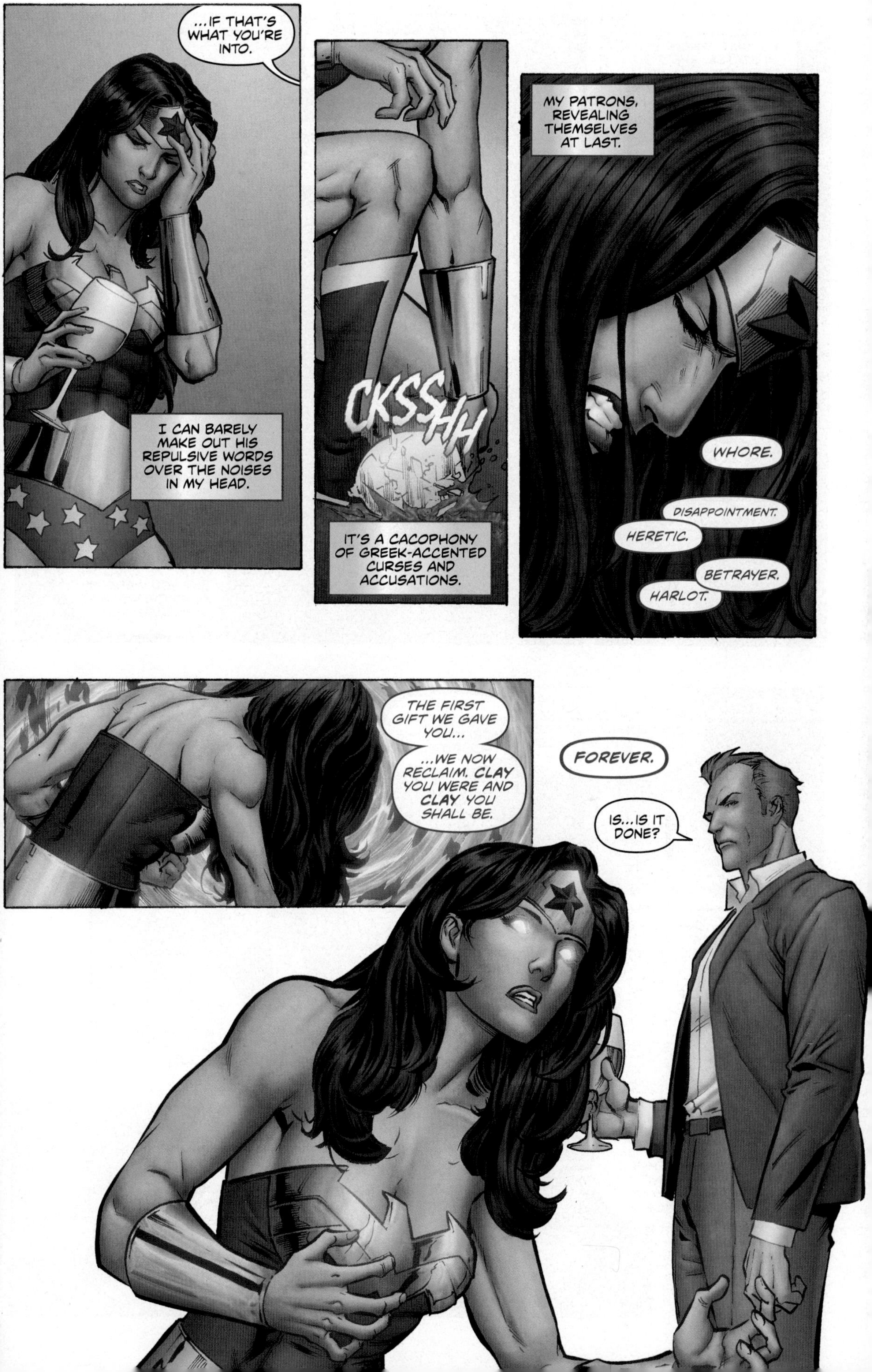
...IF THAT'S WHAT YOU'RE INTO.
I CAN BARELY MAKE OUT HIS REPULSIVE WORDS OVER THE NOISES IN MY HEAD.
CKSSHH
IT'S A CACOPHONY OF GREEK-ACCENTED CURSES AND ACCUSATIONS.
MY PATRONS, REVEALING THEMSELVES AT LAST.
WHORE.
DISAPPOINTMENT.
HERETIC.
BETRAYER.
HARLOT.
THE FIRST GIFT WE GAVE YOU...
...WE NOW RECLAIM. CLAY YOU WERE AND CLAY YOU SHALL BE.
FOREVER.
IS...IS IT DONE?

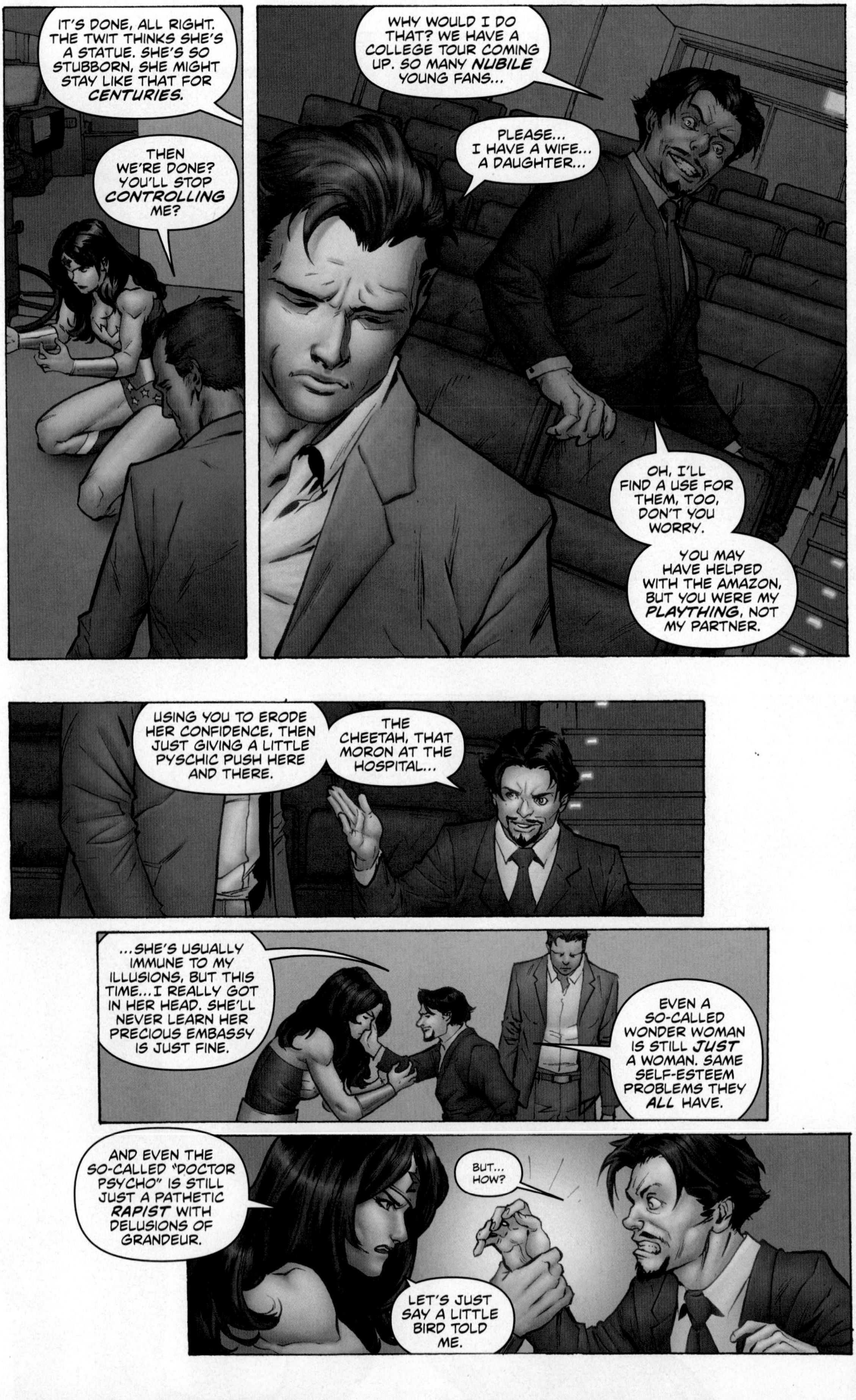
IT'S DONE, ALL RIGHT. THE TWIT THINKS SHE'S A STATUE. SHE'S SO STUBBORN, SHE MIGHT STAY LIKE THAT FOR CENTURIES.
THEN WE'RE DONE? YOU'LL STOP CONTROLLING ME?
WHY WOULD I DO THAT? WE HAVE A COLLEGE TOUR COMING UP. SO MANY NUBILE YOUNG FANS...
PLEASE... I HAVE A WIFE... A DAUGHTER...
OH, I'LL FIND A USE FOR THEM, TOO, DON'T YOU WORRY.
YOU MAY HAVE HELPED WITH THE AMAZON, BUT YOU WERE MY PLAYTHING, NOT MY PARTNER.
USING YOU TO ERODE HER CONFIDENCE, THEN JUST GIVING A LITTLE PYSCHIC PUSH HERE AND THERE.
THE CHEETAH, THAT MORON AT THE HOSPITAL...
...SHE'S USUALLY IMMUNE TO MY ILLUSIONS, BUT THIS TIME...I REALLY GOT IN HER HEAD. SHE'LL NEVER LEARN HER PRECIOUS EMBASSY IS JUST FINE.
EVEN A SO-CALLED WONDER WOMAN IS STILL JUST A WOMAN. SAME SELF-ESTEEM PROBLEMS THEY ALL HAVE.
AND EVEN THE SO-CALLED "DOCTOR PSYCHO" IS STILL JUST A PATHETIC RAPIST WITH DELUSIONS OF GRANDEUR.
BUT... HOW?
LET'S JUST SAY A LITTLE BIRD TOLD ME.

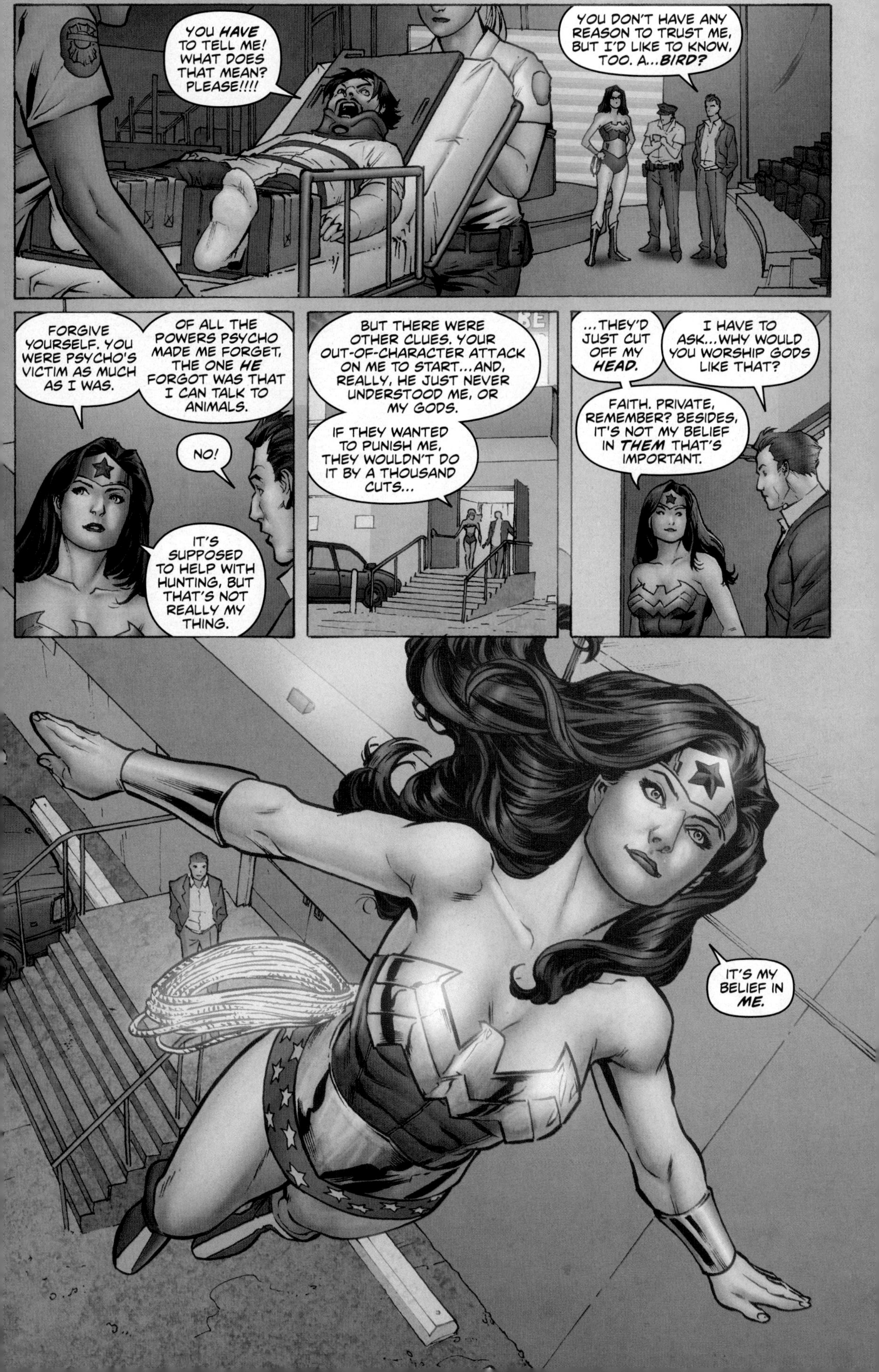
YOU HAVE TO TELL ME! WHAT DOES THAT MEAN? PLEASE!!!!
YOU DON'T HAVE ANY REASON TO TRUST ME, BUT I'D LIKE TO KNOW, TOO. A...BIRD?
FORGIVE YOURSELF. YOU WERE PSYCHO'S VICTIM AS MUCH AS I WAS.
OF ALL THE POWERS PSYCHO MADE ME FORGET, THE ONE HE FORGOT WAS THAT I CAN TALK TO ANIMALS.
NO!
IT'S SUPPOSED TO HELP WITH HUNTING, BUT THAT'S NOT REALLY MY THING.
BUT THERE WERE OTHER CLUES. YOUR OUT-OF-CHARACTER ATTACK ON ME TO START...AND, REALLY, HE JUST NEVER UNDERSTOOD ME, OR MY GODS.
IF THEY WANTED TO PUNISH ME, THEY WOULDN'T DO IT BY A THOUSAND CUTS...
...THEY'D JUST CUT OFF MY HEAD.
I HAVE TO ASK...WHY WOULD YOU WORSHIP GODS LIKE THAT?
FAITH. PRIVATE, REMEMBER? BESIDES, IT'S NOT MY BELIEF IN THEM THAT'S IMPORTANT.
IT'S MY BELIEF IN ME.

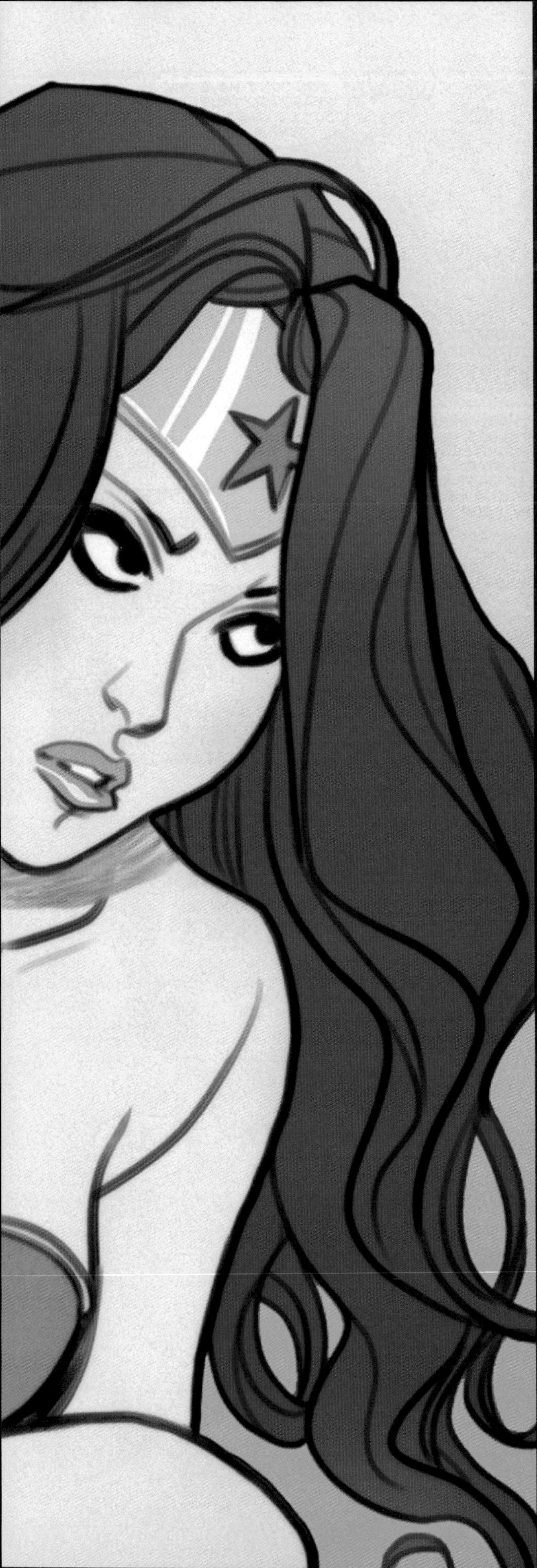

BULLETS AND BRACELETS

SEAN E. WILLIAMS
WRITER

MARGUERITE SAUVAGE
ARTIST AND COLORIST

DERON BENNETT
LETTERER

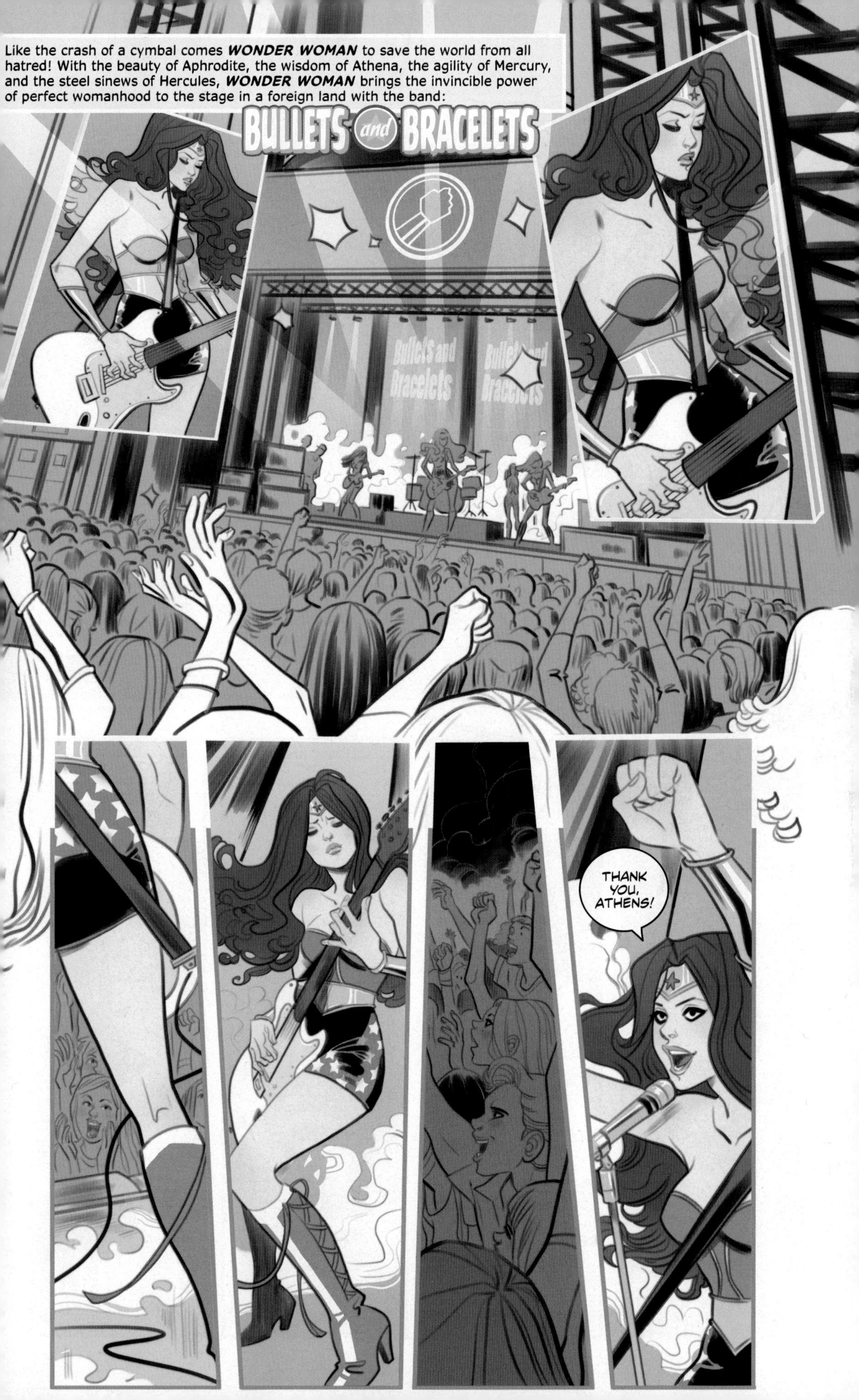
Like the crash of a cymbal comes WONDER WOMAN to save the world from all hatred! With the beauty of Aphrodite, the wisdom of Athena, the agility of Mercury, and the steel sinews of Hercules, WONDER WOMAN brings the invincible power of perfect womanhood to the stage in a foreign land with the band:
BULLETS and BRACELETS
Bullets and Bracelets
THANK YOU, ATHENS!

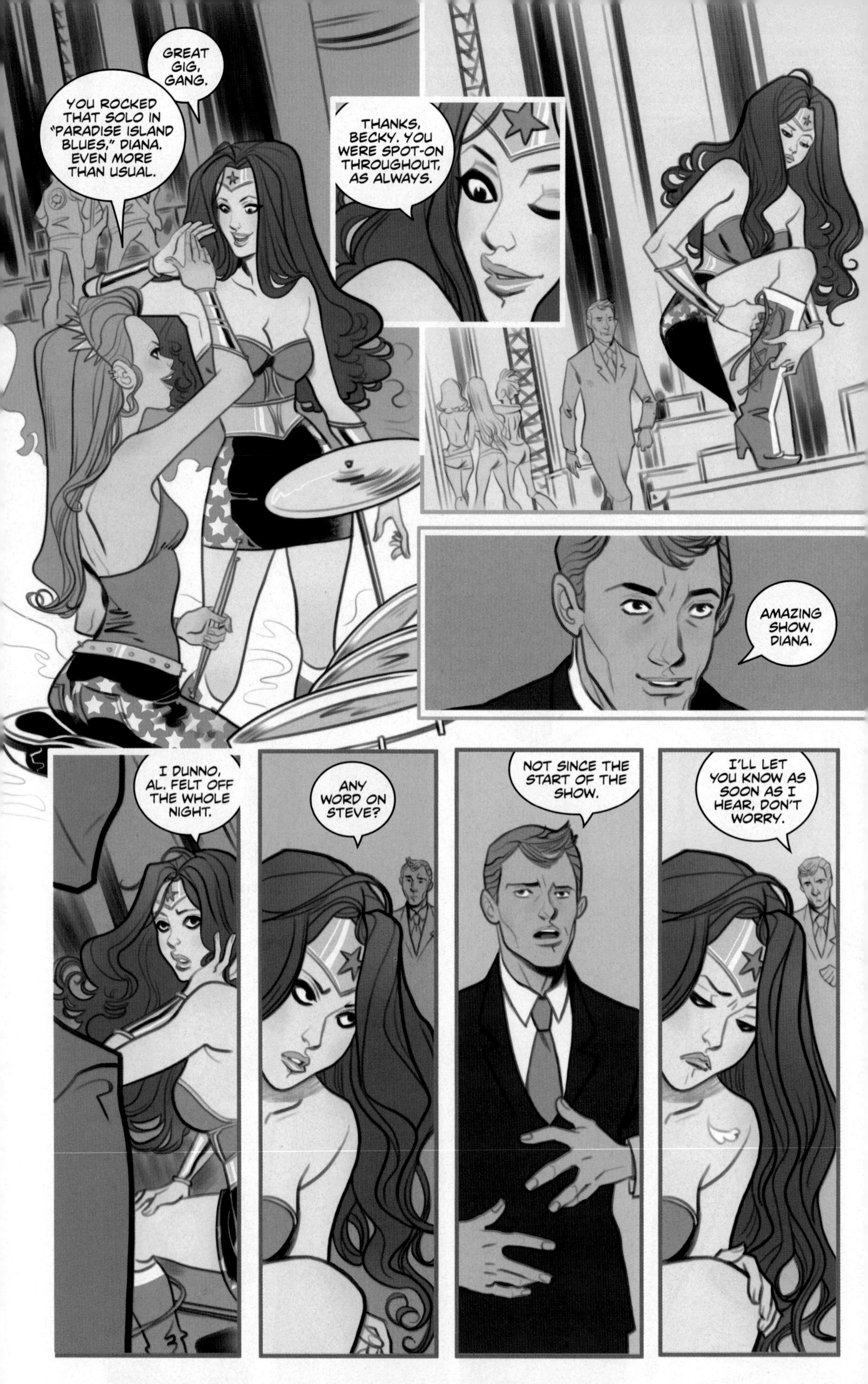
GREAT GIG, GANG.
YOU ROCKED THAT SOLO IN "PARADISE ISLAND BLUES," DIANA. EVEN MORE THAN USUAL.
THANKS, BECKY. YOU WERE SPOT-ON THROUGHOUT, AS ALWAYS.
AMAZING SHOW, DIANA.
I DUNNO, AL. FELT OFF THE WHOLE NIGHT.
ANY WORD ON STEVE?
NOT SINCE THE START OF THE SHOW.
I'LL LET YOU KNOW AS SOON AS I HEAR, DON'T WORRY.

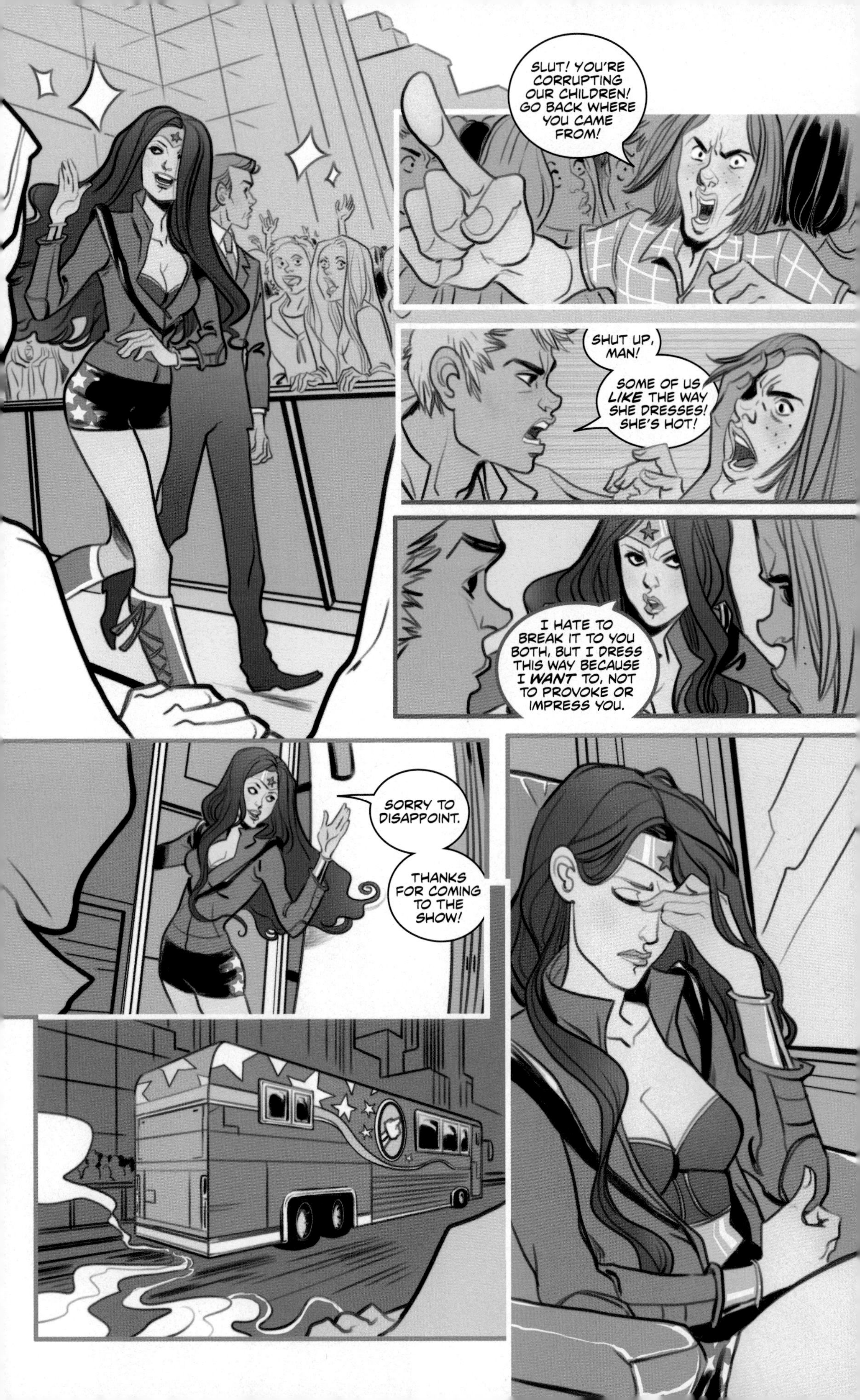
SLUT! YOU'RE CORRUPTING OUR CHILDREN! GO BACK WHERE YOU CAME FROM!
SHUT UP, MAN!
SOME OF US *LIKE* THE WAY SHE DRESSES! SHE'S HOT!
I HATE TO BREAK IT TO YOU BOTH, BUT I DRESS THIS WAY BECAUSE I *WANT* TO, NOT TO PROVOKE OR IMPRESS YOU.
SORRY TO DISAPPOINT.
THANKS FOR COMING TO THE SHOW!

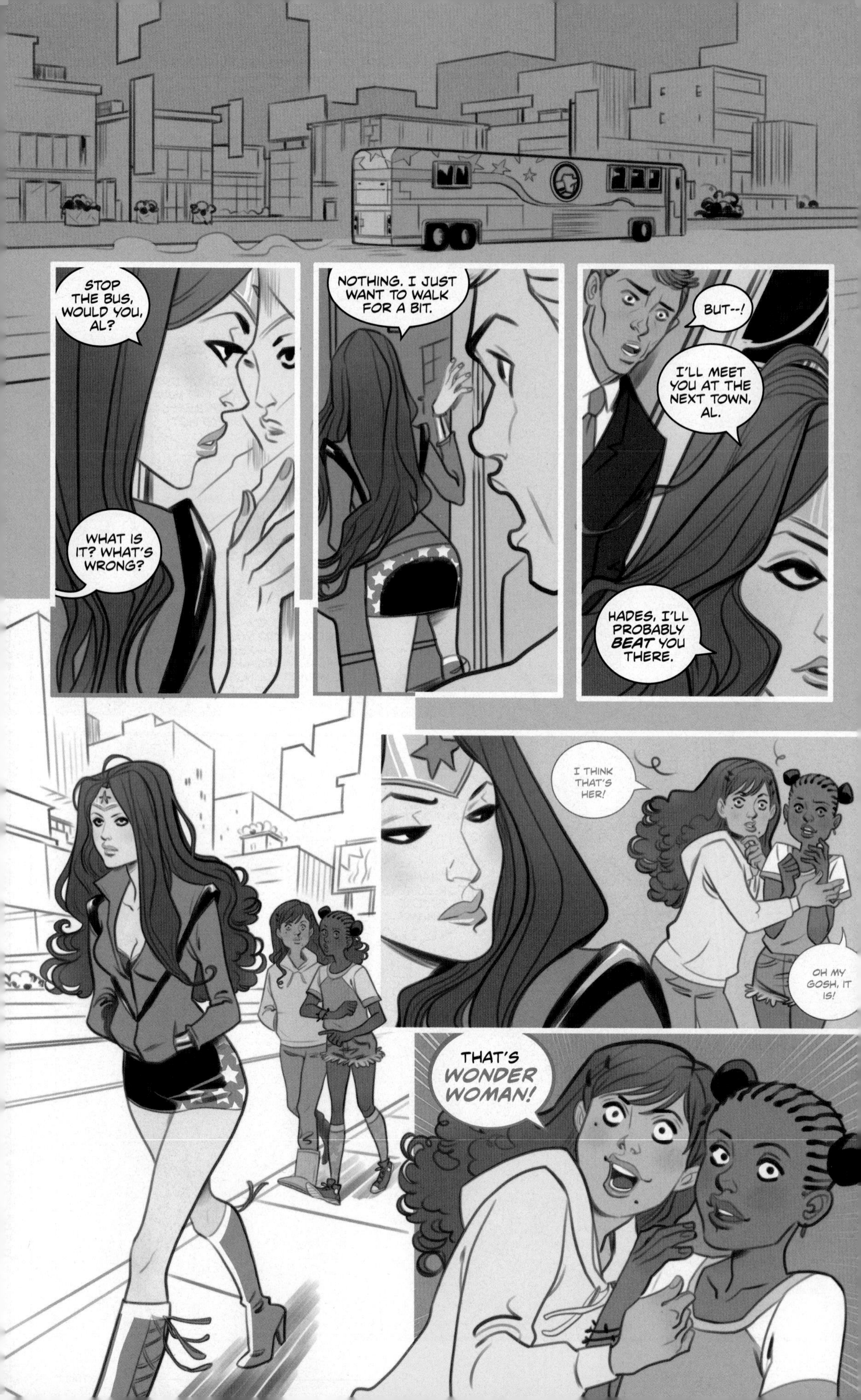
STOP THE BUS, WOULD YOU, AL?
WHAT IS IT? WHAT'S WRONG?
NOTHING. I JUST WANT TO WALK FOR A BIT.
BUT--!
I'LL MEET YOU AT THE NEXT TOWN, AL.
HADES, I'LL PROBABLY *BEAT* YOU THERE.
I THINK THAT'S HER!
OH MY GOSH, IT IS!
THAT'S *WONDER WOMAN!*

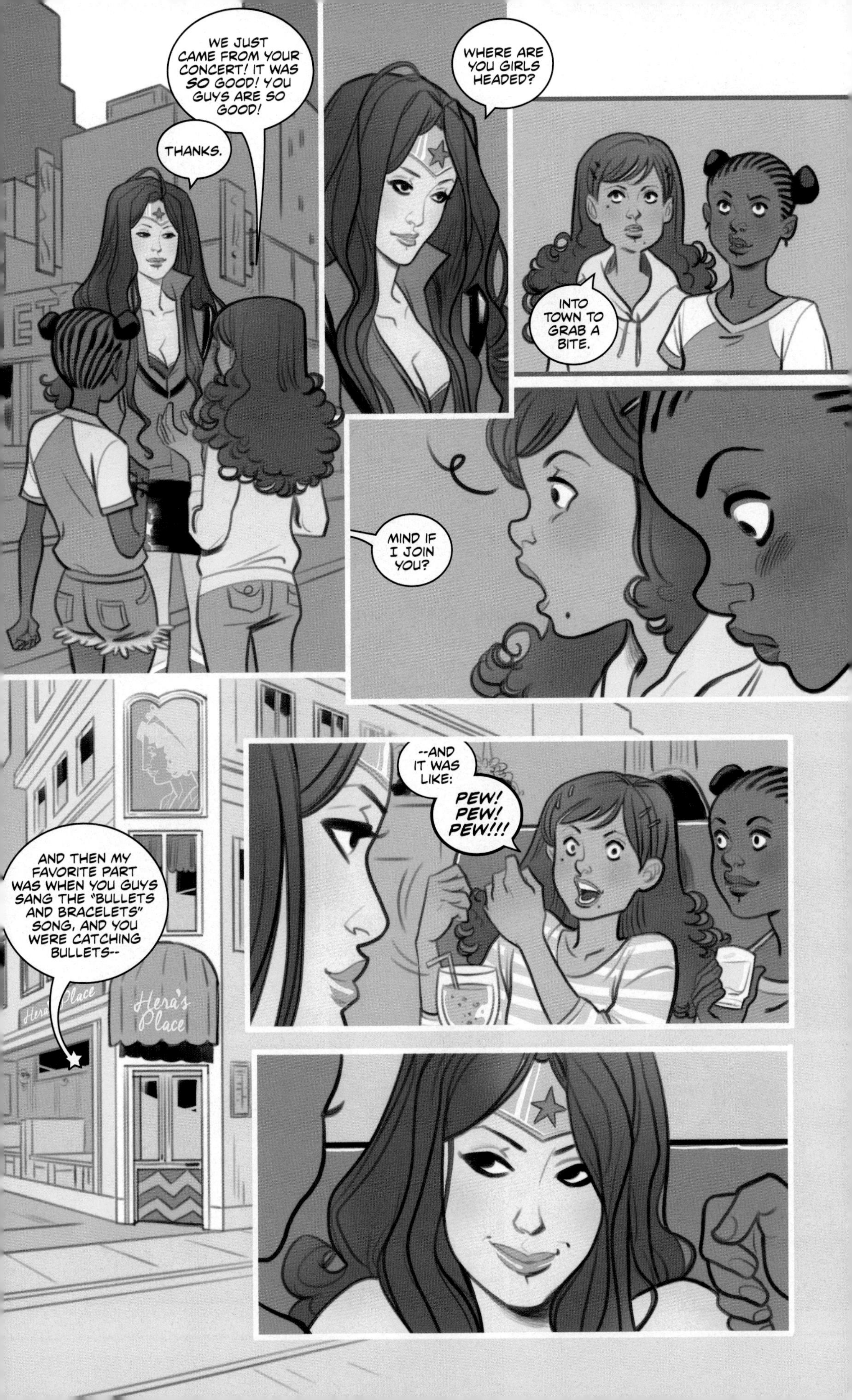
WE JUST CAME FROM YOUR CONCERT! IT WAS SO GOOD! YOU GUYS ARE SO GOOD!
THANKS.
WHERE ARE YOU GIRLS HEADED?
INTO TOWN TO GRAB A BITE.
MIND IF I JOIN YOU?
AND THEN MY FAVORITE PART WAS WHEN YOU GUYS SANG THE "BULLETS AND BRACELETS" SONG, AND YOU WERE CATCHING BULLETS--
--AND IT WAS LIKE:
PEW! PEW! PEW!!!
Hera's Place
Hera's Place

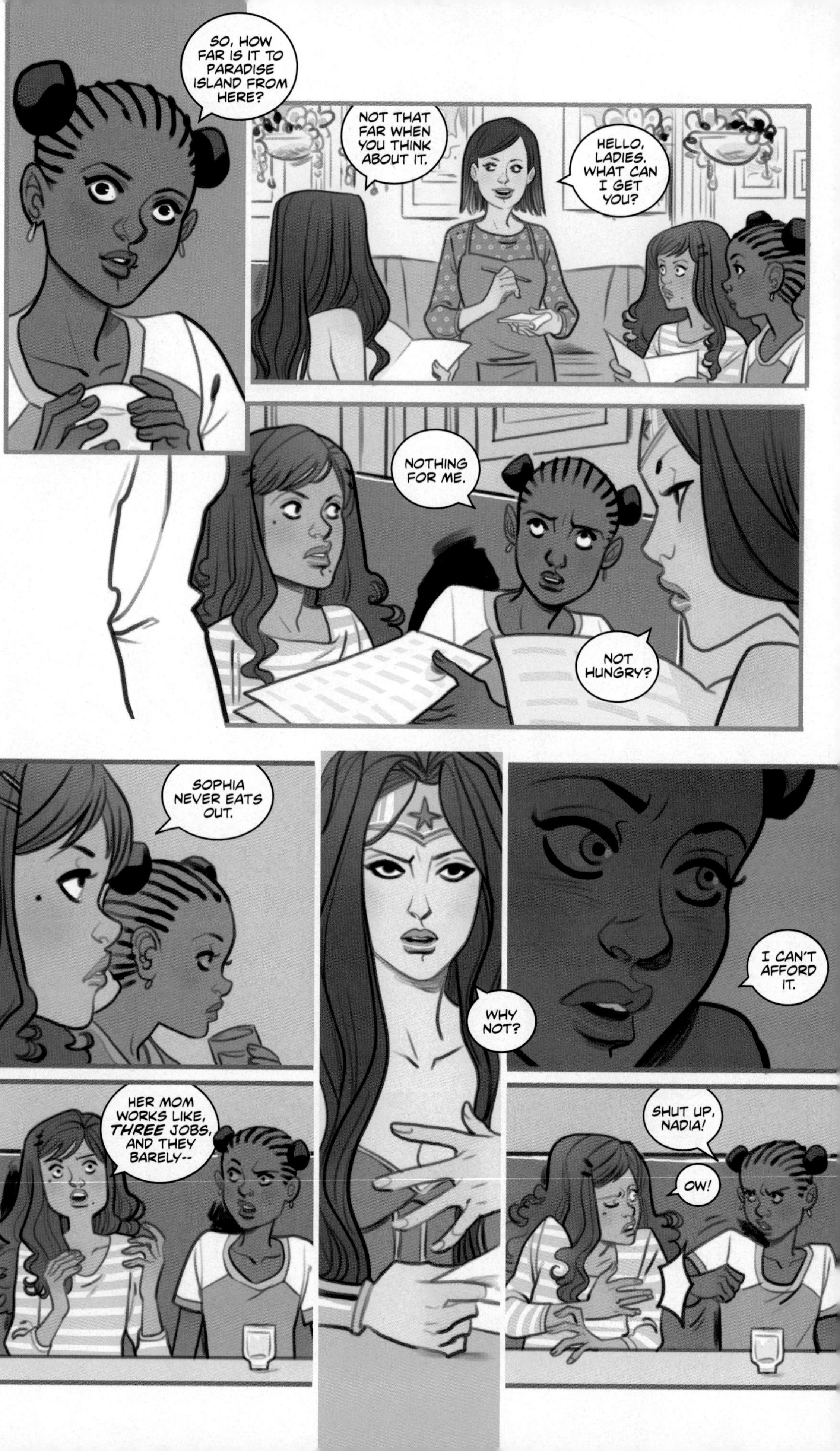
SO, HOW FAR IS IT TO PARADISE ISLAND FROM HERE?
NOT THAT FAR WHEN YOU THINK ABOUT IT.
HELLO, LADIES. WHAT CAN I GET YOU?
NOTHING FOR ME.
NOT HUNGRY?
SOPHIA NEVER EATS OUT.
WHY NOT?
I CAN'T AFFORD IT.
HER MOM WORKS LIKE, THREE JOBS, AND THEY BARELY--
SHUT UP, NADIA!
OW!

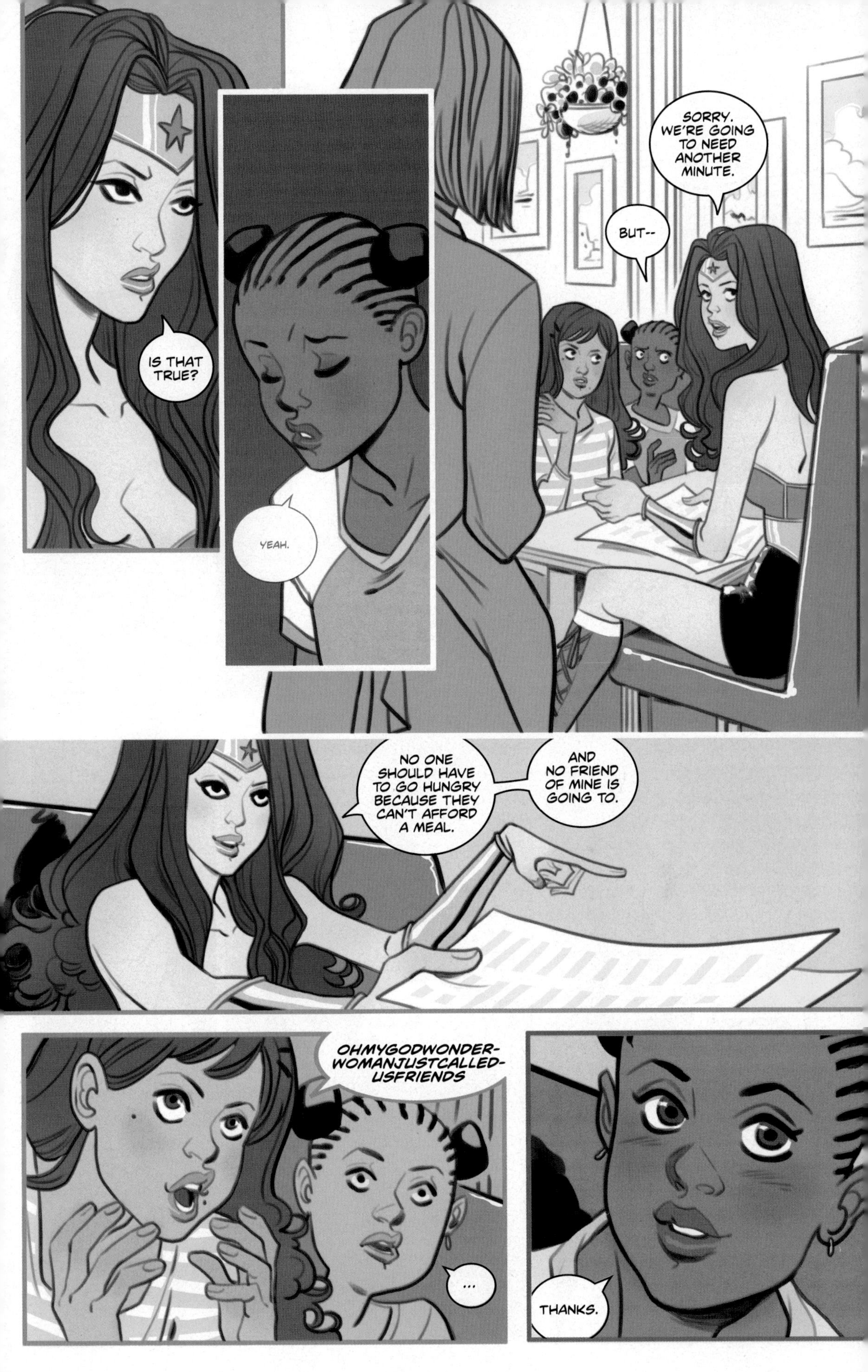
IS THAT TRUE?
YEAH.
BUT--
SORRY. WE'RE GOING TO NEED ANOTHER MINUTE.
NO ONE SHOULD HAVE TO GO HUNGRY BECAUSE THEY CAN'T AFFORD A MEAL.
AND NO FRIEND OF MINE IS GOING TO.
OHMYGODWONDER-WOMANJUSTCALLED-USFRIENDS
...
THANKS.

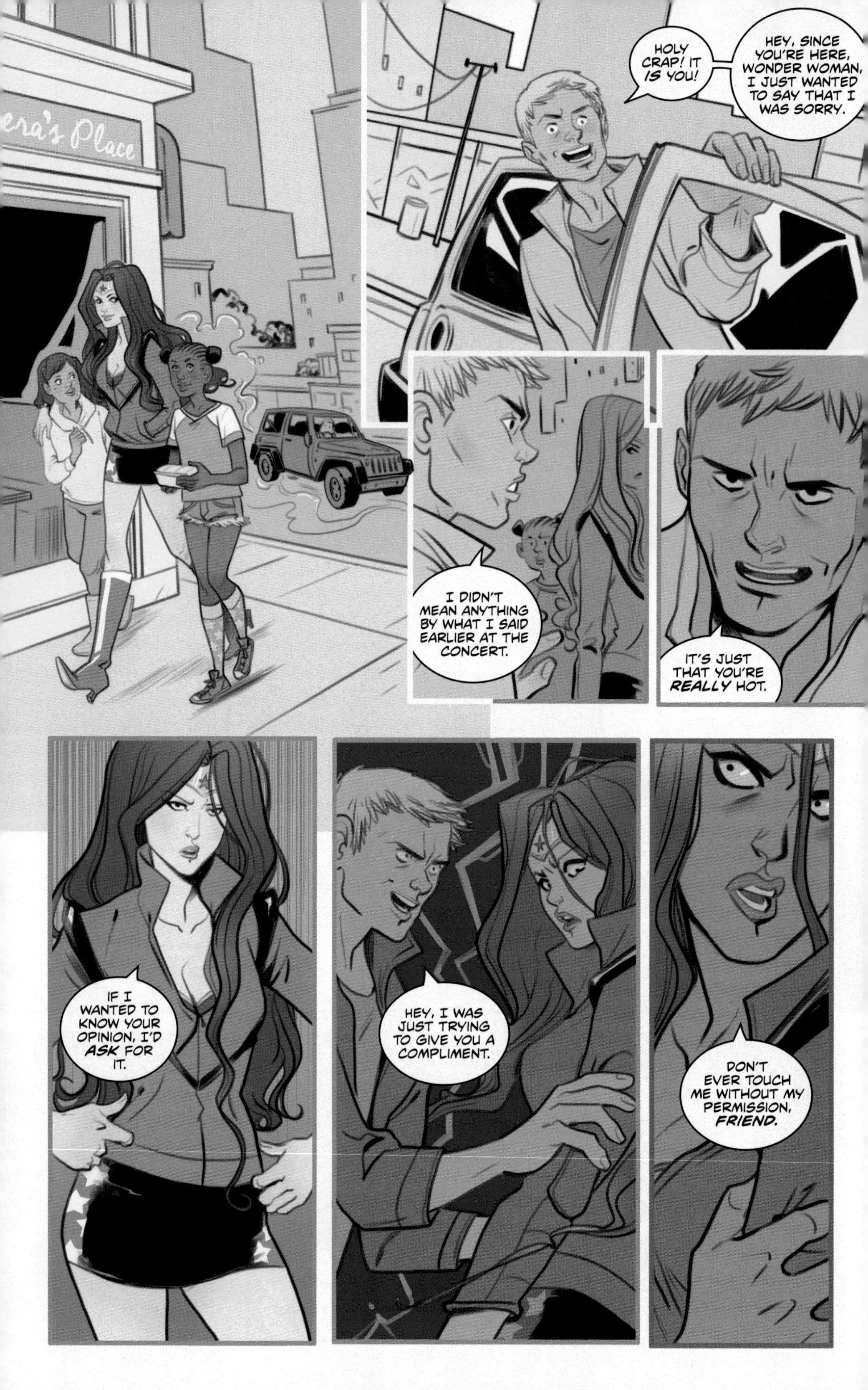

era's Place
HOLY CRAP! IT *IS* YOU!
HEY, SINCE YOU'RE HERE, WONDER WOMAN, I JUST WANTED TO SAY THAT I WAS SORRY.
I DIDN'T MEAN ANYTHING BY WHAT I SAID EARLIER AT THE CONCERT.
IT'S JUST THAT YOU'RE ***REALLY*** HOT.
IF I WANTED TO KNOW YOUR OPINION, I'D ***ASK*** FOR IT.
HEY, I WAS JUST TRYING TO GIVE YOU A COMPLIMENT.
DON'T EVER TOUCH ME WITHOUT MY PERMISSION, ***FRIEND.***

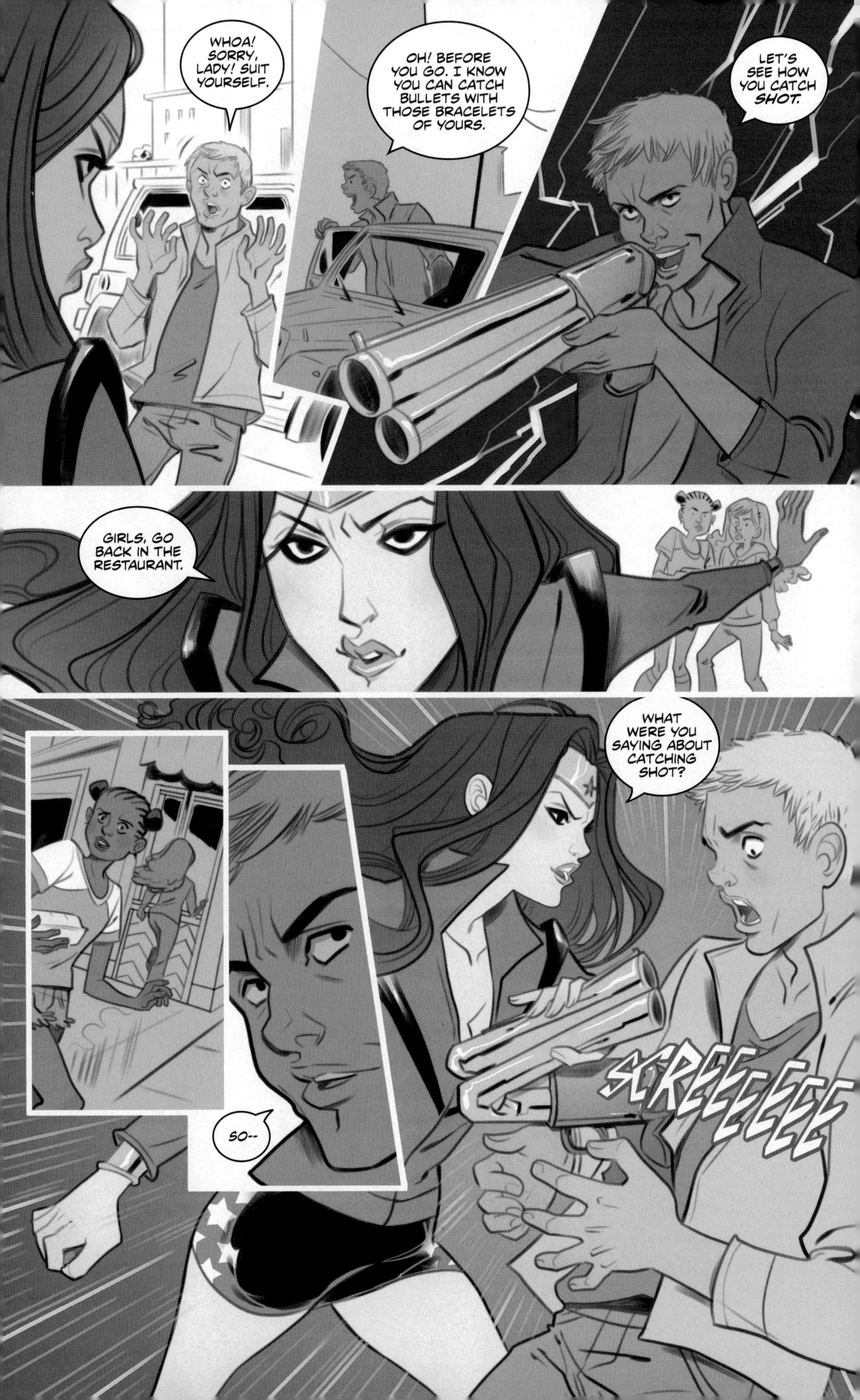
WHOA! SORRY, LADY! SUIT YOURSELF.
OH! BEFORE YOU GO. I KNOW YOU CAN CATCH BULLETS WITH THOSE BRACELETS OF YOURS.
LET'S SEE HOW YOU CATCH SHOT.
GIRLS, GO BACK IN THE RESTAURANT.
SO--
WHAT WERE YOU SAYING ABOUT CATCHING SHOT?
SCREEEEEEE

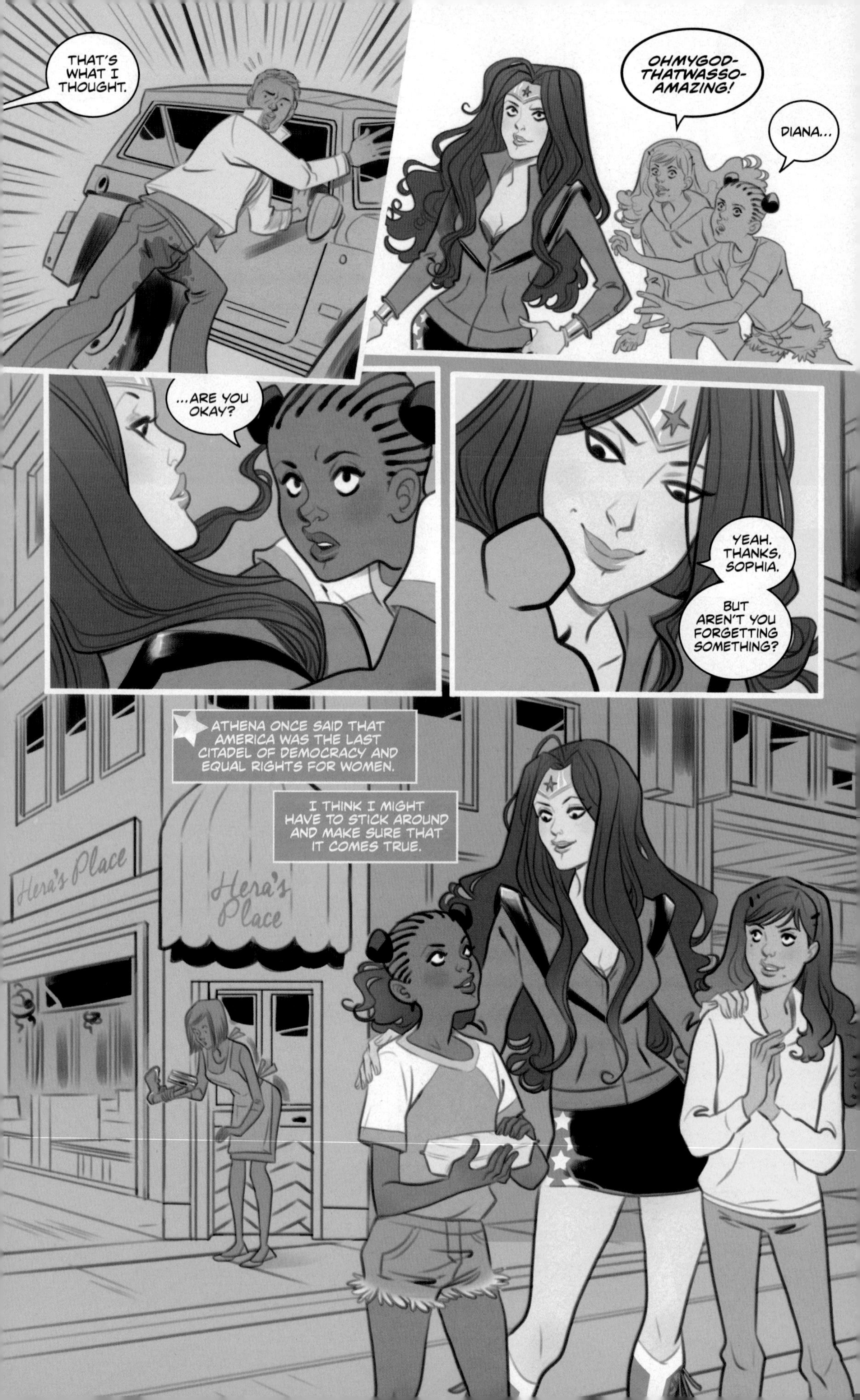
THAT'S WHAT I THOUGHT.
OHMYGOD-THATWASSO-AMAZING!
DIANA...
...ARE YOU OKAY?
YEAH. THANKS, SOPHIA.
BUT AREN'T YOU FORGETTING SOMETHING?
ATHENA ONCE SAID THAT AMERICA WAS THE LAST CITADEL OF DEMOCRACY AND EQUAL RIGHTS FOR WOMEN.
I THINK I MIGHT HAVE TO STICK AROUND AND MAKE SURE THAT IT COMES TRUE.
Hera's Place
Hera's Place

MORNING COFFEE

OLLIE MASTERS
WRITER

AMY MEBBERSON
ARTIST AND COLORIST

DERON BENNETT
LETTERER

THE BRITISH MUSEUM, LONDON.

KLICK

WOOWOOWOOWOOWOOWO

WOOWOOWOOWOO

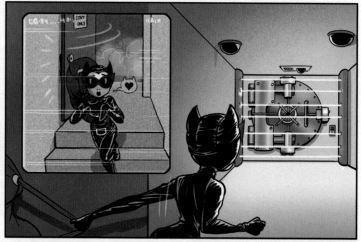

RING! RING! RING!

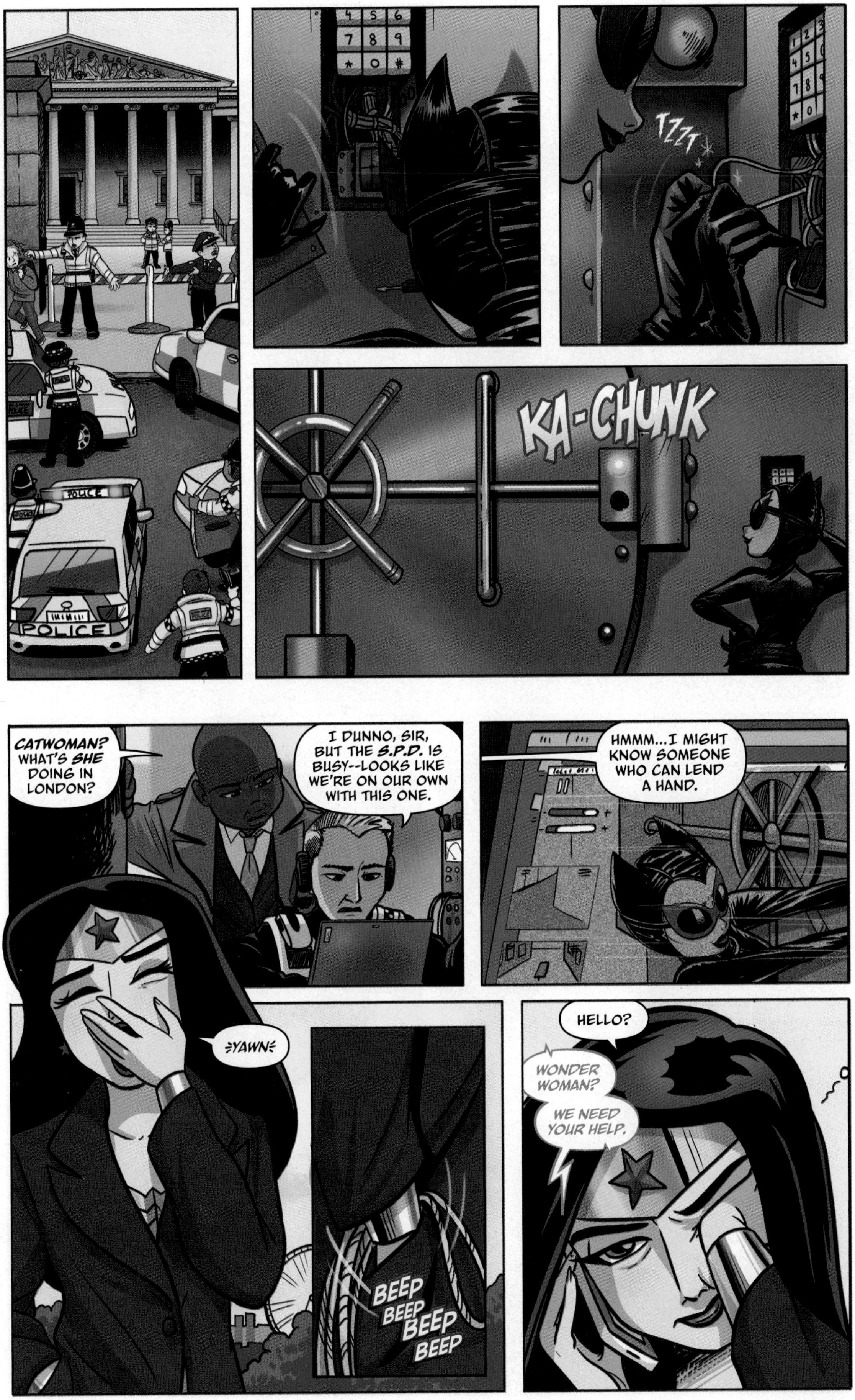

TZZT
KA-CHUNK
CATWOMAN? WHAT'S SHE DOING IN LONDON?
I DUNNO, SIR, BUT THE S.P.D. IS BUSY--LOOKS LIKE WE'RE ON OUR OWN WITH THIS ONE.
HMMM...I MIGHT KNOW SOMEONE WHO CAN LEND A HAND.
YAWN
BEEP BEEP BEEP BEEP
HELLO?
WONDER WOMAN?
WE NEED YOUR HELP.

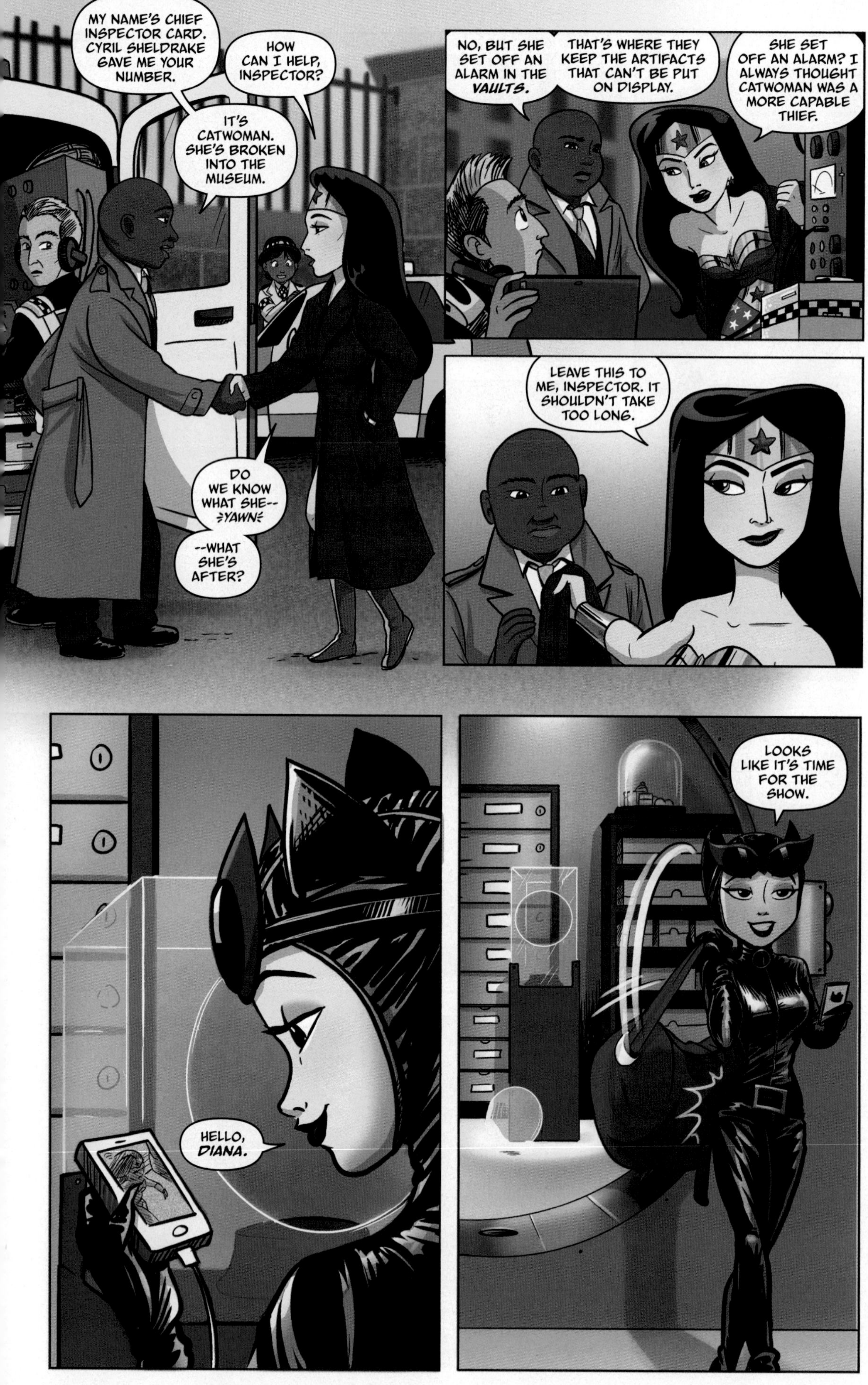
MY NAME'S CHIEF INSPECTOR CARD. CYRIL SHELDRAKE GAVE ME YOUR NUMBER.
HOW CAN I HELP, INSPECTOR?
IT'S CATWOMAN. SHE'S BROKEN INTO THE MUSEUM.
DO WE KNOW WHAT SHE--
YAWN
--WHAT SHE'S AFTER?
NO, BUT SHE SET OFF AN ALARM IN THE VAULTS.
THAT'S WHERE THEY KEEP THE ARTIFACTS THAT CAN'T BE PUT ON DISPLAY.
SHE SET OFF AN ALARM? I ALWAYS THOUGHT CATWOMAN WAS A MORE CAPABLE THIEF.
LEAVE THIS TO ME, INSPECTOR. IT SHOULDN'T TAKE TOO LONG.
HELLO, DIANA.
LOOKS LIKE IT'S TIME FOR THE SHOW.

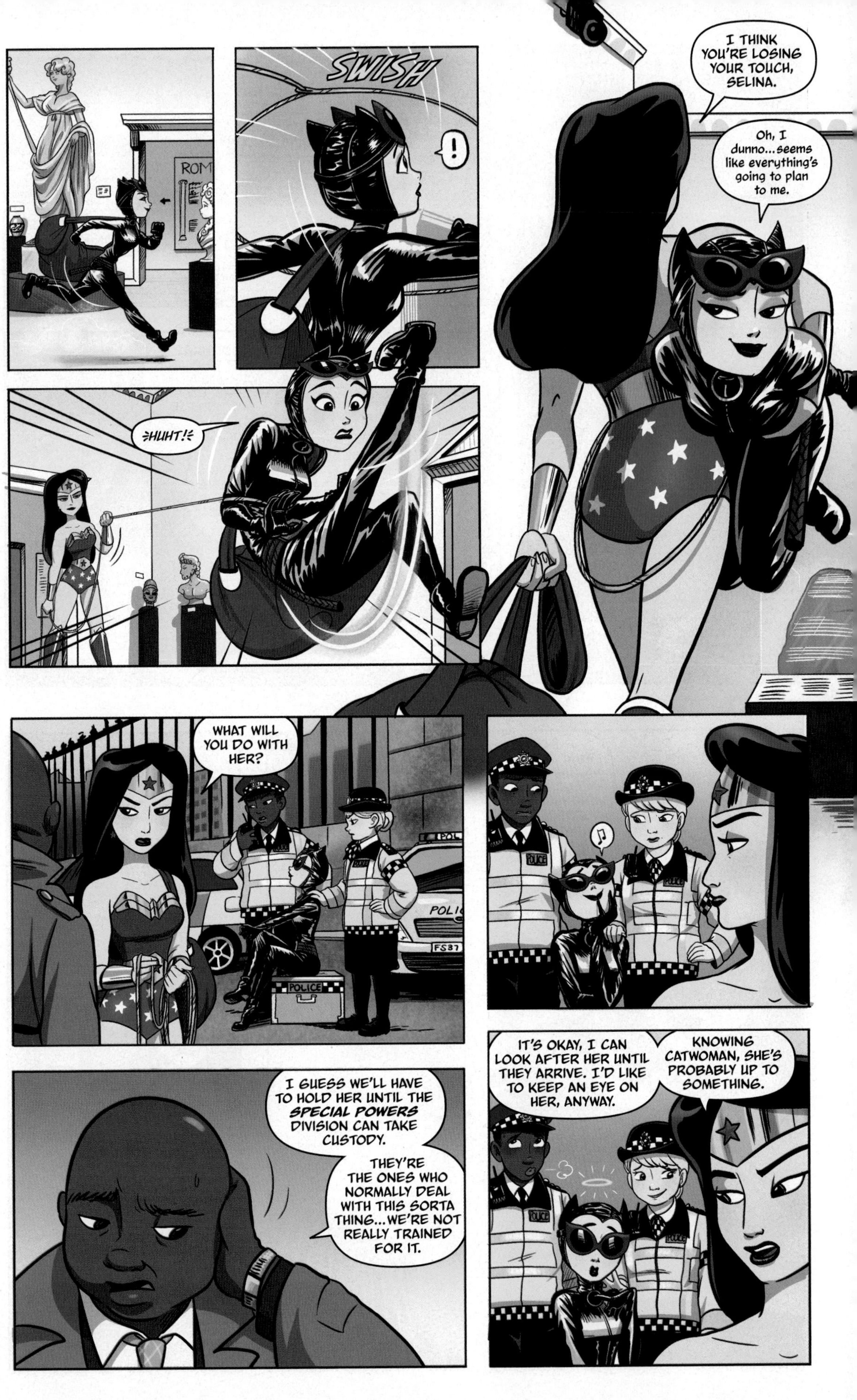
ROM
SWISH
!
I THINK YOU'RE LOSING YOUR TOUCH, SELINA.
Oh, I dunno...seems like everything's going to plan to me.
HUHT!
WHAT WILL YOU DO WITH HER?
POLICE
I GUESS WE'LL HAVE TO HOLD HER UNTIL THE SPECIAL POWERS DIVISION CAN TAKE CUSTODY.
THEY'RE THE ONES WHO NORMALLY DEAL WITH THIS SORTA THING...WE'RE NOT REALLY TRAINED FOR IT.
IT'S OKAY, I CAN LOOK AFTER HER UNTIL THEY ARRIVE. I'D LIKE TO KEEP AN EYE ON HER, ANYWAY.
KNOWING CATWOMAN, SHE'S PROBABLY UP TO SOMETHING.

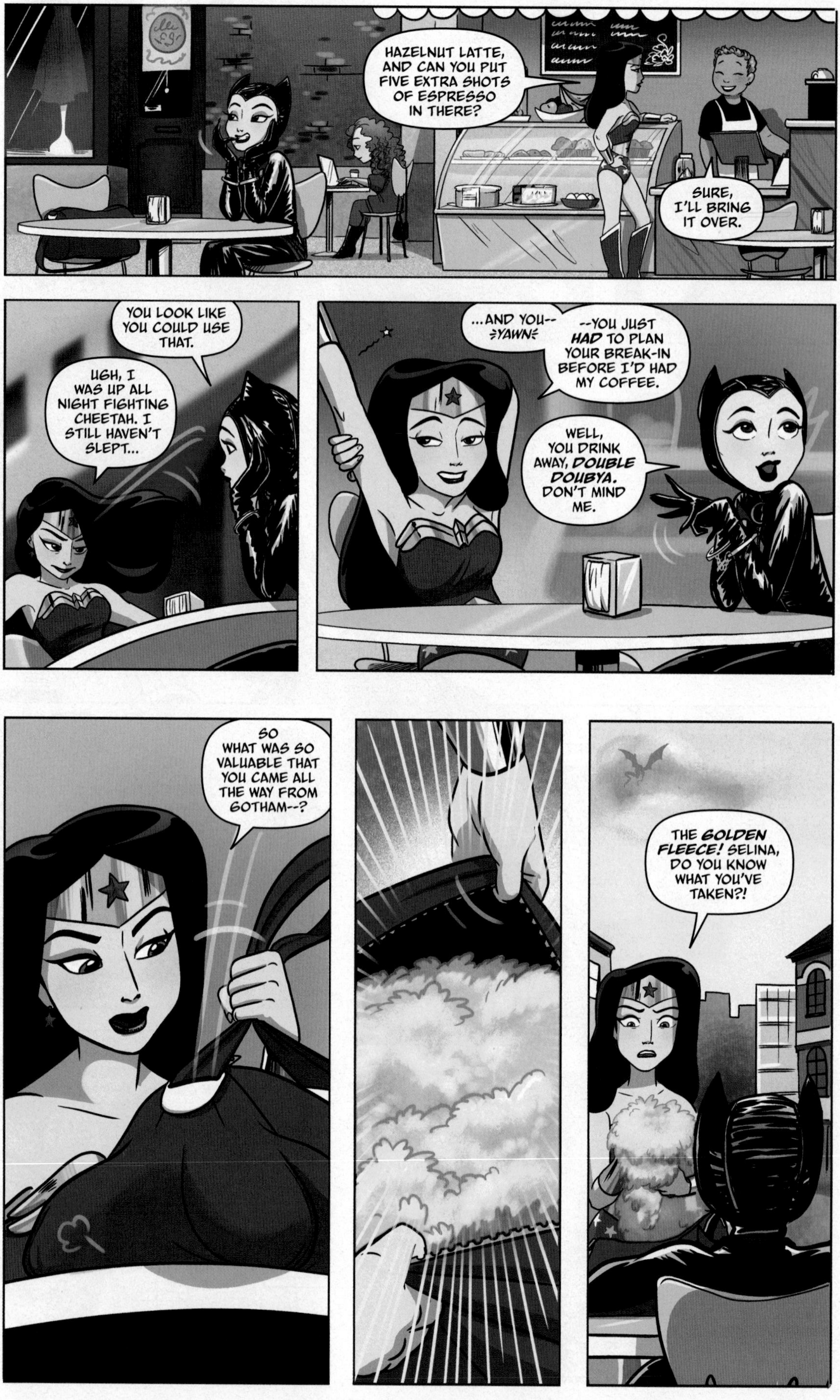
HAZELNUT LATTE, AND CAN YOU PUT FIVE EXTRA SHOTS OF ESPRESSO IN THERE?
SURE, I'LL BRING IT OVER.
YOU LOOK LIKE YOU COULD USE THAT.
UGH, I WAS UP ALL NIGHT FIGHTING CHEETAH. I STILL HAVEN'T SLEPT...
...AND YOU-- *YAWN*
--YOU JUST **HAD** TO PLAN YOUR BREAK-IN BEFORE I'D HAD MY COFFEE.
WELL, YOU DRINK AWAY, ***DOUBLE DOUBYA.*** DON'T MIND ME.
SO WHAT WAS SO VALUABLE THAT YOU CAME ALL THE WAY FROM GOTHAM--?
THE ***GOLDEN FLEECE!*** SELINA, DO YOU KNOW WHAT YOU'VE TAKEN?!

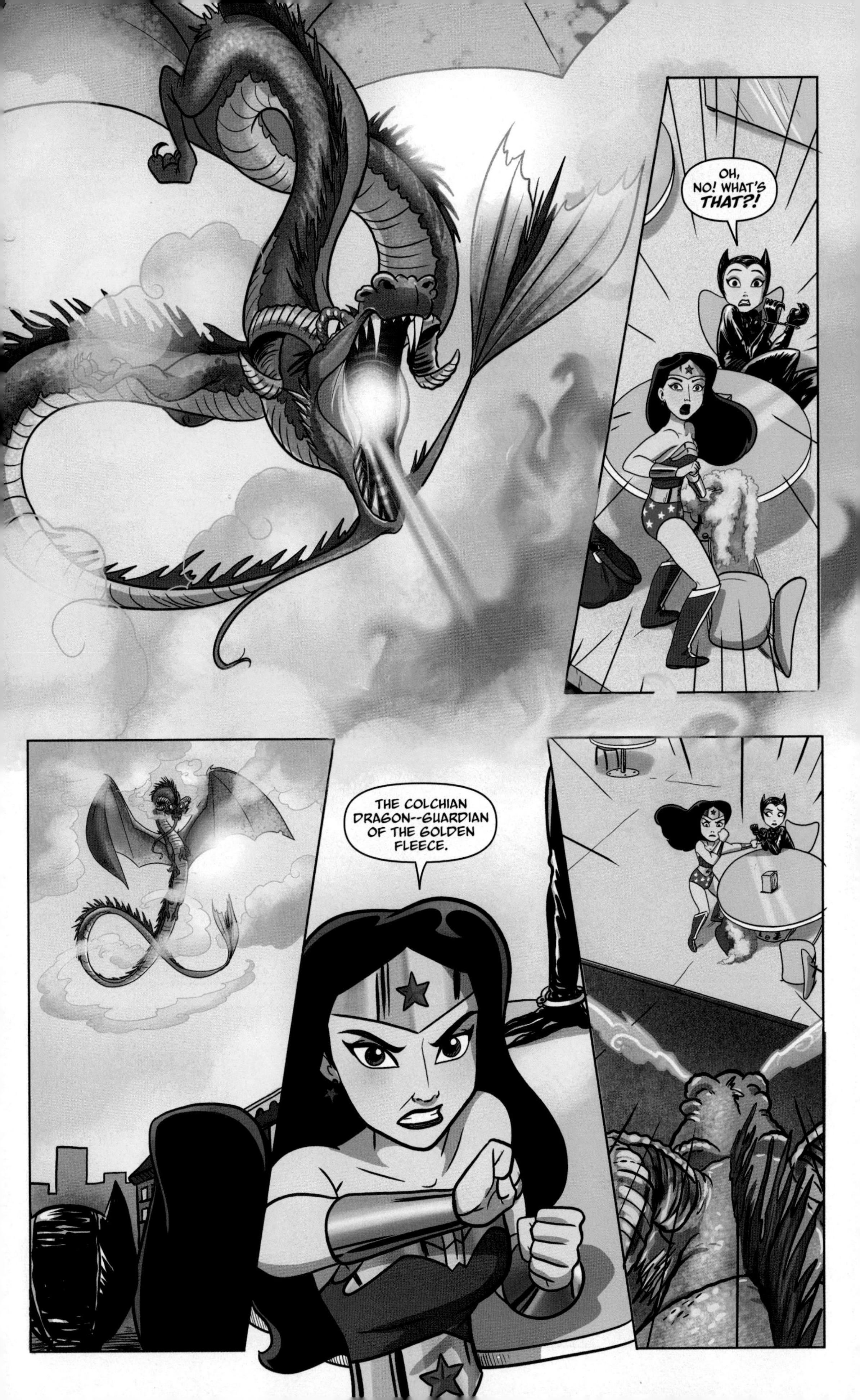
OH, NO! WHAT'S THAT?!
THE COLCHIAN DRAGON--GUARDIAN OF THE GOLDEN FLEECE.

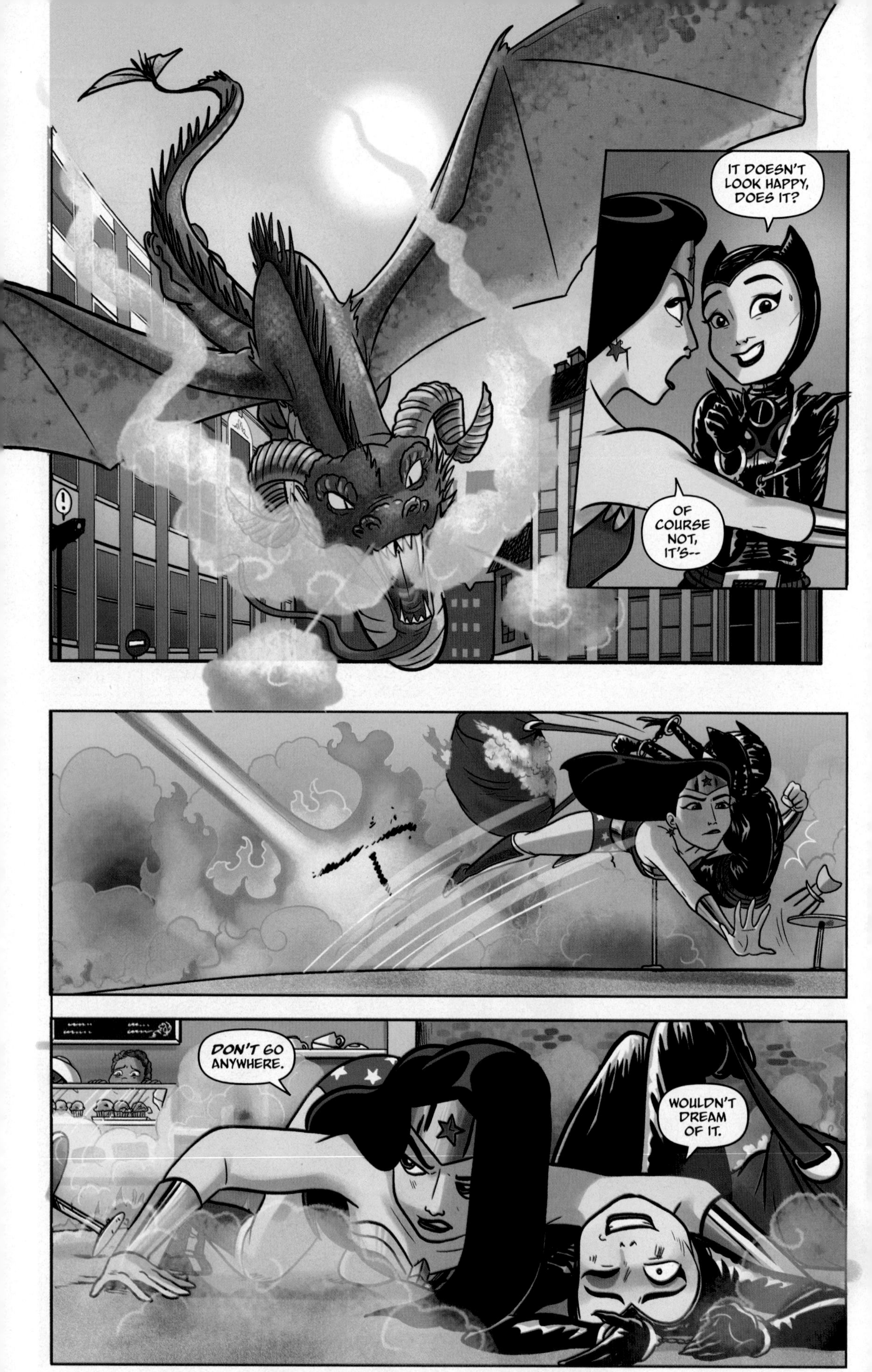

IT DOESN'T LOOK HAPPY, DOES IT?
OF COURSE NOT, IT'S--
DON'T GO ANYWHERE.
WOULDN'T DREAM OF IT.

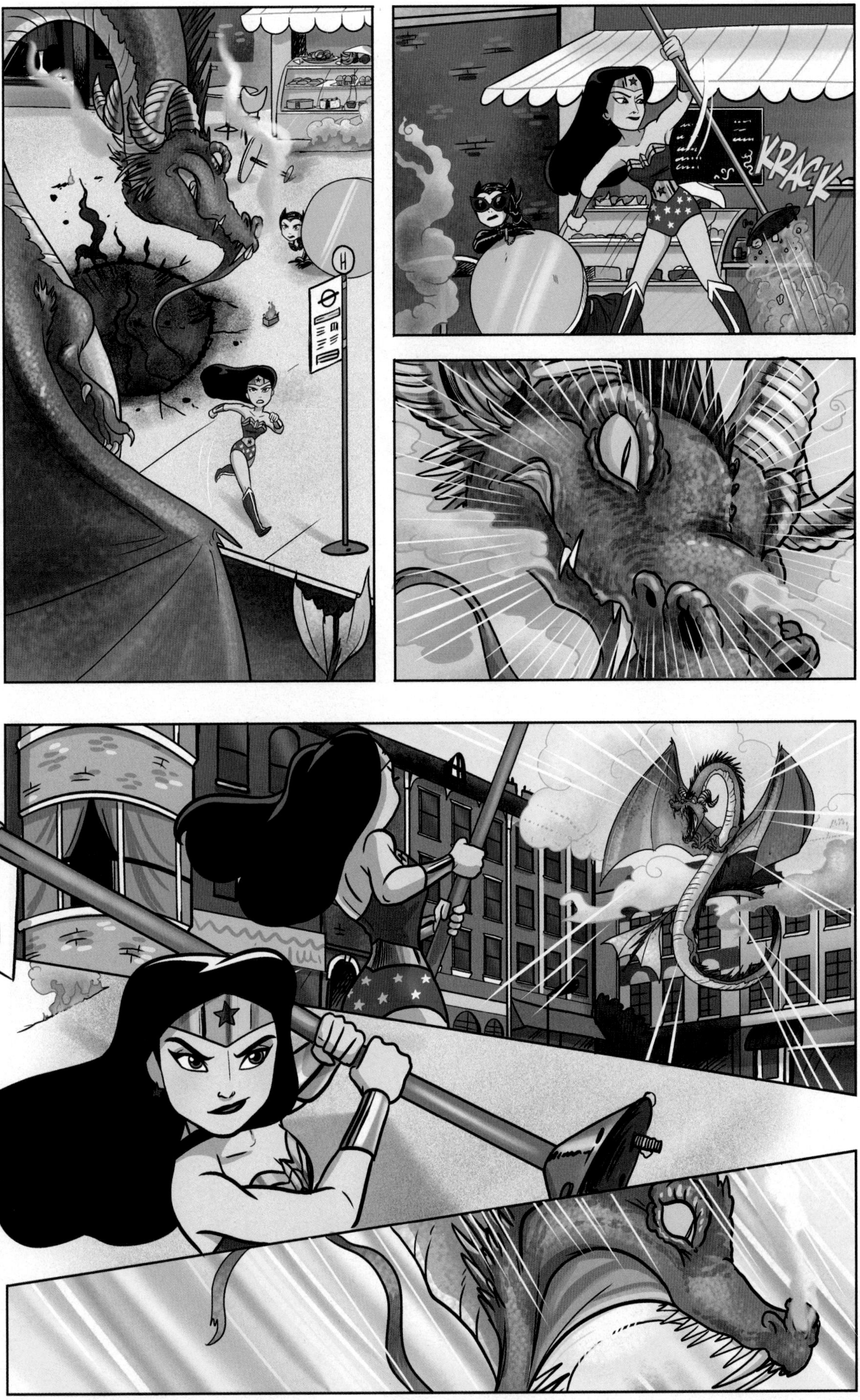
KRACK

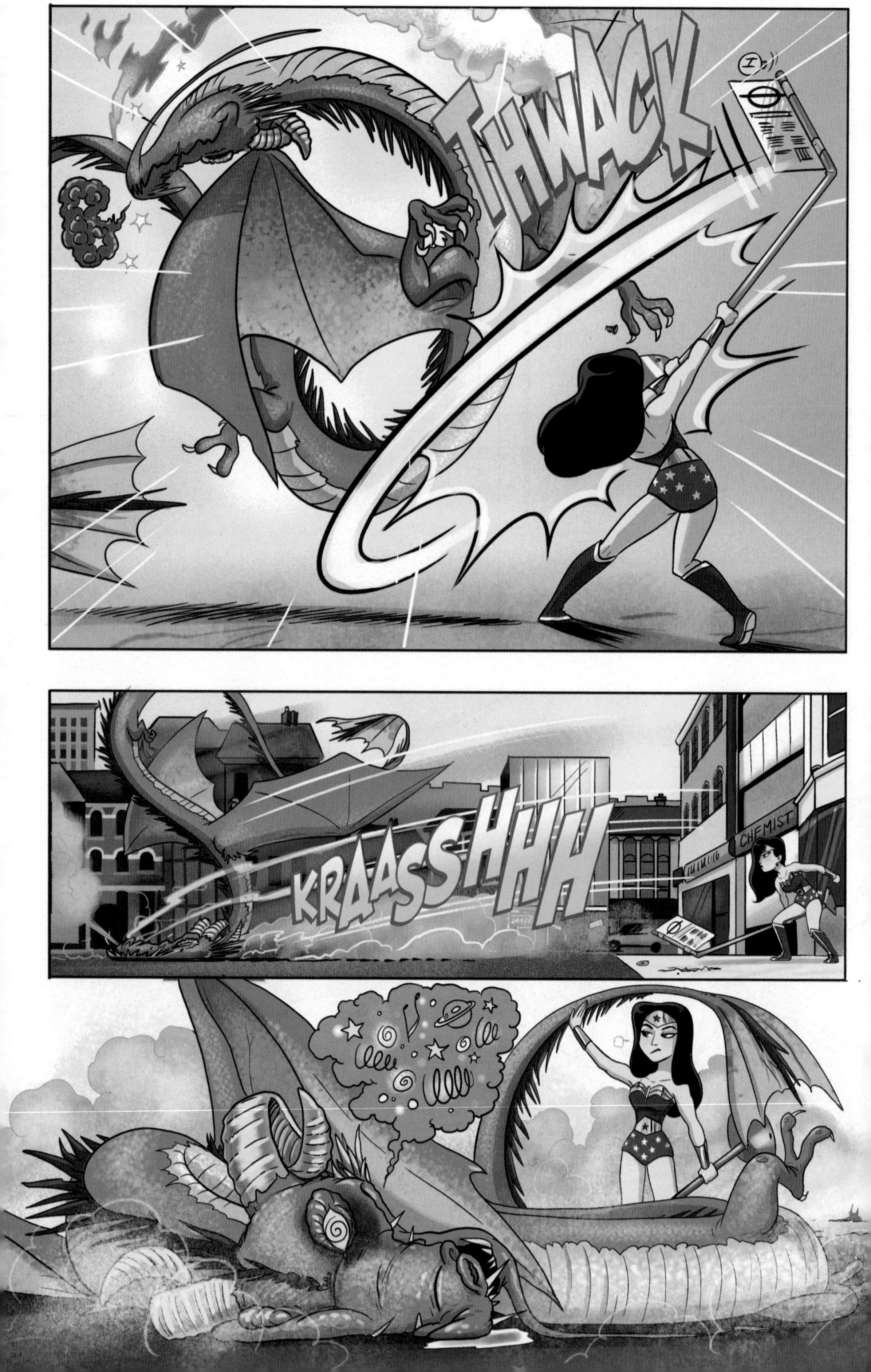
THWACK
KRAASSHHH
CHEMIST

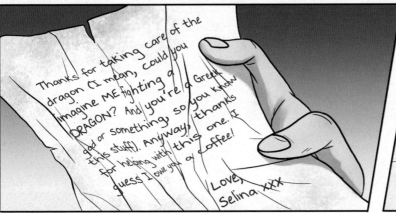

Thanks for taking care of the dragon (I mean, could you imagine ME fighting a DRAGON? And you're a Greek god or something, so you know this stuff). Anyway, thanks for helping with this one. I guess I owe you a coffee!

Love,
Selina, XXX

DO YOU KNOW HOW LONG IT TOOK ME TO SET THIS UP?! TIMING EVERYTHING PERFECTLY, MAKING SURE YOU WERE HERE AND--

SELINA, BE QUIET!

I'M TAKING YOU BACK TO GOTHAM SO YOU CAN GO BACK TO BEING BATMAN'S PROBLEM, BUT FIRST--

--YOU'RE BUYING ME THAT COFFEE.

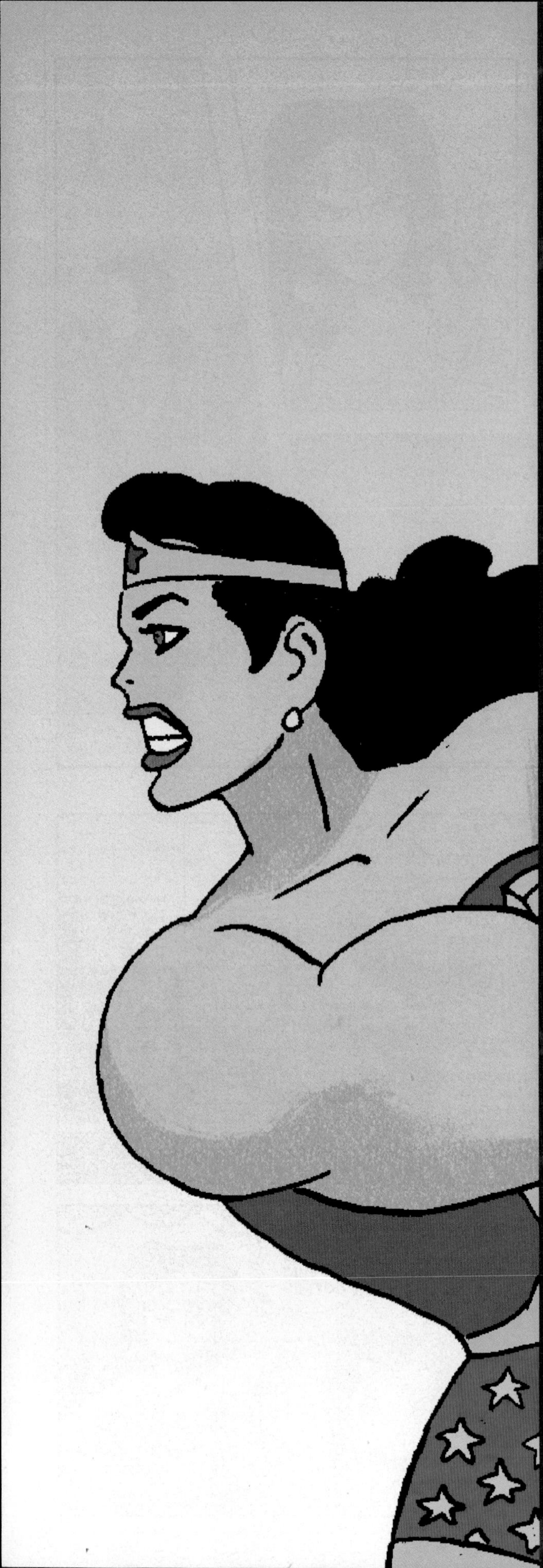

NO CHAINS CAN HOLD HER!

GILBERT HERNANDEZ
WRITER & ARTIST

JOHN RAUCH
COLORIST

DERON BENNETT
LETTERER

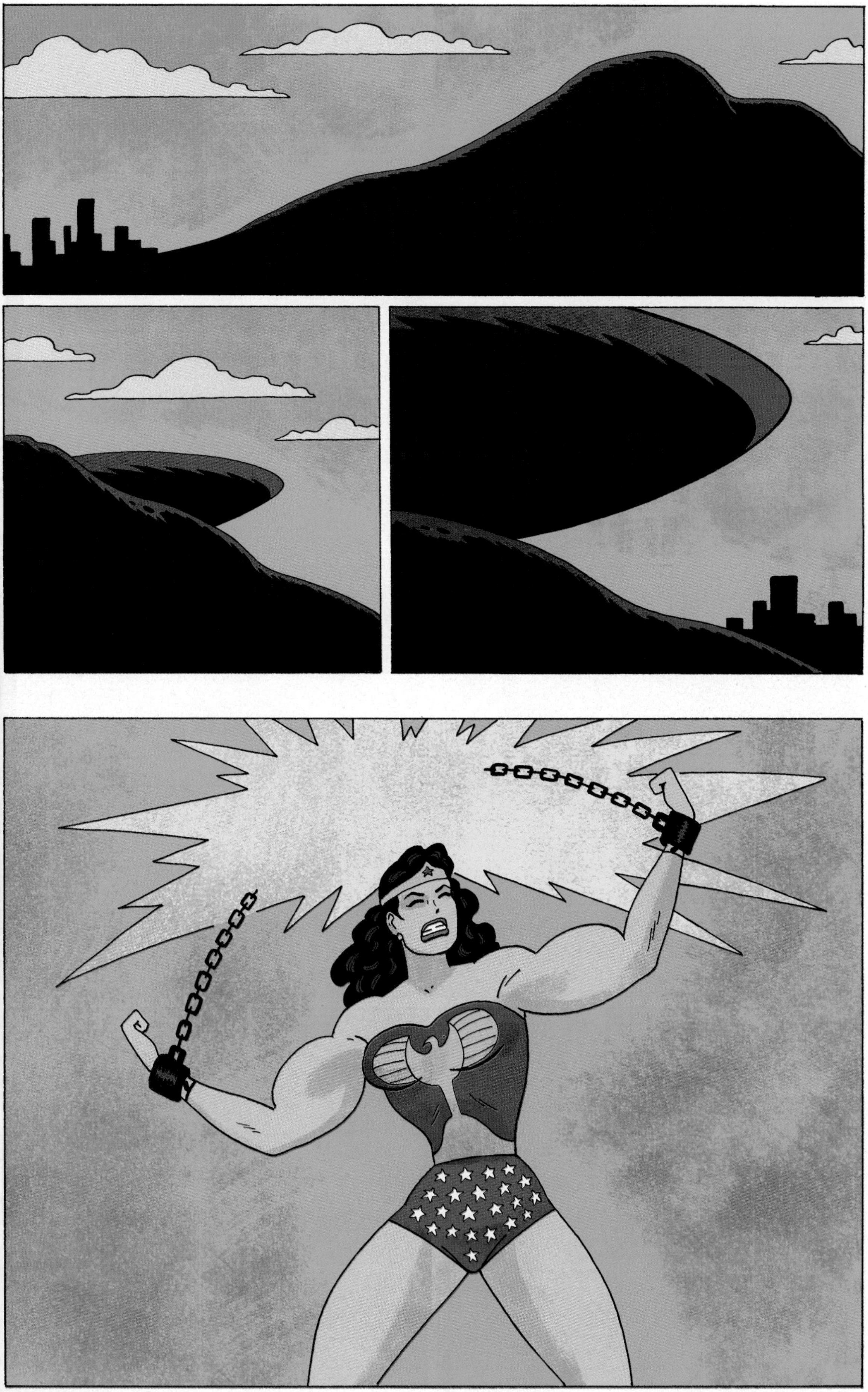

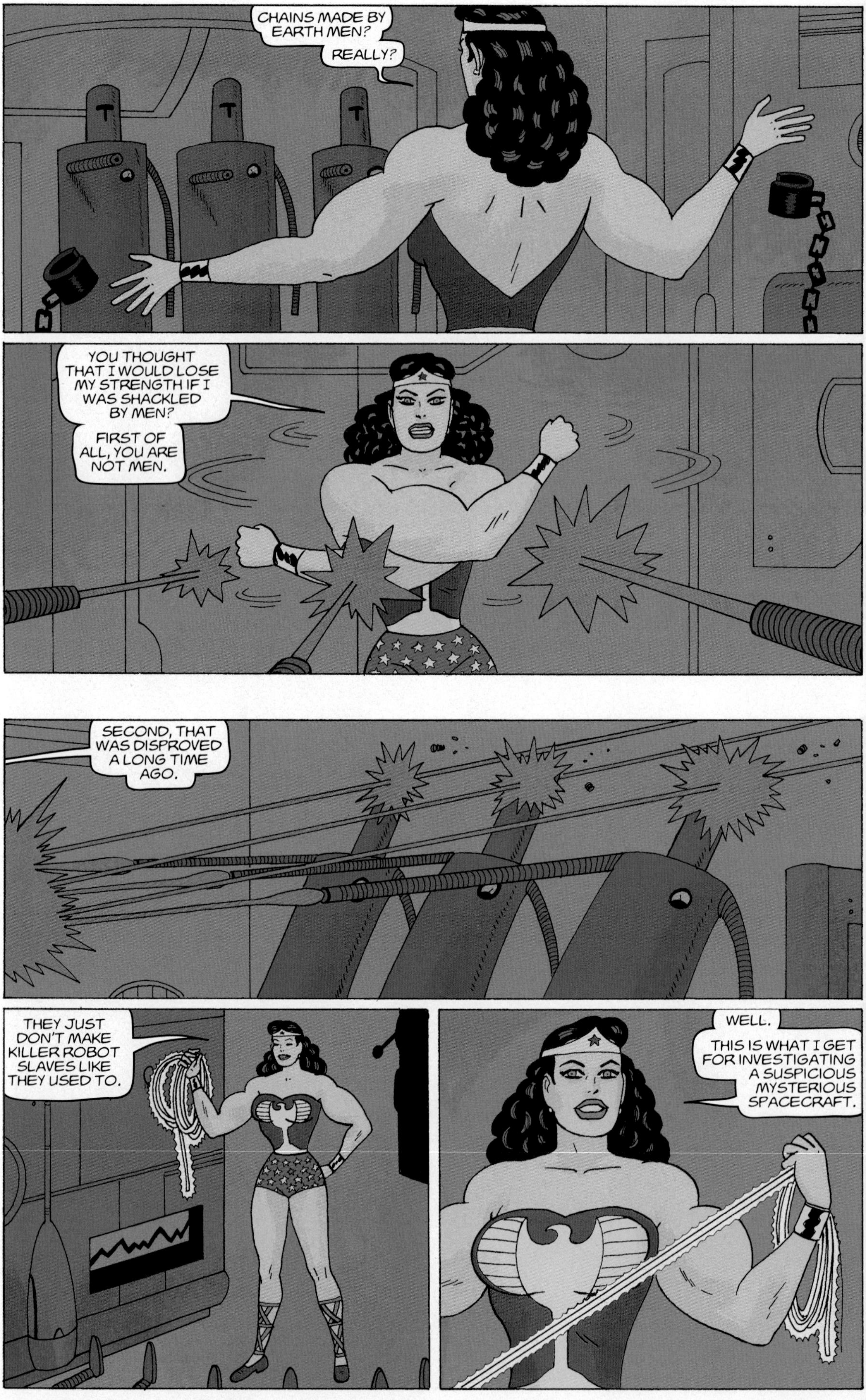
CHAINS MADE BY EARTH MEN?
REALLY?
YOU THOUGHT THAT I WOULD LOSE MY STRENGTH IF I WAS SHACKLED BY MEN?
FIRST OF ALL, YOU ARE NOT MEN.
SECOND, THAT WAS DISPROVED A LONG TIME AGO.
THEY JUST DON'T MAKE KILLER ROBOT SLAVES LIKE THEY USED TO.
WELL.
THIS IS WHAT I GET FOR INVESTIGATING A SUSPICIOUS MYSTERIOUS SPACECRAFT.

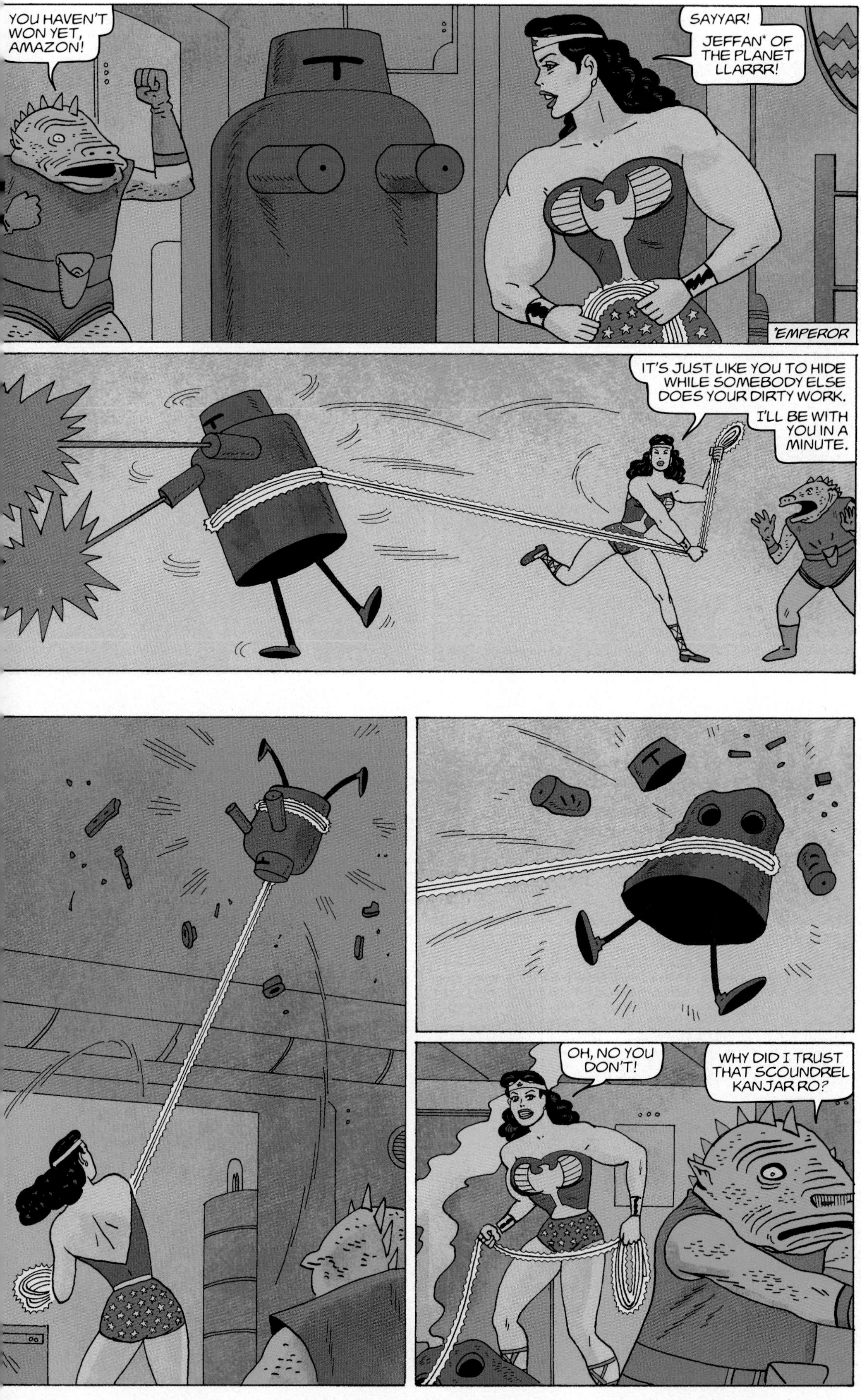
YOU HAVEN'T WON YET, AMAZON!
SAYYAR!
JEFFAN* OF THE PLANET LLARRR!
*EMPEROR
IT'S JUST LIKE YOU TO HIDE WHILE SOMEBODY ELSE DOES YOUR DIRTY WORK.
I'LL BE WITH YOU IN A MINUTE.
OH, NO YOU DON'T!
WHY DID I TRUST THAT SCOUNDREL KANJAR RO?

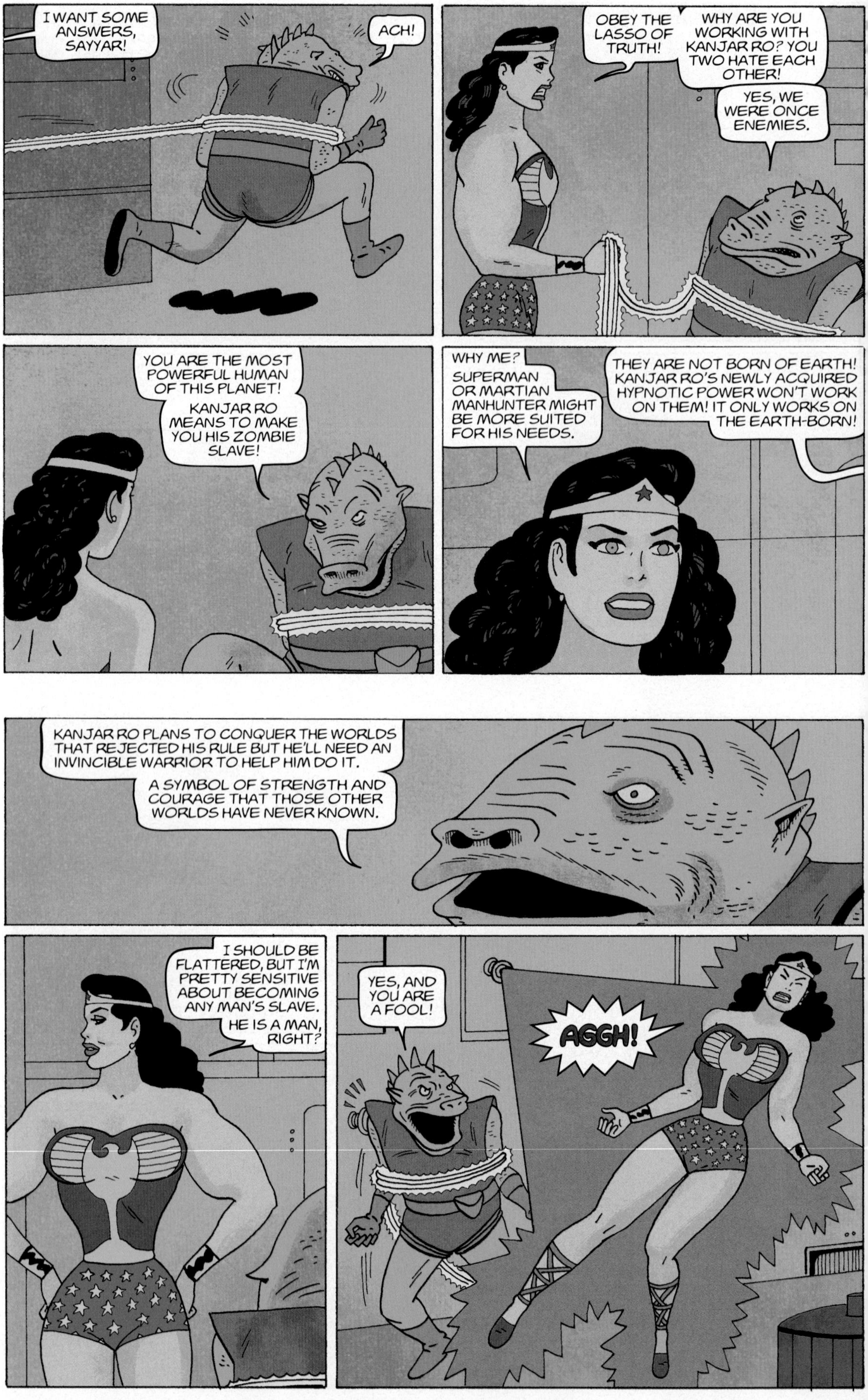

I WANT SOME ANSWERS, SAYYAR!
ACH!
OBEY THE LASSO OF TRUTH!
WHY ARE YOU WORKING WITH KANJAR RO? YOU TWO HATE EACH OTHER!
YES, WE WERE ONCE ENEMIES.
YOU ARE THE MOST POWERFUL HUMAN OF THIS PLANET!
KANJAR RO MEANS TO MAKE YOU HIS ZOMBIE SLAVE!
WHY ME? SUPERMAN OR MARTIAN MANHUNTER MIGHT BE MORE SUITED FOR HIS NEEDS.
THEY ARE NOT BORN OF EARTH! KANJAR RO'S NEWLY ACQUIRED HYPNOTIC POWER WON'T WORK ON THEM! IT ONLY WORKS ON THE EARTH-BORN!
KANJAR RO PLANS TO CONQUER THE WORLDS THAT REJECTED HIS RULE BUT HE'LL NEED AN INVINCIBLE WARRIOR TO HELP HIM DO IT.
A SYMBOL OF STRENGTH AND COURAGE THAT THOSE OTHER WORLDS HAVE NEVER KNOWN.
I SHOULD BE FLATTERED, BUT I'M PRETTY SENSITIVE ABOUT BECOMING ANY MAN'S SLAVE.
HE IS A MAN, RIGHT?
YES, AND YOU ARE A FOOL!
AGGH!

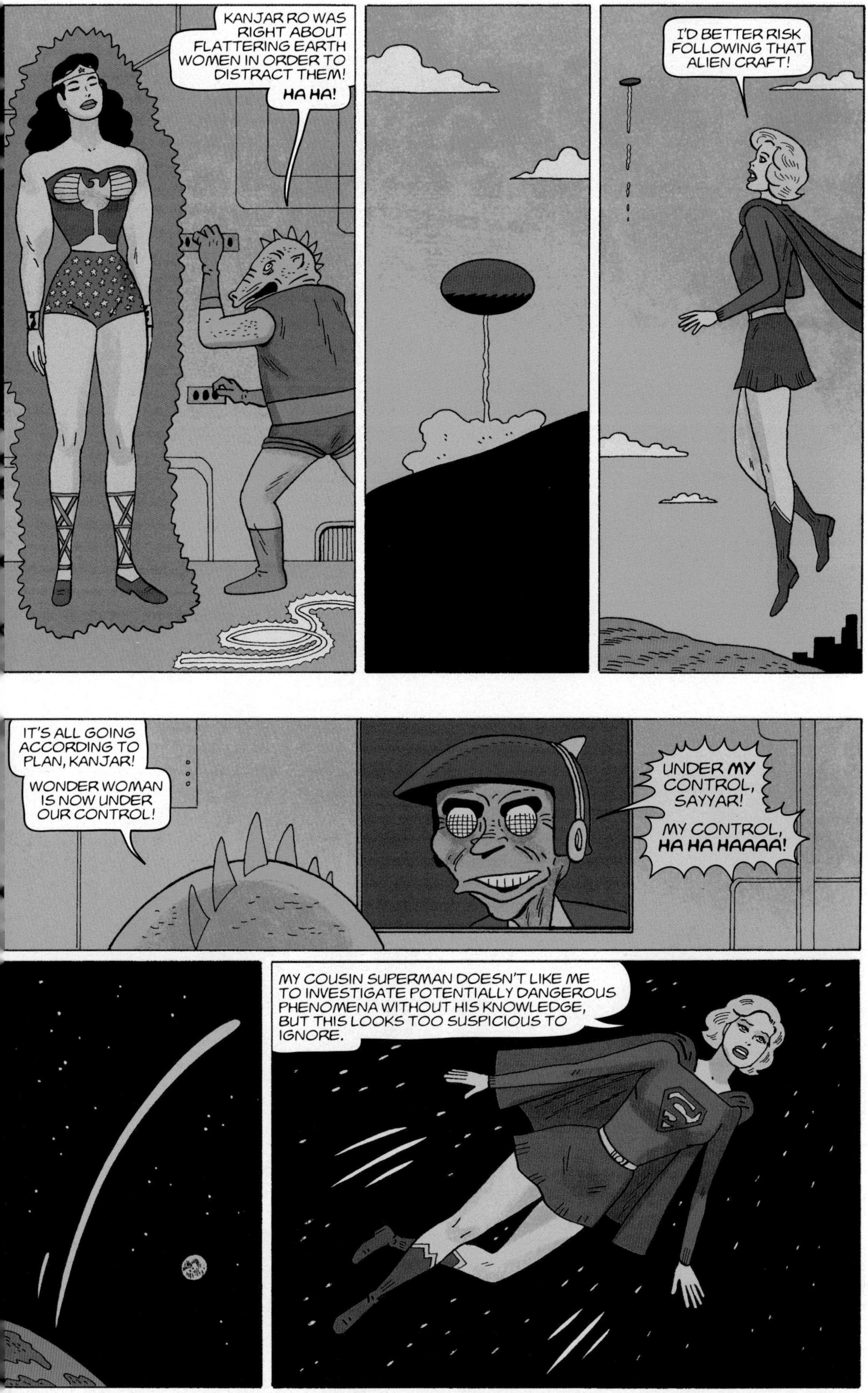

KANJAR RO WAS RIGHT ABOUT FLATTERING EARTH WOMEN IN ORDER TO DISTRACT THEM!
HA HA!
I'D BETTER RISK FOLLOWING THAT ALIEN CRAFT!
IT'S ALL GOING ACCORDING TO PLAN, KANJAR!
WONDER WOMAN IS NOW UNDER OUR CONTROL!
UNDER MY CONTROL, SAYYAR!
MY CONTROL, HA HA HAAAA!
MY COUSIN SUPERMAN DOESN'T LIKE ME TO INVESTIGATE POTENTIALLY DANGEROUS PHENOMENA WITHOUT HIS KNOWLEDGE, BUT THIS LOOKS TOO SUSPICIOUS TO IGNORE.

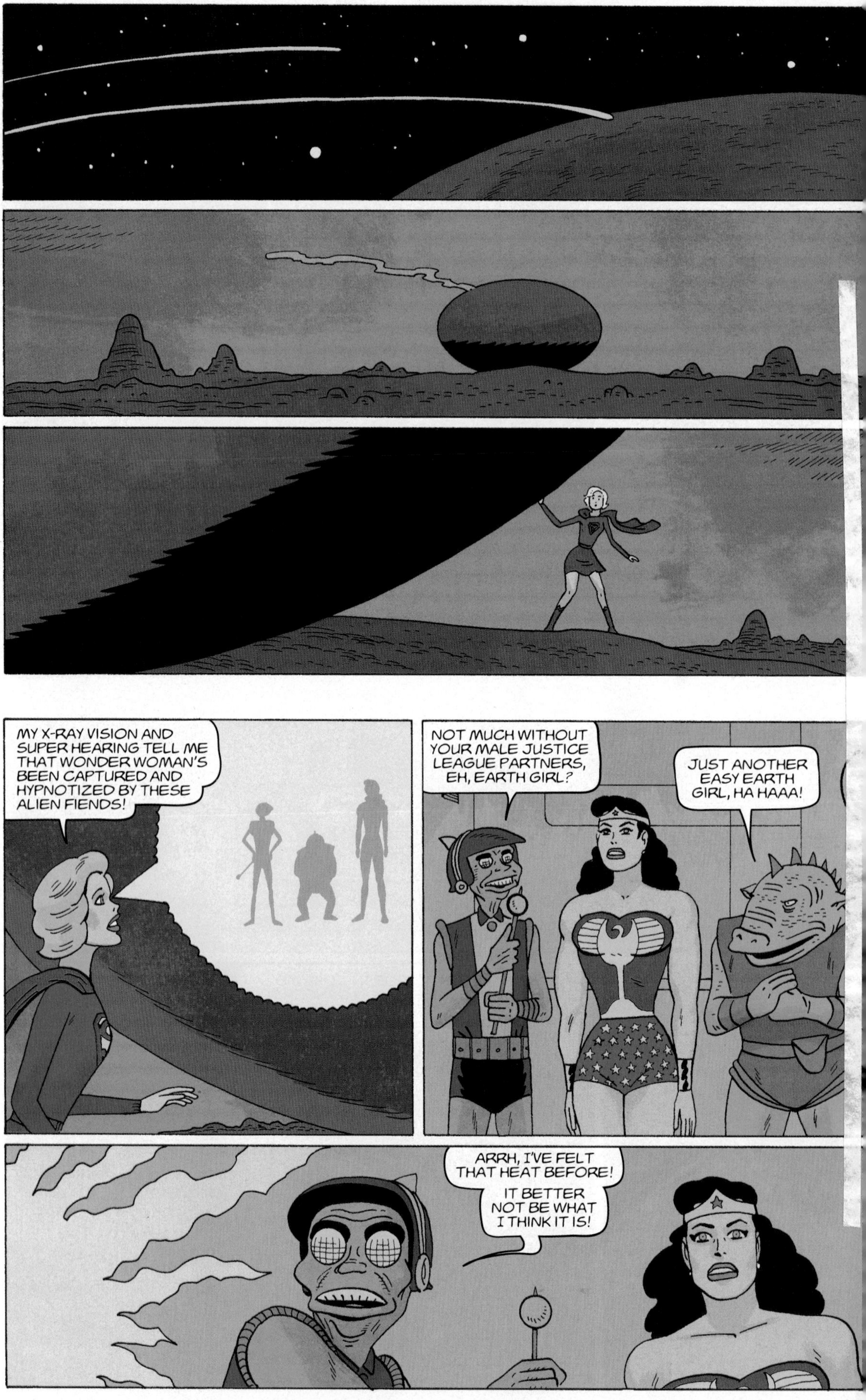
MY X-RAY VISION AND SUPER HEARING TELL ME THAT WONDER WOMAN'S BEEN CAPTURED AND HYPNOTIZED BY THESE ALIEN FIENDS!
NOT MUCH WITHOUT YOUR MALE JUSTICE LEAGUE PARTNERS, EH, EARTH GIRL?
JUST ANOTHER EASY EARTH GIRL, HA HAAA!
ARRH, I'VE FELT THAT HEAT BEFORE!
IT BETTER NOT BE WHAT I THINK IT IS!

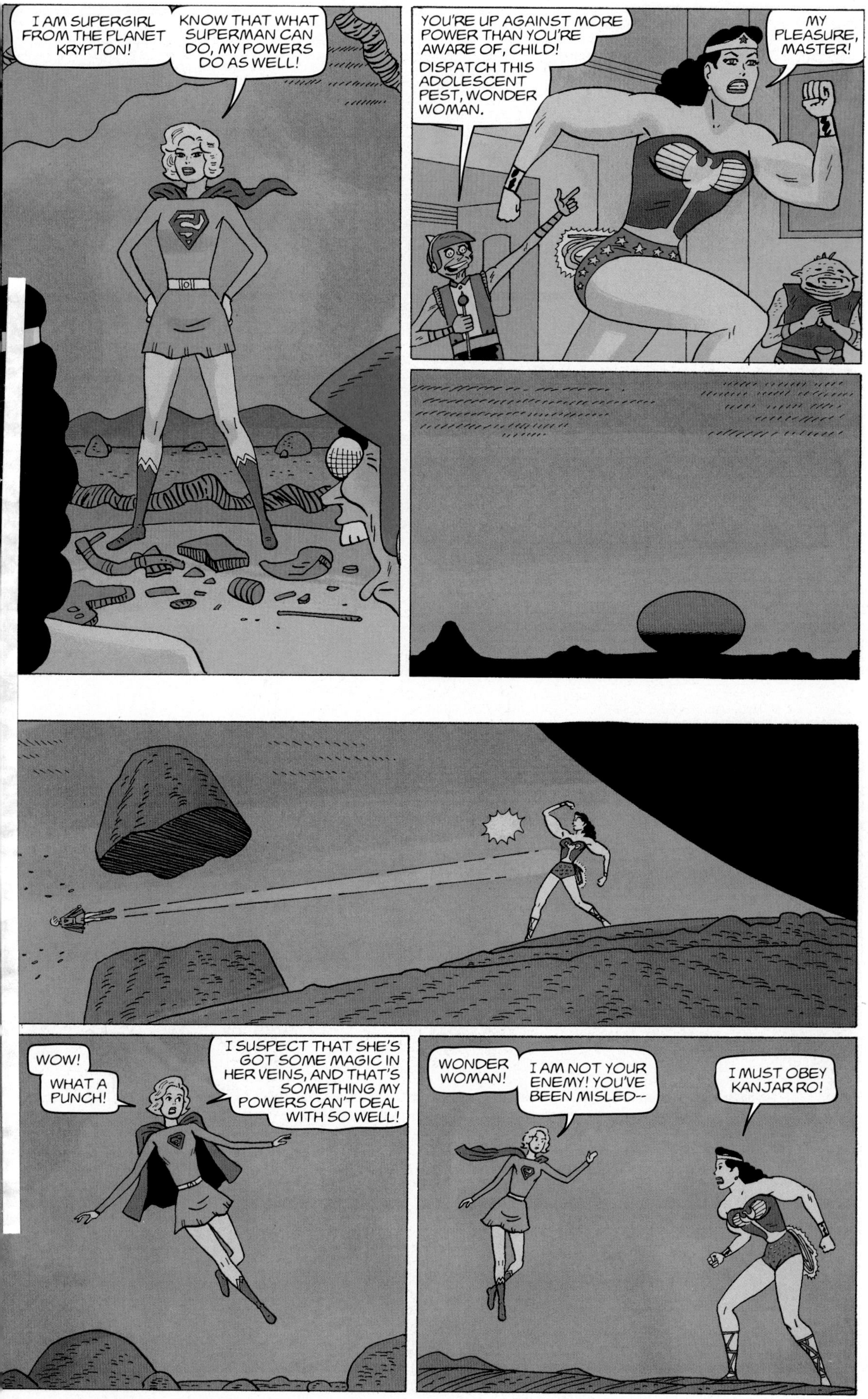
I AM SUPERGIRL FROM THE PLANET KRYPTON!
KNOW THAT WHAT SUPERMAN CAN DO, MY POWERS DO AS WELL!
YOU'RE UP AGAINST MORE POWER THAN YOU'RE AWARE OF, CHILD!
DISPATCH THIS ADOLESCENT PEST, WONDER WOMAN.
MY PLEASURE, MASTER!
WOW!
WHAT A PUNCH!
I SUSPECT THAT SHE'S GOT SOME MAGIC IN HER VEINS, AND THAT'S SOMETHING MY POWERS CAN'T DEAL WITH SO WELL!
WONDER WOMAN!
I AM NOT YOUR ENEMY! YOU'VE BEEN MISLED--
I MUST OBEY KANJAR RO!

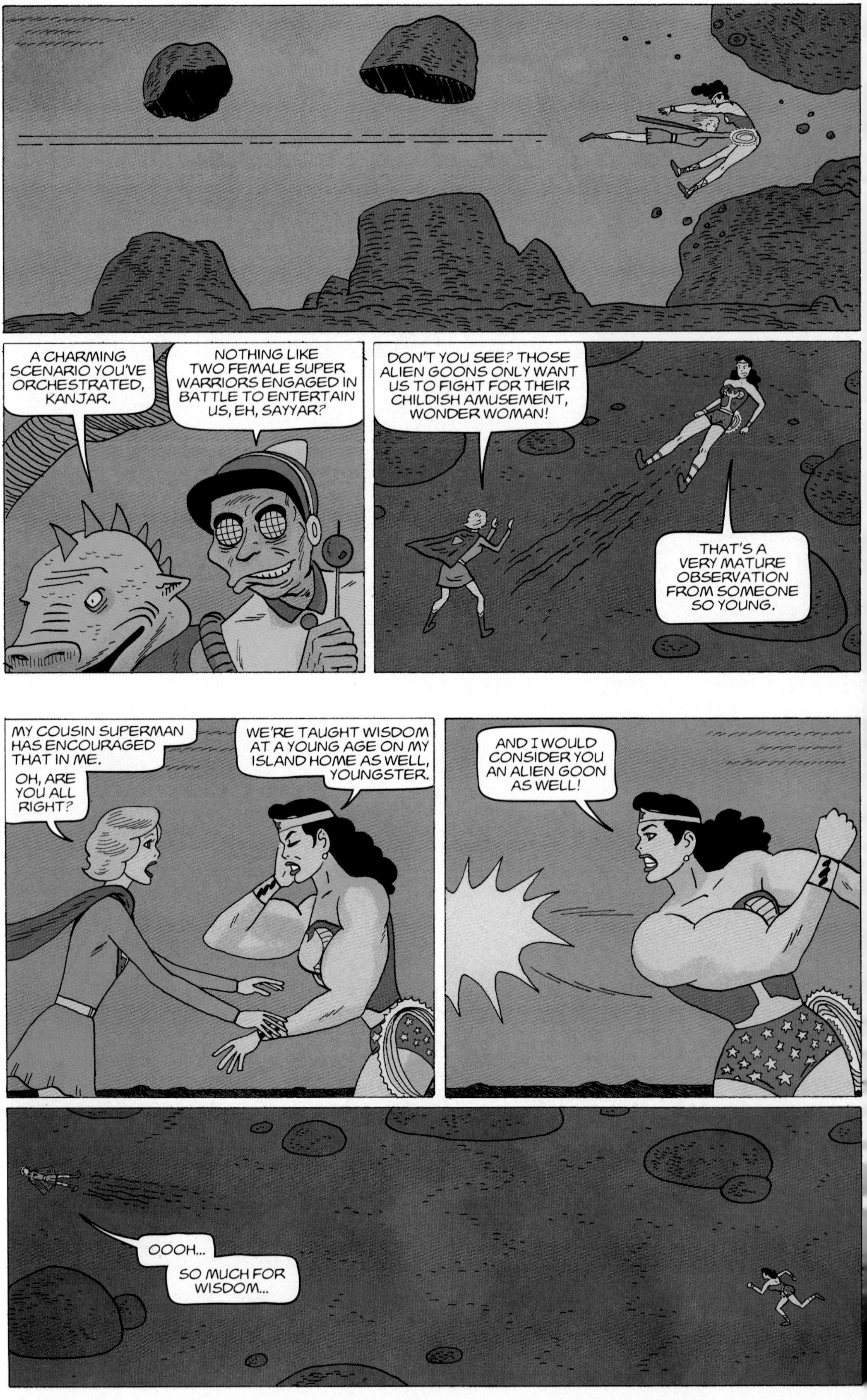
A CHARMING SCENARIO YOU'VE ORCHESTRATED, KANJAR.
NOTHING LIKE TWO FEMALE SUPER WARRIORS ENGAGED IN BATTLE TO ENTERTAIN US, EH, SAYYAR?
DON'T YOU SEE? THOSE ALIEN GOONS ONLY WANT US TO FIGHT FOR THEIR CHILDISH AMUSEMENT, WONDER WOMAN!
THAT'S A VERY MATURE OBSERVATION FROM SOMEONE SO YOUNG.
MY COUSIN SUPERMAN HAS ENCOURAGED THAT IN ME.
OH, ARE YOU ALL RIGHT?
WE'RE TAUGHT WISDOM AT A YOUNG AGE ON MY ISLAND HOME AS WELL, YOUNGSTER.
AND I WOULD CONSIDER YOU AN ALIEN GOON AS WELL!
OOOH...
SO MUCH FOR WISDOM...

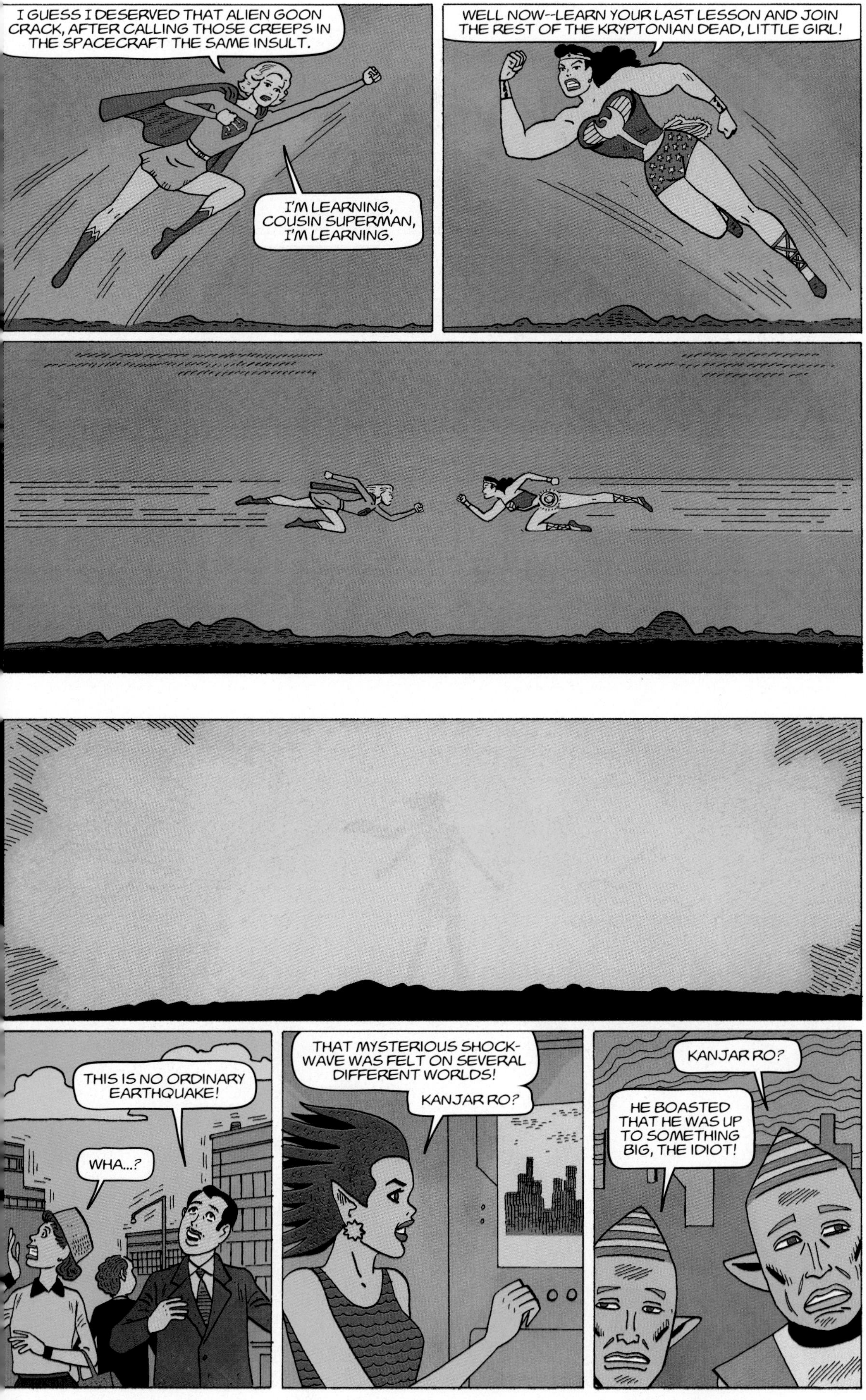
I GUESS I DESERVED THAT ALIEN GOON CRACK, AFTER CALLING THOSE CREEPS IN THE SPACECRAFT THE SAME INSULT.
I'M LEARNING, COUSIN SUPERMAN, I'M LEARNING.
WELL NOW--LEARN YOUR LAST LESSON AND JOIN THE REST OF THE KRYPTONIAN DEAD, LITTLE GIRL!
THIS IS NO ORDINARY EARTHQUAKE!
WHA...?
THAT MYSTERIOUS SHOCK-WAVE WAS FELT ON SEVERAL DIFFERENT WORLDS!
KANJAR RO?
KANJAR RO?
HE BOASTED THAT HE WAS UP TO SOMETHING BIG, THE IDIOT!

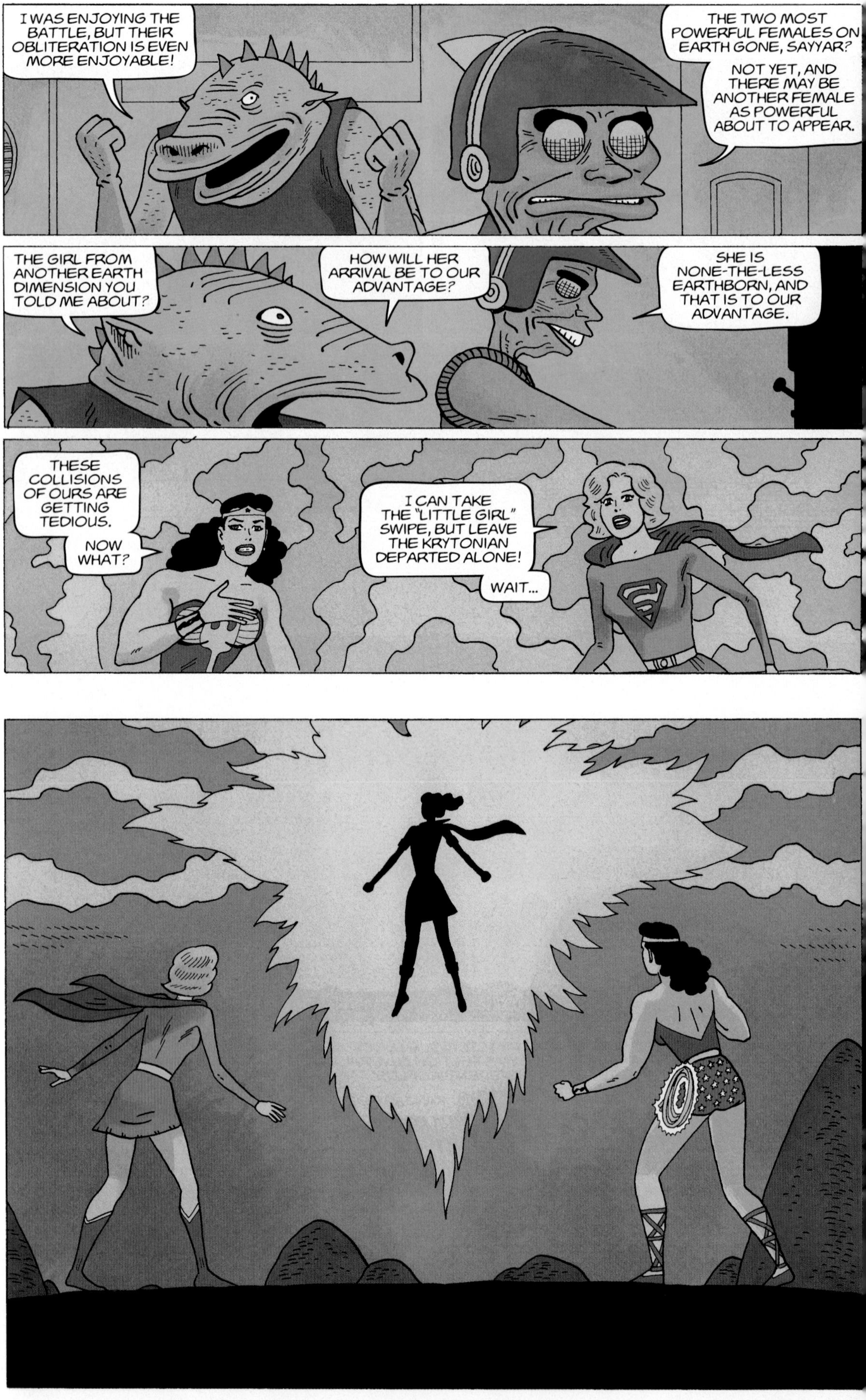
I WAS ENJOYING THE BATTLE, BUT THEIR OBLITERATION IS EVEN MORE ENJOYABLE!
THE TWO MOST POWERFUL FEMALES ON EARTH GONE, SAYYAR?
NOT YET, AND THERE MAY BE ANOTHER FEMALE AS POWERFUL ABOUT TO APPEAR.
THE GIRL FROM ANOTHER EARTH DIMENSION YOU TOLD ME ABOUT?
HOW WILL HER ARRIVAL BE TO OUR ADVANTAGE?
SHE IS NONE-THE-LESS EARTHBORN, AND THAT IS TO OUR ADVANTAGE.
THESE COLLISIONS OF OURS ARE GETTING TEDIOUS.
NOW WHAT?
I CAN TAKE THE "LITTLE GIRL" SWIPE, BUT LEAVE THE KRYTONIAN DEPARTED ALONE!
WAIT...

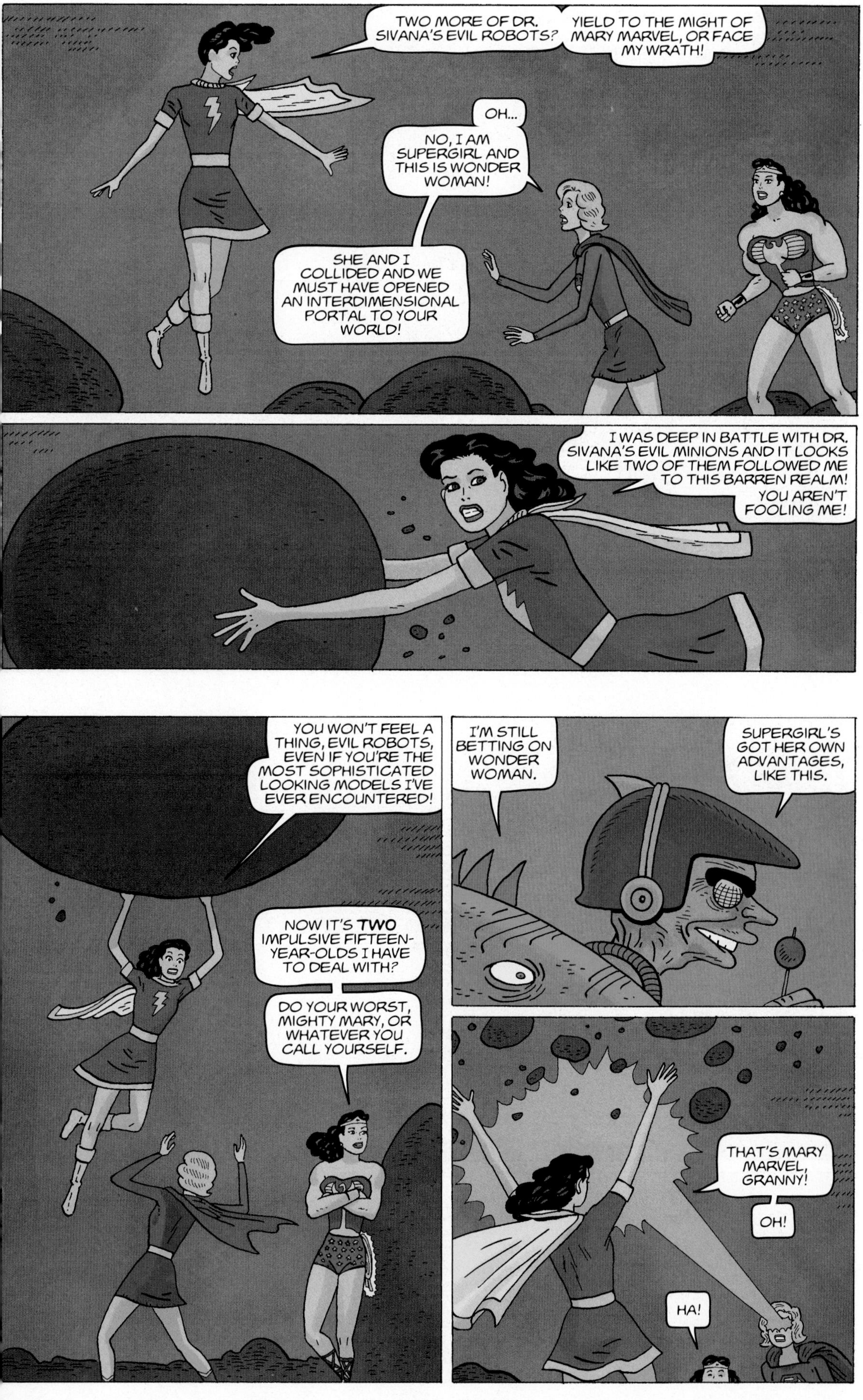

TWO MORE OF DR. SIVANA'S EVIL ROBOTS?
YIELD TO THE MIGHT OF MARY MARVEL, OR FACE MY WRATH!
OH...
NO, I AM SUPERGIRL AND THIS IS WONDER WOMAN!
SHE AND I COLLIDED AND WE MUST HAVE OPENED AN INTERDIMENSIONAL PORTAL TO YOUR WORLD!
I WAS DEEP IN BATTLE WITH DR. SIVANA'S EVIL MINIONS AND IT LOOKS LIKE TWO OF THEM FOLLOWED ME TO THIS BARREN REALM!
YOU AREN'T FOOLING ME!
YOU WON'T FEEL A THING, EVIL ROBOTS, EVEN IF YOU'RE THE MOST SOPHISTICATED LOOKING MODELS I'VE EVER ENCOUNTERED!
NOW IT'S **TWO** IMPULSIVE FIFTEEN-YEAR-OLDS I HAVE TO DEAL WITH?
DO YOUR WORST, MIGHTY MARY, OR WHATEVER YOU CALL YOURSELF.
I'M STILL BETTING ON WONDER WOMAN.
SUPERGIRL'S GOT HER OWN ADVANTAGES, LIKE THIS.
THAT'S MARY MARVEL, GRANNY!
OH!
HA!

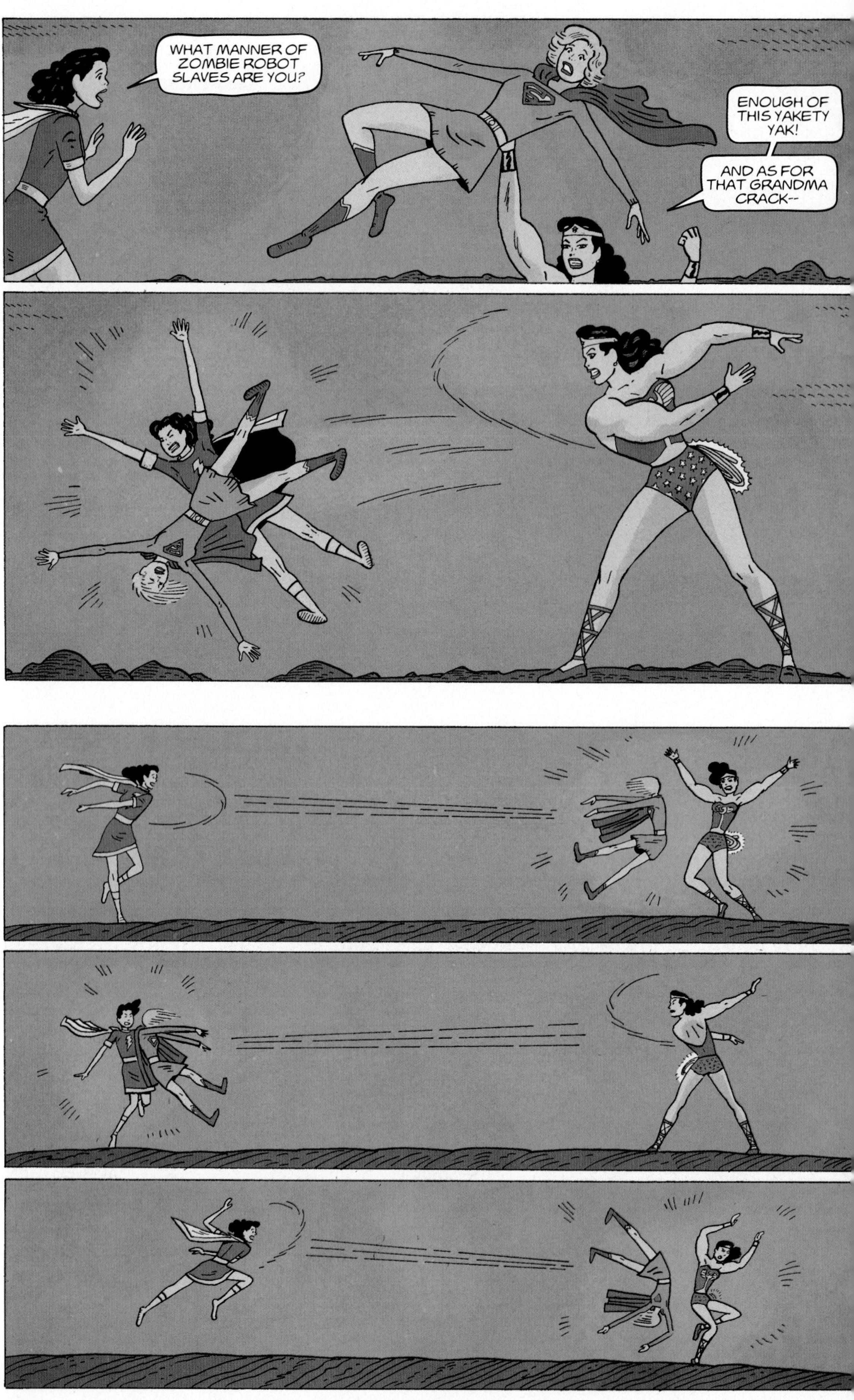
WHAT MANNER OF ZOMBIE ROBOT SLAVES ARE YOU?
ENOUGH OF THIS YAKETY YAK!
AND AS FOR THAT GRANDMA CRACK--

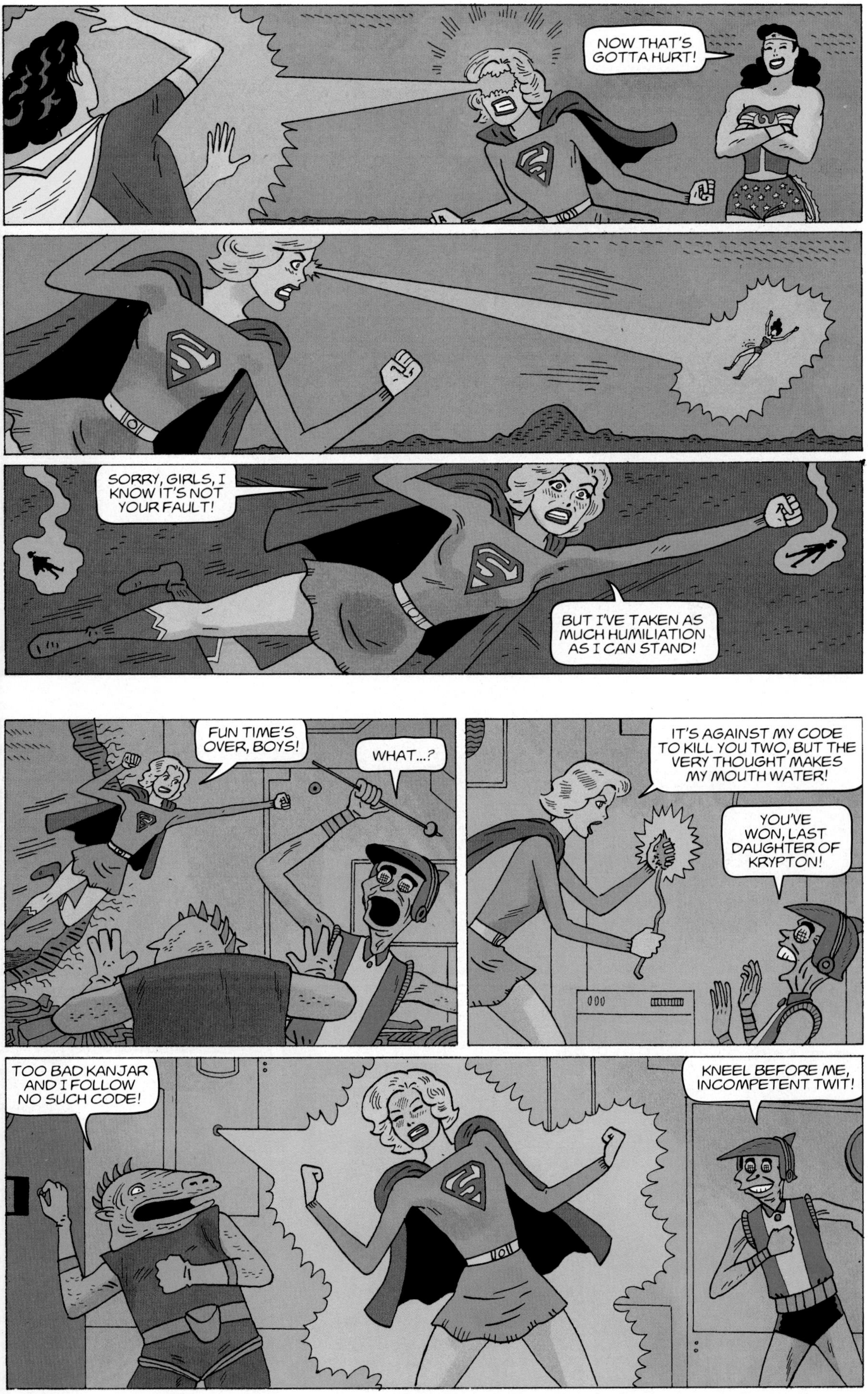
NOW THAT'S GOTTA HURT!
SORRY, GIRLS, I KNOW IT'S NOT YOUR FAULT!
BUT I'VE TAKEN AS MUCH HUMILIATION AS I CAN STAND!
FUN TIME'S OVER, BOYS!
WHAT...?
IT'S AGAINST MY CODE TO KILL YOU TWO, BUT THE VERY THOUGHT MAKES MY MOUTH WATER!
YOU'VE WON, LAST DAUGHTER OF KRYPTON!
TOO BAD KANJAR AND I FOLLOW NO SUCH CODE!
KNEEL BEFORE ME, INCOMPETENT TWIT!

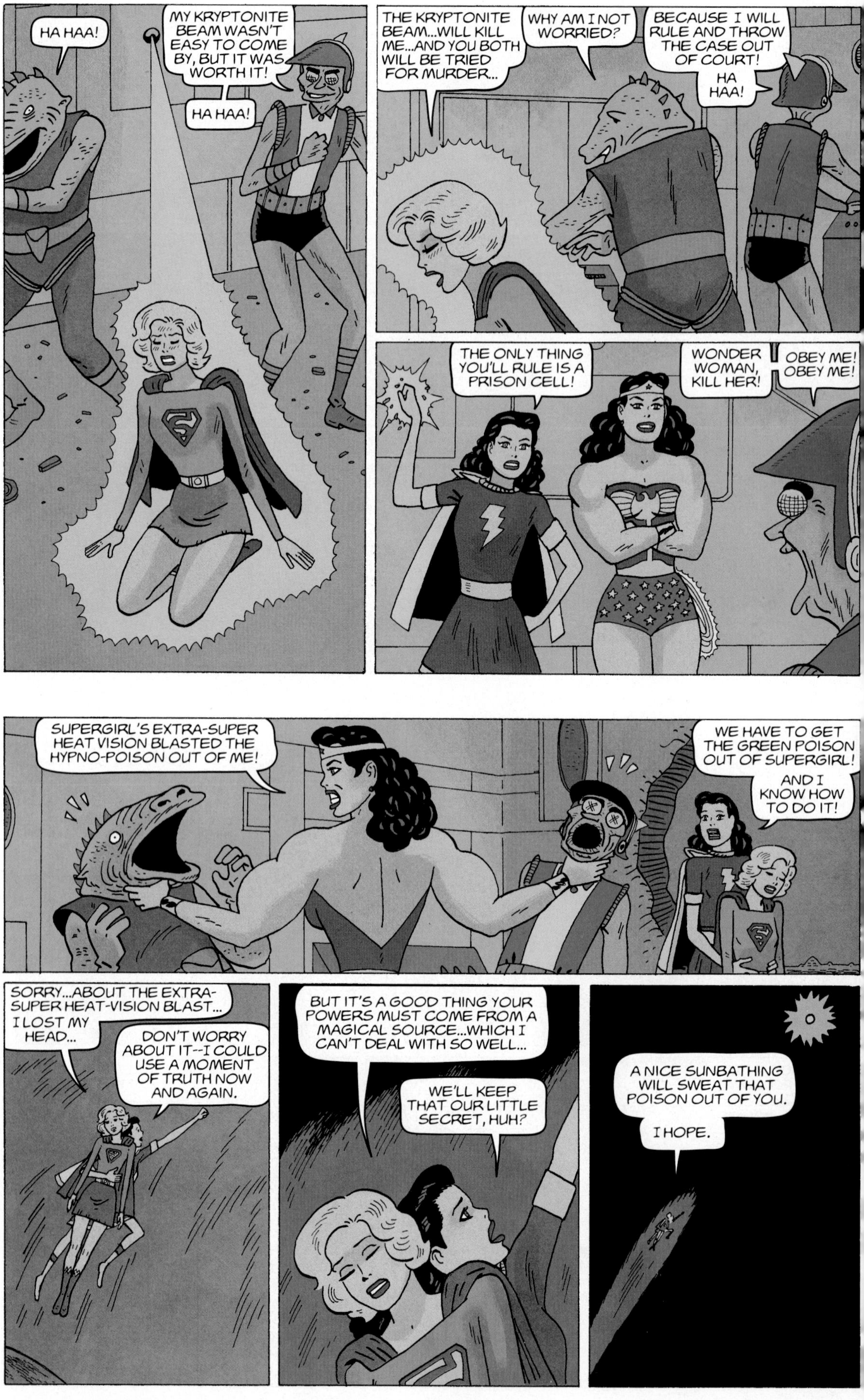
HA HAA!
MY KRYPTONITE BEAM WASN'T EASY TO COME BY, BUT IT WAS WORTH IT!
HA HAA!
THE KRYPTONITE BEAM...WILL KILL ME...AND YOU BOTH WILL BE TRIED FOR MURDER...
WHY AM I NOT WORRIED?
BECAUSE I WILL RULE AND THROW THE CASE OUT OF COURT!
HA HAA!
THE ONLY THING YOU'LL RULE IS A PRISON CELL!
WONDER WOMAN, KILL HER!
OBEY ME! OBEY ME!
SUPERGIRL'S EXTRA-SUPER HEAT VISION BLASTED THE HYPNO-POISON OUT OF ME!
WE HAVE TO GET THE GREEN POISON OUT OF SUPERGIRL!
AND I KNOW HOW TO DO IT!
SORRY...ABOUT THE EXTRA-SUPER HEAT-VISION BLAST... I LOST MY HEAD...
DON'T WORRY ABOUT IT--I COULD USE A MOMENT OF TRUTH NOW AND AGAIN.
BUT IT'S A GOOD THING YOUR POWERS MUST COME FROM A MAGICAL SOURCE...WHICH I CAN'T DEAL WITH SO WELL...
WE'LL KEEP THAT OUR LITTLE SECRET, HUH?
A NICE SUNBATHING WILL SWEAT THAT POISON OUT OF YOU.
I HOPE.

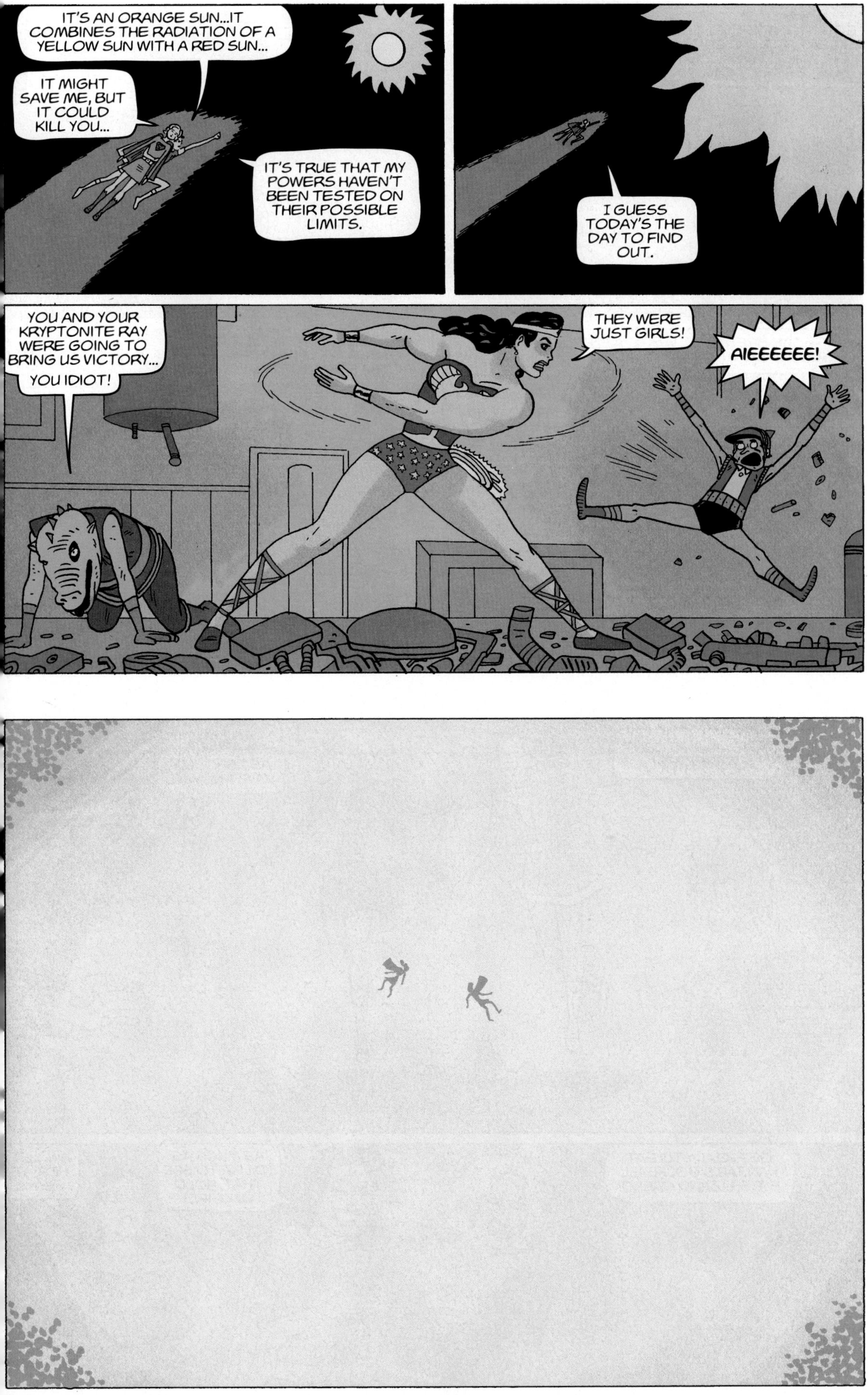
IT'S AN ORANGE SUN...IT COMBINES THE RADIATION OF A YELLOW SUN WITH A RED SUN...
IT MIGHT SAVE ME, BUT IT COULD KILL YOU...
IT'S TRUE THAT MY POWERS HAVEN'T BEEN TESTED ON THEIR POSSIBLE LIMITS.
I GUESS TODAY'S THE DAY TO FIND OUT.
YOU AND YOUR KRYPTONITE RAY WERE GOING TO BRING US VICTORY...
YOU IDIOT!
THEY WERE JUST GIRLS!
AIEEEEEE!

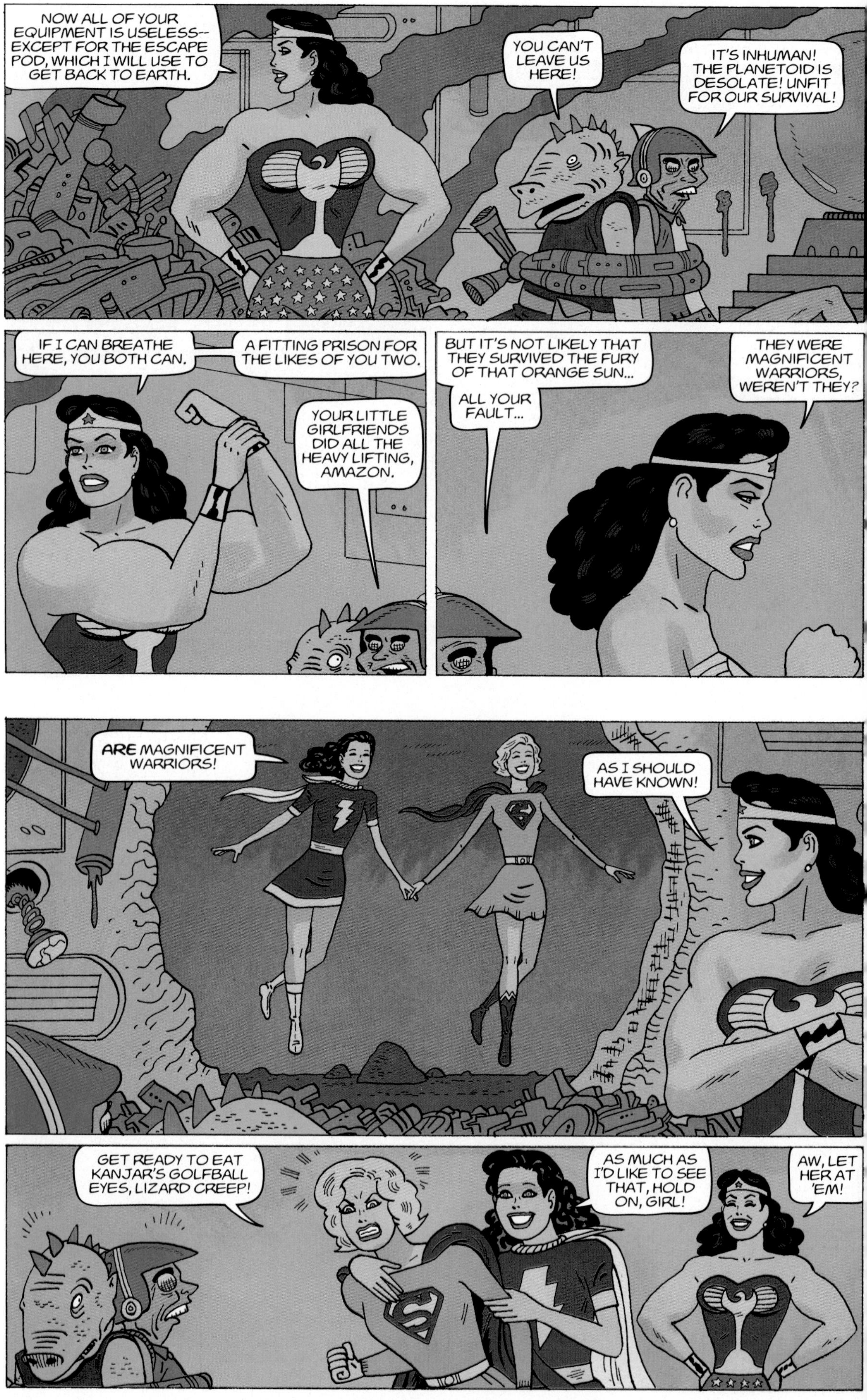
NOW ALL OF YOUR EQUIPMENT IS USELESS-- EXCEPT FOR THE ESCAPE POD, WHICH I WILL USE TO GET BACK TO EARTH.
YOU CAN'T LEAVE US HERE!
IT'S INHUMAN! THE PLANETOID IS DESOLATE! UNFIT FOR OUR SURVIVAL!
IF I CAN BREATHE HERE, YOU BOTH CAN.
A FITTING PRISON FOR THE LIKES OF YOU TWO.
YOUR LITTLE GIRLFRIENDS DID ALL THE HEAVY LIFTING, AMAZON.
BUT IT'S NOT LIKELY THAT THEY SURVIVED THE FURY OF THAT ORANGE SUN...
ALL YOUR FAULT...
THEY WERE MAGNIFICENT WARRIORS, WEREN'T THEY?
ARE MAGNIFICENT WARRIORS!
AS I SHOULD HAVE KNOWN!
GET READY TO EAT KANJAR'S GOLFBALL EYES, LIZARD CREEP!
AS MUCH AS I'D LIKE TO SEE THAT, HOLD ON, GIRL!
AW, LET HER AT 'EM!

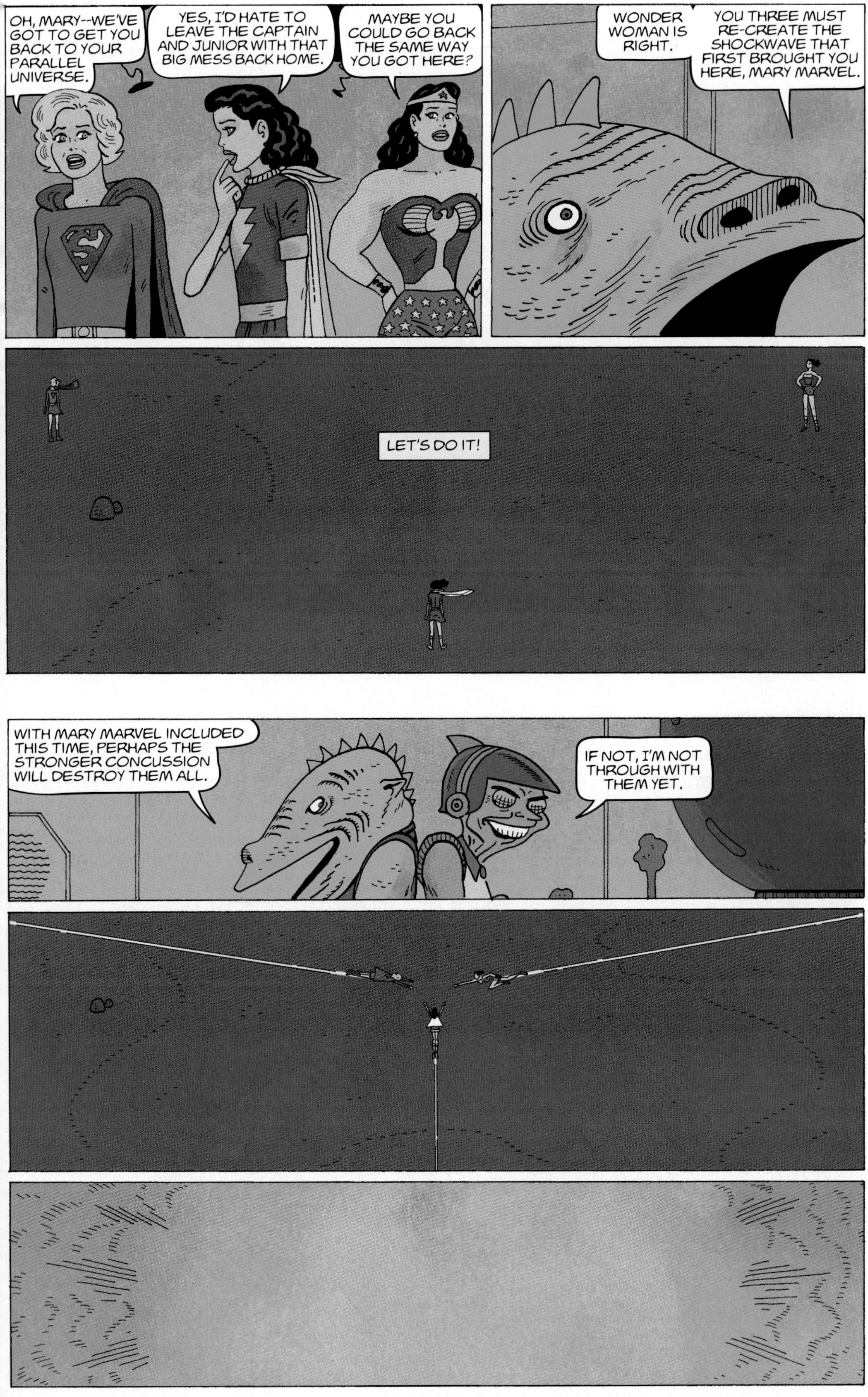
OH, MARY--WE'VE GOT TO GET YOU BACK TO YOUR PARALLEL UNIVERSE.
YES, I'D HATE TO LEAVE THE CAPTAIN AND JUNIOR WITH THAT BIG MESS BACK HOME.
MAYBE YOU COULD GO BACK THE SAME WAY YOU GOT HERE?
WONDER WOMAN IS RIGHT.
YOU THREE MUST RE-CREATE THE SHOCKWAVE THAT FIRST BROUGHT YOU HERE, MARY MARVEL.
LET'S DO IT!
WITH MARY MARVEL INCLUDED THIS TIME, PERHAPS THE STRONGER CONCUSSION WILL DESTROY THEM ALL.
IF NOT, I'M NOT THROUGH WITH THEM YET.

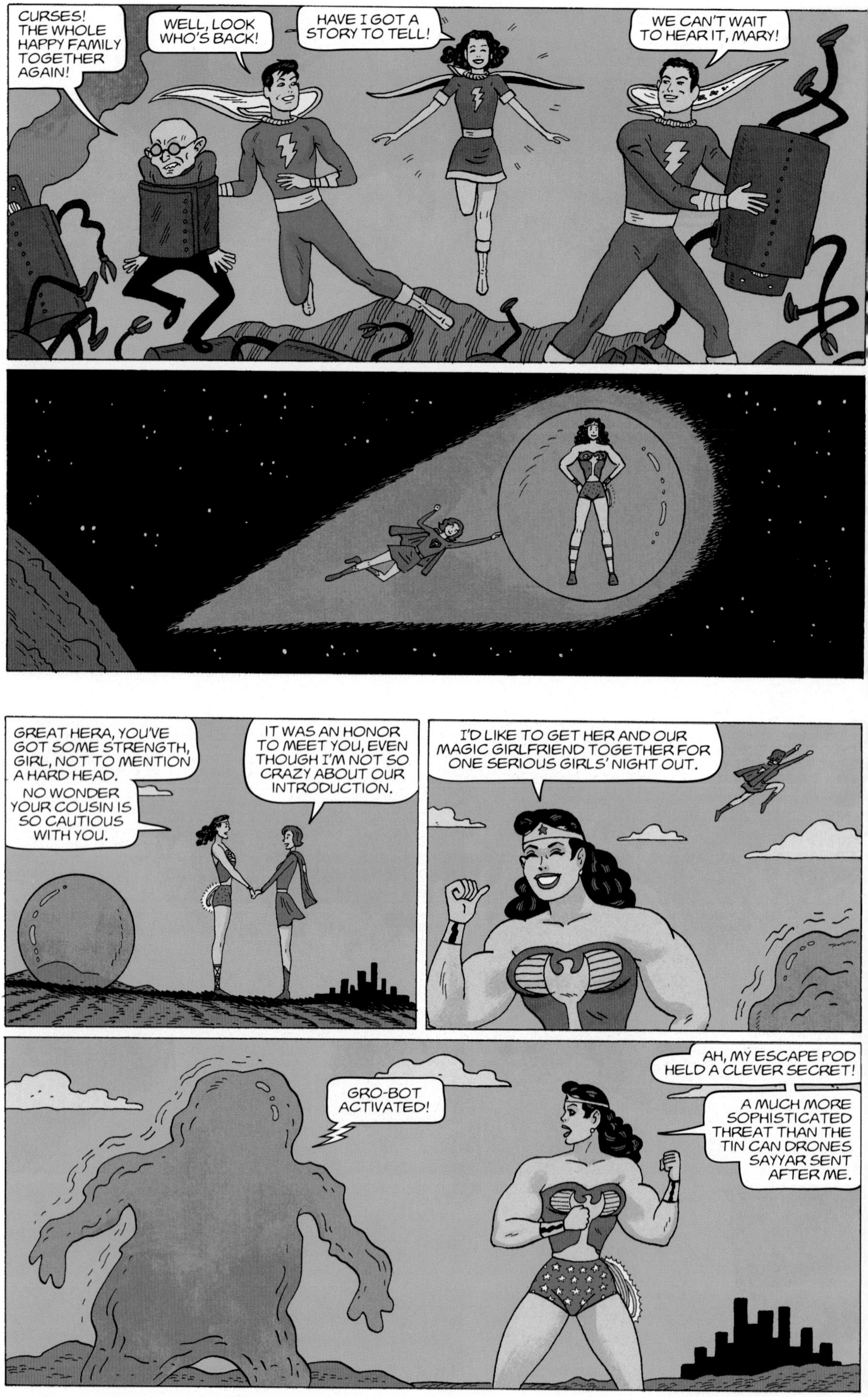
CURSES! THE WHOLE HAPPY FAMILY TOGETHER AGAIN!
WELL, LOOK WHO'S BACK!
HAVE I GOT A STORY TO TELL!
WE CAN'T WAIT TO HEAR IT, MARY!
GREAT HERA, YOU'VE GOT SOME STRENGTH, GIRL, NOT TO MENTION A HARD HEAD.
NO WONDER YOUR COUSIN IS SO CAUTIOUS WITH YOU.
IT WAS AN HONOR TO MEET YOU, EVEN THOUGH I'M NOT SO CRAZY ABOUT OUR INTRODUCTION.
I'D LIKE TO GET HER AND OUR MAGIC GIRLFRIEND TOGETHER FOR ONE SERIOUS GIRLS' NIGHT OUT.
GRO-BOT ACTIVATED!
AH, MY ESCAPE POD HELD A CLEVER SECRET!
A MUCH MORE SOPHISTICATED THREAT THAN THE TIN CAN DRONES SAYYAR SENT AFTER ME.

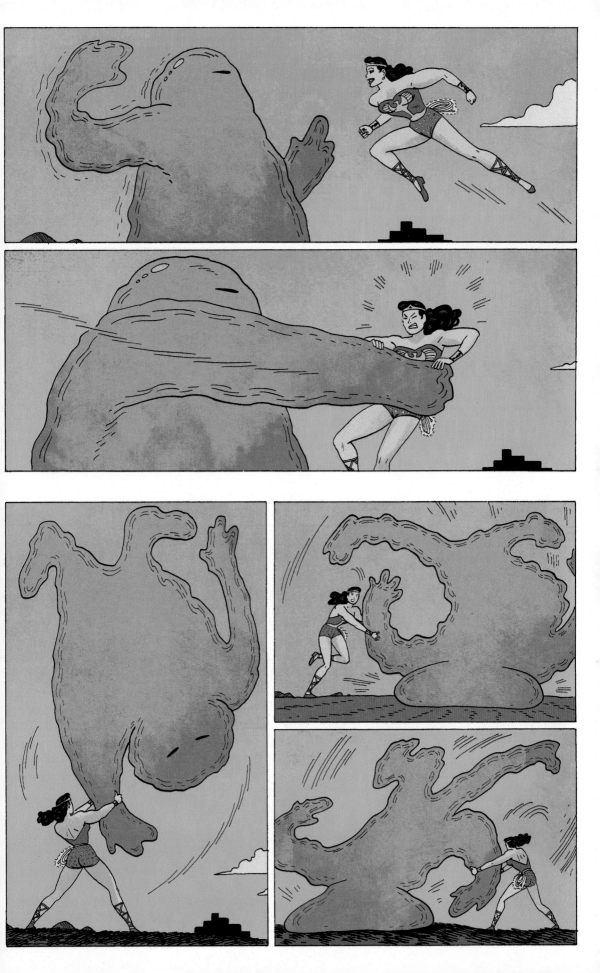

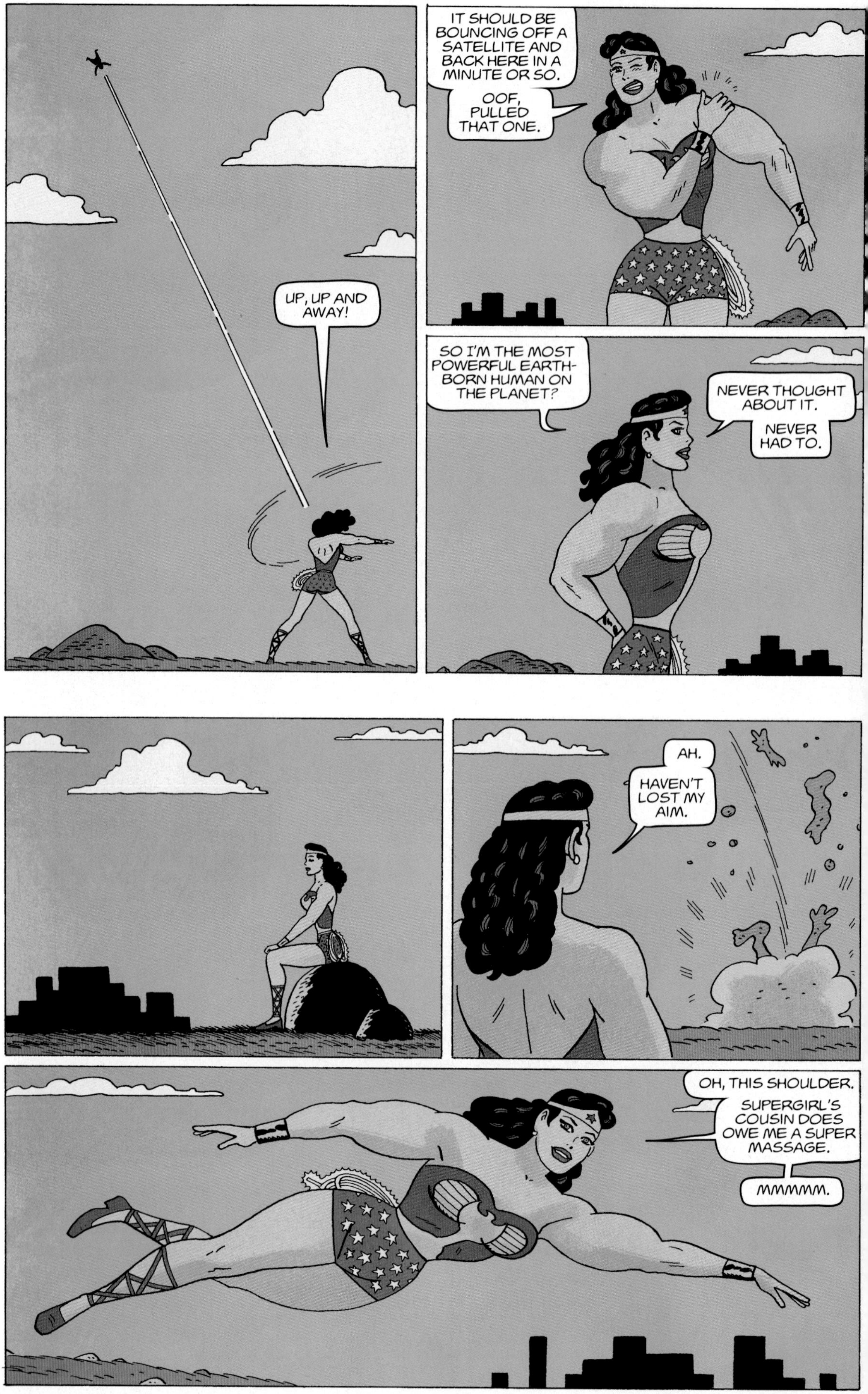
UP, UP AND AWAY!
IT SHOULD BE BOUNCING OFF A SATELLITE AND BACK HERE IN A MINUTE OR SO.
OOF, PULLED THAT ONE.
SO I'M THE MOST POWERFUL EARTH-BORN HUMAN ON THE PLANET?
NEVER THOUGHT ABOUT IT.
NEVER HAD TO.
AH.
HAVEN'T LOST MY AIM.
OH, THIS SHOULDER.
SUPERGIRL'S COUSIN DOES OWE ME A SUPER MASSAGE.
MMMMM.

ATTACK OF THE 500-FOOT WONDER WOMAN

ROB WILLIAMS
WRITER

TOM LYLE
ARTIST

WENDY BROOME
COLORIST

SAIDA TEMOFONTE
LETTERER

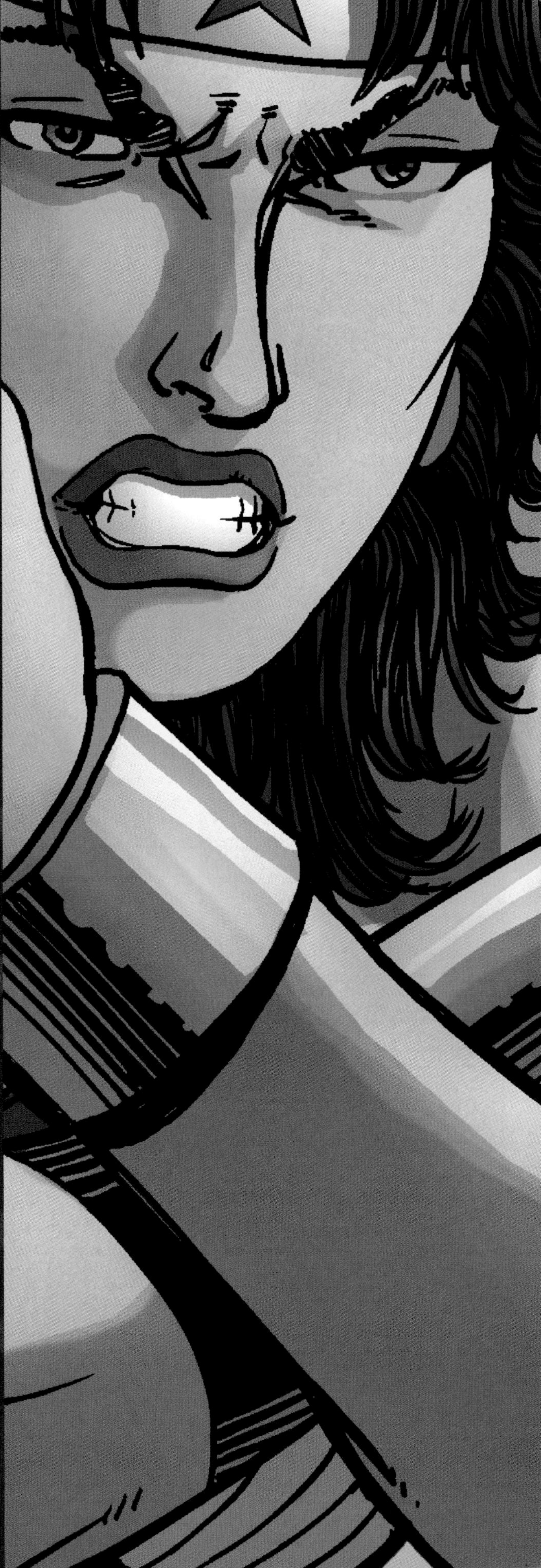

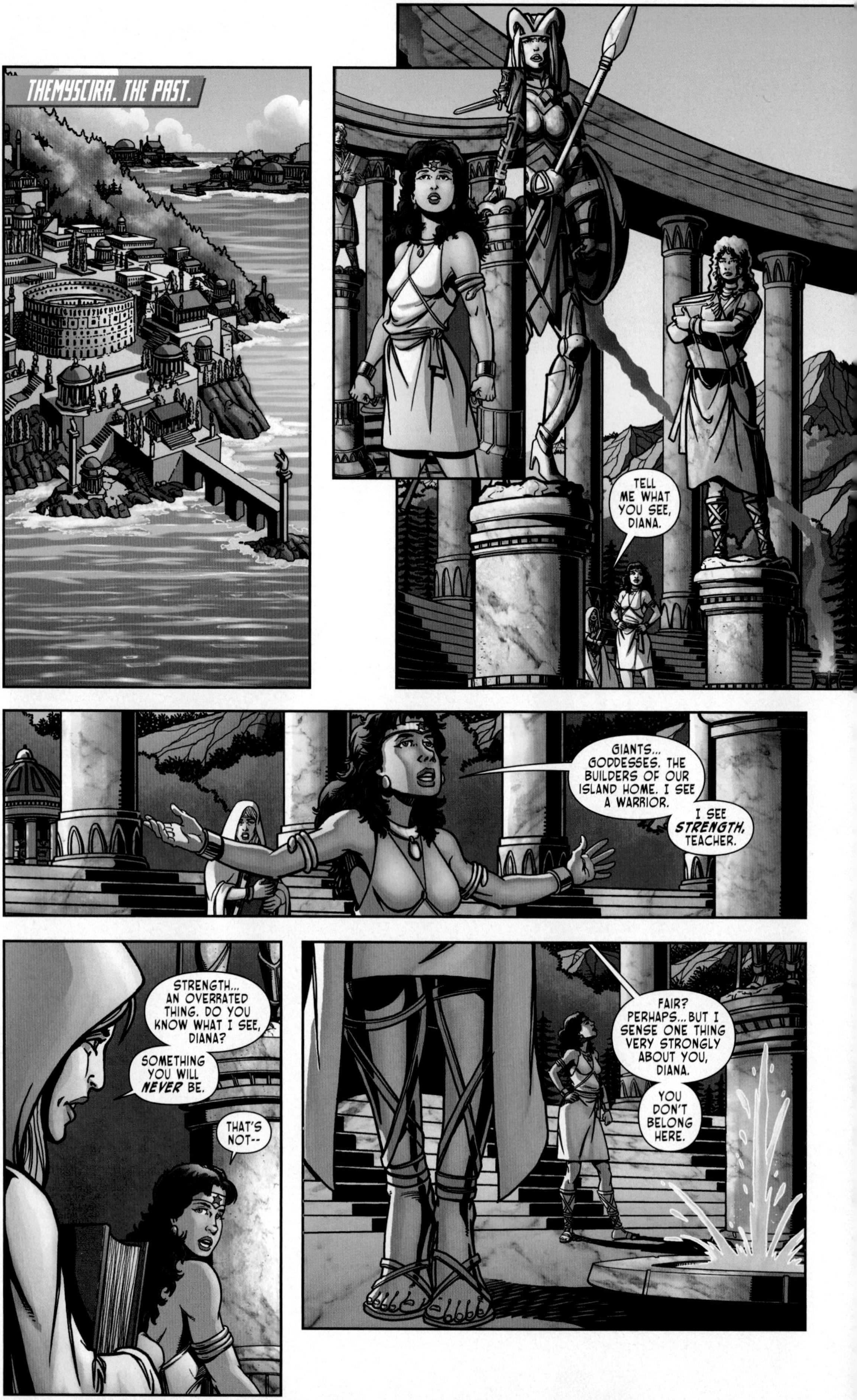
THEMYSCIRA. THE PAST.
TELL ME WHAT YOU SEE, DIANA.
GIANTS... GODDESSES. THE BUILDERS OF OUR ISLAND HOME. I SEE A WARRIOR.
I SEE *STRENGTH*, TEACHER.
STRENGTH... AN OVERRATED THING. DO YOU KNOW WHAT I SEE, DIANA?
SOMETHING YOU WILL ***NEVER*** BE.
THAT'S NOT--
FAIR? PERHAPS... BUT I SENSE ONE THING VERY STRONGLY ABOUT YOU, DIANA.
YOU DON'T BELONG HERE.

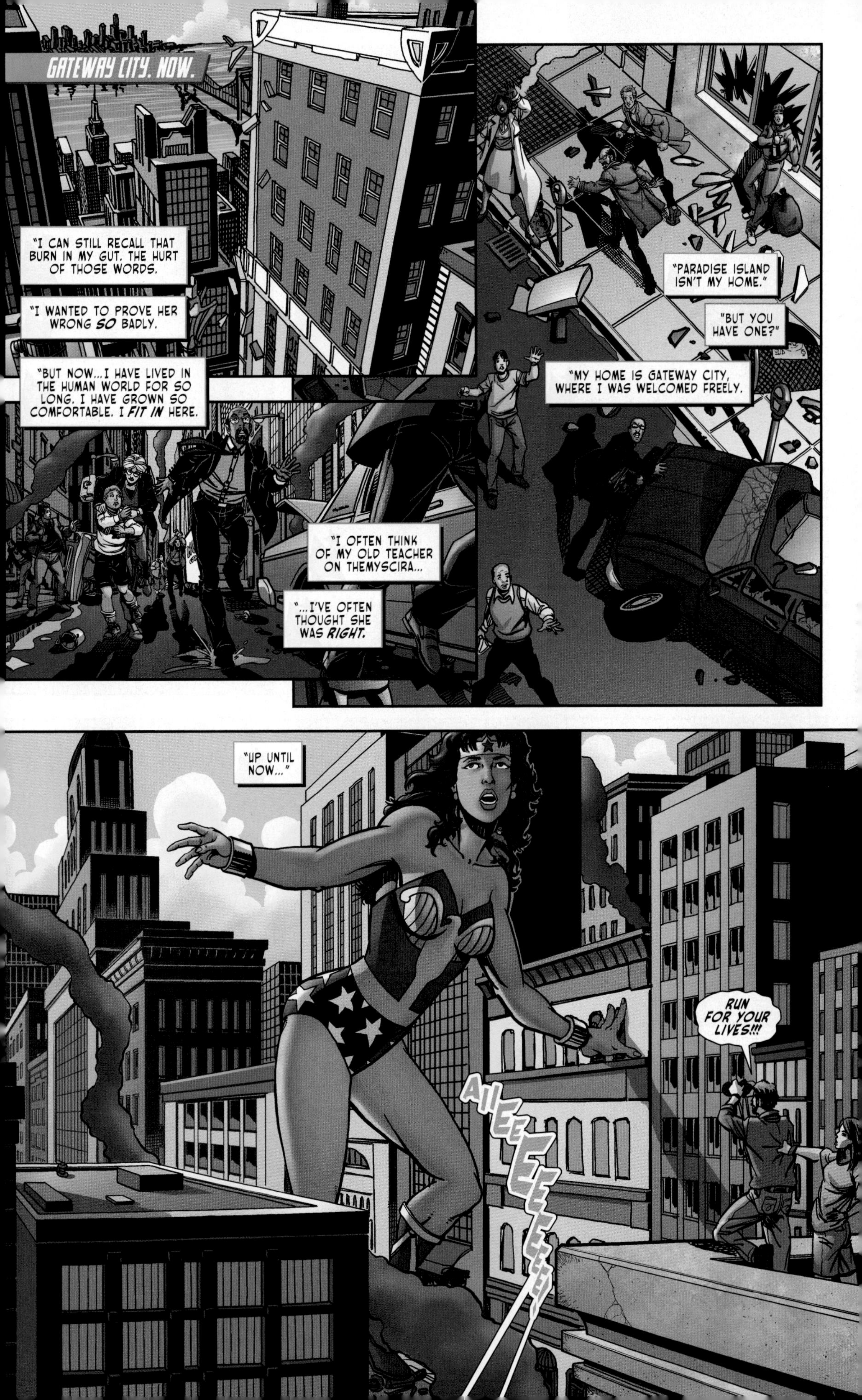
GATEWAY CITY. NOW.
"I CAN STILL RECALL THAT BURN IN MY GUT. THE HURT OF THOSE WORDS.
"I WANTED TO PROVE HER WRONG SO BADLY.
"BUT NOW...I HAVE LIVED IN THE HUMAN WORLD FOR SO LONG. I HAVE GROWN SO COMFORTABLE. I FIT IN HERE.
"PARADISE ISLAND ISN'T MY HOME."
"BUT YOU HAVE ONE?"
"MY HOME IS GATEWAY CITY, WHERE I WAS WELCOMED FREELY.
"I OFTEN THINK OF MY OLD TEACHER ON THEMYSCIRA...
"...I'VE OFTEN THOUGHT SHE WAS RIGHT.
"UP UNTIL NOW..."
RUN FOR YOUR LIVES!!!
AIIEEEEEEE

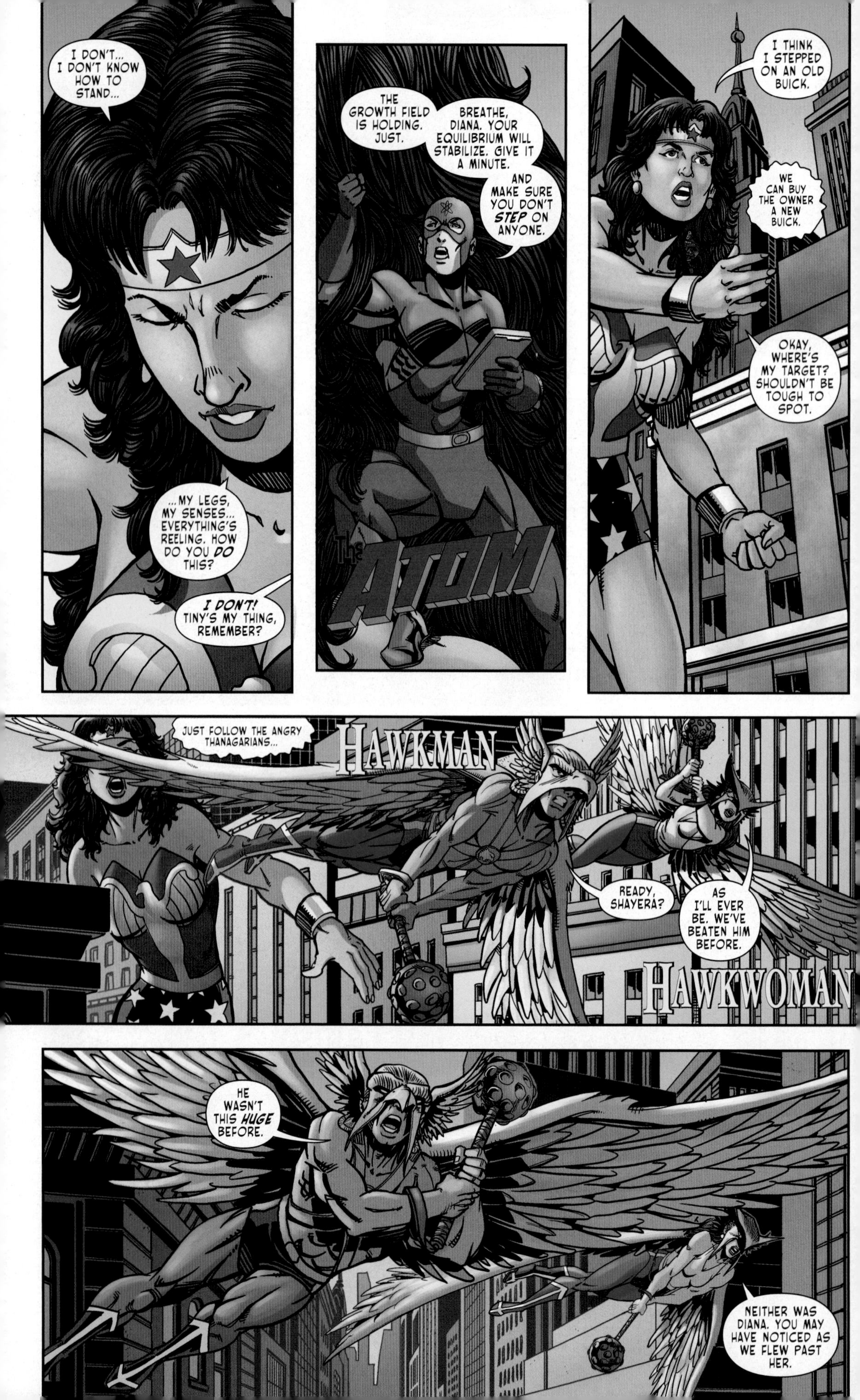
I DON'T... I DON'T KNOW HOW TO STAND...
...MY LEGS, MY SENSES... EVERYTHING'S REELING. HOW DO YOU DO THIS?
I DON'T! TINY'S MY THING, REMEMBER?
THE GROWTH FIELD IS HOLDING. JUST.
BREATHE, DIANA. YOUR EQUILIBRIUM WILL STABILIZE. GIVE IT A MINUTE.
AND MAKE SURE YOU DON'T STEP ON ANYONE.
The ATOM
I THINK I STEPPED ON AN OLD BUICK.
WE CAN BUY THE OWNER A NEW BUICK.
OKAY, WHERE'S MY TARGET? SHOULDN'T BE TOUGH TO SPOT.
JUST FOLLOW THE ANGRY THANAGARIANS...
HAWKMAN
READY, SHAYERA?
AS I'LL EVER BE. WE'VE BEATEN HIM BEFORE.
HAWKWOMAN
HE WASN'T THIS HUGE BEFORE.
NEITHER WAS DIANA. YOU MAY HAVE NOTICED AS WE FLEW PAST HER.

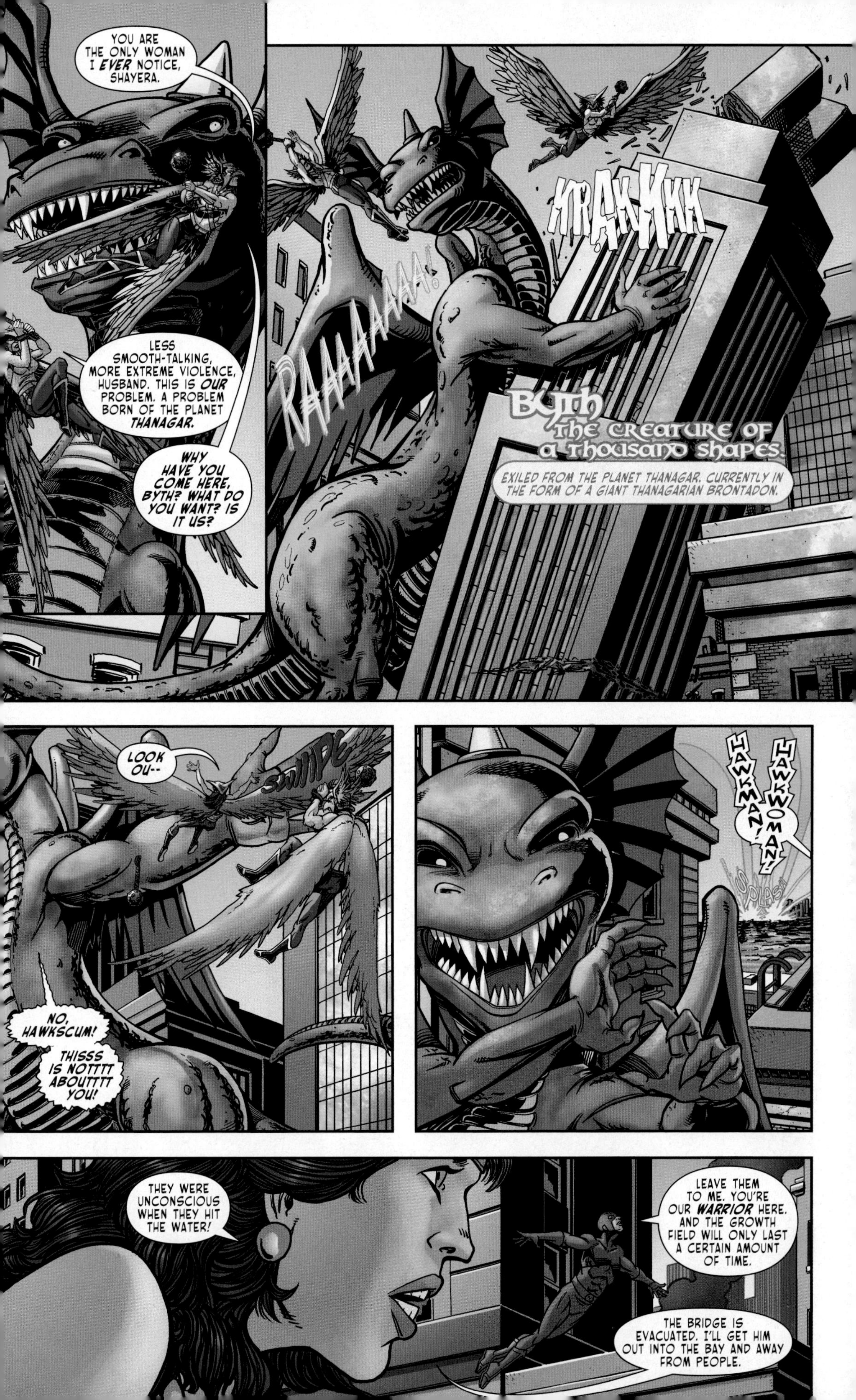
YOU ARE THE ONLY WOMAN I *EVER* NOTICE, SHAYERA.
KRAKKKK
RAAAAAAAA!
LESS SMOOTH-TALKING, MORE EXTREME VIOLENCE, HUSBAND. THIS IS *OUR* PROBLEM. A PROBLEM BORN OF THE PLANET *THANAGAR.*
WHY HAVE YOU COME HERE, BYTH? WHAT DO YOU WANT? IS IT US?
BYTH THE CREATURE OF A THOUSAND SHAPES.
EXILED FROM THE PLANET THANAGAR. CURRENTLY IN THE FORM OF A GIANT THANAGARIAN BRONTADON.
LOOK OU--
SWIIPE
NO, HAWKSCUM!
THISSS IS NOTTTT ABOUTTTT YOU!
HAWKMAN!
HAWKWOMAN!
SPLASH
THEY WERE UNCONSCIOUS WHEN THEY HIT THE WATER!
LEAVE THEM TO ME. YOU'RE OUR *WARRIOR* HERE. AND THE GROWTH FIELD WILL ONLY LAST A CERTAIN AMOUNT OF TIME.
THE BRIDGE IS EVACUATED. I'LL GET HIM OUT INTO THE BAY AND AWAY FROM PEOPLE.

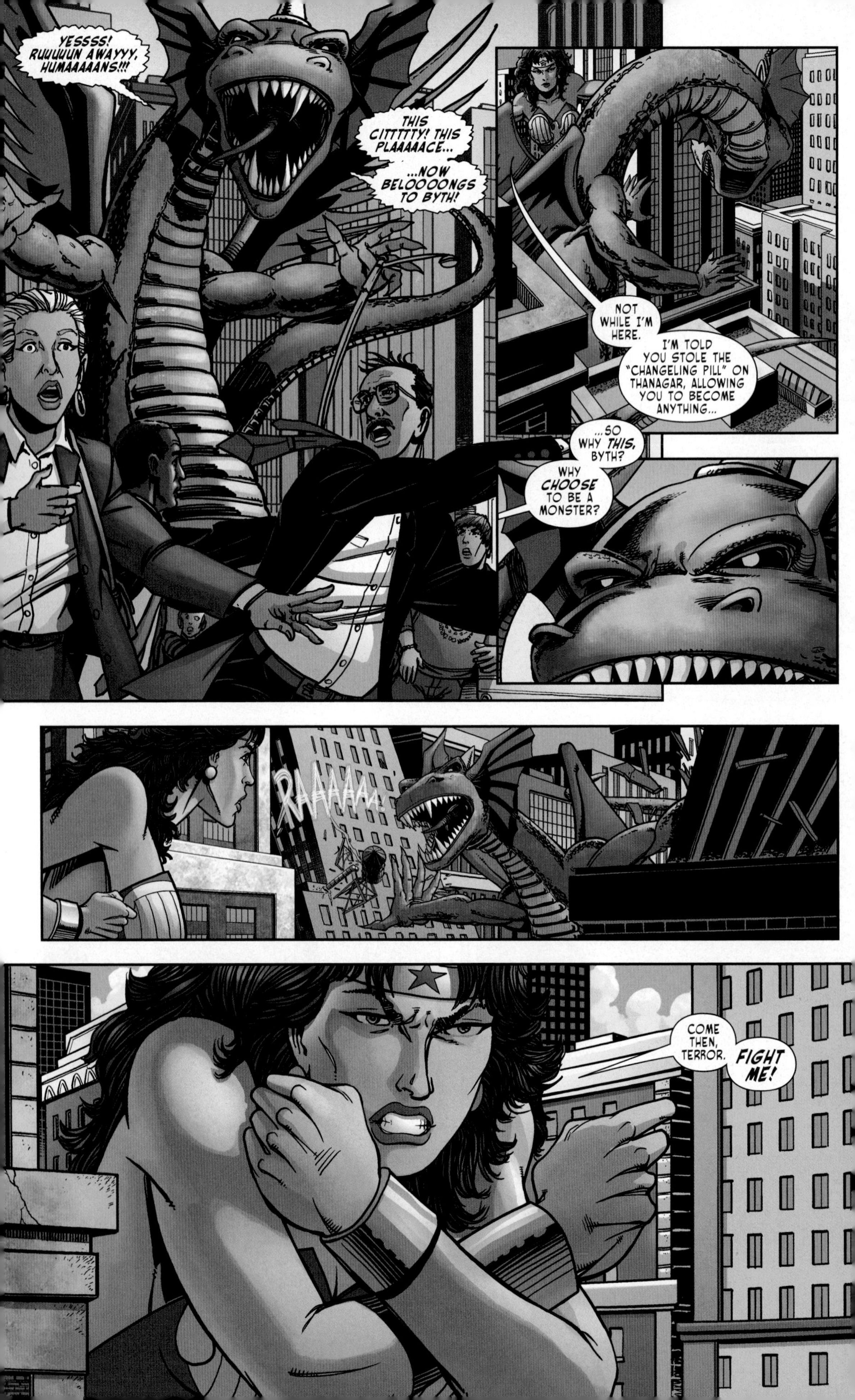
YESSSS! RUUUUUN AWAYYY, HUMAAAAAANS!!!
THIS CITTTTTY! THIS PLAAAAACE...
...NOW BELOOOONGS TO BYTH!
NOT WHILE I'M HERE.
I'M TOLD YOU STOLE THE "CHANGELING PILL" ON THANAGAR, ALLOWING YOU TO BECOME ANYTHING...
...SO WHY THIS, BYTH?
WHY CHOOSE TO BE A MONSTER?
RAAAAAA!
COME THEN, TERROR.
FIGHT ME!

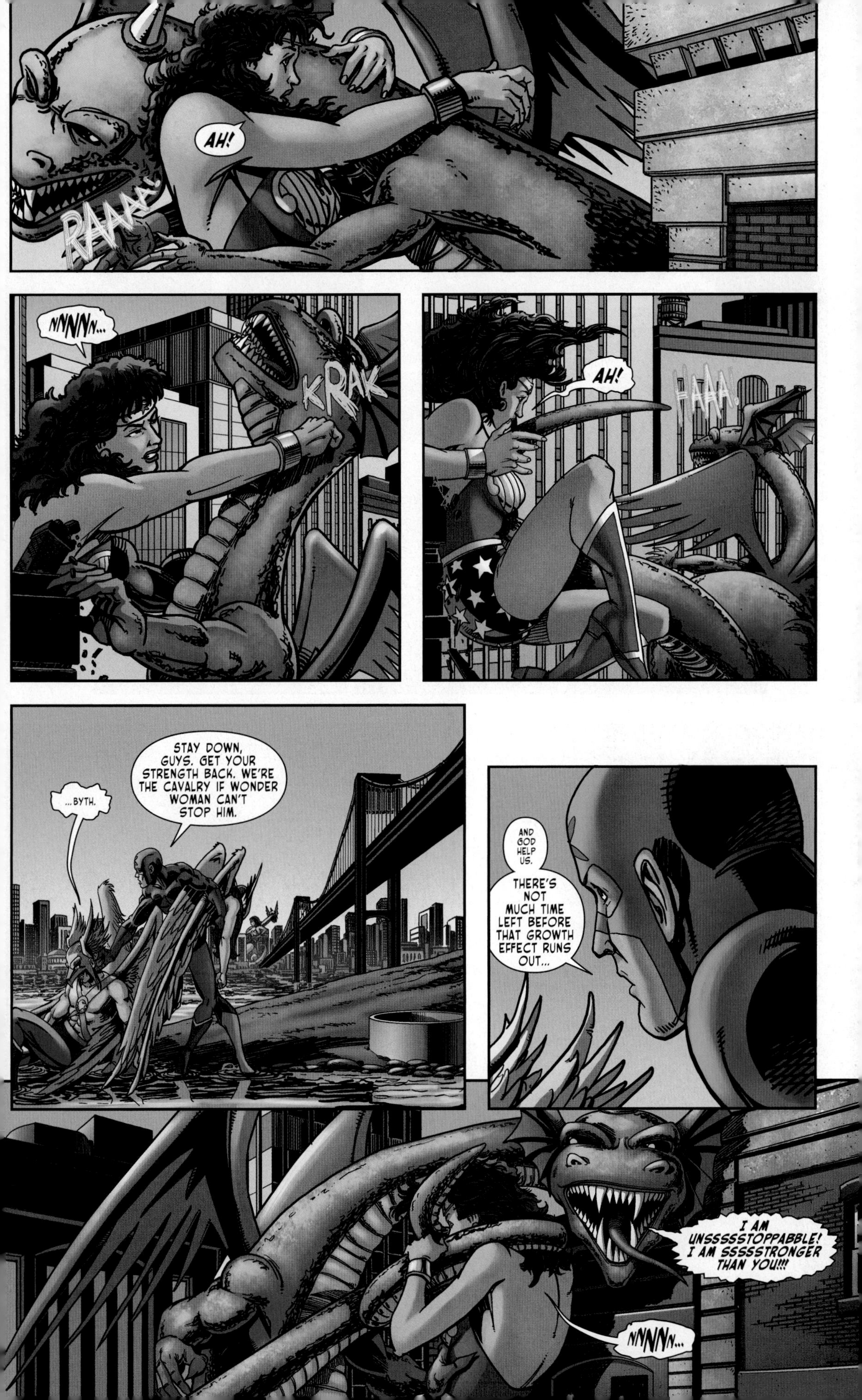
AH!
RAAAA!
NNNNN...
KRAK
AH!
HAAAA!
...BYTH.
STAY DOWN, GUYS. GET YOUR STRENGTH BACK. WE'RE THE CAVALRY IF WONDER WOMAN CAN'T STOP HIM.
AND GOD HELP US.
THERE'S NOT MUCH TIME LEFT BEFORE THAT GROWTH EFFECT RUNS OUT...
I AM UNSSSSSTOPPABBLE! I AM SSSSSTRONGER THAN YOU!!!
NNNNN...

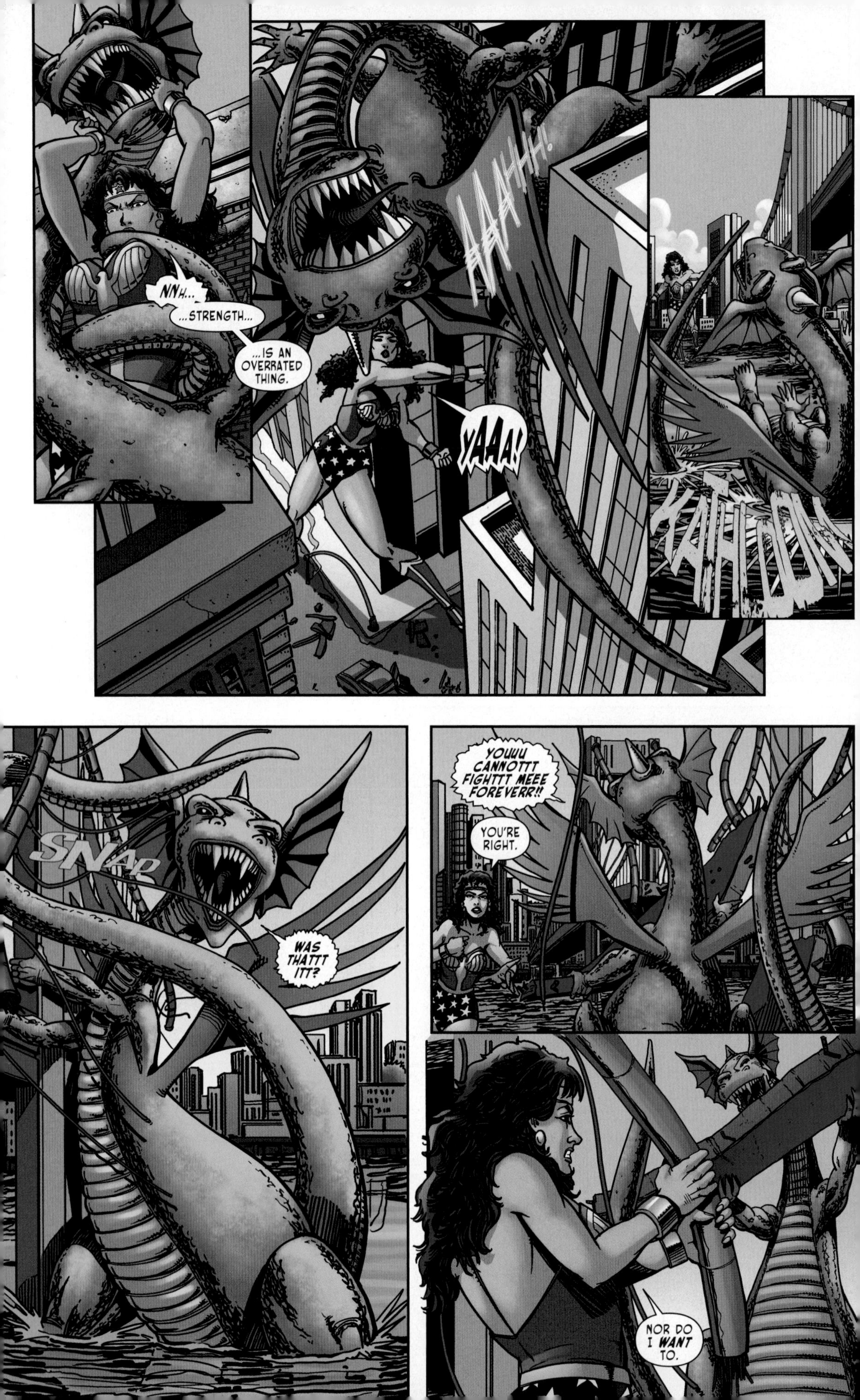
NNH...
...STRENGTH...
...IS AN OVERRATED THING.
AAAHHHH!
YAAA!
KAHOOM
SNAP
WAS THATTT ITT?
YOUUU CANNOTTT FIGHTTT MEEE FOREVERR!!
YOU'RE RIGHT.
NOR DO I WANT TO.

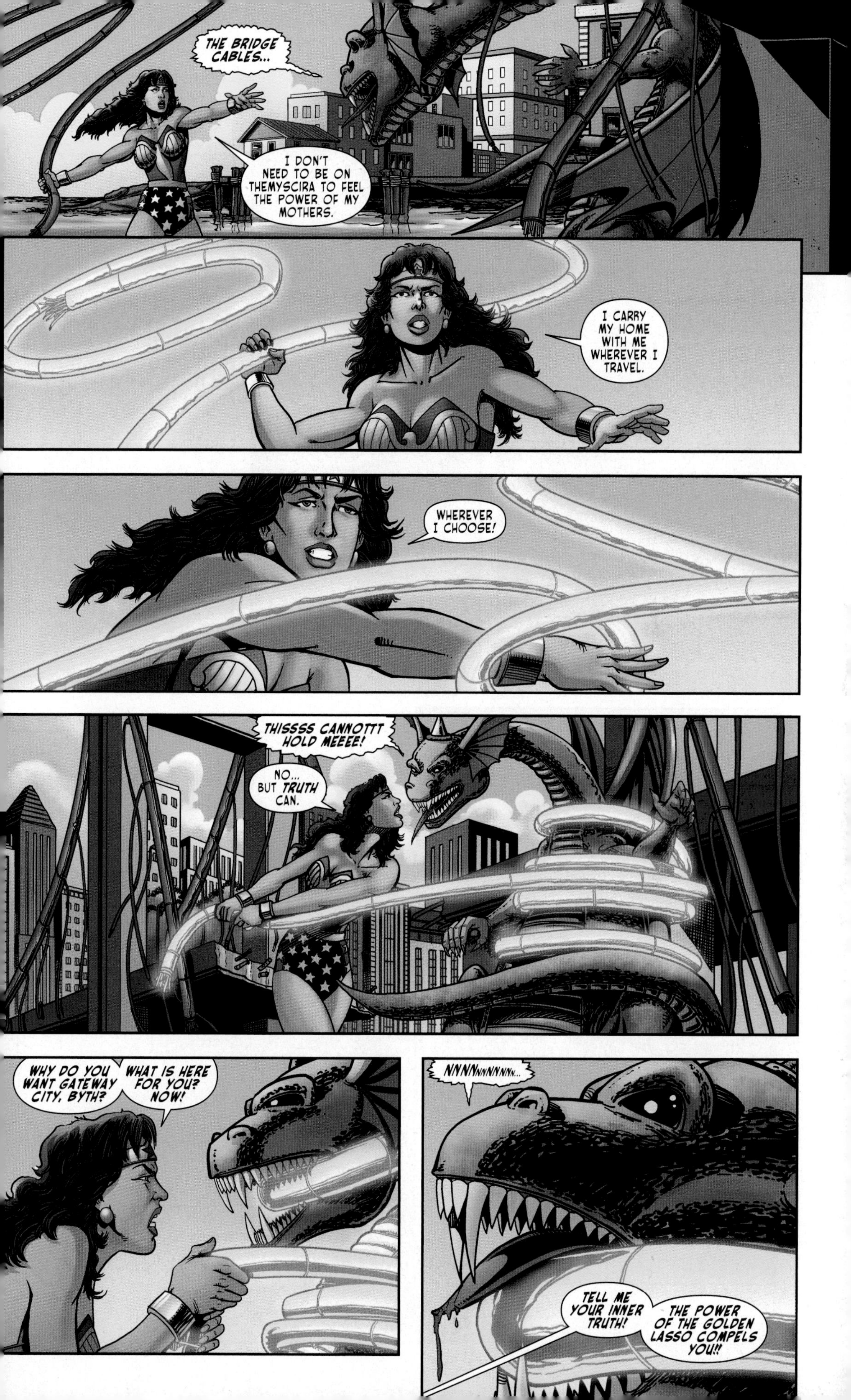

THE BRIDGE CABLES...
I DON'T NEED TO BE ON THEMYSCIRA TO FEEL THE POWER OF MY MOTHERS.
I CARRY MY HOME WITH ME WHEREVER I TRAVEL.
WHEREVER I CHOOSE!
THISSSS CANNOTTT HOLD MEEEE!
NO... BUT TRUTH CAN.
WHY DO YOU WANT GATEWAY CITY, BYTH?
WHAT IS HERE FOR YOU? NOW!
NNNNNNNNNN...
TELL ME YOUR INNER TRUTH!
THE POWER OF THE GOLDEN LASSO COMPELS YOU!!

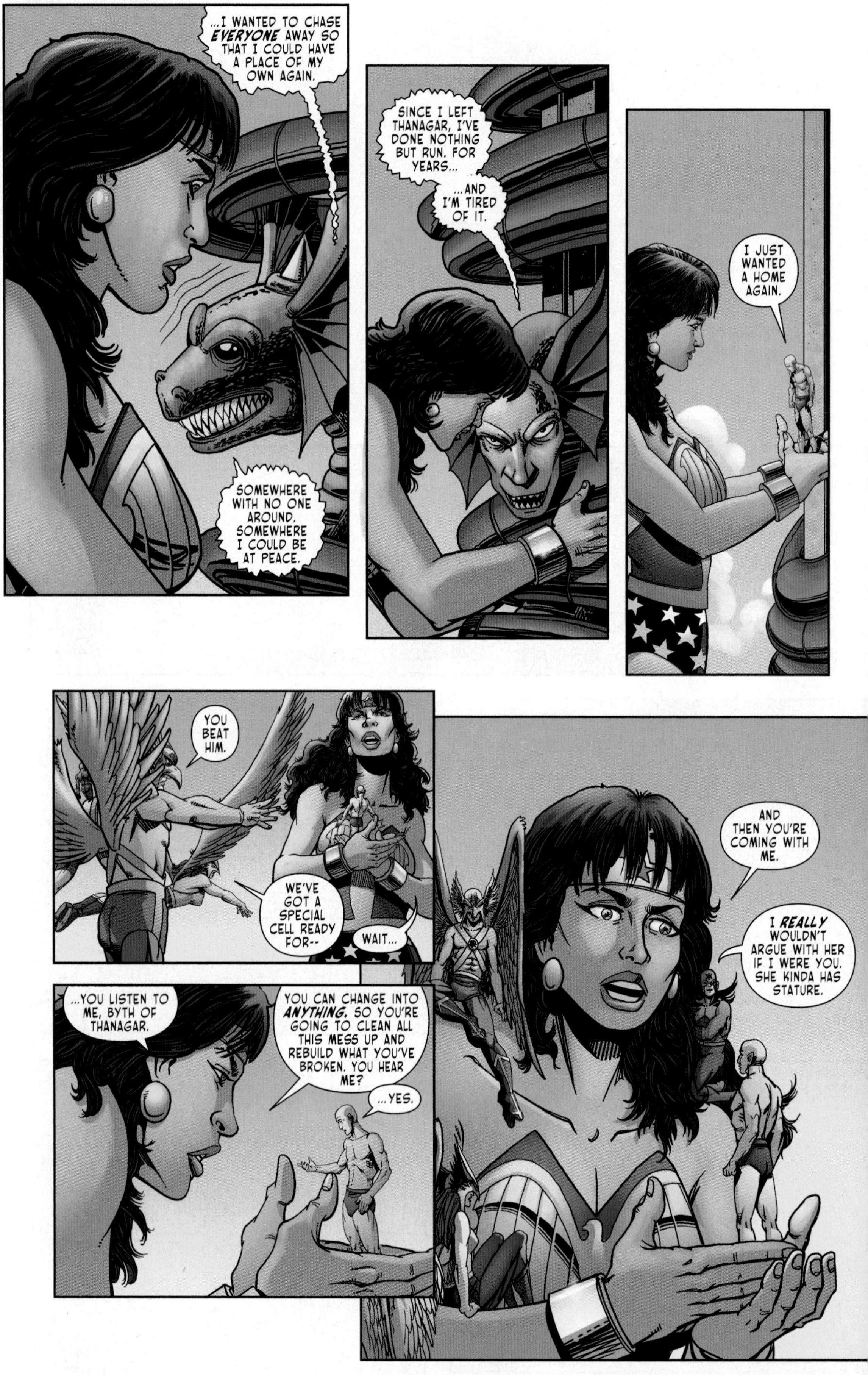
...I WANTED TO CHASE EVERYONE AWAY SO THAT I COULD HAVE A PLACE OF MY OWN AGAIN.
SOMEWHERE WITH NO ONE AROUND. SOMEWHERE I COULD BE AT PEACE.
SINCE I LEFT THANAGAR, I'VE DONE NOTHING BUT RUN. FOR YEARS...
...AND I'M TIRED OF IT.
I JUST WANTED A HOME AGAIN.
YOU BEAT HIM.
WE'VE GOT A SPECIAL CELL READY FOR--
WAIT...
...YOU LISTEN TO ME, BYTH OF THANAGAR.
YOU CAN CHANGE INTO ANYTHING. SO YOU'RE GOING TO CLEAN ALL THIS MESS UP AND REBUILD WHAT YOU'VE BROKEN. YOU HEAR ME?
...YES.
AND THEN YOU'RE COMING WITH ME.
I REALLY WOULDN'T ARGUE WITH HER IF I WERE YOU. SHE KINDA HAS STATURE.

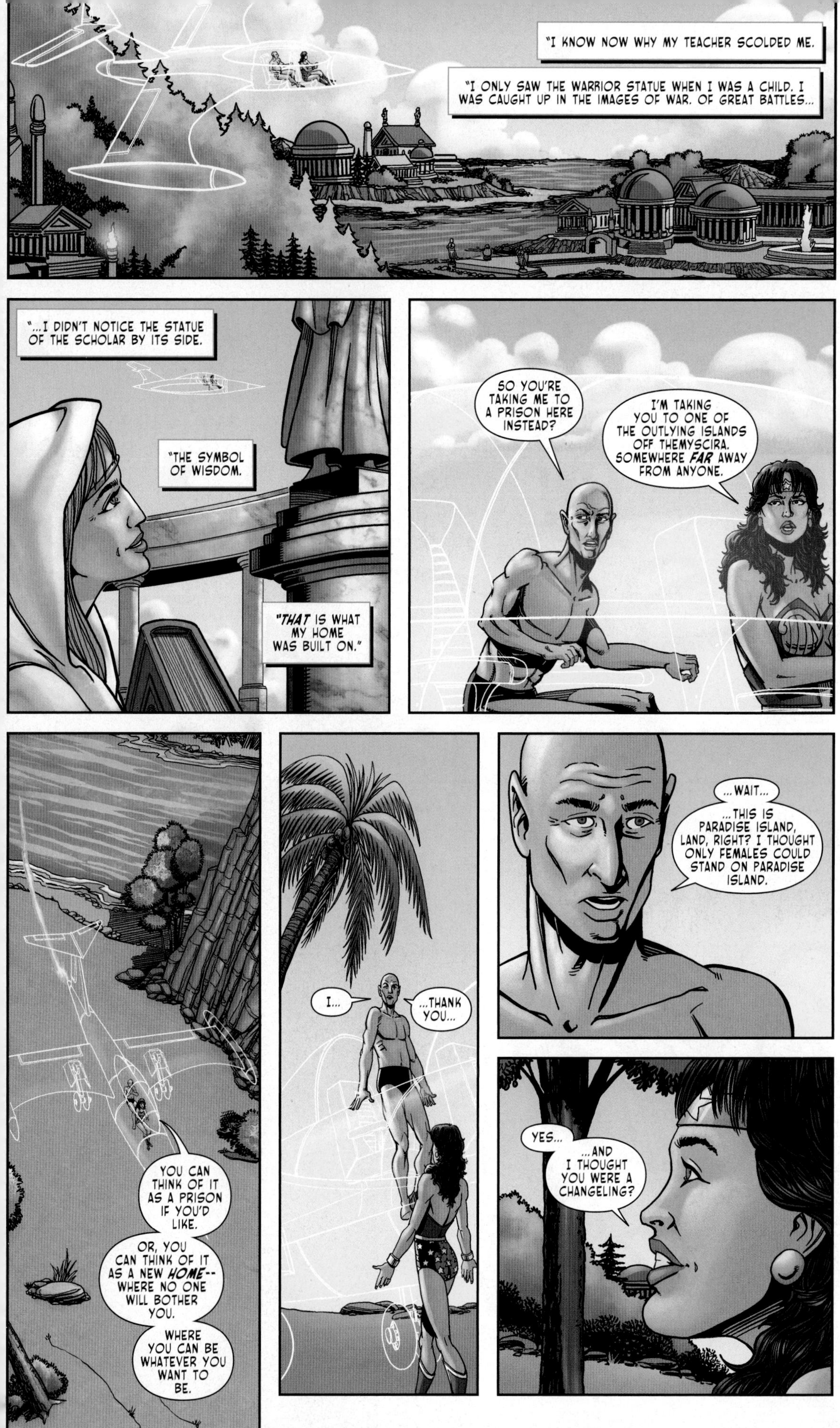
"I KNOW NOW WHY MY TEACHER SCOLDED ME.
"I ONLY SAW THE WARRIOR STATUE WHEN I WAS A CHILD. I WAS CAUGHT UP IN THE IMAGES OF WAR. OF GREAT BATTLES...
"...I DIDN'T NOTICE THE STATUE OF THE SCHOLAR BY ITS SIDE.
"THE SYMBOL OF WISDOM.
"*THAT* IS WHAT MY HOME WAS BUILT ON."
SO YOU'RE TAKING ME TO A PRISON HERE INSTEAD?
I'M TAKING YOU TO ONE OF THE OUTLYING ISLANDS OFF THEMYSCIRA. SOMEWHERE *FAR* AWAY FROM ANYONE.
YOU CAN THINK OF IT AS A PRISON IF YOU'D LIKE.
OR, YOU CAN THINK OF IT AS A NEW *HOME*-- WHERE NO ONE WILL BOTHER YOU.
WHERE YOU CAN BE WHATEVER YOU WANT TO BE.
I...
...THANK YOU...
...WAIT...
...THIS IS PARADISE ISLAND, LAND, RIGHT? I THOUGHT ONLY FEMALES COULD STAND ON PARADISE ISLAND.
YES...
...AND I THOUGHT YOU WERE A CHANGELING?

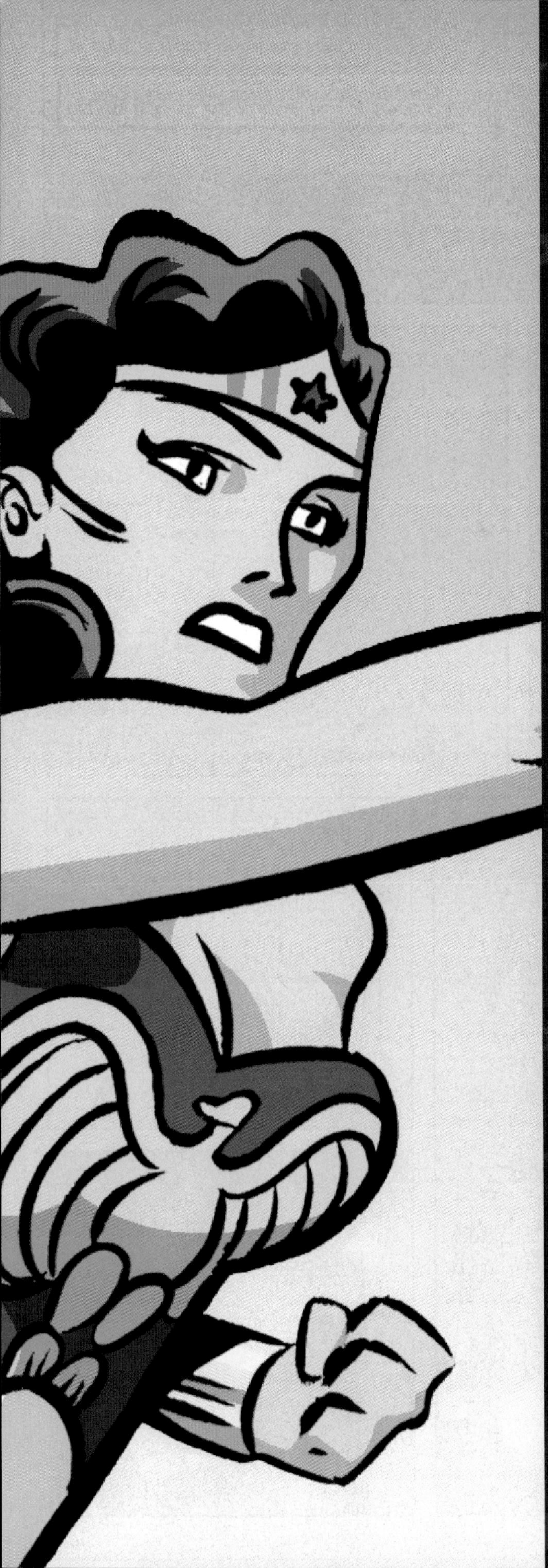

GHOSTS AND GODS

NEIL KLEID
WRITER

DEAN HASPIEL
ARTIST

ALLEN PASSALAQUA
COLORIST

SAIDA TEMOFONTE
LETTERER

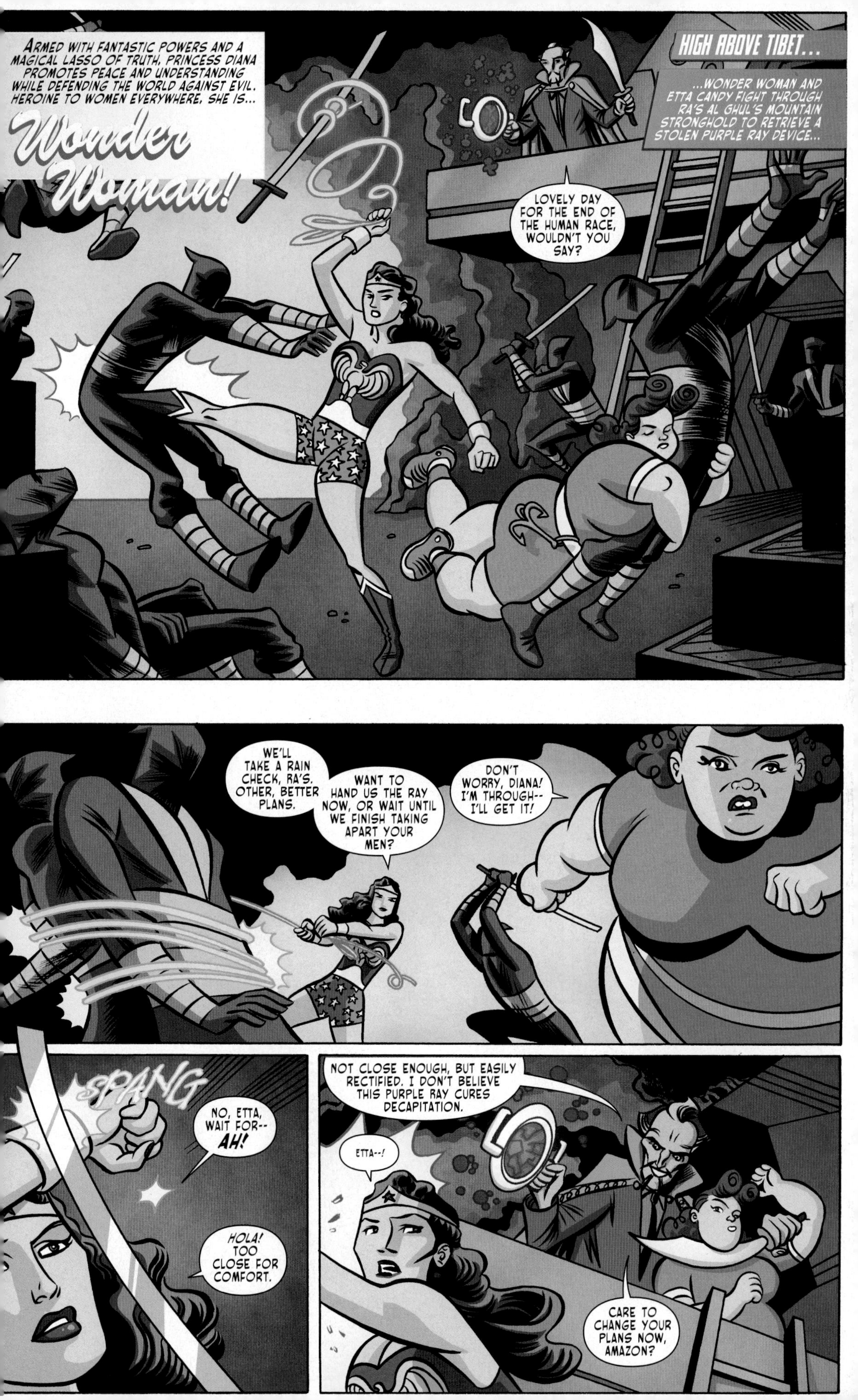
ARMED WITH FANTASTIC POWERS AND A MAGICAL LASSO OF TRUTH, PRINCESS DIANA PROMOTES PEACE AND UNDERSTANDING WHILE DEFENDING THE WORLD AGAINST EVIL. HEROINE TO WOMEN EVERYWHERE, SHE IS...
Wonder Woman!
HIGH ABOVE TIBET...
...WONDER WOMAN AND ETTA CANDY FIGHT THROUGH RA'S AL GHUL'S MOUNTAIN STRONGHOLD TO RETRIEVE A STOLEN PURPLE RAY DEVICE...
LOVELY DAY FOR THE END OF THE HUMAN RACE, WOULDN'T YOU SAY?
WE'LL TAKE A RAIN CHECK, RA'S. OTHER, BETTER PLANS.
WANT TO HAND US THE RAY NOW, OR WAIT UNTIL WE FINISH TAKING APART YOUR MEN?
DON'T WORRY, DIANA! I'M THROUGH-- I'LL GET IT!
SPANG
NO, ETTA, WAIT FOR-- AH!
HOLA! TOO CLOSE FOR COMFORT.
NOT CLOSE ENOUGH, BUT EASILY RECTIFIED. I DON'T BELIEVE THIS PURPLE RAY CURES DECAPITATION.
ETTA--!
CARE TO CHANGE YOUR PLANS NOW, AMAZON?

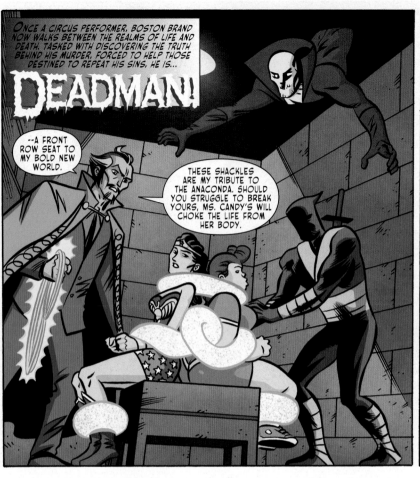

ONCE A CIRCUS PERFORMER, BOSTON BRAND NOW WALKS BETWEEN THE REALMS OF LIFE AND DEATH. TASKED WITH DISCOVERING THE TRUTH BEHIND HIS MURDER. FORCED TO HELP THOSE DESTINED TO REPEAT HIS SINS, HE IS...

DEADMAN!

--A FRONT ROW SEAT TO MY BOLD NEW WORLD.

THESE SHACKLES ARE MY TRIBUTE TO THE ANACONDA. SHOULD YOU STRUGGLE TO BREAK YOURS, MS. CANDY'S WILL CHOKE THE LIFE FROM HER BODY.

I'M OFF TO IMBUE YOUR RAY'S HEALING POWERS INTO AN ARMY OF IMMORTAL ASSASSINS. AU REVOIR.

UNLESS YOU'D CARE TO JOIN ME AS MY AMAZON BRIDE...?

I'D SOONER WED THE ANACONDA.

PITY. OUR CHILDREN WOULD HAVE BEEN BENEFICENT RULERS.

I DOUBT THAT.

I'M HOLDING A LASSO OF TRUTH, MY DEAR. I CAN HARDLY LIE.

SIT TIGHT, ETTA. I'LL FREE US OF THIS CRAZY TIN CAN.

HEY, I CAN HELP. JUST LET ME GNYYAGH--!

ETTA? ARE YOU ALL RIGHT?

ETTA'S TAKING A BREAK RIGHT NOW. NO WORRIES--I'VE GOT THE CONTROLS.

THE NAME'S BOSTON. I'M A GHOST. HOWYADOIN'?

NICE STARS, BY THE WAY.

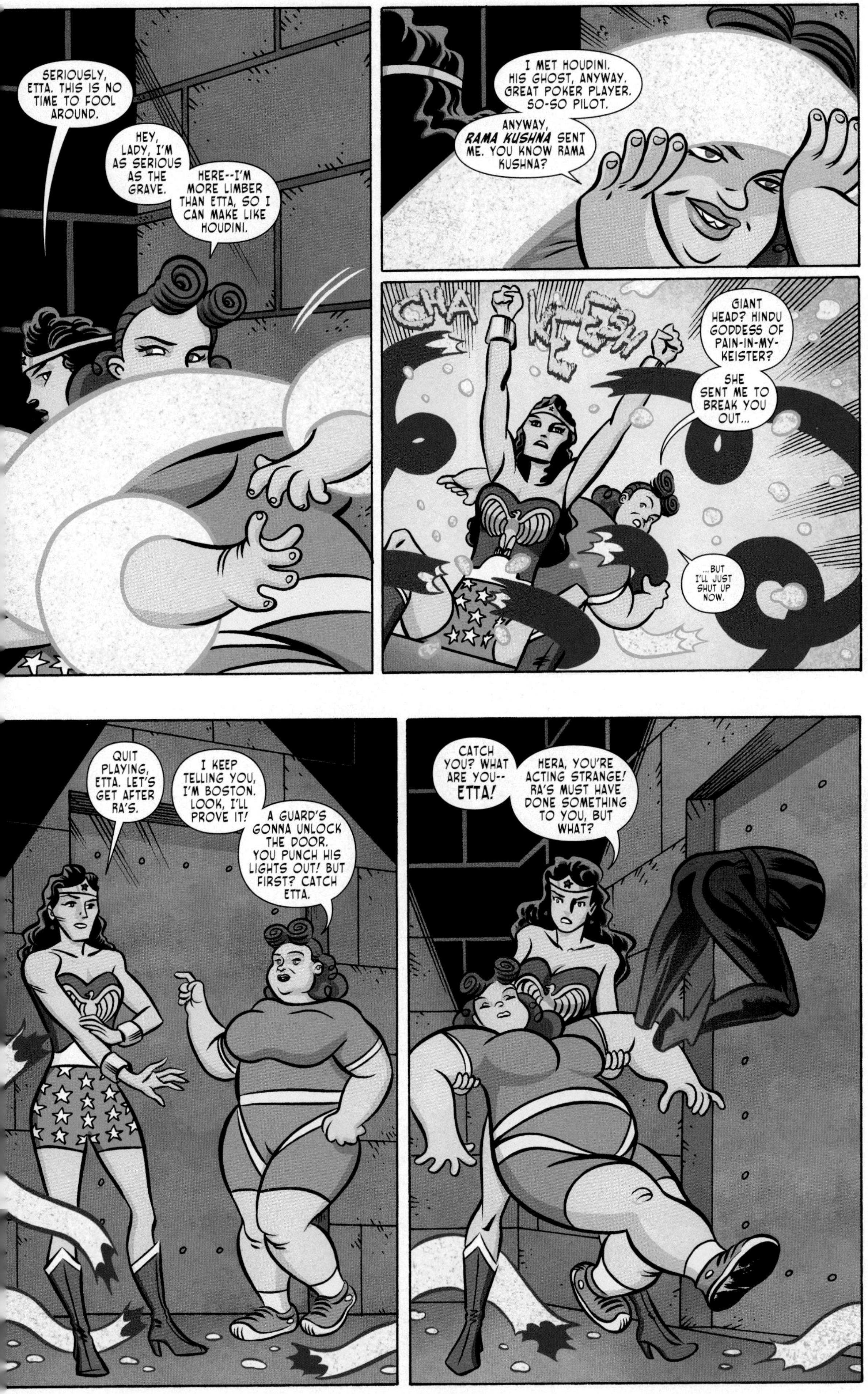
SERIOUSLY, ETTA. THIS IS NO TIME TO FOOL AROUND.
HEY, LADY, I'M AS SERIOUS AS THE GRAVE.
HERE--I'M MORE LIMBER THAN ETTA, SO I CAN MAKE LIKE HOUDINI.
I MET HOUDINI. HIS GHOST, ANYWAY. GREAT POKER PLAYER. SO-SO PILOT.
ANYWAY, RAMA KUSHNA SENT ME. YOU KNOW RAMA KUSHNA?
CHA KRESH
GIANT HEAD? HINDU GODDESS OF PAIN-IN-MY-KEISTER?
SHE SENT ME TO BREAK YOU OUT...
...BUT I'LL JUST SHUT UP NOW.
QUIT PLAYING, ETTA. LET'S GET AFTER RA'S.
I KEEP TELLING YOU, I'M BOSTON. LOOK, I'LL PROVE IT!
A GUARD'S GONNA UNLOCK THE DOOR. YOU PUNCH HIS LIGHTS OUT! BUT FIRST? CATCH ETTA.
CATCH YOU? WHAT ARE YOU-- ETTA!
HERA, YOU'RE ACTING STRANGE! RA'S MUST HAVE DONE SOMETHING TO YOU, BUT WHAT?

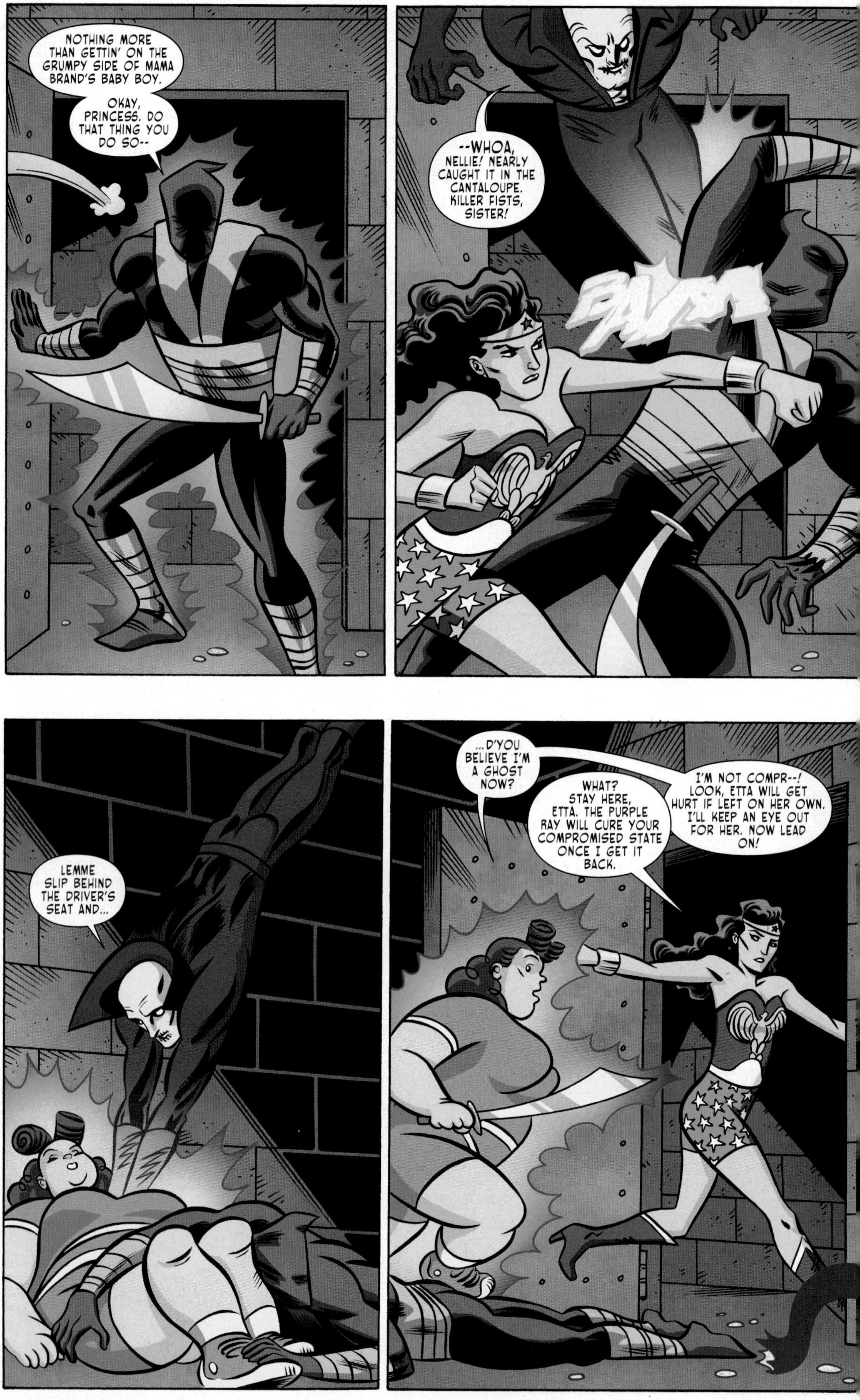
NOTHING MORE THAN GETTIN' ON THE GRUMPY SIDE OF MAMA BRAND'S BABY BOY.
OKAY, PRINCESS. DO THAT THING YOU DO SO--
--WHOA, NELLIE! NEARLY CAUGHT IT IN THE CANTALOUPE. KILLER FISTS, SISTER!
BAM
LEMME SLIP BEHIND THE DRIVER'S SEAT AND...
...D'YOU BELIEVE I'M A GHOST NOW?
WHAT? STAY HERE, ETTA. THE PURPLE RAY WILL CURE YOUR COMPROMISED STATE ONCE I GET IT BACK.
I'M NOT COMPR--! LOOK, ETTA WILL GET HURT IF LEFT ON HER OWN. I'LL KEEP AN EYE OUT FOR HER. NOW LEAD ON!

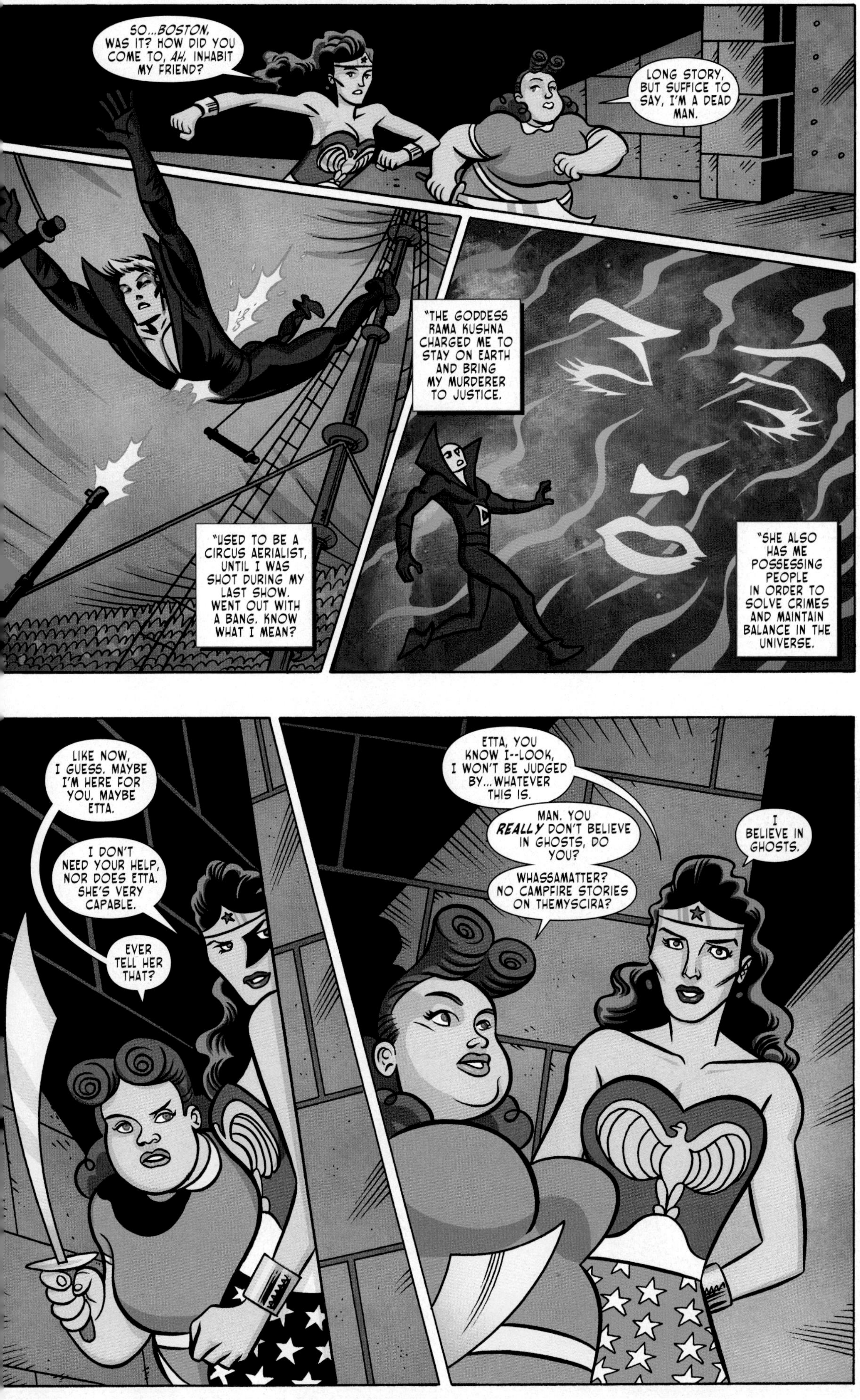

SO...BOSTON, WAS IT? HOW DID YOU COME TO, AH, INHABIT MY FRIEND?
LONG STORY, BUT SUFFICE TO SAY, I'M A DEAD MAN.
"USED TO BE A CIRCUS AERIALIST, UNTIL I WAS SHOT DURING MY LAST SHOW. WENT OUT WITH A BANG. KNOW WHAT I MEAN?
"THE GODDESS RAMA KUSHNA CHARGED ME TO STAY ON EARTH AND BRING MY MURDERER TO JUSTICE.
"SHE ALSO HAS ME POSSESSING PEOPLE IN ORDER TO SOLVE CRIMES AND MAINTAIN BALANCE IN THE UNIVERSE.
LIKE NOW, I GUESS. MAYBE I'M HERE FOR YOU. MAYBE ETTA.
I DON'T NEED YOUR HELP, NOR DOES ETTA. SHE'S VERY CAPABLE.
EVER TELL HER THAT?
ETTA, YOU KNOW I--LOOK, I WON'T BE JUDGED BY...WHATEVER THIS IS.
MAN. YOU REALLY DON'T BELIEVE IN GHOSTS, DO YOU?
WHASSAMATTER? NO CAMPFIRE STORIES ON THEMYSCIRA?
I BELIEVE IN GHOSTS.

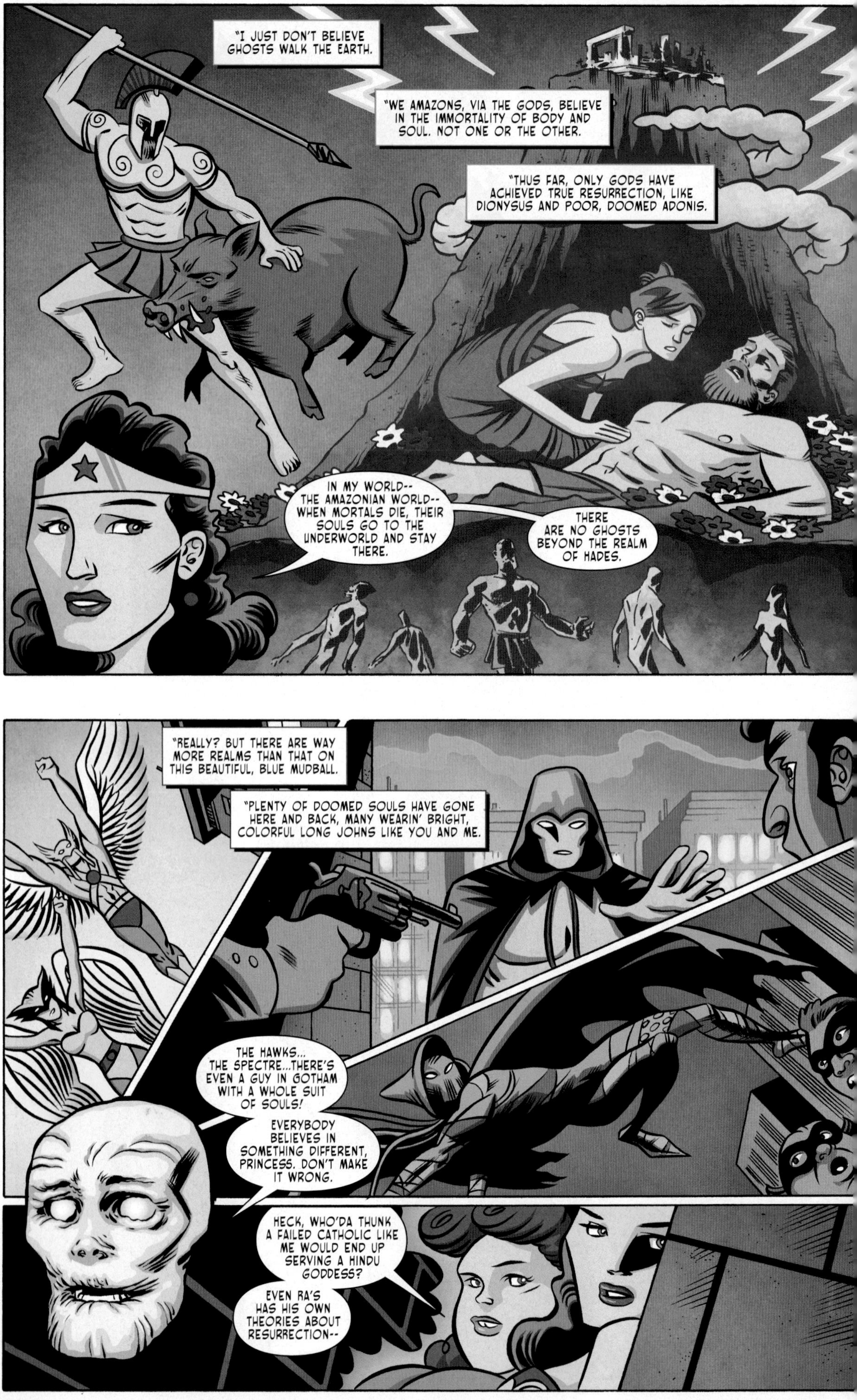
"I JUST DON'T BELIEVE GHOSTS WALK THE EARTH.
"WE AMAZONS, VIA THE GODS, BELIEVE IN THE IMMORTALITY OF BODY AND SOUL. NOT ONE OR THE OTHER.
"THUS FAR, ONLY GODS HAVE ACHIEVED TRUE RESURRECTION, LIKE DIONYSUS AND POOR, DOOMED ADONIS.
IN MY WORLD-- THE AMAZONIAN WORLD-- WHEN MORTALS DIE, THEIR SOULS GO TO THE UNDERWORLD AND STAY THERE.
THERE ARE NO GHOSTS BEYOND THE REALM OF HADES.
"REALLY? BUT THERE ARE WAY MORE REALMS THAN THAT ON THIS BEAUTIFUL, BLUE MUDBALL.
"PLENTY OF DOOMED SOULS HAVE GONE HERE AND BACK, MANY WEARIN' BRIGHT, COLORFUL LONG JOHNS LIKE YOU AND ME.
THE HAWKS... THE SPECTRE...THERE'S EVEN A GUY IN GOTHAM WITH A WHOLE SUIT OF SOULS!
EVERYBODY BELIEVES IN SOMETHING DIFFERENT, PRINCESS. DON'T MAKE IT WRONG.
HECK, WHO'DA THUNK A FAILED CATHOLIC LIKE ME WOULD END UP SERVING A HINDU GODDESS?
EVEN RA'S HAS HIS OWN THEORIES ABOUT RESURRECTION--

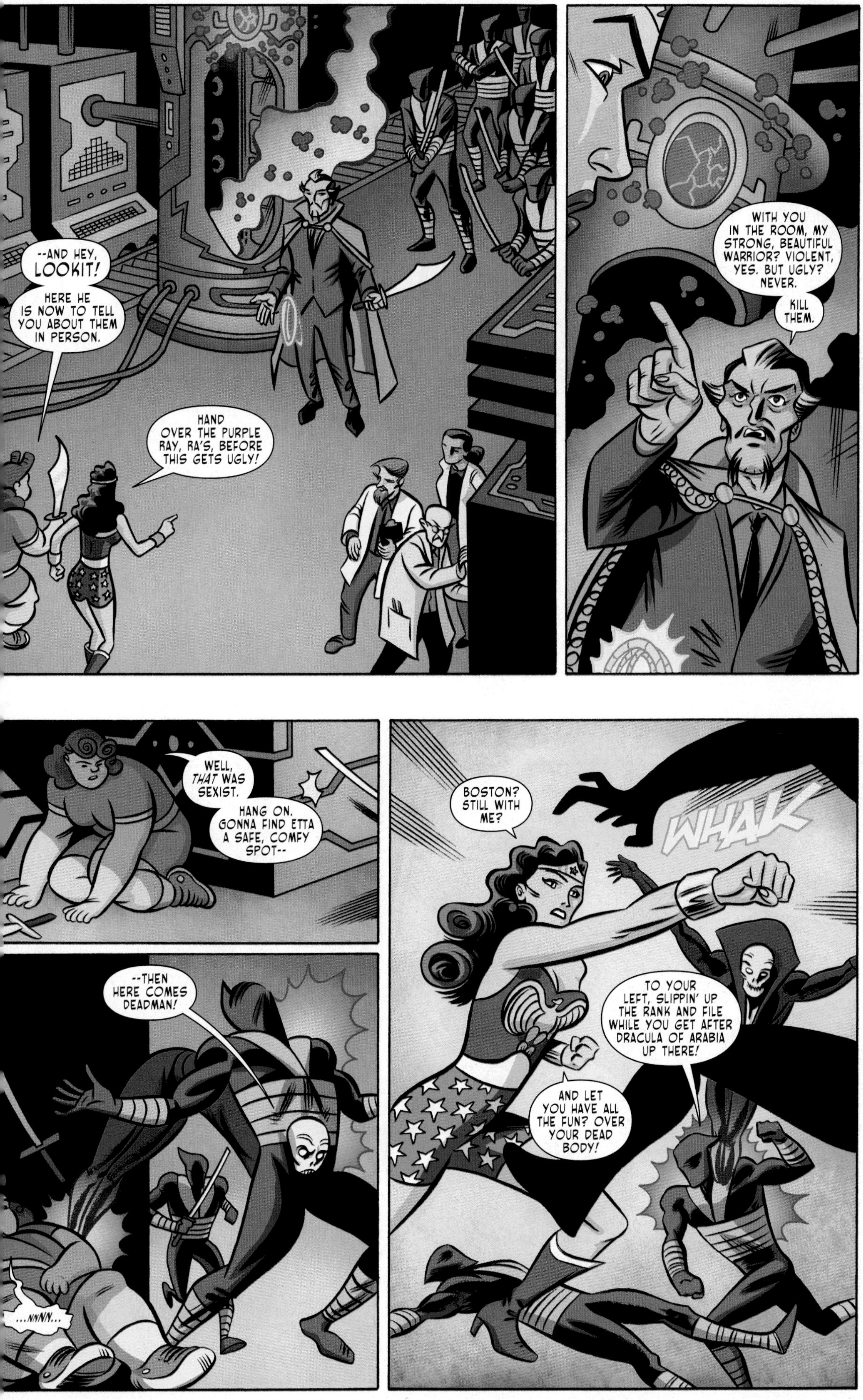
--AND HEY, LOOKIT!
HERE HE IS NOW TO TELL YOU ABOUT THEM IN PERSON.
HAND OVER THE PURPLE RAY, RA'S, BEFORE THIS GETS UGLY!
WITH YOU IN THE ROOM, MY STRONG, BEAUTIFUL WARRIOR? VIOLENT, YES. BUT UGLY? NEVER.
KILL THEM.
WELL, THAT WAS SEXIST.
HANG ON. GONNA FIND ETTA A SAFE, COMFY SPOT--
--THEN HERE COMES DEADMAN!
...NNNN...
BOSTON? STILL WITH ME?
WHAK
TO YOUR LEFT, SLIPPIN' UP THE RANK AND FILE WHILE YOU GET AFTER DRACULA OF ARABIA UP THERE!
AND LET YOU HAVE ALL THE FUN? OVER YOUR DEAD BODY!

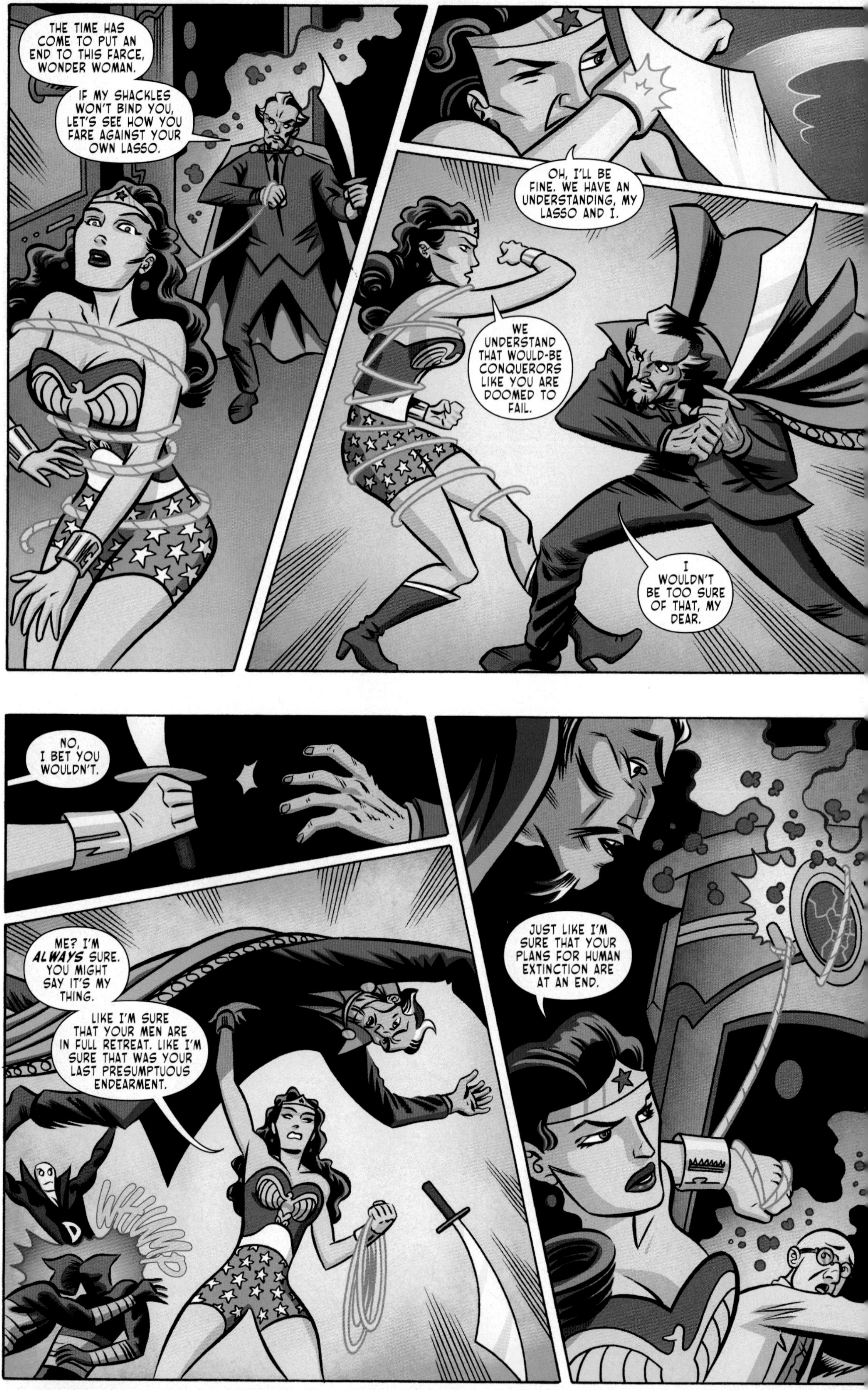

THE TIME HAS COME TO PUT AN END TO THIS FARCE, WONDER WOMAN.
IF MY SHACKLES WON'T BIND YOU, LET'S SEE HOW YOU FARE AGAINST YOUR OWN LASSO.
OH, I'LL BE FINE. WE HAVE AN UNDERSTANDING, MY LASSO AND I.
WE UNDERSTAND THAT WOULD-BE CONQUERORS LIKE YOU ARE DOOMED TO FAIL.
I WOULDN'T BE TOO SURE OF THAT, MY DEAR.
NO, I BET YOU WOULDN'T.
ME? I'M *ALWAYS* SURE. YOU MIGHT SAY IT'S MY THING.
LIKE I'M SURE THAT YOUR MEN ARE IN FULL RETREAT. LIKE I'M SURE THAT WAS YOUR LAST PRESUMPTUOUS ENDEARMENT.
WHUMP
JUST LIKE I'M SURE THAT YOUR PLANS FOR HUMAN EXTINCTION ARE AT AN END.

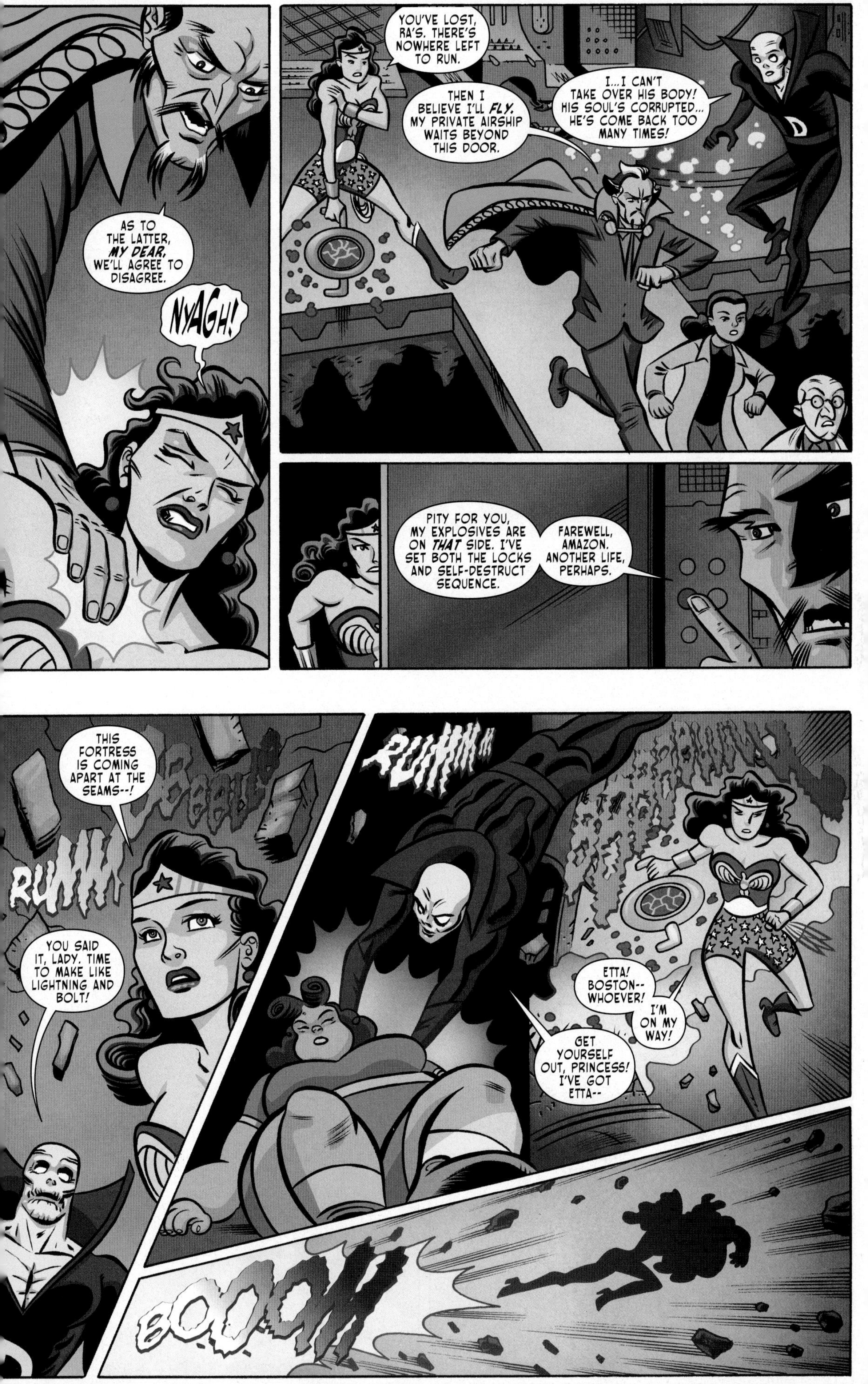
AS TO THE LATTER, MY DEAR, WE'LL AGREE TO DISAGREE.
NYAGH!
YOU'VE LOST, RA'S. THERE'S NOWHERE LEFT TO RUN.
THEN I BELIEVE I'LL FLY. MY PRIVATE AIRSHIP WAITS BEYOND THIS DOOR.
I...I CAN'T TAKE OVER HIS BODY! HIS SOUL'S CORRUPTED... HE'S COME BACK TOO MANY TIMES!
PITY FOR YOU, MY EXPLOSIVES ARE ON THAT SIDE. I'VE SET BOTH THE LOCKS AND SELF-DESTRUCT SEQUENCE.
FAREWELL, AMAZON. ANOTHER LIFE, PERHAPS.
THIS FORTRESS IS COMING APART AT THE SEAMS--!
RUHH
YOU SAID IT, LADY. TIME TO MAKE LIKE LIGHTNING AND BOLT!
RUHHM
ETTA! BOSTON-- WHOEVER!
I'M ON MY WAY!
GET YOURSELF OUT, PRINCESS! I'VE GOT ETTA--
BOOOM

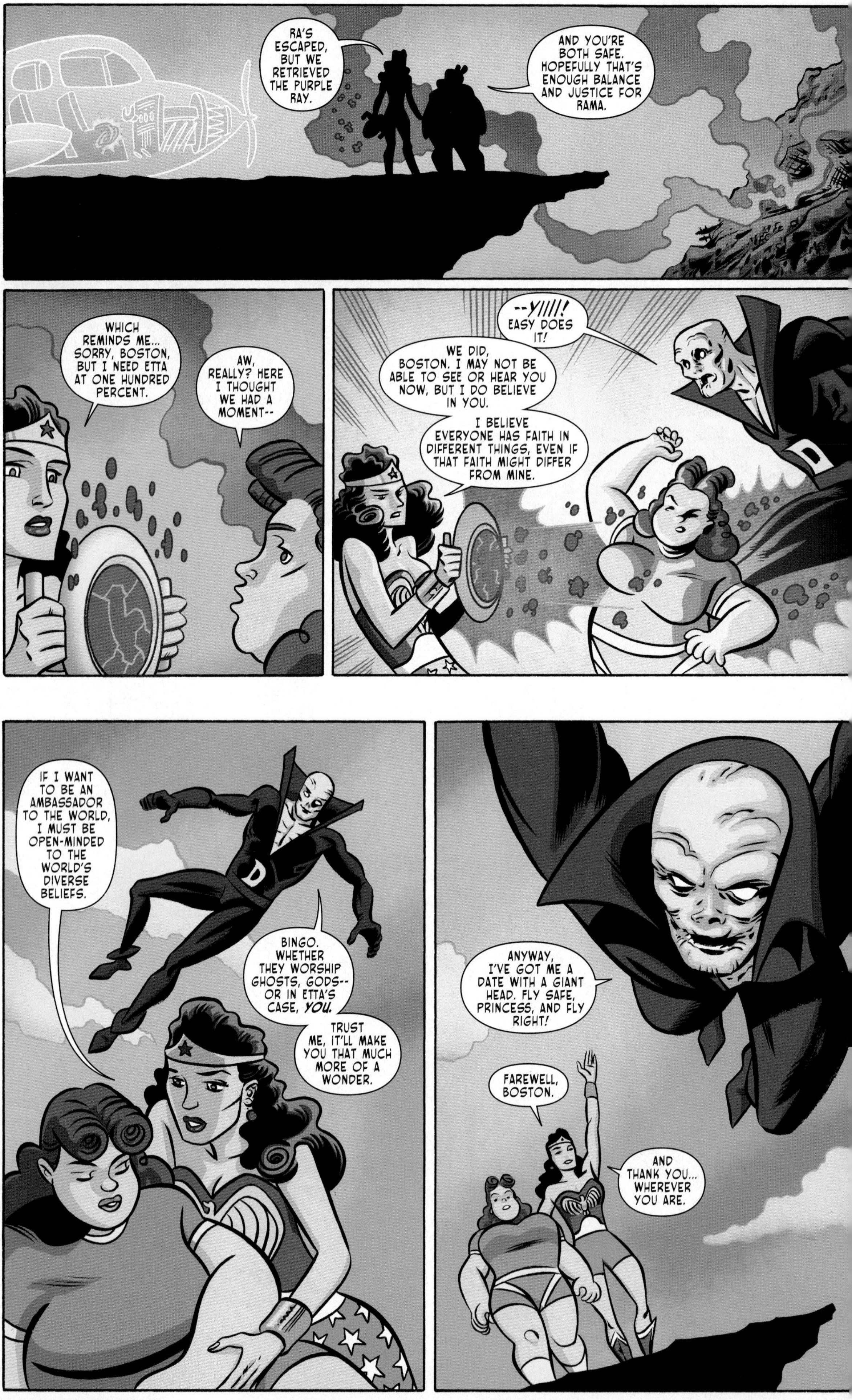
RA'S ESCAPED, BUT WE RETRIEVED THE PURPLE RAY.
AND YOU'RE BOTH SAFE. HOPEFULLY THAT'S ENOUGH BALANCE AND JUSTICE FOR RAMA.
WHICH REMINDS ME... SORRY, BOSTON, BUT I NEED ETTA AT ONE HUNDRED PERCENT.
AW, REALLY? HERE I THOUGHT WE HAD A MOMENT--
--YIIII! EASY DOES IT!
WE DID, BOSTON. I MAY NOT BE ABLE TO SEE OR HEAR YOU NOW, BUT I DO BELIEVE IN YOU.
I BELIEVE EVERYONE HAS FAITH IN DIFFERENT THINGS, EVEN IF THAT FAITH MIGHT DIFFER FROM MINE.
IF I WANT TO BE AN AMBASSADOR TO THE WORLD, I MUST BE OPEN-MINDED TO THE WORLD'S DIVERSE BELIEFS.
BINGO. WHETHER THEY WORSHIP GHOSTS, GODS-- OR IN ETTA'S CASE, YOU.
TRUST ME, IT'LL MAKE YOU THAT MUCH MORE OF A WONDER.
ANYWAY, I'VE GOT ME A DATE WITH A GIANT HEAD. FLY SAFE, PRINCESS, AND FLY RIGHT!
FAREWELL, BOSTON.
AND THANK YOU... WHEREVER YOU ARE.

DIG FOR FIRE

CORINNA BECHKO
&
GABRIEL HARDMAN
WRITERS

GABRIEL HARDMAN
ARTIST

JORDAN BOYD
COLORIST

SAIDA TEMOFONTE

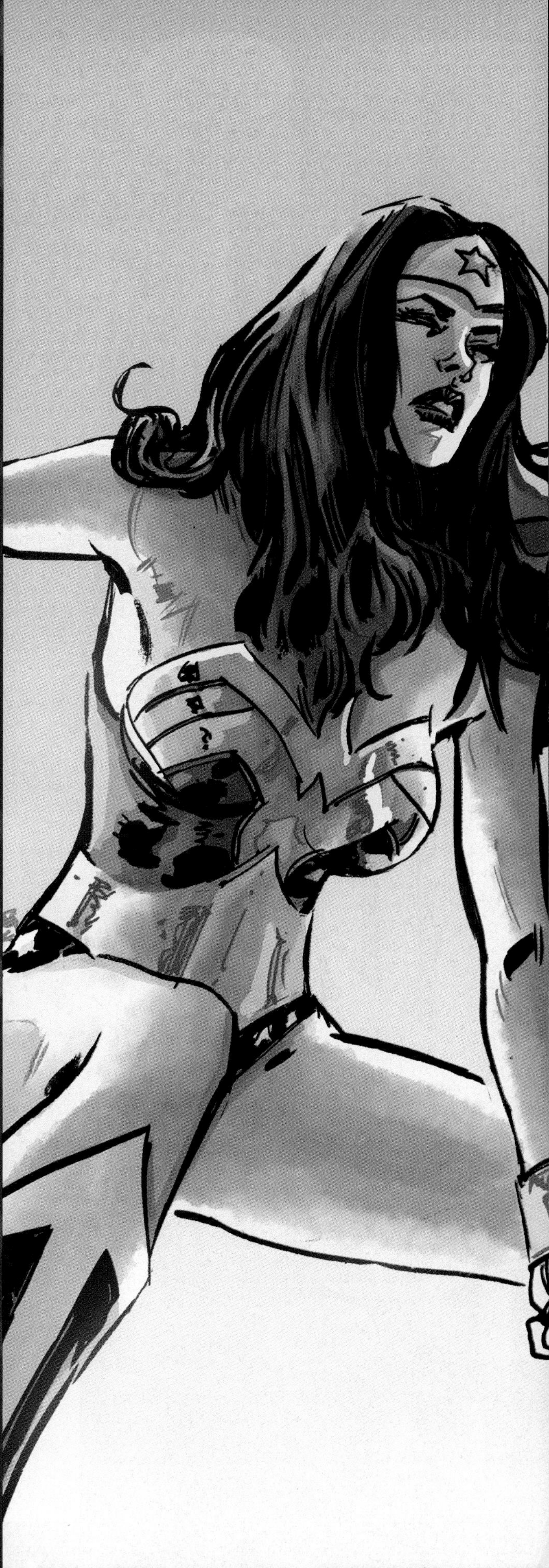

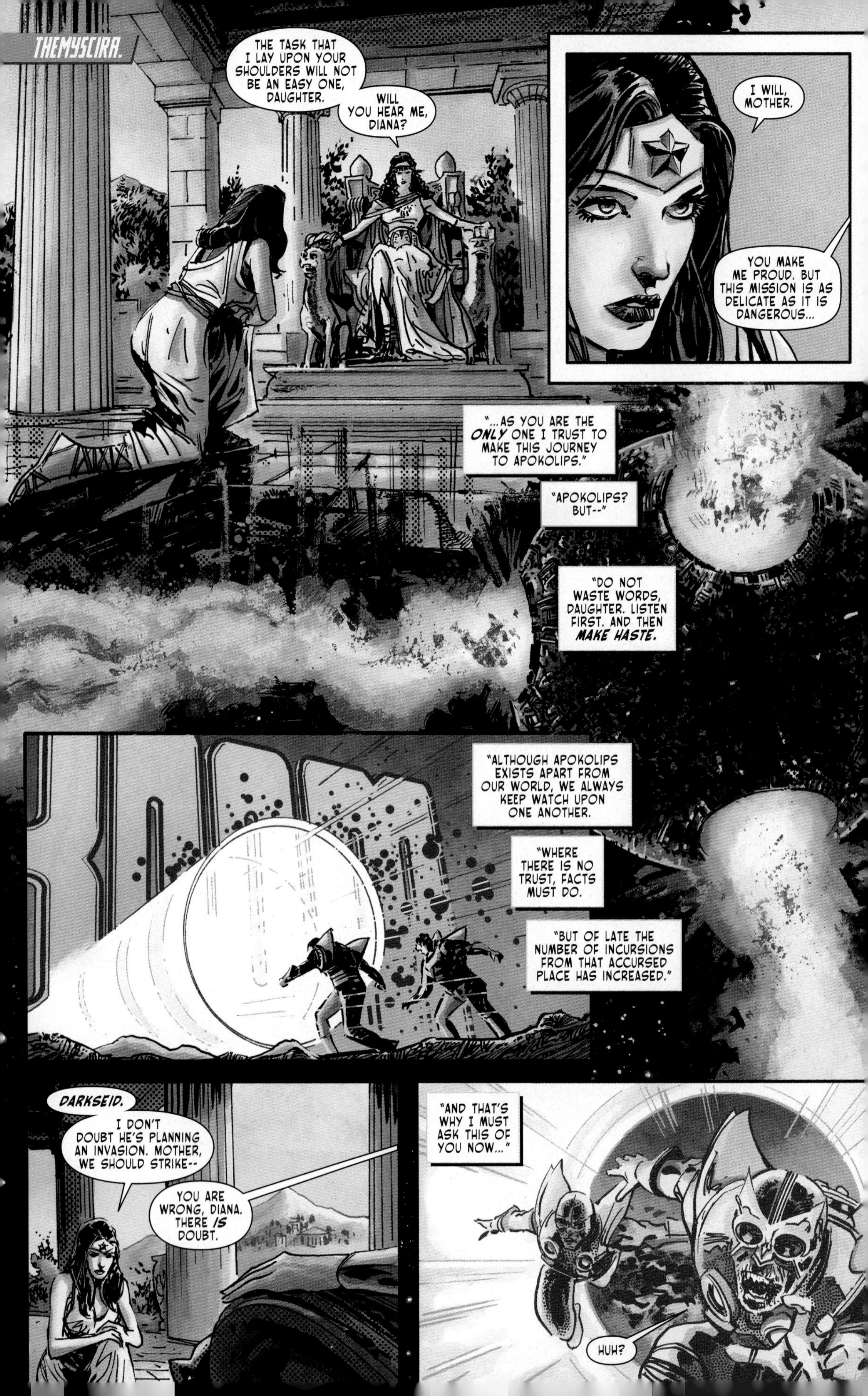
THEMYSCIRA.
THE TASK THAT I LAY UPON YOUR SHOULDERS WILL NOT BE AN EASY ONE, DAUGHTER.
WILL YOU HEAR ME, DIANA?
I WILL, MOTHER.
YOU MAKE ME PROUD. BUT THIS MISSION IS AS DELICATE AS IT IS DANGEROUS...
"...AS YOU ARE THE ONLY ONE I TRUST TO MAKE THIS JOURNEY TO APOKOLIPS."
"APOKOLIPS? BUT--"
"DO NOT WASTE WORDS, DAUGHTER. LISTEN FIRST. AND THEN MAKE HASTE.
"ALTHOUGH APOKOLIPS EXISTS APART FROM OUR WORLD, WE ALWAYS KEEP WATCH UPON ONE ANOTHER.
"WHERE THERE IS NO TRUST, FACTS MUST DO.
"BUT OF LATE THE NUMBER OF INCURSIONS FROM THAT ACCURSED PLACE HAS INCREASED."
DARKSEID.
I DON'T DOUBT HE'S PLANNING AN INVASION. MOTHER, WE SHOULD STRIKE--
YOU ARE WRONG, DIANA. THERE IS DOUBT.
"AND THAT'S WHY I MUST ASK THIS OF YOU NOW..."
HUH?

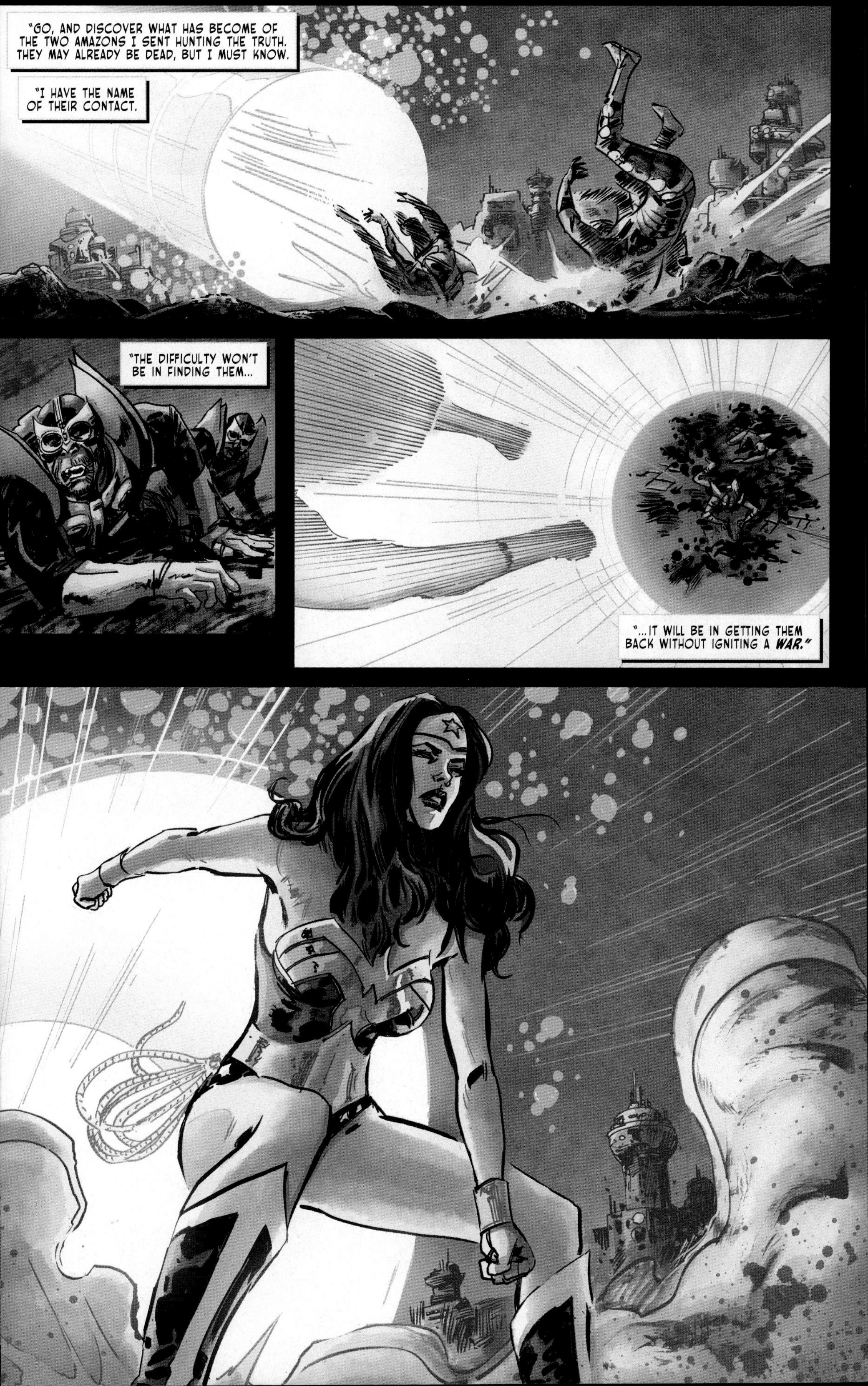
"GO, AND DISCOVER WHAT HAS BECOME OF THE TWO AMAZONS I SENT HUNTING THE TRUTH. THEY MAY ALREADY BE DEAD, BUT I MUST KNOW.
"I HAVE THE NAME OF THEIR CONTACT.
"THE DIFFICULTY WON'T BE IN FINDING THEM...
"...IT WILL BE IN GETTING THEM BACK WITHOUT IGNITING A WAR."

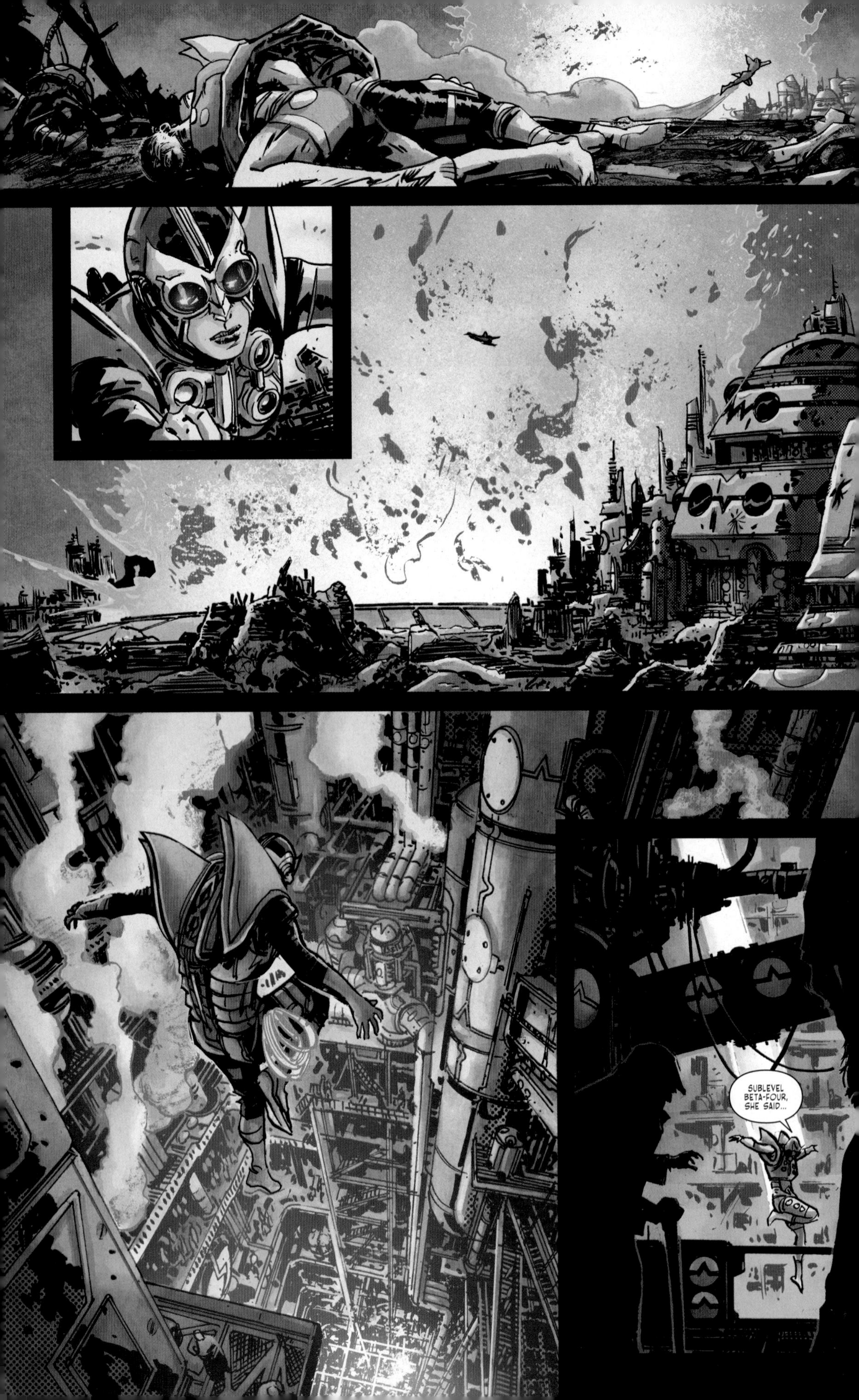
SUBLEVEL BETA-FOUR, SHE SAID...

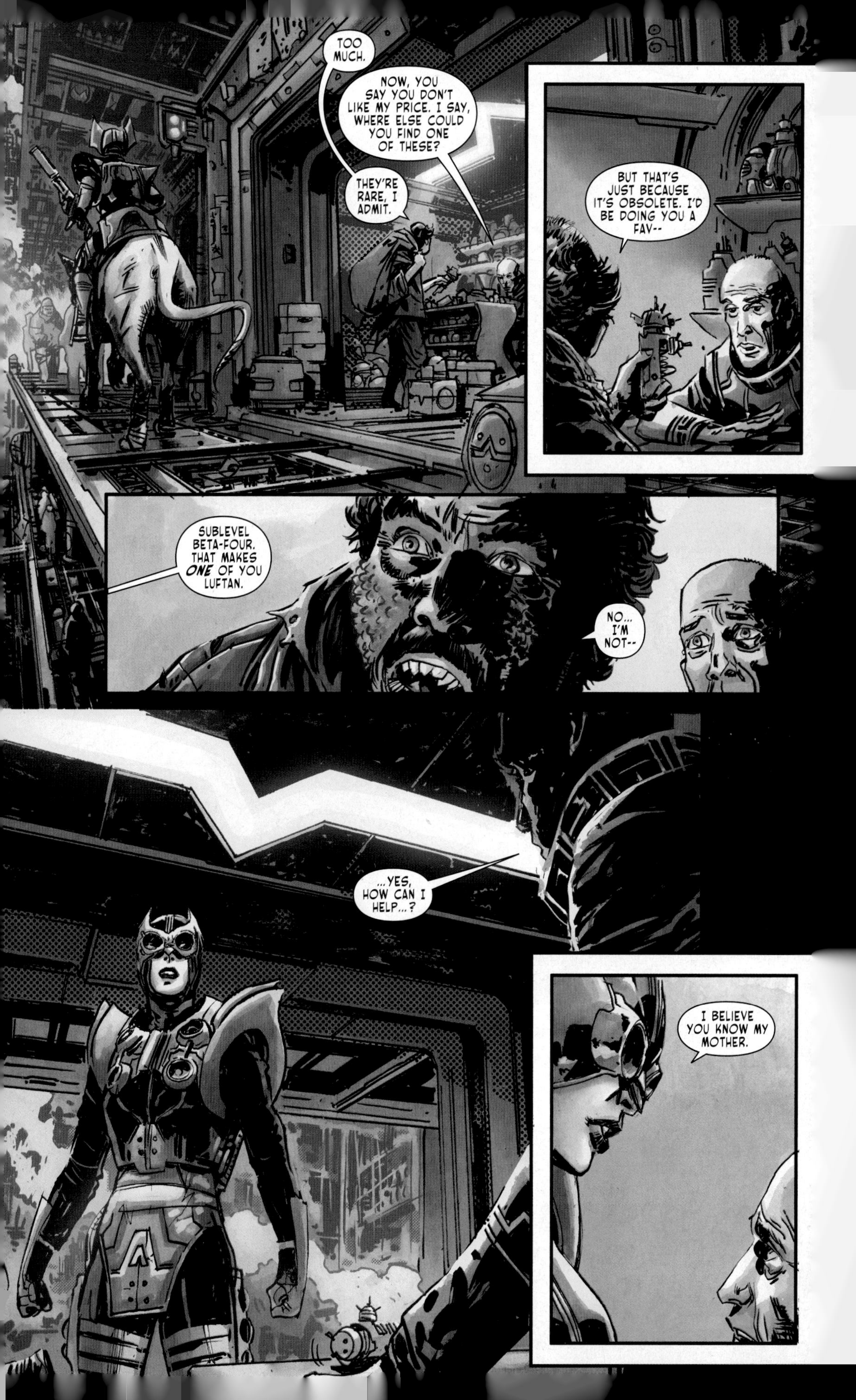
TOO MUCH.
NOW, YOU SAY YOU DON'T LIKE MY PRICE. I SAY, WHERE ELSE COULD YOU FIND ONE OF THESE?
THEY'RE RARE, I ADMIT.
BUT THAT'S JUST BECAUSE IT'S OBSOLETE. I'D BE DOING YOU A FAV--
SUBLEVEL BETA-FOUR. THAT MAKES ONE OF YOU LUFTAN.
NO... I'M NOT--
...YES, HOW CAN I HELP...?
I BELIEVE YOU KNOW MY MOTHER.

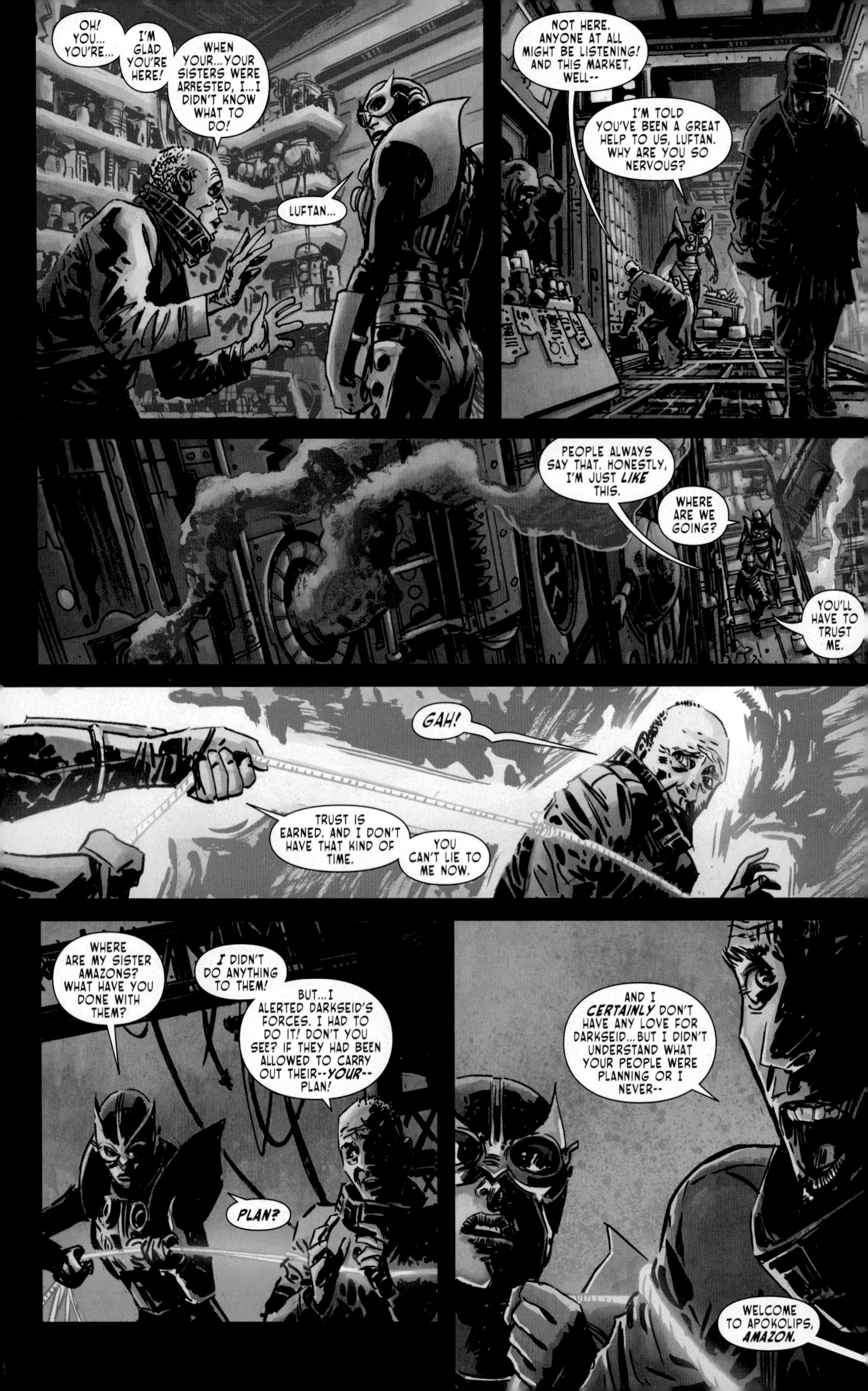
OH! YOU... YOU'RE...
I'M GLAD YOU'RE HERE!
WHEN YOUR...YOUR SISTERS WERE ARRESTED, I...I DIDN'T KNOW WHAT TO DO!
LUFTAN...
NOT HERE. ANYONE AT ALL MIGHT BE LISTENING! AND THIS MARKET, WELL--
I'M TOLD YOU'VE BEEN A GREAT HELP TO US, LUFTAN. WHY ARE YOU SO NERVOUS?
PEOPLE ALWAYS SAY THAT. HONESTLY, I'M JUST LIKE THIS.
WHERE ARE WE GOING?
YOU'LL HAVE TO TRUST ME.
GAH!
TRUST IS EARNED. AND I DON'T HAVE THAT KIND OF TIME.
YOU CAN'T LIE TO ME NOW.
WHERE ARE MY SISTER AMAZONS? WHAT HAVE YOU DONE WITH THEM?
I DIDN'T DO ANYTHING TO THEM!
BUT...I ALERTED DARKSEID'S FORCES. I HAD TO DO IT! DON'T YOU SEE? IF THEY HAD BEEN ALLOWED TO CARRY OUT THEIR--YOUR--PLAN!
PLAN?
AND I CERTAINLY DON'T HAVE ANY LOVE FOR DARKSEID...BUT I DIDN'T UNDERSTAND WHAT YOUR PEOPLE WERE PLANNING OR I NEVER--
WELCOME TO APOKOLIPS, AMAZON.

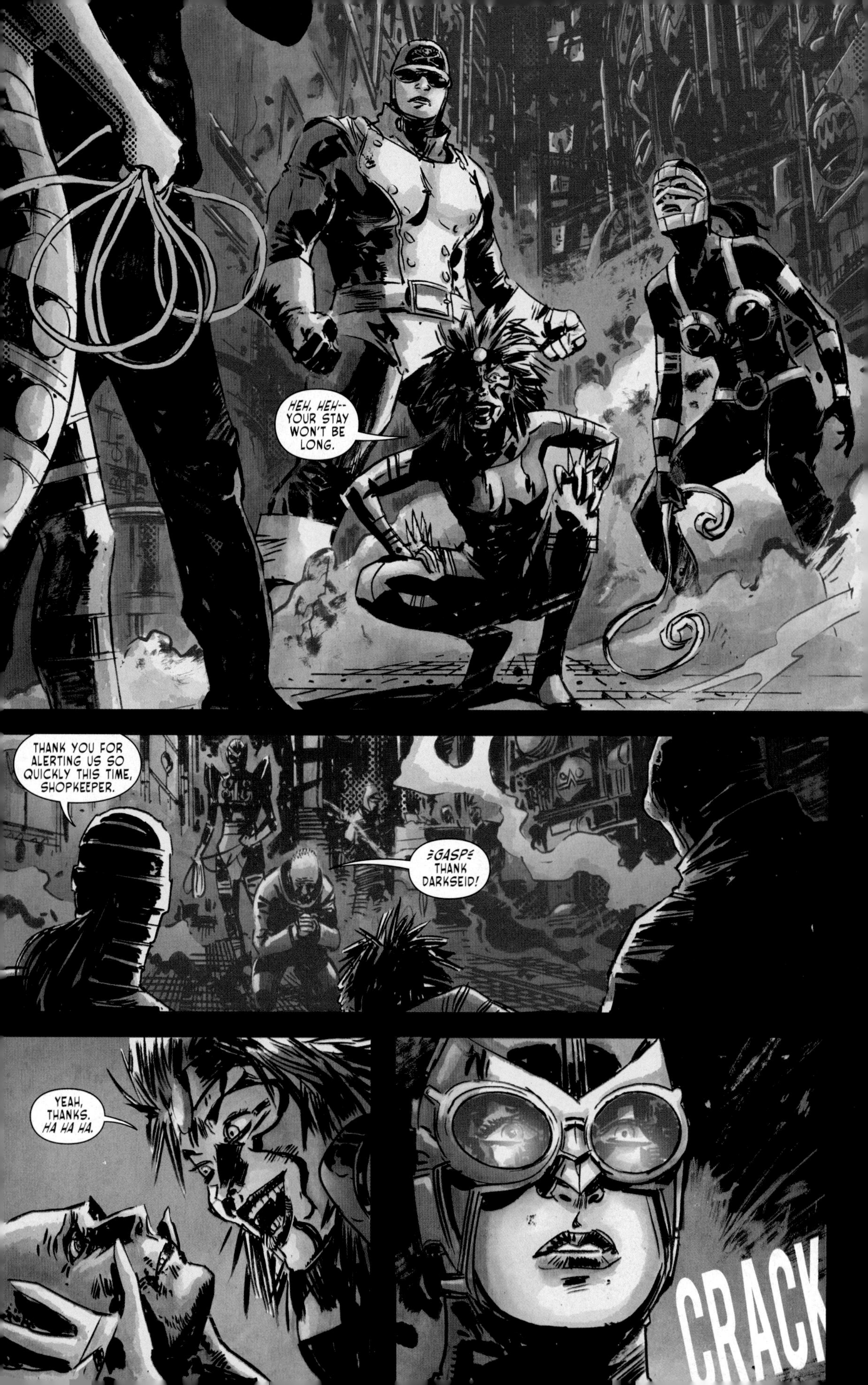
HEH, HEH--
YOUR STAY WON'T BE LONG.
THANK YOU FOR ALERTING US SO QUICKLY THIS TIME, SHOPKEEPER.
≡GASP≡ THANK DARKSEID!
YEAH, THANKS. HA HA HA.
CRACK

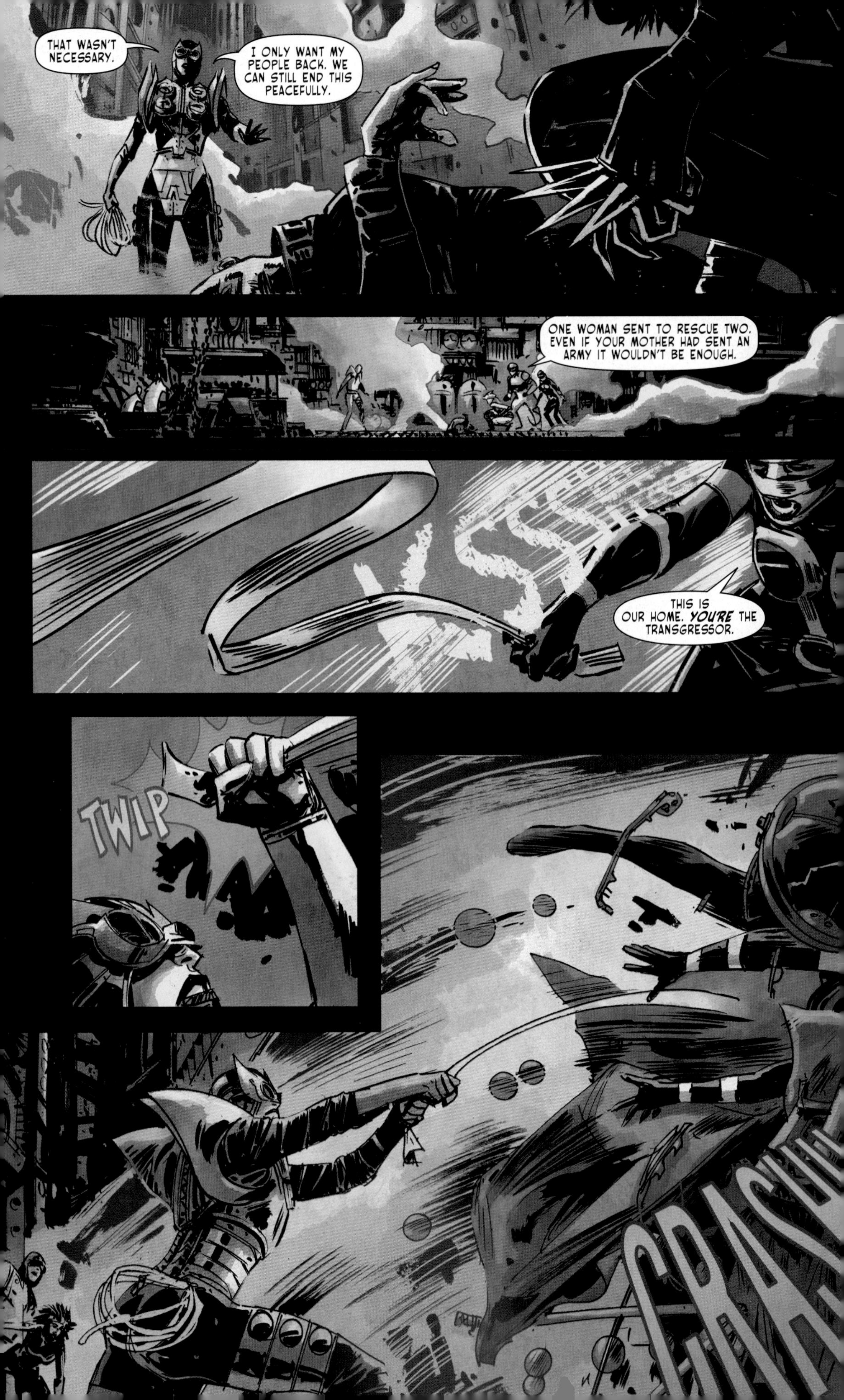
THAT WASN'T NECESSARY.
I ONLY WANT MY PEOPLE BACK. WE CAN STILL END THIS PEACEFULLY.
ONE WOMAN SENT TO RESCUE TWO. EVEN IF YOUR MOTHER HAD SENT AN ARMY IT WOULDN'T BE ENOUGH.
THIS IS OUR HOME. *YOU'RE* THE TRANSGRESSOR.
TWIP

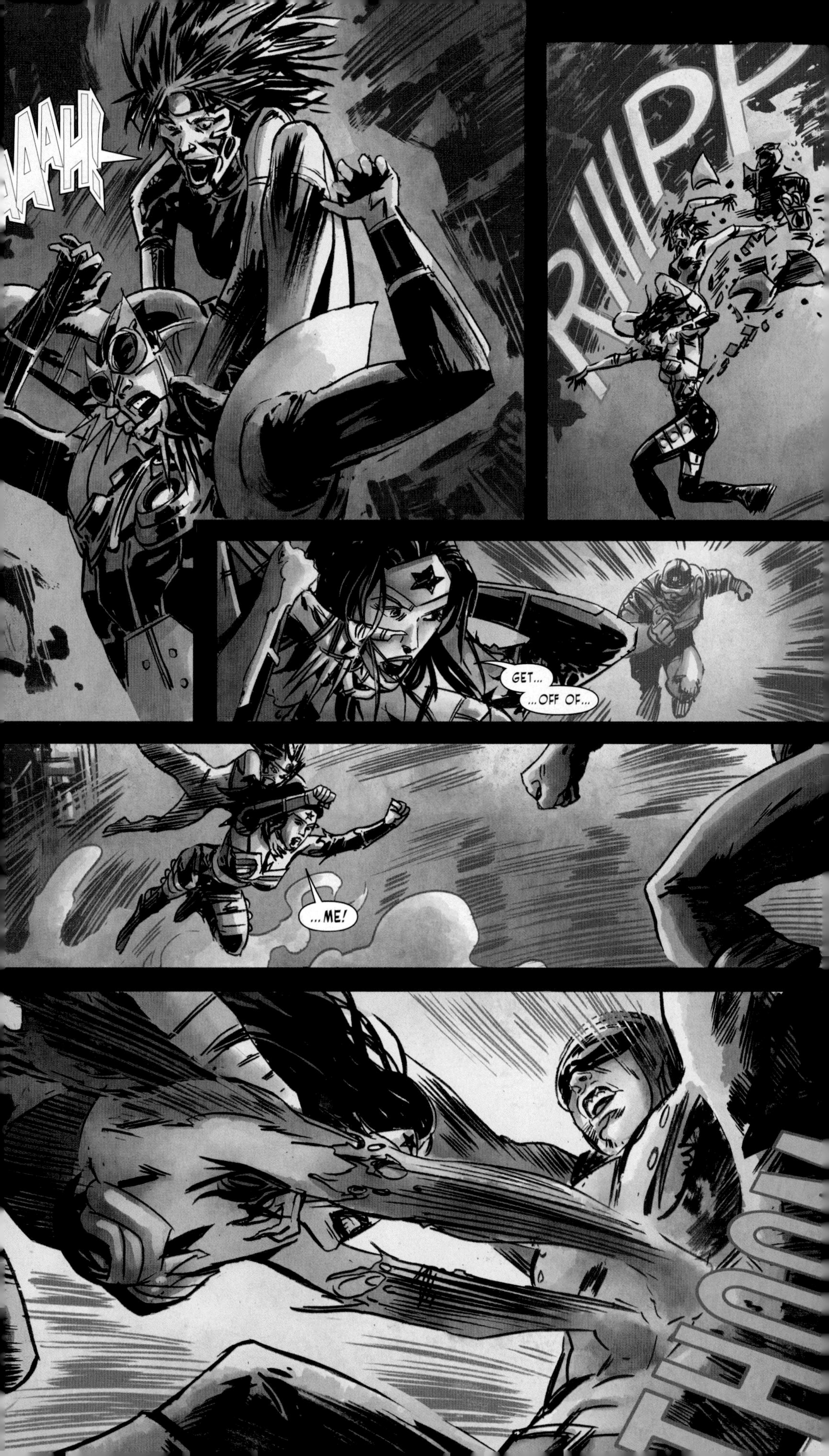
GET...
...OFF OF...
...ME!

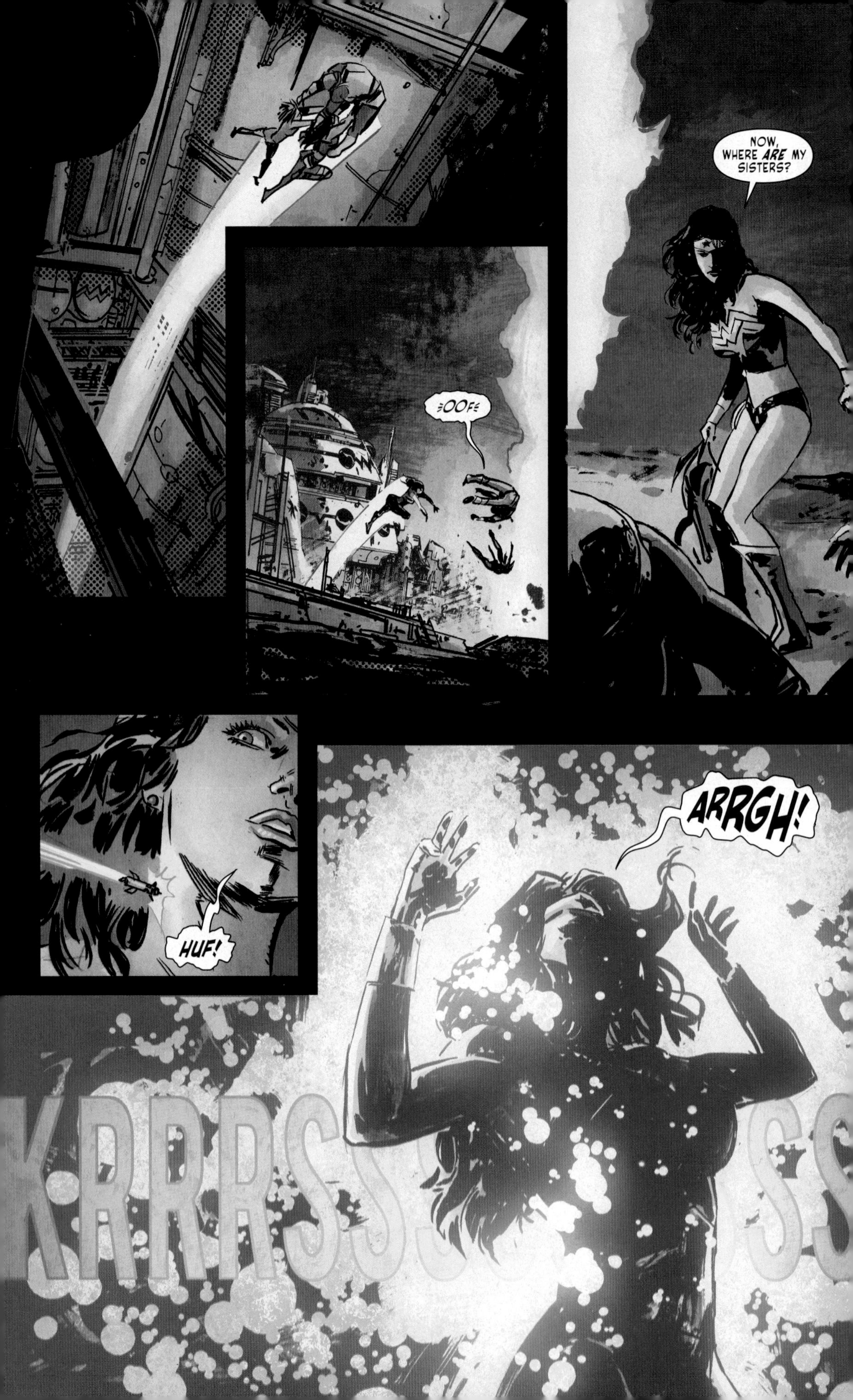

OOF
NOW, WHERE ARE MY SISTERS?
HUF!
ARRGH!
KRRSSSSSS

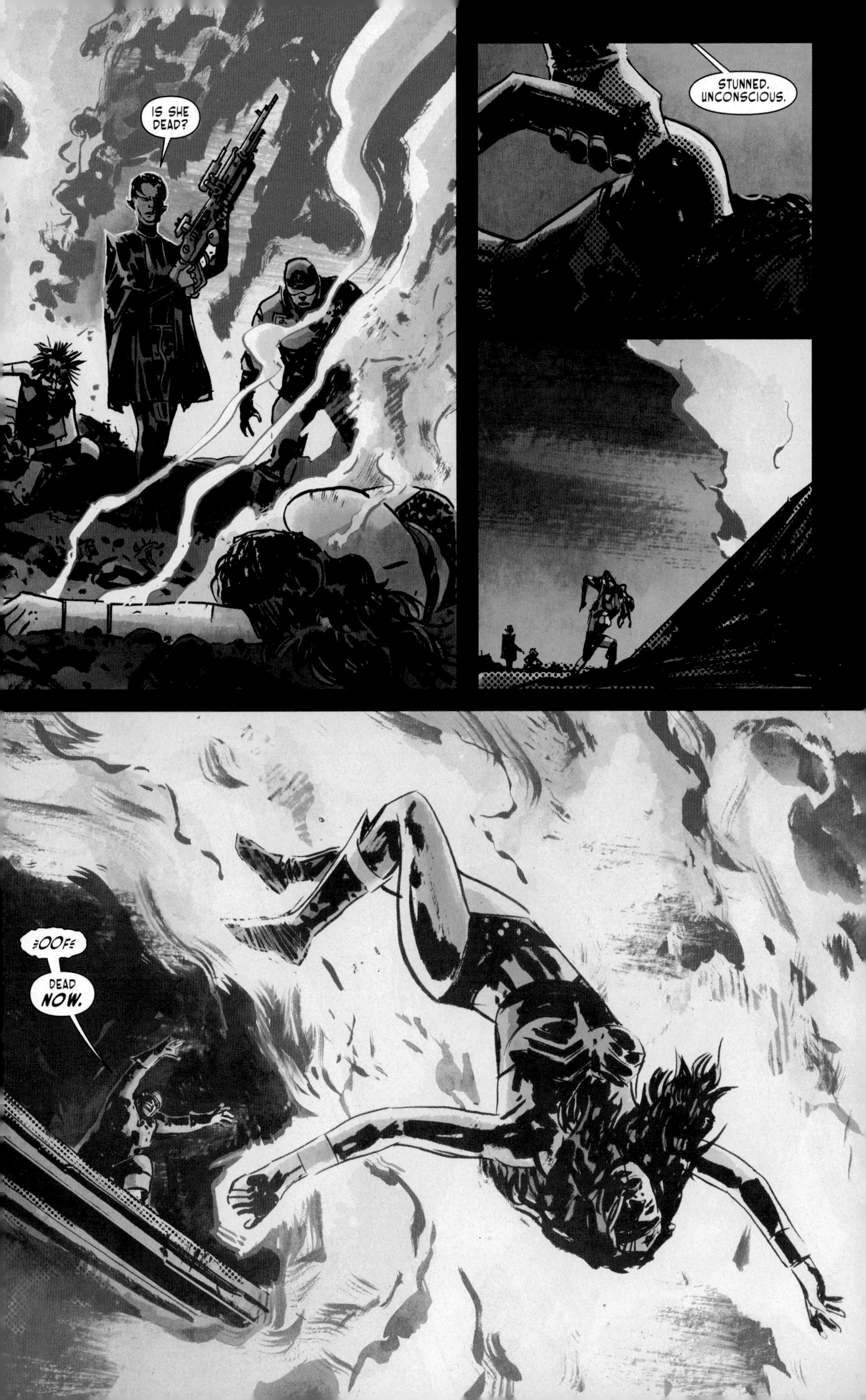
IS SHE DEAD?
STUNNED. UNCONSCIOUS.
OOF
DEAD NOW.

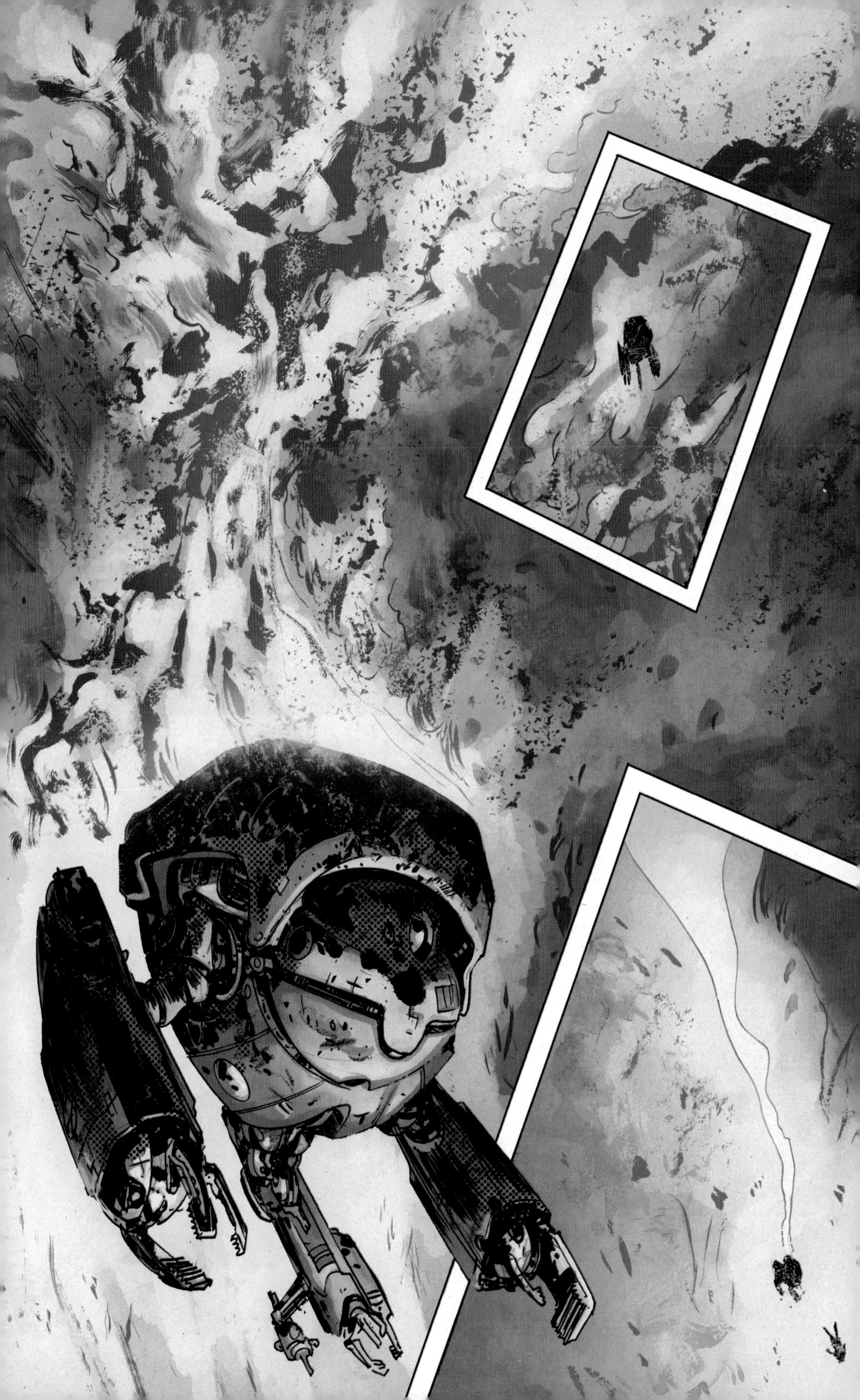

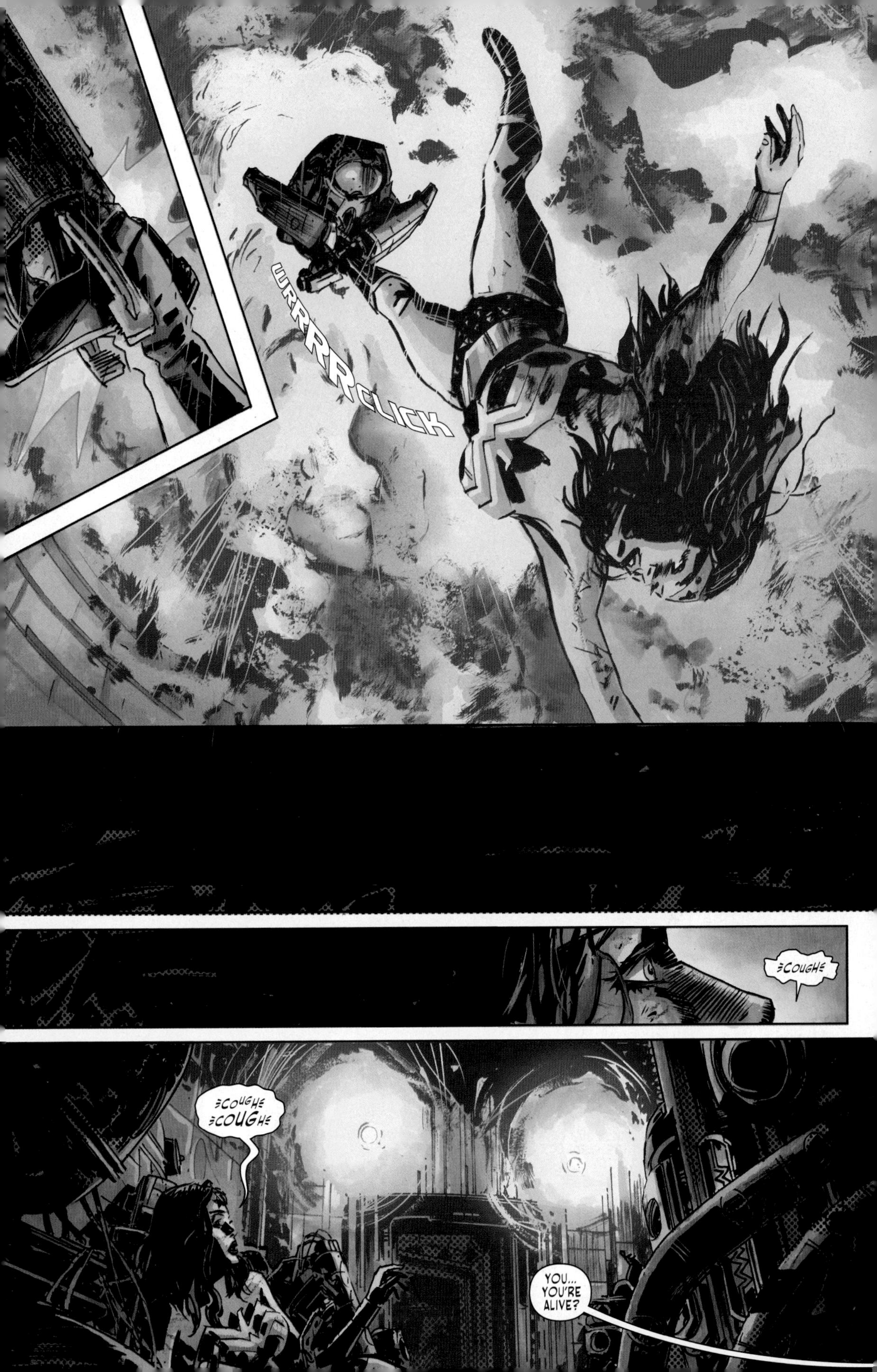
URRRRRCLICK
COUGH
COUGH
COUGH
YOU... YOU'RE ALIVE?

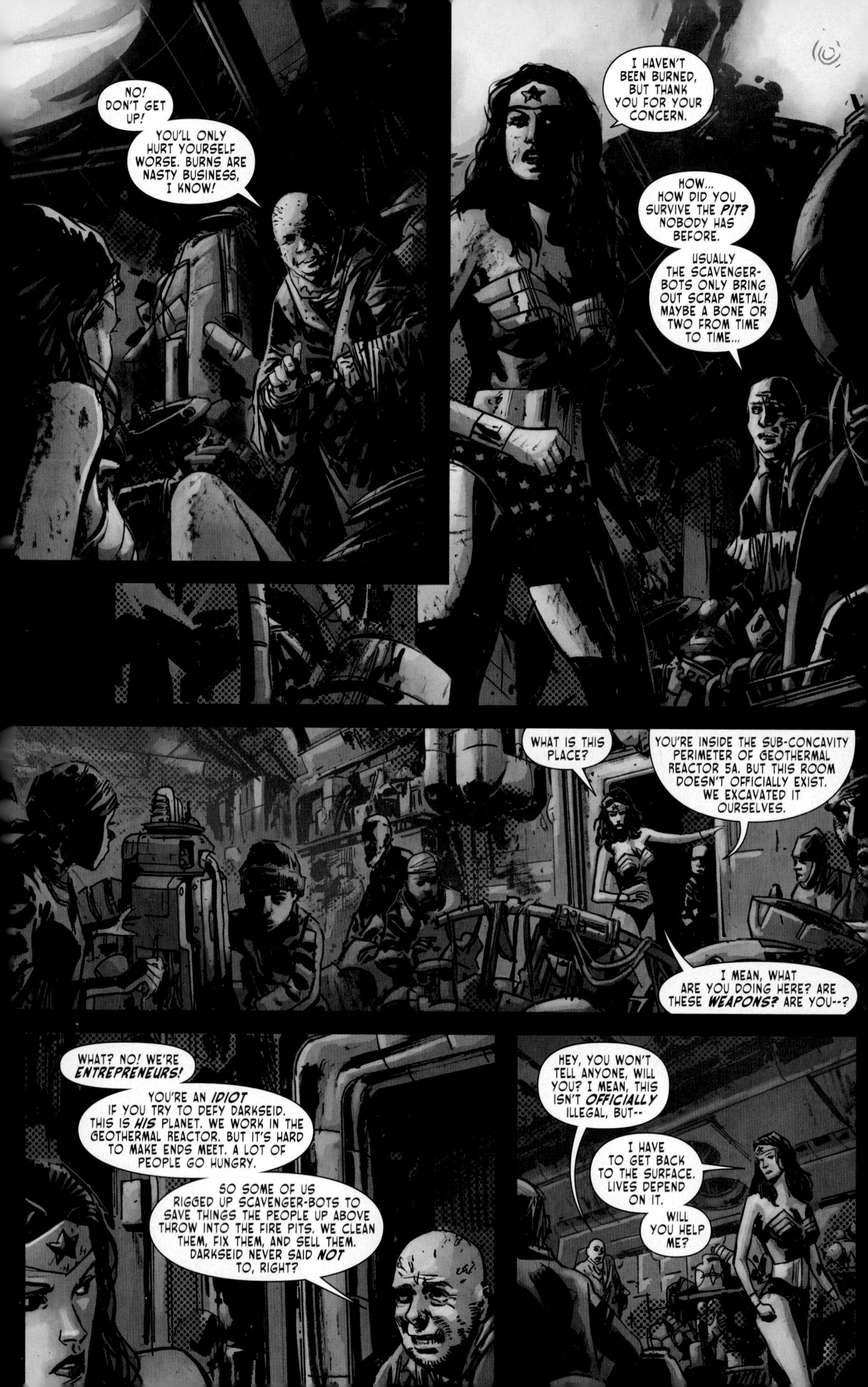
NO! DON'T GET UP!
YOU'LL ONLY HURT YOURSELF WORSE. BURNS ARE NASTY BUSINESS, I KNOW!
I HAVEN'T BEEN BURNED, BUT THANK YOU FOR YOUR CONCERN.
HOW... HOW DID YOU SURVIVE THE *PIT?* NOBODY HAS BEFORE.
USUALLY THE SCAVENGER-BOTS ONLY BRING OUT SCRAP METAL! MAYBE A BONE OR TWO FROM TIME TO TIME...
WHAT IS THIS PLACE?
YOU'RE INSIDE THE SUB-CONCAVITY PERIMETER OF GEOTHERMAL REACTOR 5A. BUT THIS ROOM DOESN'T OFFICIALLY EXIST. WE EXCAVATED IT OURSELVES.
I MEAN, WHAT ARE YOU DOING HERE? ARE THESE ***WEAPONS?*** ARE YOU--?
WHAT? NO! WE'RE ***ENTREPRENEURS!***
YOU'RE AN *IDIOT* IF YOU TRY TO DEFY DARKSEID. THIS IS *HIS* PLANET. WE WORK IN THE GEOTHERMAL REACTOR. BUT IT'S HARD TO MAKE ENDS MEET. A LOT OF PEOPLE GO HUNGRY.
SO SOME OF US RIGGED UP SCAVENGER-BOTS TO SAVE THINGS THE PEOPLE UP ABOVE THROW INTO THE FIRE PITS. WE CLEAN THEM, FIX THEM, AND SELL THEM. DARKSEID NEVER SAID *NOT* TO, RIGHT?
HEY, YOU WON'T TELL ANYONE, WILL YOU? I MEAN, THIS ISN'T *OFFICIALLY* ILLEGAL, BUT--
I HAVE TO GET BACK TO THE SURFACE. LIVES DEPEND ON IT.
WILL YOU HELP ME?

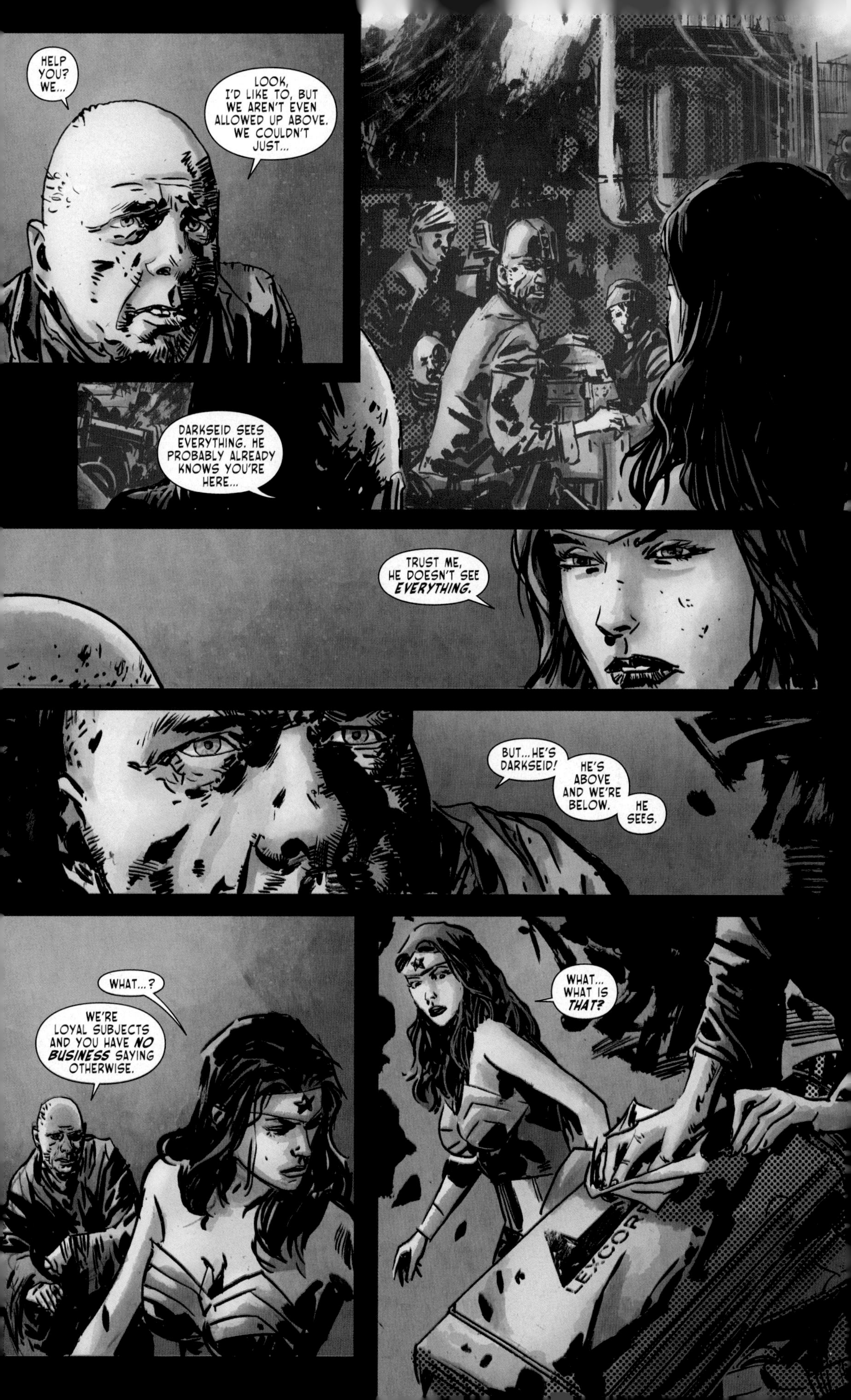
HELP YOU? WE...
LOOK, I'D LIKE TO, BUT WE AREN'T EVEN ALLOWED UP ABOVE. WE COULDN'T JUST...
DARKSEID SEES EVERYTHING. HE PROBABLY ALREADY KNOWS YOU'RE HERE...
TRUST ME, HE DOESN'T SEE *EVERYTHING.*
BUT...HE'S DARKSEID!
HE'S ABOVE AND WE'RE BELOW.
HE SEES.
WHAT...?
WE'RE LOYAL SUBJECTS AND YOU HAVE *NO BUSINESS* SAYING OTHERWISE.
WHAT... WHAT IS *THAT?*
LEXCOR

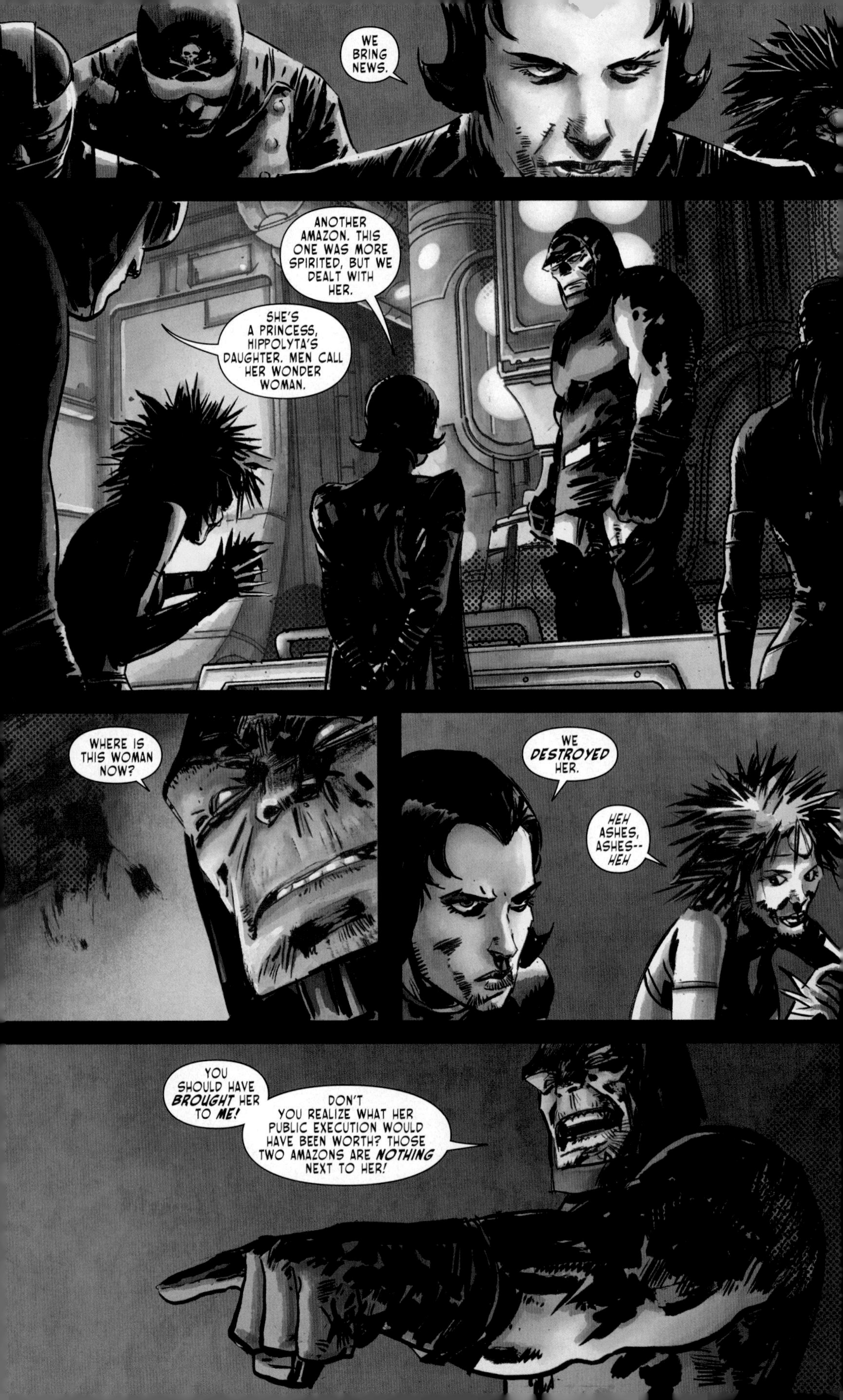
WE BRING NEWS.
ANOTHER AMAZON. THIS ONE WAS MORE SPIRITED, BUT WE DEALT WITH HER.
SHE'S A PRINCESS, HIPPOLYTA'S DAUGHTER. MEN CALL HER WONDER WOMAN.
WHERE IS THIS WOMAN NOW?
WE *DESTROYED* HER.
HEH ASHES, ASHES-- *HEH*
YOU SHOULD HAVE ***BROUGHT*** HER TO ***ME!***
DON'T YOU REALIZE WHAT HER PUBLIC EXECUTION WOULD HAVE BEEN WORTH? THOSE TWO AMAZONS ARE ***NOTHING*** NEXT TO HER!

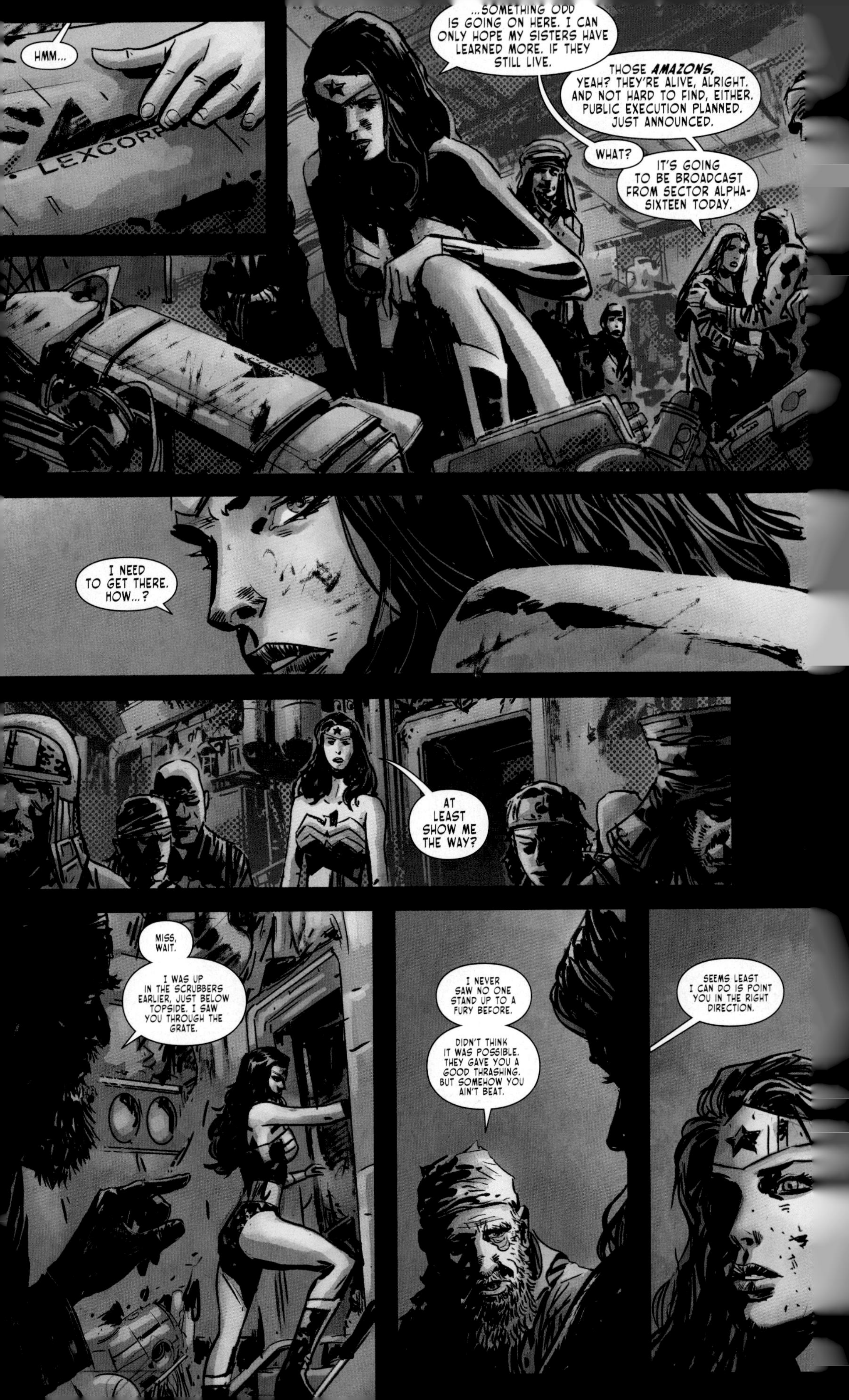
HMM...
...SOMETHING ODD IS GOING ON HERE. I CAN ONLY HOPE MY SISTERS HAVE LEARNED MORE. IF THEY STILL LIVE.
THOSE AMAZONS, YEAH? THEY'RE ALIVE, ALRIGHT. AND NOT HARD TO FIND, EITHER. PUBLIC EXECUTION PLANNED. JUST ANNOUNCED.
WHAT?
IT'S GOING TO BE BROADCAST FROM SECTOR ALPHA-SIXTEEN TODAY.
I NEED TO GET THERE. HOW...?
AT LEAST SHOW ME THE WAY?
MISS, WAIT.
I WAS UP IN THE SCRUBBERS EARLIER, JUST BELOW TOPSIDE. I SAW YOU THROUGH THE GRATE.
I NEVER SAW NO ONE STAND UP TO A FURY BEFORE.
DIDN'T THINK IT WAS POSSIBLE. THEY GAVE YOU A GOOD THRASHING. BUT SOMEHOW YOU AIN'T BEAT.
SEEMS LEAST I CAN DO IS POINT YOU IN THE RIGHT DIRECTION.

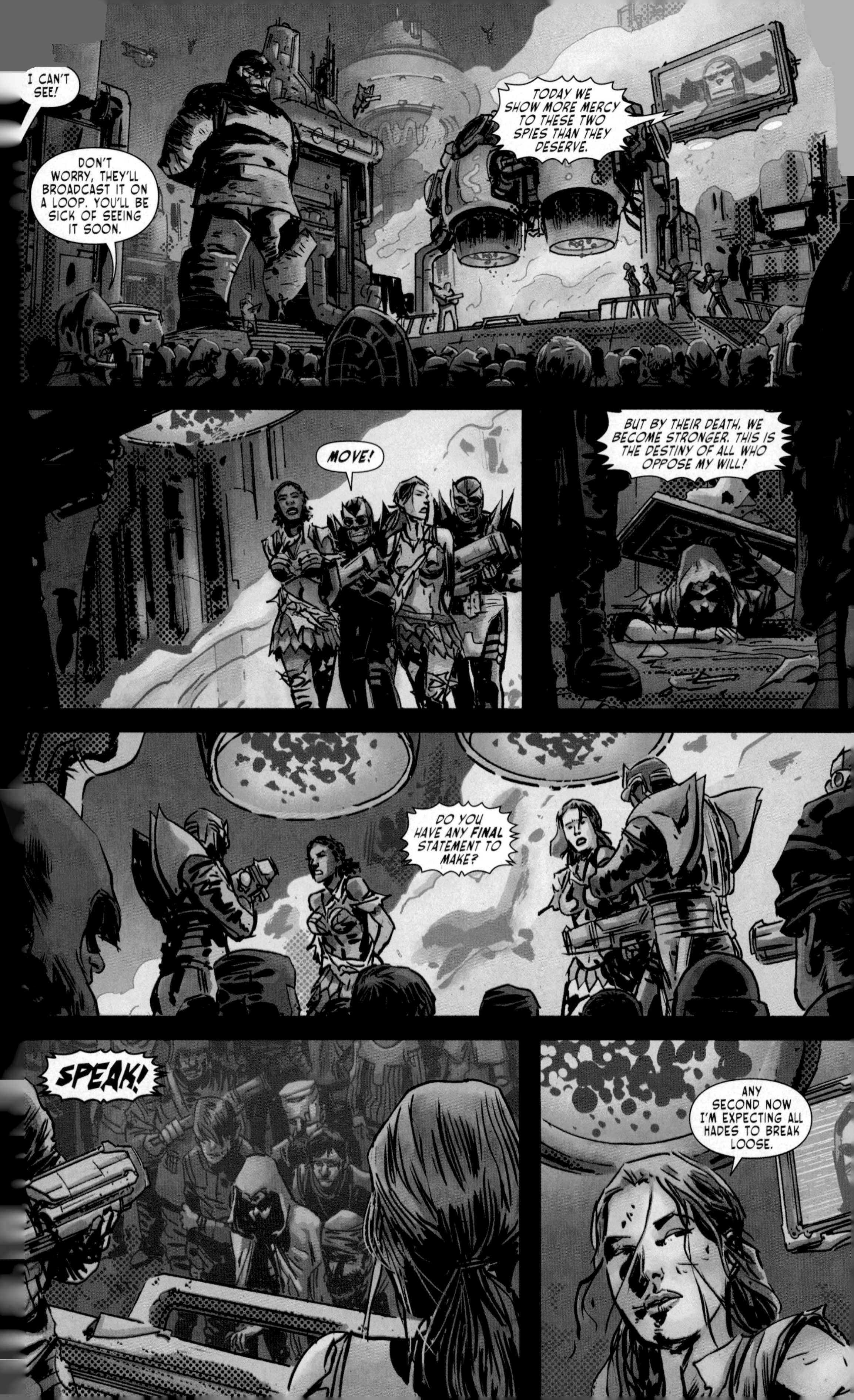
I CAN'T SEE!
DON'T WORRY, THEY'LL BROADCAST IT ON A LOOP. YOU'LL BE SICK OF SEEING IT SOON.
TODAY WE SHOW MORE MERCY TO THESE TWO SPIES THAN THEY DESERVE.
MOVE!
BUT BY THEIR DEATH, WE BECOME STRONGER. THIS IS THE DESTINY OF ALL WHO OPPOSE MY WILL!
DO YOU HAVE ANY FINAL STATEMENT TO MAKE?
SPEAK!
ANY SECOND NOW I'M EXPECTING ALL HADES TO BREAK LOOSE.

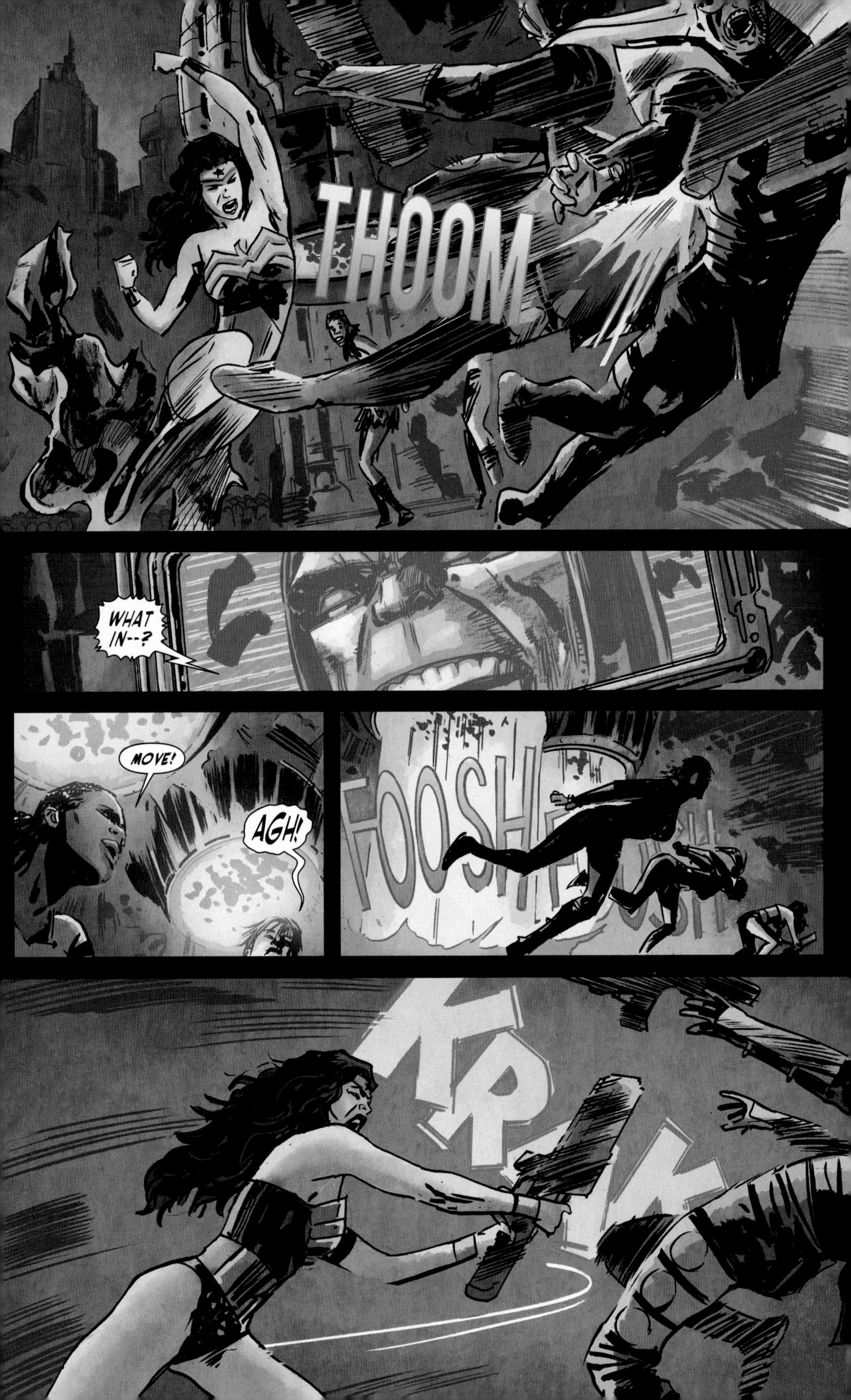
THOOM
WHAT IN--?
MOVE!
AGH!
FOOSH
KRAK

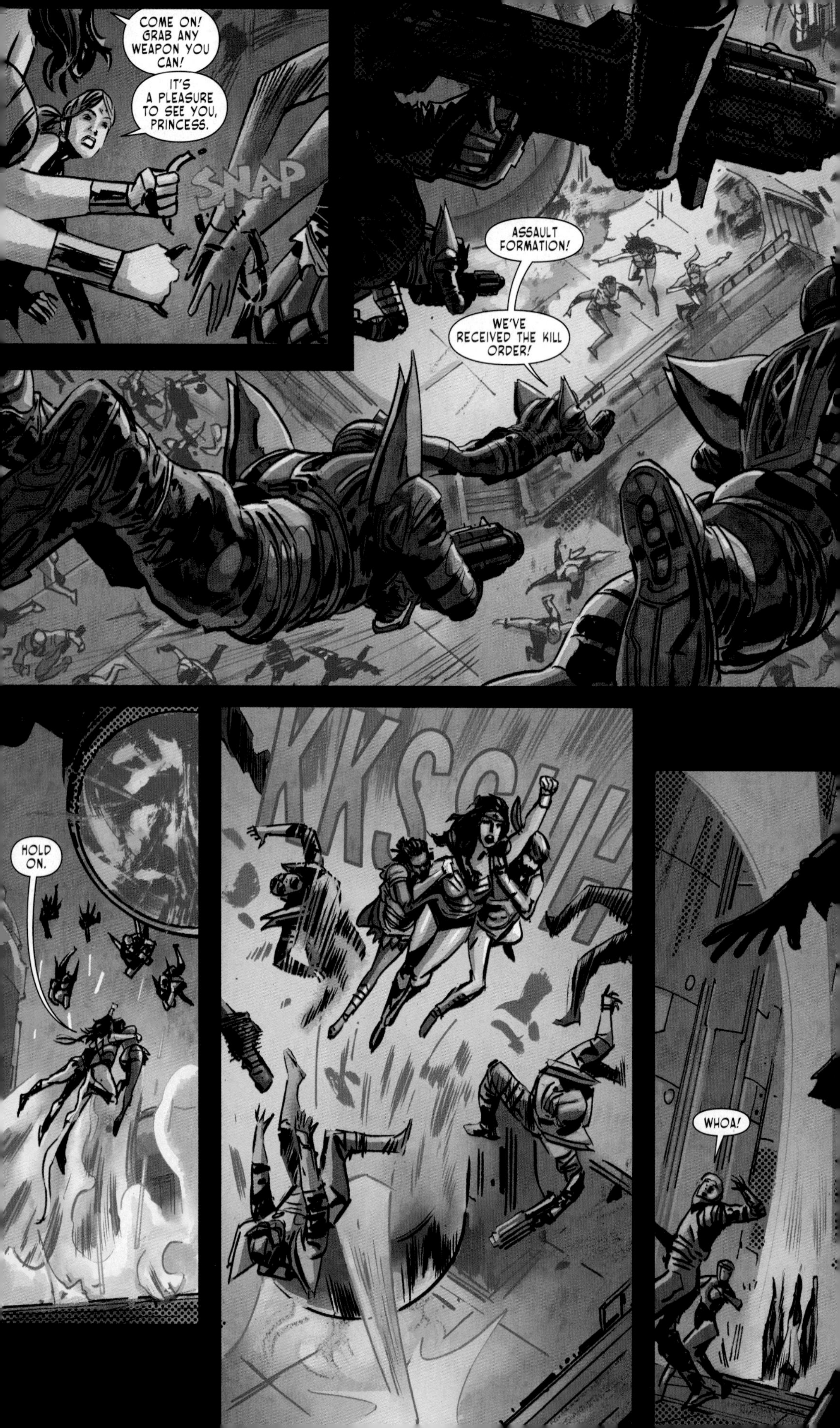
COME ON! GRAB ANY WEAPON YOU CAN!
IT'S A PLEASURE TO SEE YOU, PRINCESS.
SNAP
ASSAULT FORMATION!
WE'VE RECEIVED THE KILL ORDER!
HOLD ON.
KKSCHH
WHOA!

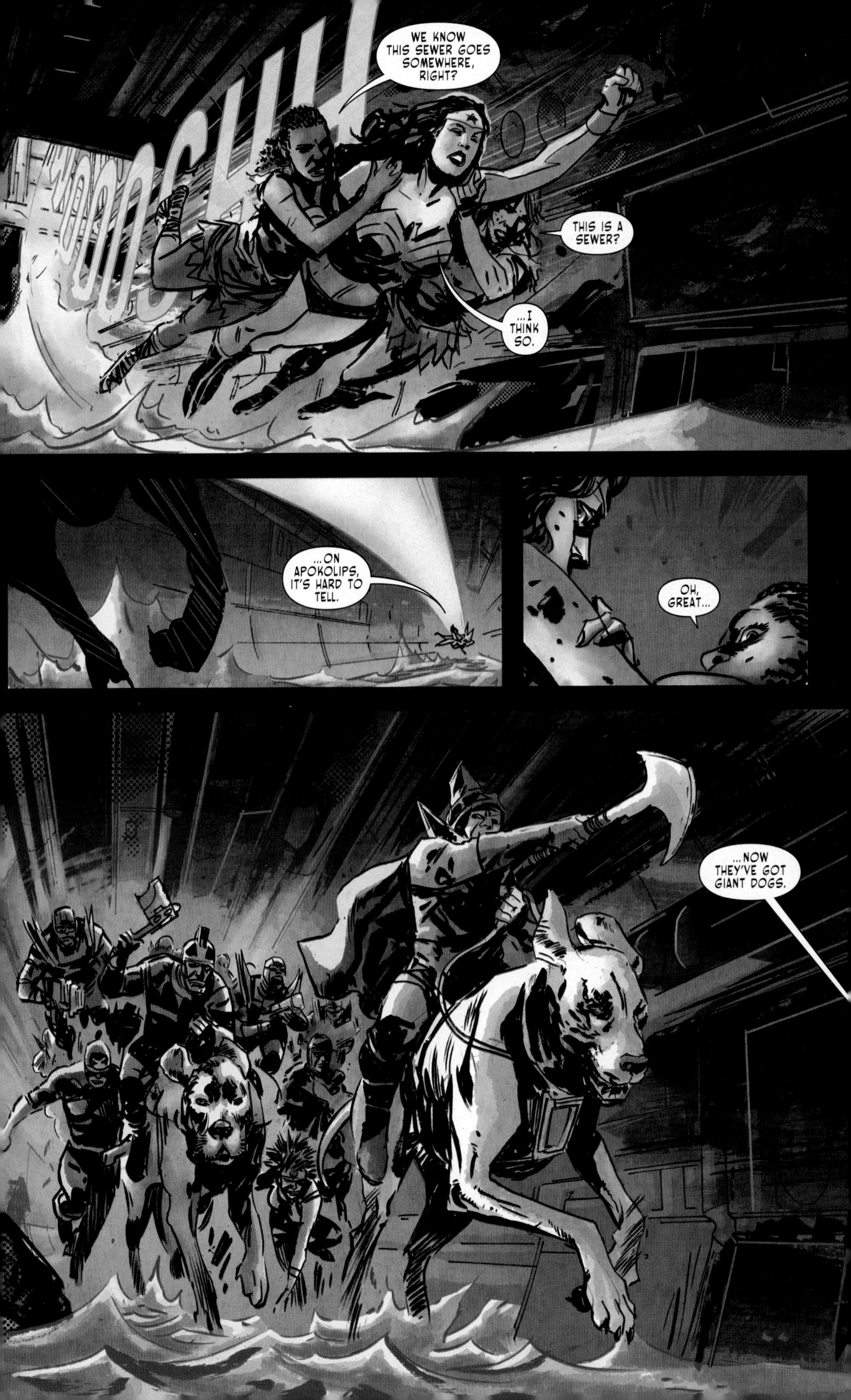
WE KNOW THIS SEWER GOES SOMEWHERE, RIGHT?
THIS IS A SEWER?
...I THINK SO.
...ON APOKOLIPS, IT'S HARD TO TELL.
OH, GREAT...
...NOW THEY'VE GOT GIANT DOGS.

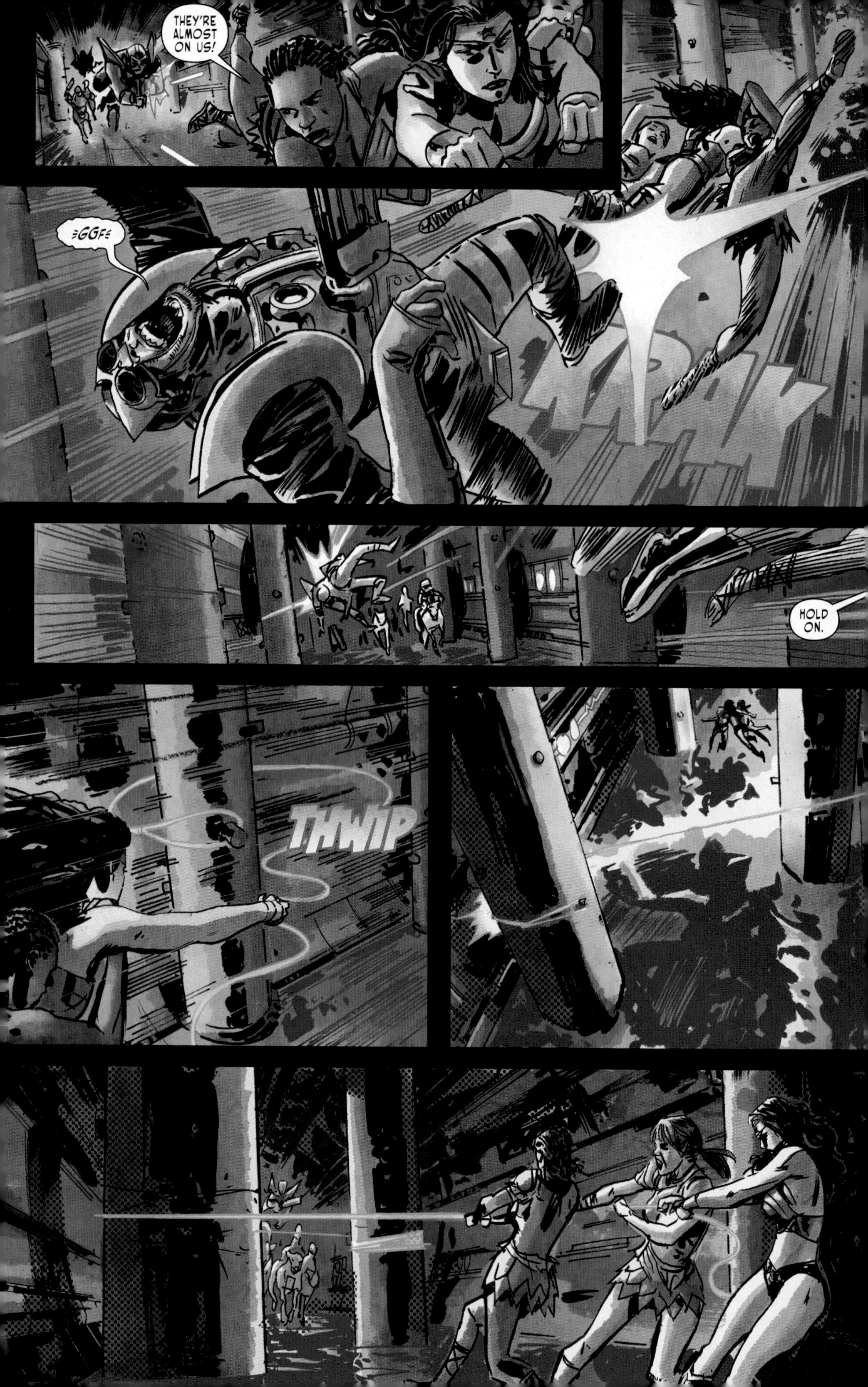
THEY'RE ALMOST ON US!
GGF
KRAK
HOLD ON.
THWIP

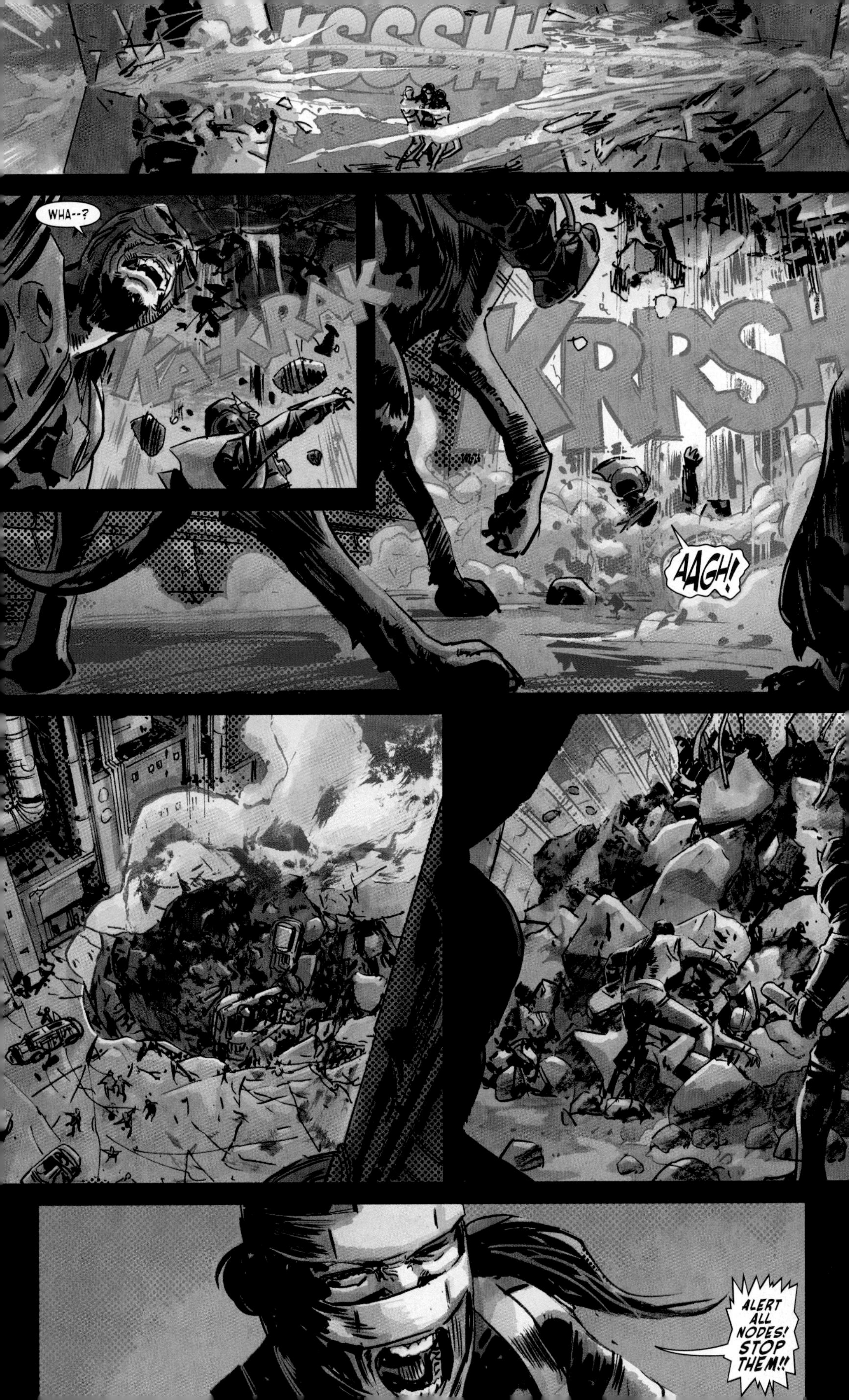
KSSSHH
WHA--?
KAKRAK
KRRSH
AAGH!
ALERT ALL NODES! STOP THEM!!

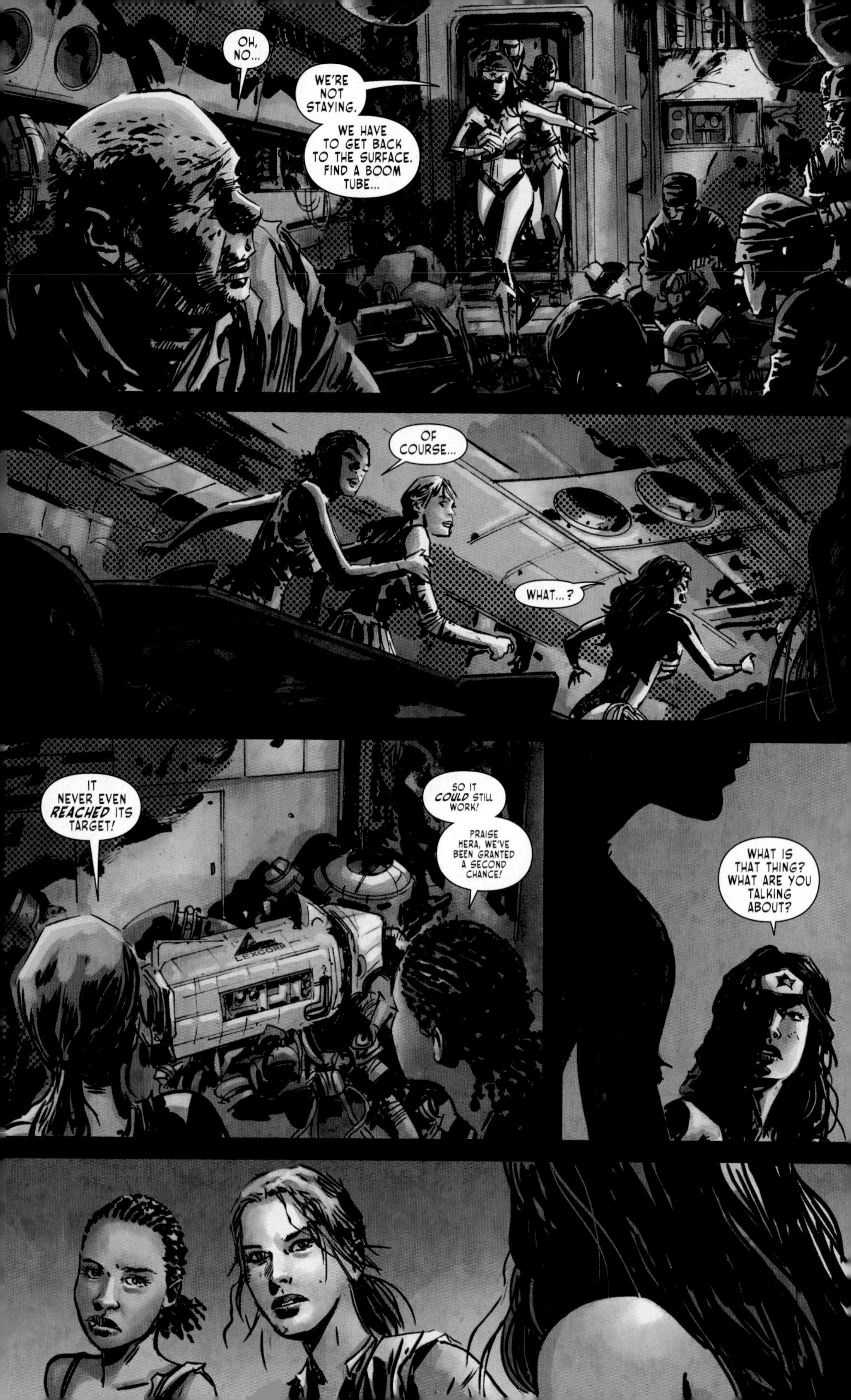
OH, NO...
WE'RE NOT STAYING.
WE HAVE TO GET BACK TO THE SURFACE. FIND A BOOM TUBE...
OF COURSE...
WHAT...?
IT NEVER EVEN REACHED ITS TARGET!
SO IT COULD STILL WORK!
PRAISE HERA, WE'VE BEEN GRANTED A SECOND CHANCE!
WHAT IS THAT THING? WHAT ARE YOU TALKING ABOUT?
LEXCORP

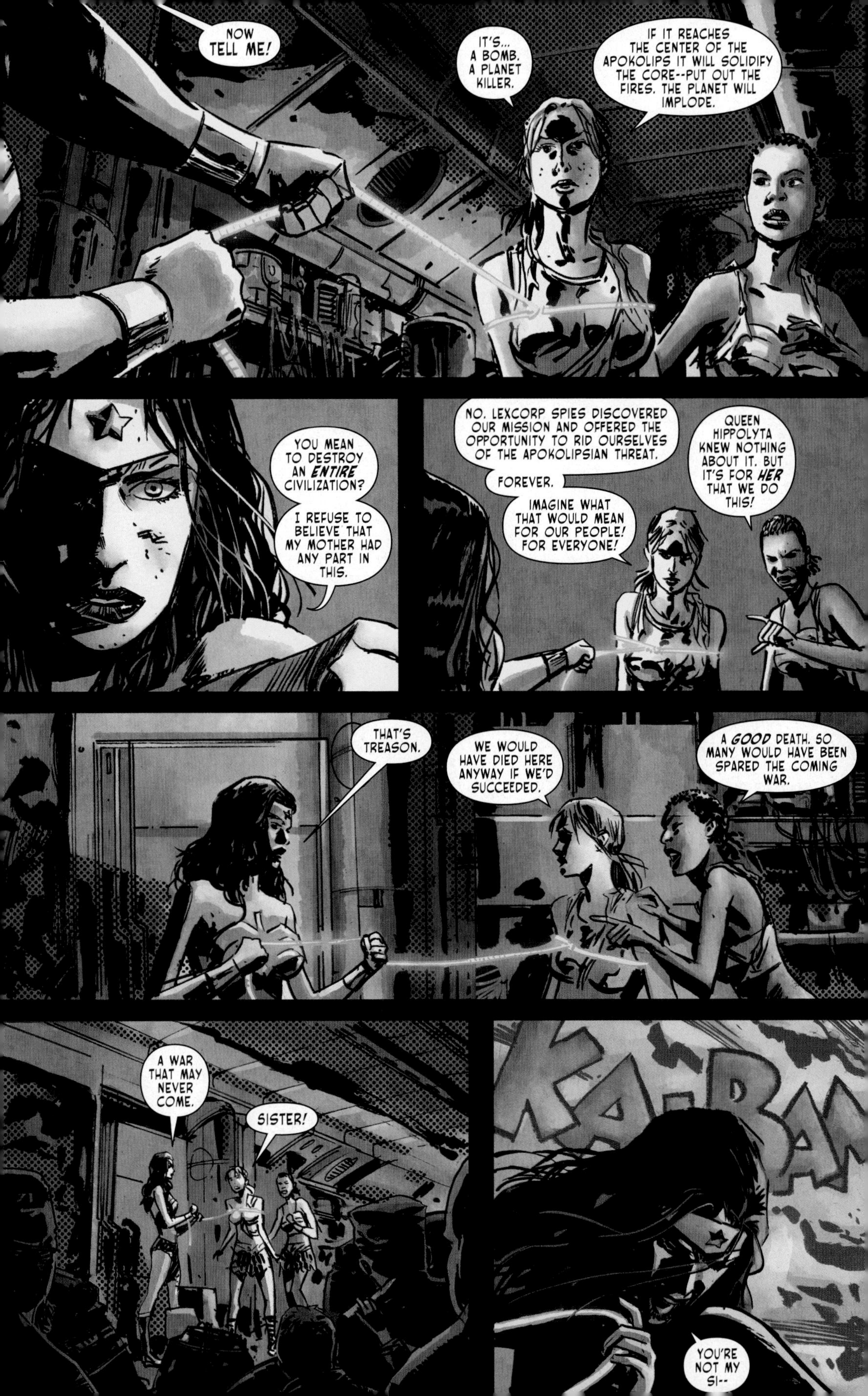
NOW TELL ME!
IT'S... A BOMB. A PLANET KILLER.
IF IT REACHES THE CENTER OF THE APOKOLIPS IT WILL SOLIDIFY THE CORE--PUT OUT THE FIRES. THE PLANET WILL IMPLODE.
YOU MEAN TO DESTROY AN ENTIRE CIVILIZATION?
I REFUSE TO BELIEVE THAT MY MOTHER HAD ANY PART IN THIS.
NO. LEXCORP SPIES DISCOVERED OUR MISSION AND OFFERED THE OPPORTUNITY TO RID OURSELVES OF THE APOKOLIPSIAN THREAT.
FOREVER.
IMAGINE WHAT THAT WOULD MEAN FOR OUR PEOPLE! FOR EVERYONE!
QUEEN HIPPOLYTA KNEW NOTHING ABOUT IT. BUT IT'S FOR HER THAT WE DO THIS!
THAT'S TREASON.
WE WOULD HAVE DIED HERE ANYWAY IF WE'D SUCCEEDED.
A GOOD DEATH. SO MANY WOULD HAVE BEEN SPARED THE COMING WAR.
A WAR THAT MAY NEVER COME.
SISTER!
KA-BA
YOU'RE NOT MY SI--

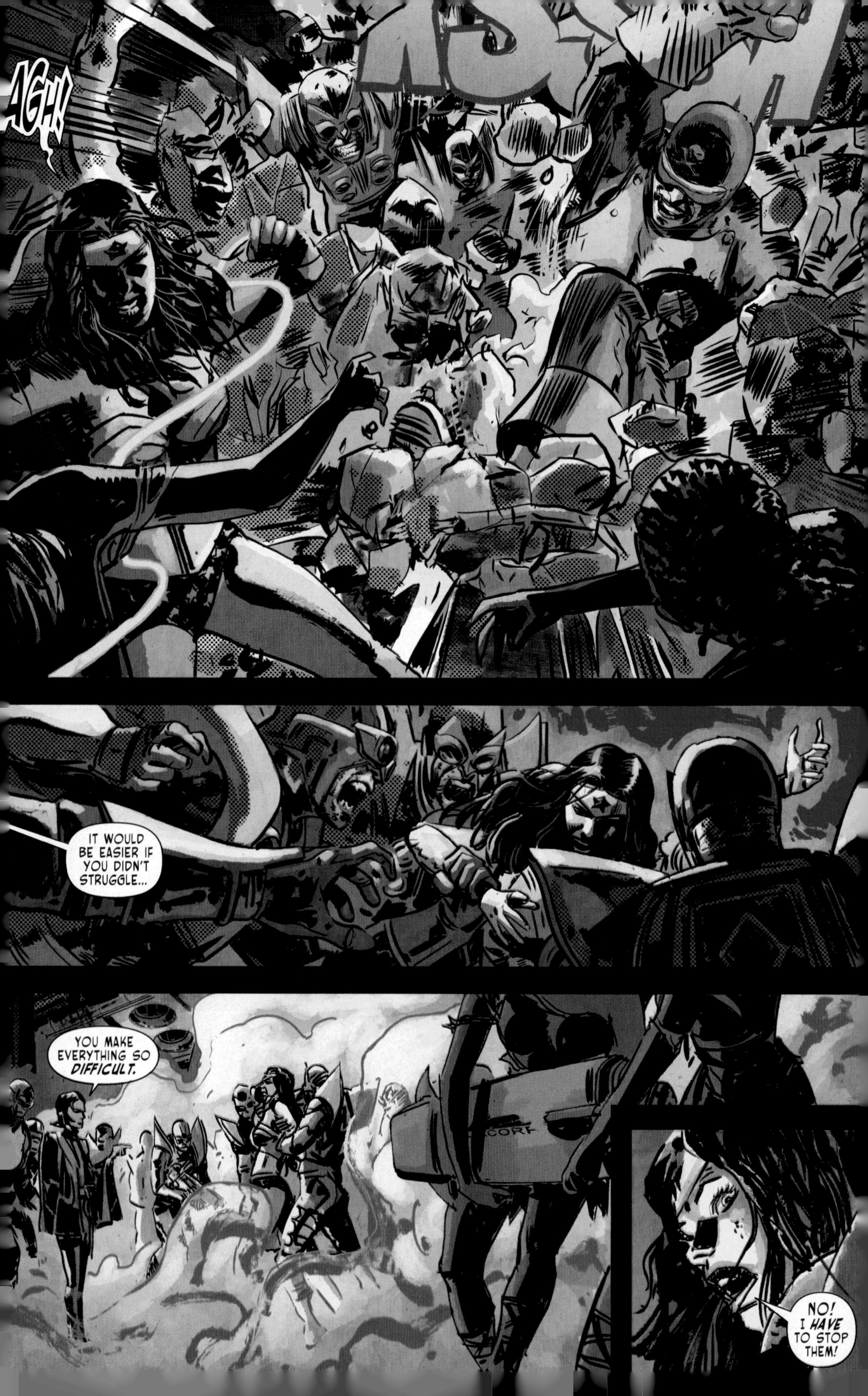
AGH!
IT WOULD BE EASIER IF YOU DIDN'T STRUGGLE...
YOU MAKE EVERYTHING SO *DIFFICULT*.
NO! I *HAVE* TO STOP THEM!

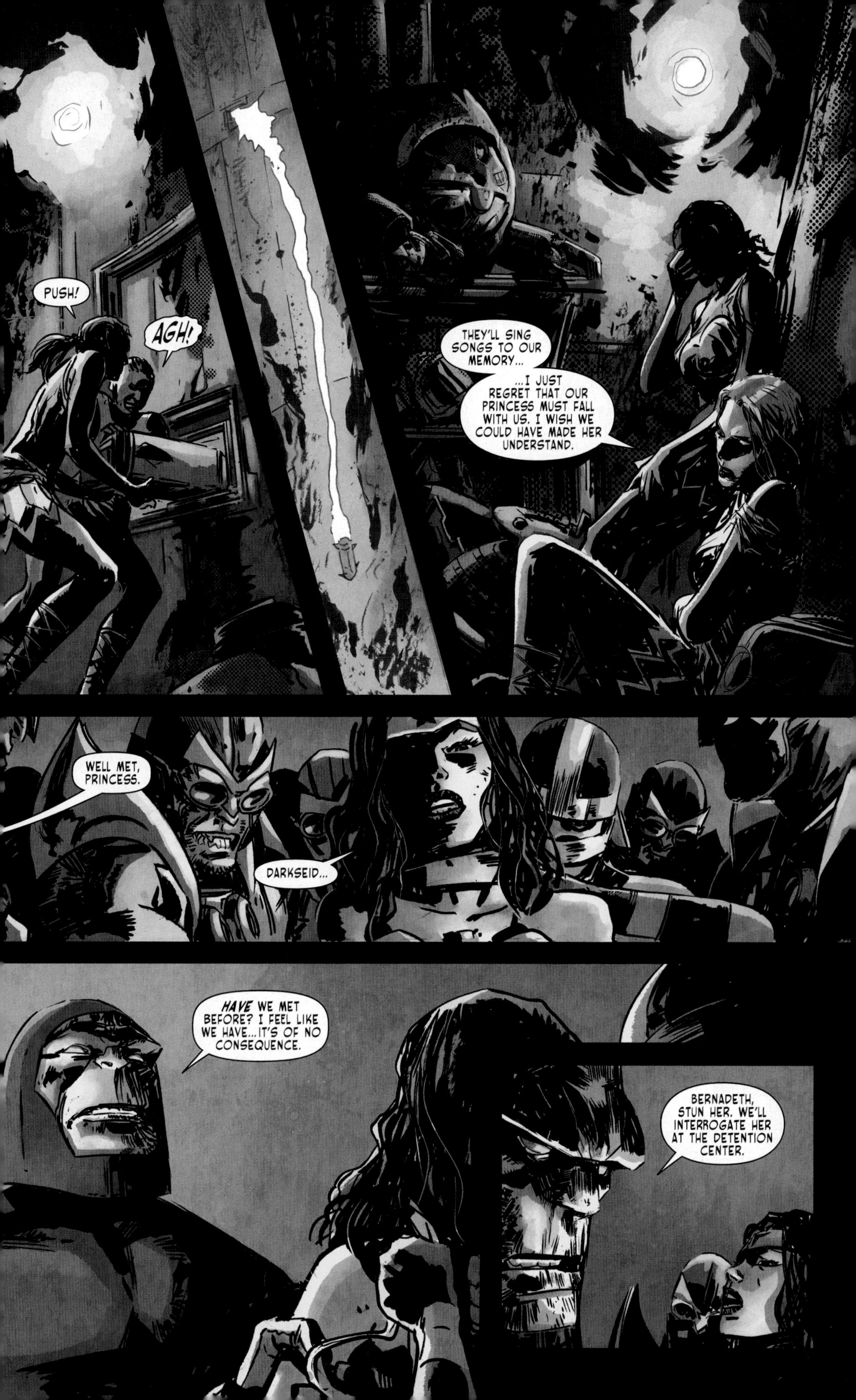
PUSH!
AGH!
THEY'LL SING SONGS TO OUR MEMORY...
...I JUST REGRET THAT OUR PRINCESS MUST FALL WITH US. I WISH WE COULD HAVE MADE HER UNDERSTAND.
WELL MET, PRINCESS.
DARKSEID...
HAVE WE MET BEFORE? I FEEL LIKE WE HAVE...IT'S OF NO CONSEQUENCE.
BERNADETH, STUN HER. WE'LL INTERROGATE HER AT THE DETENTION CENTER.

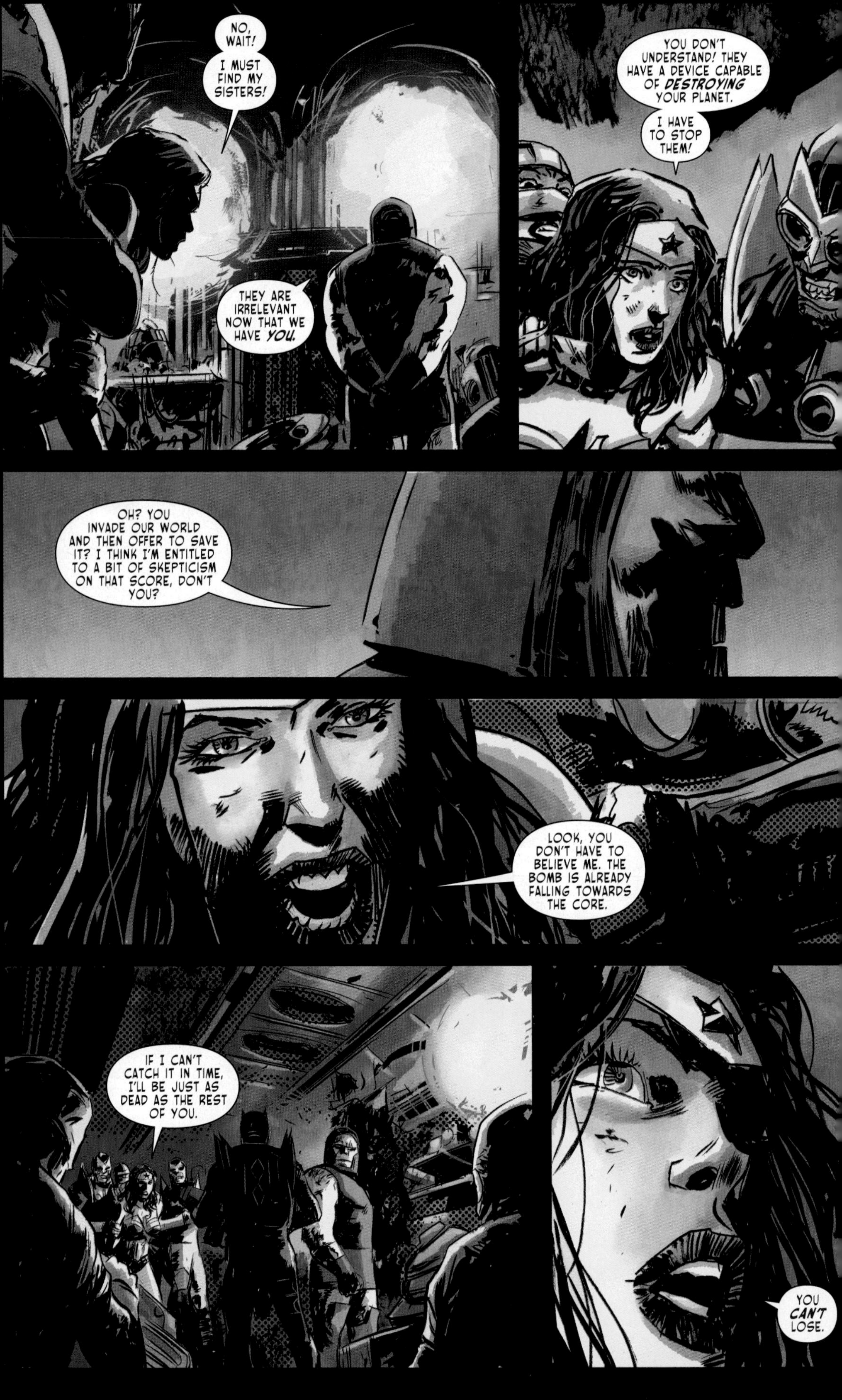
NO, WAIT!
I MUST FIND MY SISTERS!
THEY ARE IRRELEVANT NOW THAT WE HAVE YOU.
YOU DON'T UNDERSTAND! THEY HAVE A DEVICE CAPABLE OF DESTROYING YOUR PLANET.
I HAVE TO STOP THEM!
OH? YOU INVADE OUR WORLD AND THEN OFFER TO SAVE IT? I THINK I'M ENTITLED TO A BIT OF SKEPTICISM ON THAT SCORE, DON'T YOU?
LOOK, YOU DON'T HAVE TO BELIEVE ME. THE BOMB IS ALREADY FALLING TOWARDS THE CORE.
IF I CAN'T CATCH IT IN TIME, I'LL BE JUST AS DEAD AS THE REST OF YOU.
YOU CAN'T LOSE.

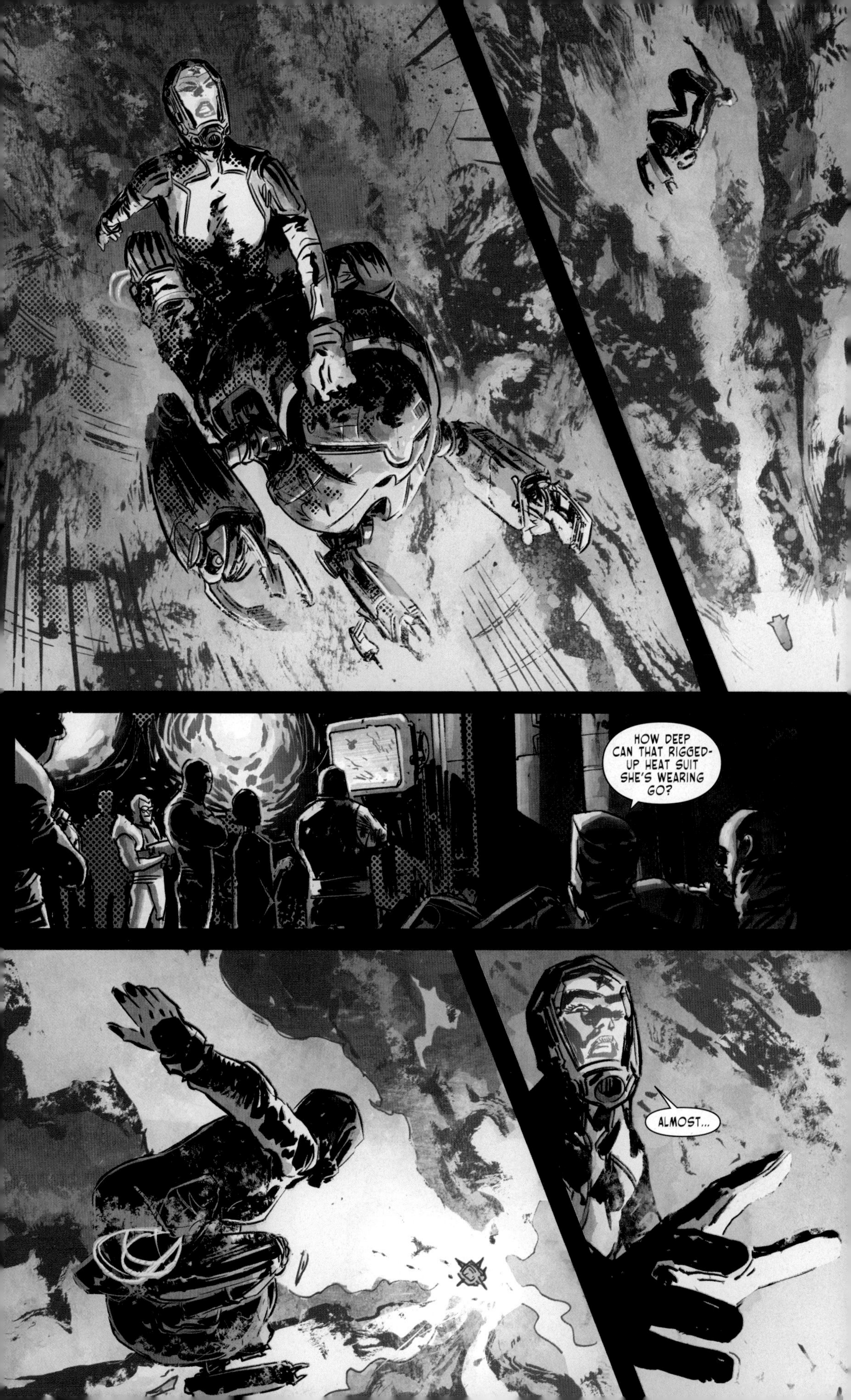
HOW DEEP CAN THAT RIGGED-UP HEAT SUIT SHE'S WEARING GO?
ALMOST...

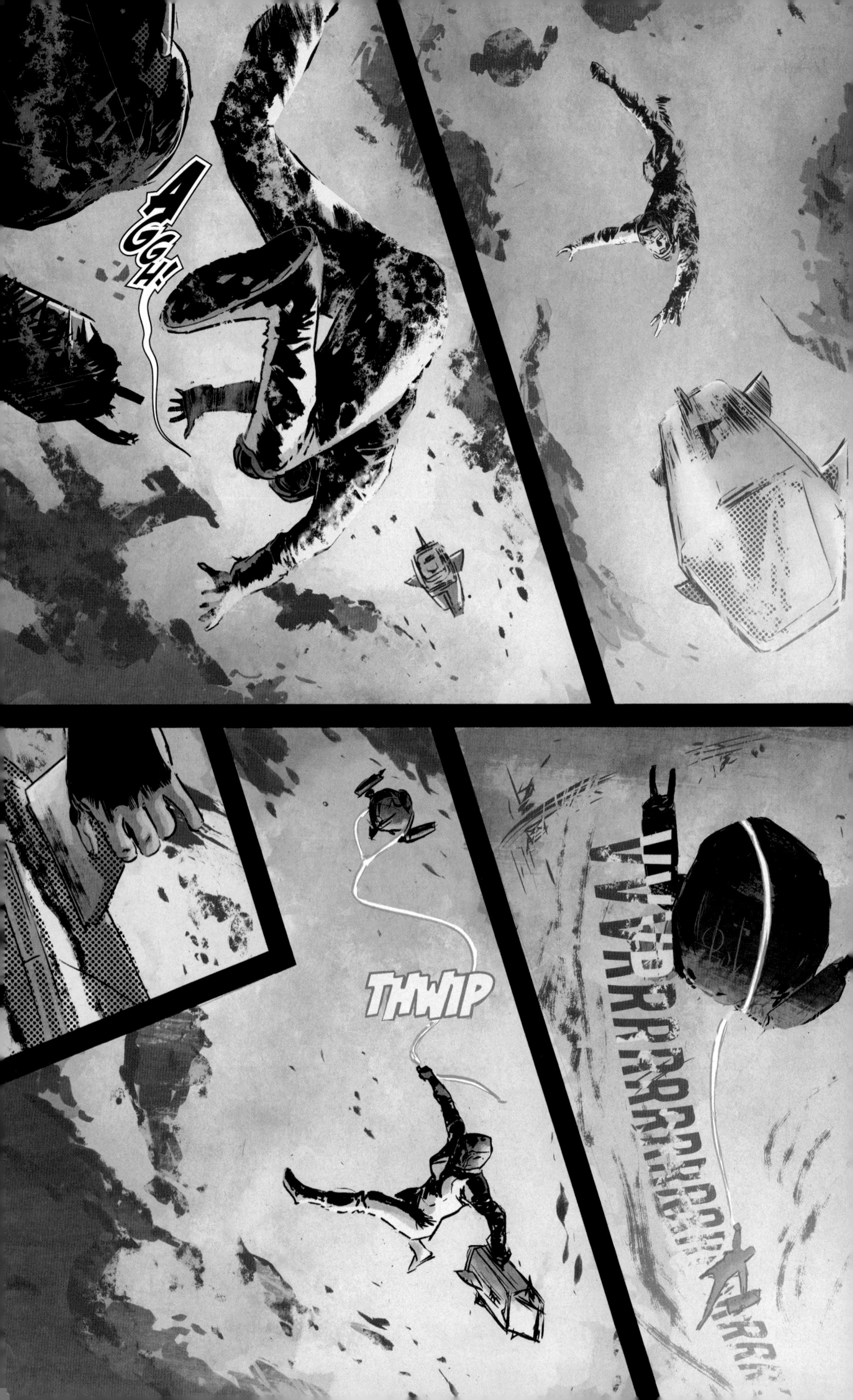
AGGH!
THWIP
VVVRRRRRRRRRRRR

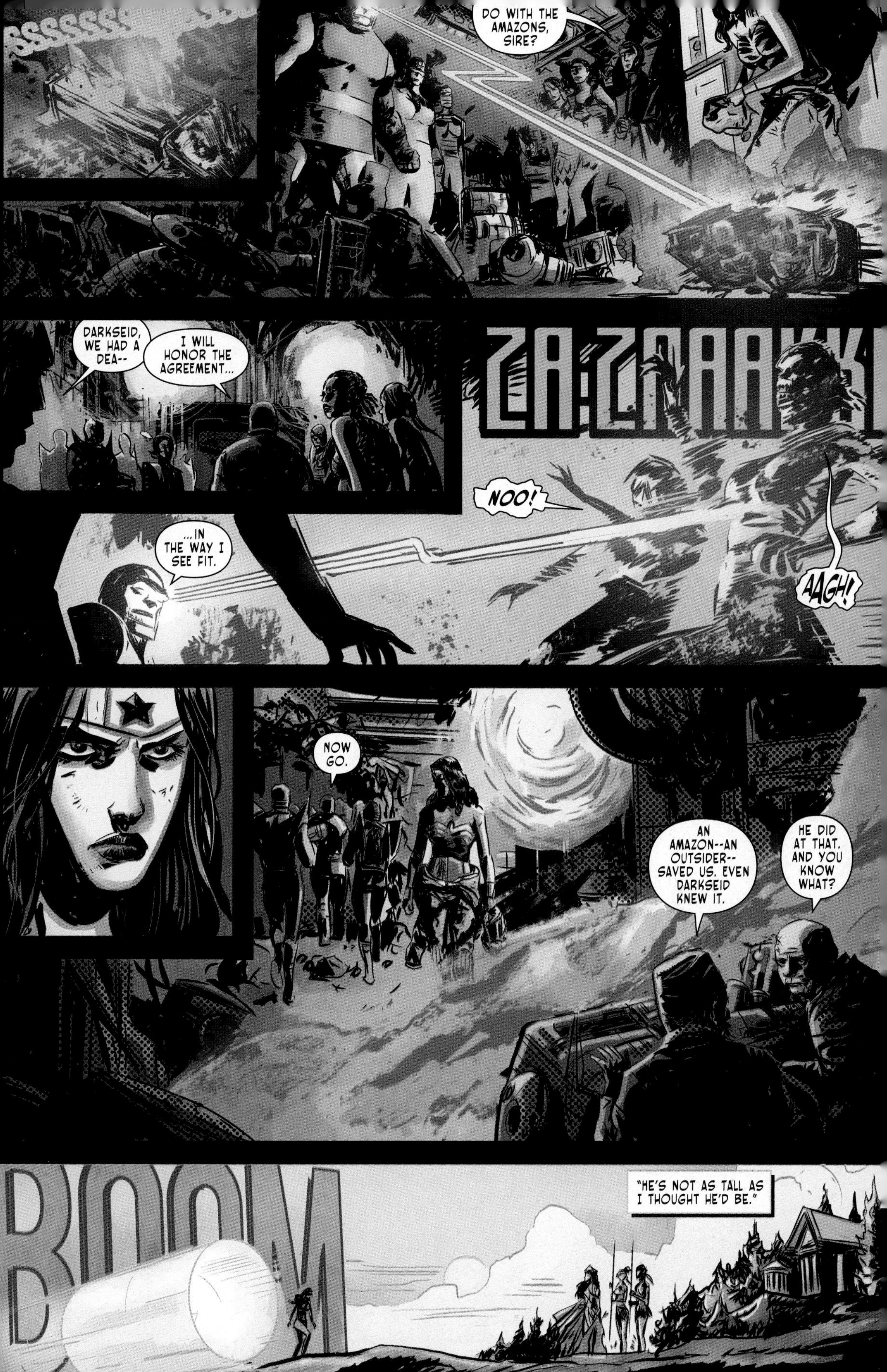

SSSSSSS
DO WITH THE AMAZONS, SIRE?
DARKSEID, WE HAD A DEA--
I WILL HONOR THE AGREEMENT...
ZA-ZAAKK!
NOO!
...IN THE WAY I SEE FIT.
AAGH!
NOW GO.
AN AMAZON--AN OUTSIDER--SAVED US. EVEN DARKSEID KNEW IT.
HE DID AT THAT. AND YOU KNOW WHAT?
BOOM
"HE'S NOT AS TALL AS I THOUGHT HE'D BE."

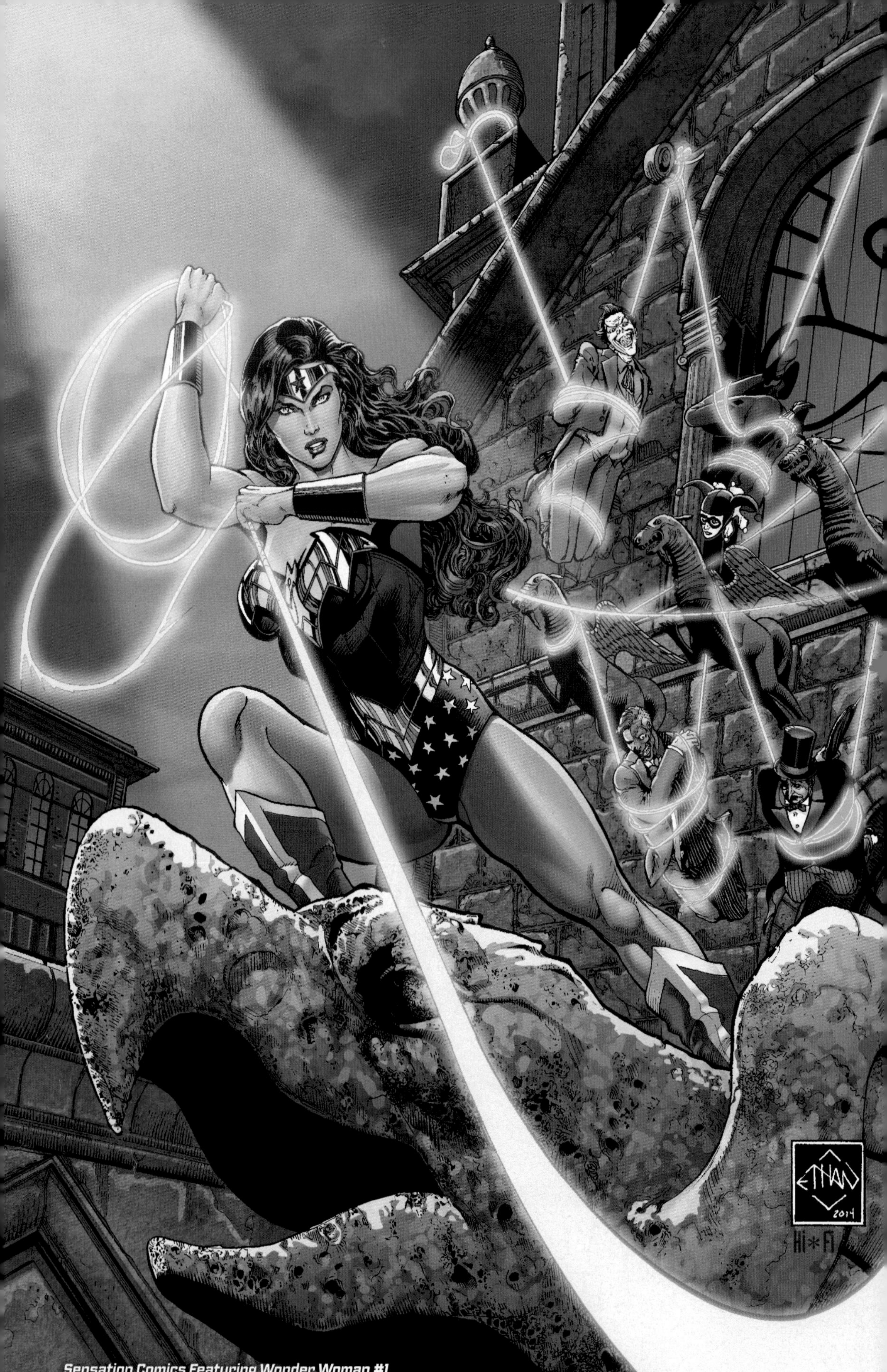
ETHAN
2014
Hi*Fi

Sensation Comics Featuring Wonder Woman #1
Cover by Ethan Van Sciver & Brian Miller of Hi-Fi Colour Design

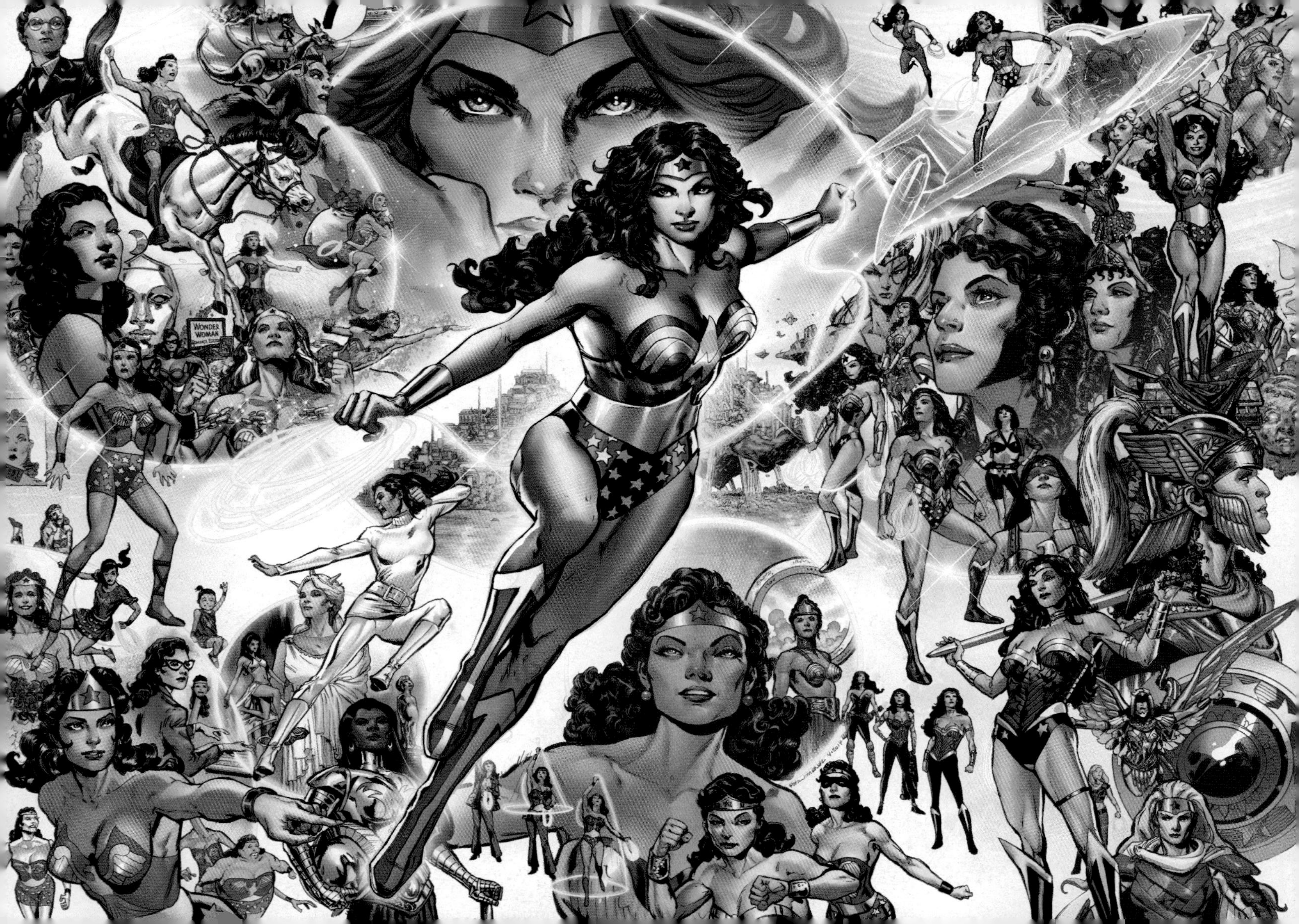
WONDER WOMAN

Sensation Comics Featuring Wonder Woman #3
Cover by Ivan Reis, Joe Prado and Carrie Strachan

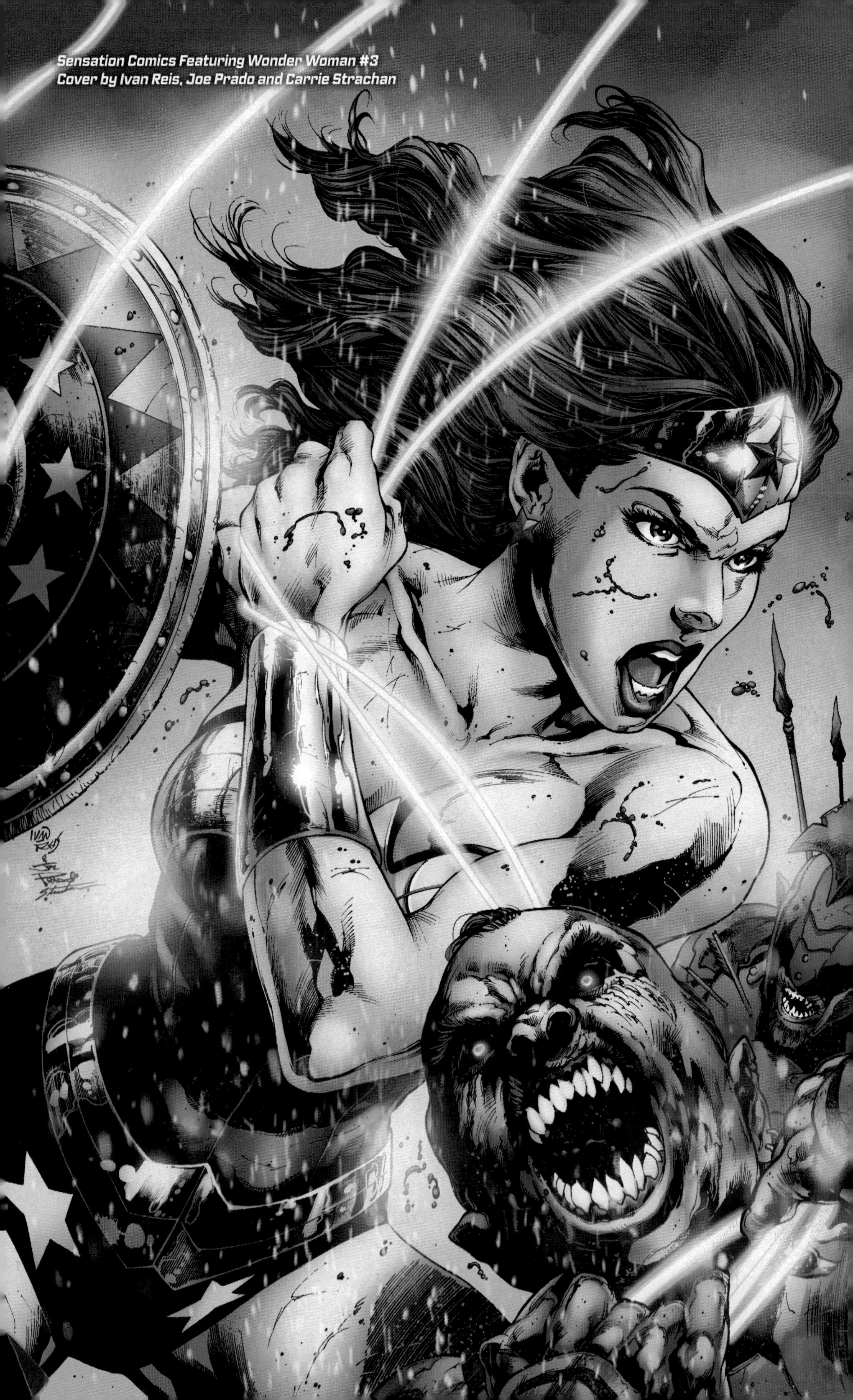

Sensation Comics Featuring Wonder Woman #4 Cover by Adam Hughes

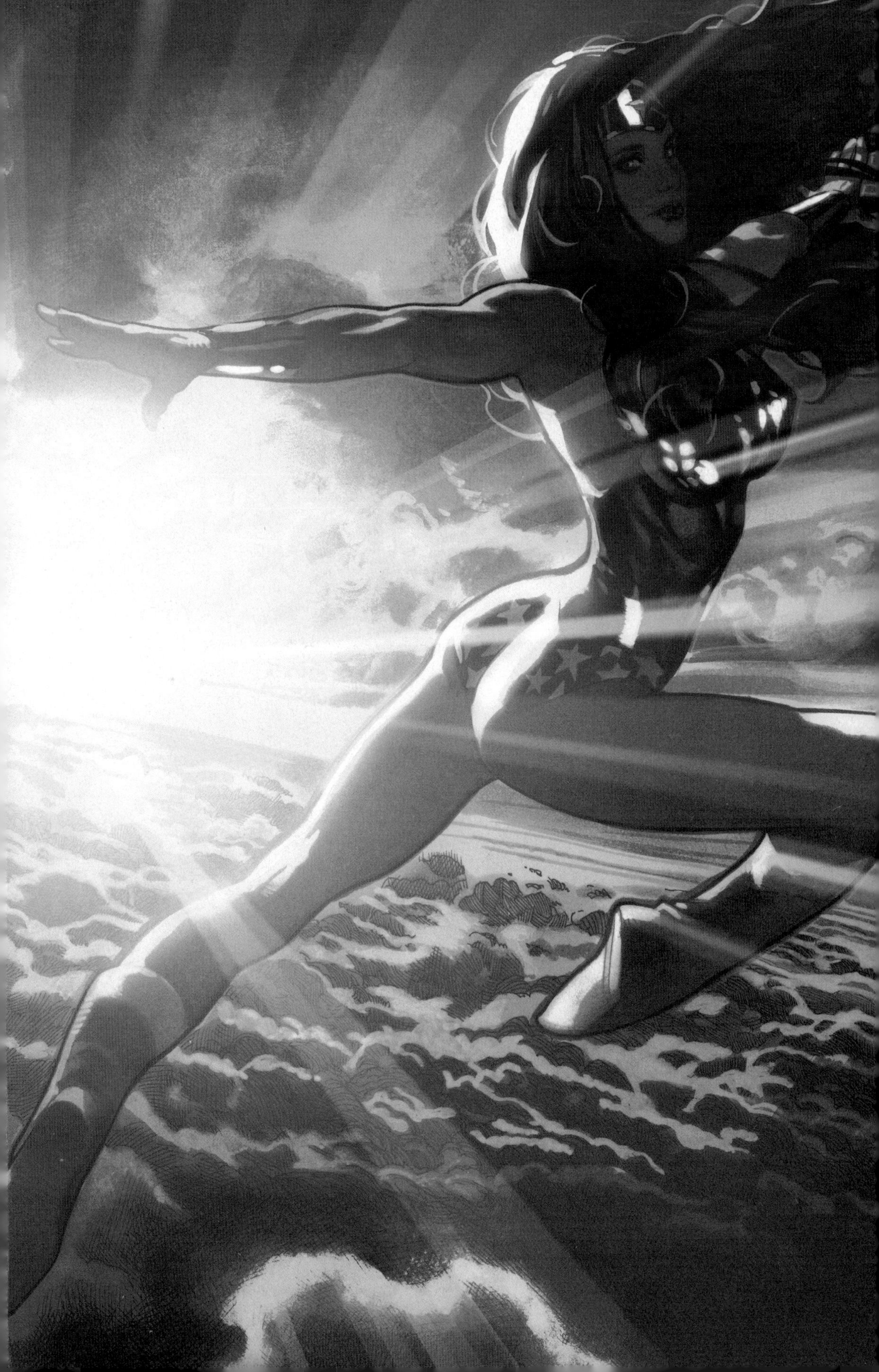

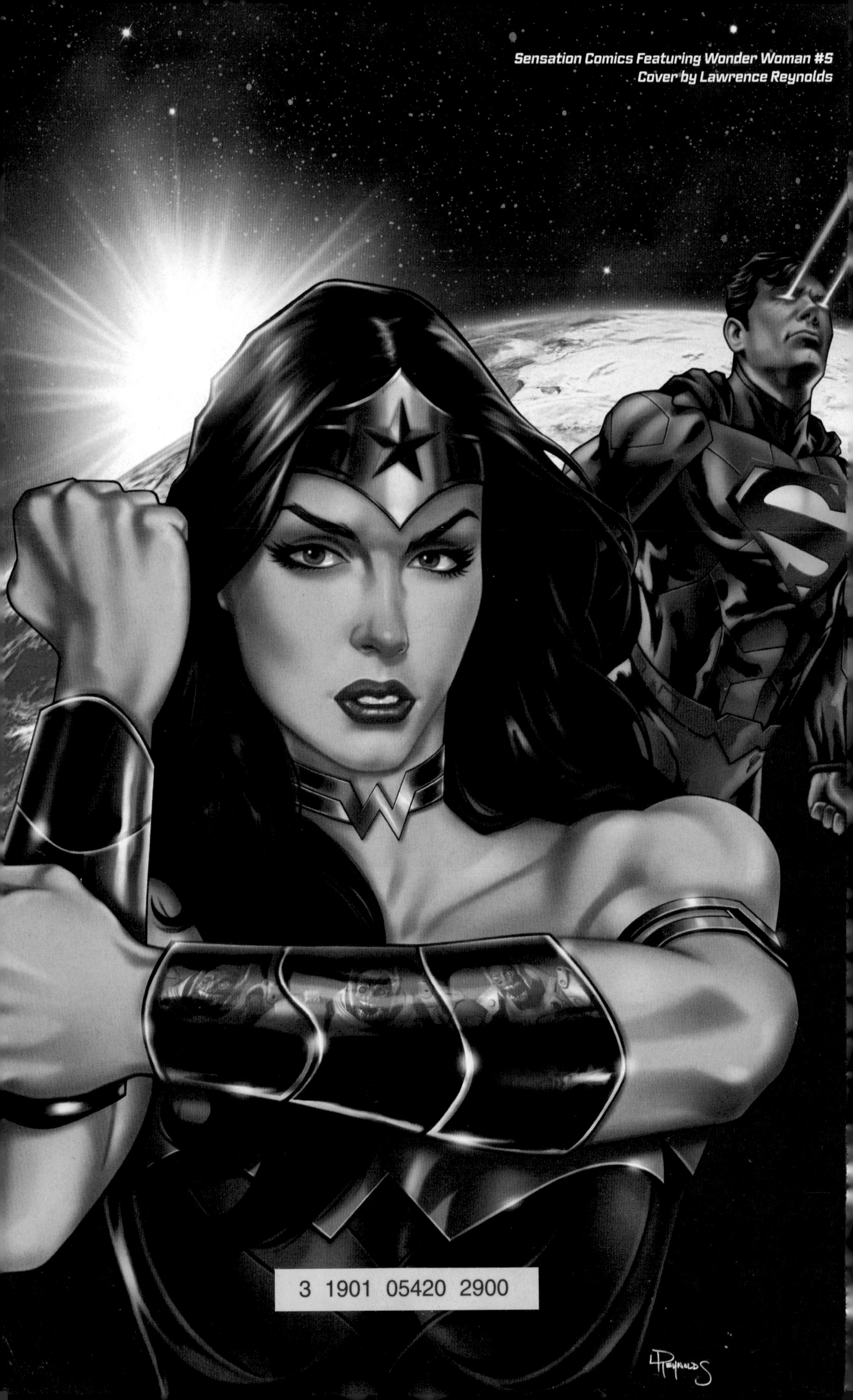

Sensation Comics Featuring Wonder Woman #5
Cover by Lawrence Reynolds